SURE&STEDFAST

SURE&STEDFAST

A History of The Boys' Brigade
◆ 1883 to 1983 ◆

by
John Springhall
coordinating editor

Brian Fraser
Michael Hoare

Which *hope* we have as an anchor of the soul,
both sure and stedfast,
and which entereth into that within the veil.

— Hebrews, 6:19 —

Collins
London and Glasgow

Published by William Collins Sons and Company Limited
Text copyright © 1983 The Boys' Brigade
First published 1983

Printed in Great Britain by Collins Glasgow

ISBN 0 00 434280 1

*To those anonymous workers
in the voluntary youth service,
the officers of The Boys' Brigade,
past, present and future,
both in Britain and overseas.*

ACKNOWLEDGEMENTS

THE AUTHORS would wish to acknowledge with grateful thanks the following individuals who have granted permission for extensive quotation from their published writings or private correspondence:

Major-General D.J. Wilson-Haffenden for use of his confidential quarterly *Newsletter* sent to B.B. district and overseas organizers; Ian Jack for use of his article on 'Youth: Scenes from the Life of a Beleaguered Generation' which appeared in the *Sunday Times Magazine* of 1 November 1981; T.R. Fyvel for use of his article on 'The "Insecure Offenders" in Retrospect', which appeared in *New Society* of 20 July 1978; Matt Stewart, Church of Scotland Minister at Boat of Garten, Inverness-shire, for use of his private letter of 29 December 1965 to D.J. Wilson-Haffenden; Tom Sharman for use of an address delivered to the Wigan Battalion on 29 October 1979; those B.B. officers who responded to the 1978 Survey of Battalion Secretaries in the U.K. and the International Survey of Overseas Organizers and Secretaries.

FOREWORD

By the President of The Boys' Brigade

WHEN ONE MAN'S shout arrests the attention of a motley crowd of boys, it is well worth while considering today how his voice denied the generation gap a century ago. This history has taken the story of the founding of The Boys' Brigade from the busy, bursting seams of Glasgow — the 'Second City of the Empire'. It begins at a time when there were many manifestations of Christian leadership in the field, but the names of William Smith and his contemporaries stand out for their firm, cheerful responsibility.

It is equally of profound interest that The Boys' Brigade — or some similar movement — might well have been started in one of another four cities in Britain. The men were there, and their enthusiasm burning. Consequently, when knowledge of what William Smith was doing became of interest in the newspapers, the Movement was taken up seriously in wide ranging locations; nor should it be overlooked that the first leaders seemed to come most strongly from the business and commercial scene. The Volunteer system which had been formed for Home Defence also provided the idea of discipline, and a simple, distinctive equipment which we now, perhaps thoughtlessly, call uniform.

In the clogged, fumy atmosphere of nineteenth-century industrial towns the idea of a camp under canvas once a year, together with organized weekly games and football, must have sounded sweetly to Boys; nor did the high standard of attendance deter.

Nonetheless, the struggle in the early days was intense, and had it not been for a cross-relationship creating a mutual understanding and support between the founding officers and their Churches the idea might have been snuffed out. It can be seen how this nearly happened in Edinburgh, and only quite superhuman endeavour secured the early successes elsewhere.

While the revelations about the founding officers are most rewarding, those of the Boys are even more so. For those, at the start, were sturdy, sharp children, whose fathers were skilled in their professions, and from a wide range of industry. The kind of Boy who, in all ages, has possessed the most penetrating ability to see the true heart of his adult mentor, and to judge what he sees with a ruthless candour — and then accept or reject what he has found.

It was, however, an acceptance which occurred, and the unfolding story of this acceptance is the warm, pulsing, Christian soul of the leadership and following of our Movement until now.

The Earl of Elgin and Kincardine

CONTENTS

PREFACE

'IT DISTRESSES ME how little publicity the [Boys'] Brigade generally receives. The Scouts receive far more space and yet they were formed by Baden-Powell after he learned about the Boys' Brigade,' lamented a sixteen year old in the 2nd Southampton Company to the *Daily Mail* recently. 'If it weren't for the Boys' Brigade there might have been no Scouts!' Certainly the pioneering role of The Boys' Brigade as the world's first successful *voluntary* uniformed youth organization has been given far less attention than it merits in the general historical and sociological writing about youth and youth movements. It is this apparent neglect which the present history sets out to remedy by attempting to present the development of The Boys' Brigade over the past hundred years, both in Britain and overseas, in a form which is both readable and easily understood but which is also accurate and scholarly. 'We have all heard of The Boys' Brigade,' the *Daily Herald* informed its readers in 1933,

> and have some hazy recollection of seeing the boys on parade, with their bugle band. Some of us have a vivid recollection of their 'pill box' hats. They must be losing their advertising value now that women wear hats at a seemingly perilous angle.

The Boys' Brigade forage cap or 'pillbox' hat disappeared after 1970-71 but still remains firmly planted, like the Boy Scouts' shorts, in the public imagination. In what follows, it is our intention to help clarify the 'hazy recollection' which is all that The Boys' Brigade may represent for a great many non-B.B. people, and possibly to provide some sort of historical perspective on the movement for the ordinary member.[1]

'I had not, in fact, expected to like The Boys' Brigade,' confessed *Sunday Times* reporter Ian Jack in 1981, after spending a day at the Lambeth and Southwark Battalion camp on the Isle of Wight:

> I share a common prejudice about an organization which combines military drill with evangelic Christianity. The truth is I was touched by a simple notice which had been pinned to the mess-tent wall. 'Remember our motto,' it said: *'Think of the other fellow first.'*

Until recently, The Boys' Brigade has received little attention from historians, and when it has been mentioned it has been misleadingly portrayed. For example, it has been described as 'a scout-like, militaristic organization for Sunday school scholars', an organization which in general 'fostered the traits of working-class jingoism'; or, again, as 'highly disciplinarian with much emphasis on drill and little concern for the development of individual character'. This history sets out to correct such false assumptions about the militarism and evangelism that have so frequently been attributed to the Brigade, assumptions which are all too often based on hearsay rather than on direct historical evidence or observation. The primary reason for compiling this historical account of The Boys' Brigade, however, apart from a genuine desire to celebrate the centenary of its birth, is to help increase public knowledge and awareness of a movement that even today has a world membership (including kindred movements in Scandanavia and the U.S.A.) in all ranks of over 400,000 in some sixty countries, and in the past has sent at least two million young men out into the world.[2]

At another level, this study is intended to contribute towards the revaluation of the history of British youth movements that has been going on since the late 1960s. It also attempts to examine and narrate the history of The Boys' Brigade as a voluntary church youth movement located within a broader social and historical context, an element usually lacking in most authorized accounts of youth organizations. More specifically, this has entailed an attempt to examine The Boys' Brigade in the light of recent academic interest in the relationship between religion and society, and in the historical development of the concepts of 'adolescence' and 'youth'. If it is asked why this particular task has had to await the centenary of The Boys' Brigade, perhaps it is not so difficult to understand when one considers the disregard by modern British historians of instinctively conservative organizations in our society, such as the uniformed youth movements themselves. For, as Brian Harrison pointed out in his account of the opposition to women's suffrage in Britain, when historians reach middle age they lack the time and enthusiasm necessary for doing justice to such topics, and when they are young they are not tempted by them. Hence inherently traditional, church-centred, establishment-supported youth organizations, such as The Boys' Brigade, are hardly likely to inspire the more leftward-leaning social historian. On the other hand, the very fact that a movement dedicated to a 'true Christian manliness' for boys could have arisen in the late nineteenth century and remained in existence to meet the entirely different circumstances of the late twentieth century provides a fascinating challenge to the understanding of the inquiring historian, however much 'the B.B. spirit' may or may not agree with his or her own temperament and general outlook.[3]

An analysis of those historical forces which act as a mechanism for social stability rather than for change, for the traditional values of discipline and obedience rather than for those of disorder and rejection of authority, can be a useful means to comprehend not only the political, moral and social conservatism of so much of modern British society, but also the respect of its members, until recent times, for the institutional forms of authority by which they are governed. 'The custom of saluting Officers in the streets by the Boys of The Boys' Brigade has spread to most of the lads in the vicinity of its operations,' wrote a satisfied Sunday School superintendent in the mid-1890s of the 1st Aston Manor Company, Birmingham, 'and has caused a respectful salute to the Clergy and [Sunday School] teachers to take the place of a disrespectful "Hallo!" in many of our streets.' Reports in the log book of the same company make the association between The Boys' Brigade and church discipline even more prominent:

> It [the B.B.] has an exceedingly beneficial effect upon its members. They are brighter, smarter, and certainly more respectful, and amenable to discipline. As the late Vicar remarked, 'He could always tell a Vicarage Road Sunday School Boy, he was so polite.' This, I take it, is a standing testimony of the good derived from The Boys' Brigade.
>
> The habits of discipline (including punctuality, etc.) engendered is beyond all praise. This is invaluable when we remember that this habit is a direct help to Sunday School work in teaching, since it makes that work so much easier when we

have a large number of Boys in a school who are well behaved and obedient. In this particular Midlands church, The Boys' Brigade had clearly performed one of the functions for which it was originally founded, to instill order and discipline into the often unmanageable adolescents attending Sunday School.[4]

Over the past century or so, youth movements have also functioned as extremely sensitive barometers of shifts in public and political attitudes towards the role of the military in society. Thus The Boys' Brigade in Britain were able successfully to resist government pressure to become Cadets and act as feeders for the Territorials before the First World War, whereas in Australia and New Zealand the B.B. succumbed very often to more stringent government legislation concerning compulsory military training. In New Zealand the Defence Act of 1909 decimated the few remaining B.B. companies and similar regulations did the same in Australia. In Britain the patriotic mobilization of wartime led to Cadet affiliation by nearly thirty per cent of B.B. companies in 1917, although the postwar reaction against militarism contributed in 1924 to their withdrawal from the scheme. Some may doubt its ultimate relevance but the ability to test and explore both Church and Nonconformist tolerance for military values and practices may be one of the least publicized but nonetheless real bequeathals of the B.B. to the history of religion. Of course, for an organization born, like The Boys' Brigade, during the 1880s to survive in such a different world environment as existed after the First World War illustrates not only the longevity of the conservative and traditional aspects of British society mentioned above, but also their ability to adapt with some success to the conditions of a more democratic, less class-bound, and less religious age. It is this remarkable process of adaptation by The Boys' Brigade to the pronounced historical changes which have occurred since it was founded a century ago that this history sets out to chart. Along the way, we shall be making some assessment of the changing contribution of The Boys' Brigade to national life both in Britain and overseas.[5]

It has to be admitted at the outset that, in comparison to the much-renowned founder of Scouting, Lord Robert Baden-Powell, his colleague, the less publicity-seeking Sir William Alexander Smith, founder of The Boys' Brigade, is not such a well-known historical figure. Yet it is worth remembering that William Smith started The Boys' Brigade in Glasgow as early as October 1883, almost a quarter of a century before the first Boy Scout took up his wooden pole and put on his bush hat. Baden-Powell was also indebted to The Boys' Brigade for providing a forum, the *B.B. Gazette*, in which to try out his early ideas, and to William Smith in particular he owed the encouragement without which he might not have converted his army manual, *Aids to Scouting*, into the classic best-selling *Scouting for Boys*. Unfortunately, the virtual absence of family correspondence and autobiographical or even published writings by William Smith — unlike the more prolific output of the Chief Scout — meant that at an early stage the publication of a fresh biography of the Founder of The Boys' Brigade was dismissed by the present authors as lacking in sufficient viability, although we would not wish this to deter anyone else from attempting such a task. Wherever fresh biographical evidence has come to light since the now-dated biographies by Smith's fellow staff officers Frederick P. Gibbon (1934) and Roger S. Peacock (1954), it has been incorporated into the opening chapters of the present volume. In any case, William Smith lived so much of his life through The Boys' Brigade — of which he became full-time

Secretary in 1888 after giving up his business — that any history of the movement of necessity becomes a history of its Founder at the same time.[6]

Similarly, after the research for this work had commenced, it was found that there were some fairly large gaps in the historical record which even the ever-resourceful Brigade Archivist, Muriel Ellis, was unable to supplement. Thus important minutes of the Brigade Executive, from its establishment until 1916, are no longer extant — unless they lie mouldering unrecognized in a cupboard somewhere in Glasgow — and little remains of the day-to-day office correspondence of Stanley Smith, Brigade Secretary from 1925 until 1954, most of it probably having been lost in the mid-1960s when the B.B.'s London Headquarters moved from Westminster to Fulham. On the other hand, the authors received unlimited assistance from Brigade staff both in London and Glasgow, as well as open access to all the records that are still available, and this is gratefully acknowledged elsewhere. William Smith's handwritten, press copy letter books, for example, provide a meticulous record of his own period as Secretary, particularly for the late 1880s, and Roger S. Peacock, who served on the Brigade staff in London from 1902 until 1947, also kept extensive files which have fortunately survived virtually intact. When it comes to the overseas history of The Boys' Brigade, the most deeply felt inadequacy has been the absence of secondary literature on the history of international youth work, let alone Brigade development, although there is no absence of primary research materials available to the historian. What is required in the future are studies of The Boys' Brigade by country, territory or region in the majority of the places mentioned in the overseas chapters. Lastly, some B.B. readers may feel that the authors have given insufficient recognition in places to the contribution of particular companies or individual officers to the history of the movement as compared with others. Our defence must be that to write such a history at all in the time and space available has meant that a certain amount of selectivity was necessary in order to prevent the non-B.B. reader from being overwhelmed by excessive detail.

Because histories of youth organizations are generally written by 'insiders', self-congratulation is often their dominant characteristic. Research into episodes in their past which might point to adversely critical conclusions have seldom been undertaken, while systematic efforts to set youth organizations in their full social, economic and political contexts usually remain unattempted. The Boys' Brigade, therefore, demonstrated a certain amount of courage (or foolhardiness!) in commissioning a professional historian, an 'outsider' with no previous affiliation to the Brigade, to act as the coordinating editor and contributor to this study. It is a common occurrence that the members of any organization fail to recognize it when it is described by someone who is not a member. However, in the case of this history, the authors come from a mixed academic and Boys' Brigade background which should combine the approach of the 'insider' with that of the more detached scholar. The coordinating editor, Dr John Springhall, is a Lecturer in History at the New University of Ulster, Coleraine, Northern Ireland, and is the author of a social history of British youth movements from 1883 to 1940, *Youth, Empire and Society* (Croom Helm, 1977). His co-authors are both B.B. officers. Dr Brian M. Fraser is currently a senior administrator in the University of Glasgow, a B.B. officer in the 205th Glasgow (Eaglesham) Company and, during 1981, was awarded his Ph.D from the University of Strathclyde for a thesis on the origins and history of The Boys' Brigade from 1883 to 1914. Dr Michael E. Hoare is the Head of the

Manuscripts Section at the Alexander Turnbull Library, Wellington, New Zealand, a former member of the B.B. Executive in Australia, and since 1981 official Brigade Historian in New Zealand. He was formerly Chairman of the Development Planning Committee (1978-81) of the B.B. in New Zealand and is the author of *Boys, Urchins, Men* (Reed, 1980), a history of The Boys' Brigade in Australia and Papua New Guinea from 1882 to 1976. He has also recently published *Faces of Boyhood* (B.B. in New Zealand, 1982), a pictorial record of the movement in New Zealand and the Southwest Pacific from 1886 to 1982. Broadly speaking, our initial briefs were for Brian Fraser to handle the pre-1914 material dealt with in his thesis, John Springhall to deal with the post-1918 history of the Brigade in Britain, and Michael Hoare to undertake the overseas history; however, it will be apparent that, in order to deal with the First World War period, for example, some overlapping did take place. To further clarify our various contributions, John Springhall and Brian Fraser collaborated together on the Introduction, Conclusions and Chapter 4; Brian Fraser is solely responsible for Chapters 1 and 2; John Springhall for Chapters 5, 7 and 9; and Michael Hoare for all the overseas chapters, that is, 3, 6 and 8.

Thanks are due to the following staff officers of The Boys' Brigade in London for their unstinting and gratefully received cooperation during the preparation and research for this work: the present Brigade Secretary, Alfred A.J. Hudson, who initiated and followed this project through to its completion, both for his time during a busy schedule and for the encouragement he has given to the editor over the years; and to John Digby, Finance and General Purposes Secretary; John Edbrooke, Development Secretary; Don West, Training Secretary; Gerald Walker, Programme Secretary; and Leslie Rawson, Executive Secretary to the World Conference, for all their help and advice. Long-serving officers and ex-officers who have provided information or allowed interviews are mentioned in the text or in references but particular thanks should be given to: Peter Ford of the Brighton and Hove Battalion; Richard Early of the 1st Witney Company; Fred Price and Frank Jackson of Bristol; Dennis Webb of the Northampton Battalion; Tom Sharman, ex-Assistant Secretary Administration, and the late J.J. Barlow, Honorary Vice-President of the Mid-Suffolk Battalion. Special thanks are also due to the following field officers for their hospitality and the guidance given to the editor while visiting their districts: Harry Overton, Southern District; Allan Percival, North of England District; and Roy Barson, Yorkshire and Humberside District. In Scotland, we would like to thank the following staff officers of The Boys' Brigade for their assistance with research: the Secretary for Scotland, Henry T. Shirley, and staff at Scottish Headquarters; Glasgow Battalion Secretary, John Neil, and former Secretary, John M. Leggat, and Duncan McLachlan and staff at Glasgow Battalion Headquarters; Edinburgh Battalion Secretary, D.C. Macnab, and Veronica W. Cassie and staff at Edinburgh Battalion Headquarters. The following officers, former officers and friends also provided valuable information and help: Douglas G.A. Rolland, Captain 1st Glasgow Company; Frank Gardiner, Captain 1st Hamilton Company; J.B. Smith, ex-Captain 1st Beith Company; Alexander Martin and Arthur Reid, ex-1st Glasgow Company; James McGregor and Dr Dan McFarlane of Glasgow; and Mrs Dora Stirling of Helensburgh. In Northern Ireland, assistance has been received from: District Secretary, W. Alex Hunter, and former Secretary, Jack McClure; former Belfast Battalion Secretaries Robert G. Greig and Albert Fogarty; and William R. Kelly, ex-Captain of the 21st Belfast

Company. The Headquarters staff in London and Glasgow of the following youth organizations also allowed access to their records: the Church Lads' Brigade, the Jewish Lads' Brigade, the Foundry Boys' and Girls' Religious Society, the Scouts, the Guides and the Girls' Brigade.

During 1978 Michael Hoare received support as a Canadian Commonwealth Fellow which enabled him to visit Brigade centres in Toronto and Montreal. He wishes to express particular thanks to Danny and Lilian Reesor and family in Toronto and to J. Howard Richardson and John Miller in Montreal for greatly facilitating access to a wide range of Canadian records. On the same visit, Dr Hoare was also able to do research and interviewing on the history of the Brigade in America, for which especial thanks go to Frank and Grace Butt, John Schlee and General Walter A. Koerber of Baltimore, Maryland, and C. Guy Smith of Swissvale, Pennsylvania. Mention should also be made of thanks due to the staff of Brigade national and state Headquarters in Australia and Geoff Lindsay of Sydney for his constant support. Help has also been received from the B.B. in Singapore recently and during the author's stays there and in Hong Kong and Malaysia in 1970-71. In New Zealand, much assistance has been received from B.B. staff past and present, including Alford Dornan, Blair Stewart, Robert Baird and Noel D. Shakespeare. Interviews have been readily granted by many other people, including Roland Hill, Mervyn Dearsley, Howard Trotman, Sid George, and the late Bob Challis, Mervyn Branks and Bruce Patchett. The author of the overseas sections of this history would especially like to thank his wife for her usual support in typing drafts and in many other ways and also Stewart Gray of Wellington for helpful comments.

The international content of this book, like all the other sections, owes much to Muriel D. Ellis, Brigade Archivist in London, who has selflessly provided answers to questions, assisted in literature and archival searches and done literally reams of photocopying for all three authors — without Muriel's invaluable help this book would not have been possible. The following historians and colleagues have also performed one of the essential penances of academic life in offering their comments and suggestions on various chapters in draft form for which the editor is duly grateful: Dr Kenneth Brown of the Department of Economic and Social History at the Queen's University of Belfast, and Dr Peter Roebuck and Dr Tom Fraser in the School of Humanities of the New University of Ulster. From 1979 to 1980 the coordinating editor, John Springhall, held a Fellowship which allowed him to take leave from his teaching duties to research, write and edit the present work, for which generous support he would like to make acknowledgement to the Leverhulme Trust Fund. It is also appropriate to mention that whatever uniformity of style and clarity of treatment has emerged from our combined efforts in writing this history owes a great deal to our patient and painstaking editor at Collins Publishers, Ian Crofton. A presentable typescript has only been made possible through the part-time skills of Rosemary Curtis in London, Marion Hoggan and Ann Doonan in Glasgow, and Tita Gatrell in Coleraine, for which many thanks. Finally, the editor would like to express sincere thanks to Prue Stevens, his family, and to Steve, Graham and Dennis, for ensuring his continuing ability to complete this book in time for the centenary.

John Springhall, July 1982.

INTRODUCTION

The Historical Background

THE GENERAL AIM in writing this book has been to place the origins, development and achievements of The Boys' Brigade, both in Britain and overseas, within the broad historical framework of the past hundred years or so. Thus it will be helpful, in seeking to understand why the B.B. should have appeared precisely when and where it did, to say something about the social, economic and religious environment of late nineteenth-century Britain. For if the B.B. is to be regarded as a product of its times, although it was to prove to be much more, then it is necessary to look at some of the general trends in late Victorian society that contributed towards the Brigade's foundation. Of particular significance were, for example, the more favourable public image of the military, and also the forceful impact of evangelical Christianity on late Victorian attitudes towards the guidance of the young. It is also important to consider those historical changes that helped to shape both the intentions behind the creation of the B.B. and also the reasons it was felt such an organization for boys was needed. Hence shifts in the relationship between religion and society, particularly in Scotland, and the appearance of the new 'problem' of adolescence both played their part in creating the historical climate which gave birth to the B.B. in late Victorian Glasgow. Other factors recently highlighted by historians include the downward percolation of the public-school ideal of Christian manliness for boys via the B.B., and the increasing association between religion and the military in British society at this time.

The Boys' Brigade was started as long ago as 1883, during Gladstone's second ministry and at the height of the European 'scramble' for colonial possessions in Africa. It took root in a society undergoing a period of rapid transition and economic change, a society which historians now see as increasingly uncertain of its future direction. At the 1881 census the population of England and Wales was almost twice what it had been half a century earlier, and over forty-six per cent of that population was under twenty years of age. Society had also become predominantly urban rather than rural, and the major cities in which the B.B. was shortly to establish itself — Glasgow, London, Manchester, Sheffield, Aberdeen — were still expanding in numbers. There was, in particular, a rapid increase during the late nineteenth century in the number of white-collar workers to be found in city offices and shops. This new breed of clerks, shop assistants, teachers and public-service employees helped to form the emerging 'lower middle class'. This status-conscious class aspired to the values and life style of the late Victorian middle class in an effort to distinguish themselves from a skilled working class whose income levels often matched their own. A substantial proportion of Brigade officers and recruits were eventually to come from this white-collar social grouping, and membership may have supplied one method of affirming their social respectability. Conditions in the overcrowded urban environment contributed to the concern felt by the better off for the poorest sections of society. The substandard level of housing and medical facilities in many industrial cities meant that any agency, such as The Boys' Brigade, which promised to promote physical as well as moral fitness among the young was bound to command attention.[1]

The notion of an economic 'Great Depression' during the last quarter of the nineteenth century has been seriously called into doubt by recent historical investigation, but there remains plenty of evidence to suggest that the mid-Victorian self-confidence of the owners of business and industry began to waver as prices and profits fell appreciably. At the lower end of the social scale, however, the ordinary skilled artisan was not so adversely affected by the so-called 'depression' and may indeed have seen his *real* income rise by some thirty per cent during this period. His middle-class contemporaries appear to have been far more influenced by short term crises of confidence, indicating that the 'depression' in the last twenty years of the century was in fact largely a depression in the morale of the business community. On the other hand, Glasgow, the second city of the Empire, exemplified in a dynamic fashion how far the traditional areas of British superiority, such as ship-building and heavy engineering, continued to hold their own against growing foreign competition. For Britain as a whole, this was equally true of the growth sectors of the so-called 'Second Industrial Revolution', such as machine tools, new synthetic materials, chemicals, and electrical goods. Formerly prosperous businessmen and major industrialists may have seen growth rates slowing down and prices falling, but the innovation of new techniques and new products in fact enabled Britain to match the performance of Germany and America. Leaving agriculture aside, if one examines the statistics relating to the results achieved by the national economy, one is bound to conclude that they do not support the gloomy view of a 'depression'. Yet industrial competition from abroad certainly undermined the fabric of British business confidence, whatever the benefit of hindsight on the actual state of the economy. It is undeniable that, as the other Great Powers became industrialized, Britain's former monopoly of world markets was challenged and gradually disappeared.[2]

The business and governing classes (the two were by no means inter-changeable) were beginning to feel nervous that their previously unassailable position in Victorian society might now be threatened by the newly educated and enfranchized urban masses. The increasing strength of organized labour, the expanding influence of socialist doctrines and the gradual evolution of the Labour Party by the turn of the century did little to allay middle-class fears of an intensification of class conflict in the years to come. While defending the training and discipline brought by war, William Smith claimed he was 'not at all sure that there are not the elements of just as much real evil . . . and bitterness of spirit in the industrial wars between class and class which many signs point to as the conflicts of the future but which, like other wars, may have their part to play in the progress of the race'. Among Glasgow's mercantile business community the repercussions of economic uncertainty were further exacerbated by the various social tensions associated with the overcrowding of the city's working-class tenements, which were often immediately adjacent to middle-class residential housing. It was from such an apprehensive middle class that, in the first instance, many B.B. officers were recruited. Despite middle-class uncertainties, Glasgow, as we shall see, was still a developing industrial and commercial centre. The city was being rapidly transformed by new technology, and a revolution in transport and communications was taking place. In religion and politics, Glasgow was to be deeply affected by a combination of liberal dissenting politics and evangelical Christianity.[3]

While the social and economic environment of the late Victorian age was undoubtedly a formative influence on the establishment of a uniformed youth movement, the technical innovations of the period also contributed to its extension. Improvements in transport and communications helped to spread the Brigade idea outside of Scotland and the urban areas where it was initially to be found. By 1880 the expansion of the national and international telegraph network had already shortened distances, and the filling in of the main framework of the railway system was to create a hitherto unknown mobility for the leaders of new voluntary bodies like The Boys' Brigade. As more lines were built and competition grew keener, excursions with cheap third-class tickets were made available to Sunday School and other church groups, enabling them to take young people out of their squalid urban environments, if only for a few hours. The expanded railway network also allowed easier communication between B.B. Headquarters and local units, thereby increasing personal contact between Brigade Executive members and the ordinary rank and file. Thus William Smith and his colleagues were to accept many invitations to travel to new locations where inaugural meetings of companies were being held, and a fast, efficient transport system enabled the 'message' to be spread more easily.

Of similar benefit to office correspondence was the improvement in the postal service, with the decrease of the penny post to a halfpenny in 1880. Yet William Smith failed to utilize another modern development, the Remington typewriter, and undertook all the drudgery of routine B.B. correspondence in his own strong handwriting. The communication of the Brigade idea was also facilitated by the growth of the popular press during this period. In the 1880s chatty magazines, such as George Newnes' popular *Tit-Bits* (1881), were first published. The format was later adapted by such newspapers as Alfred Harmsworth's *Daily Mail* (1896), which supposedly made its appeal to the lower middle-class audience already identified as a source of B.B. recruitment. At the same time, popular fiction for boys, such as G.A. Henty's *With Kitchener in the Soudan* (1903) or his *By Sheer Pluck: A Tale of the Ashanti War* (1884), brought to many young lives that were drab and ordinary the splendour of military and imperial adventure, and possibly created a frame of mind receptive to uniformed organizations.

Almost any voluntary movement directed at the adolescent in the late Victorian period has to be seen in relation to the religious, yet progressively urban and secular, environment of the time. This particularly applies to the B.B., which required affiliation to a church or other religious body as a condition of company enrolment. Church-going in the last decades of the nineteenth century was largely restricted to the upper and middle classes and the 'respectable' sections of the labouring population, but the Churches still sought to retain the illusion of exercising a supervisory role over a largely irreligious and indifferent urban working class. There remains some doubt among historians as to the real strength of the late nineteenth-century Churches, and the vast increase in new and restored church buildings need not, of course, reflect a commensurate increase in membership — hence the 'empty pews' often referred to during this period. On the one hand a slackening of momentum in religious enthusiasm can be demonstrated, while on the other hand statistics can be shown to reveal what appears to be remarkable activity. Nonconformist congregations, so prominent in early support for the B.B., certainly increased their membership in *absolute* terms until the turn of the century, but from the 1880s Methodists, Congregationalists and Baptists saw their numbers declining in proportion to the total adult population. Thus any organization, such as the B.B., that claimed to recruit young men into church membership was bound to receive close attention from the Protestant Churches in a time of declining, if more active and devout, congregations.

What concerns us here primarily is not the established Anglican and Presbyterian Churches but the impact of a revived evangelical Christianity on the various movements set up by Nonconformists and others for the training and guidance of the young in the late Victorian period. The evangelical revival is associated both with Wesleyan Methodism in the late eighteenth century and the response to its challenge within the Church of England, and a similar spirit also took hold among the Congregationalists and Baptists. The most famous group of evangelicals were the Clapham Sect, among whom was William Wilberforce, the chief spokesman for the movement in Parliament, who carried through the greatest reform connected with evangelicalism — the abolition of the slave trade in 1807. It was the evangelical movement, emphasizing the experience of conversion and dedication to service, that did much to promote the spread of domestic missionary work among the working classes which in many urban areas provided the spiritual and physical environment within which B.B. companies were to take root. Evangelical campaigns, such as those of the Americans Moody and Sankey, who visited Britain in 1867, 1873-75, 1881-83 and 1891-92, urged a new personal faith as a means of solving urban problems of immorality, drink and destitution, and converts often turned to philanthropy in working-class areas of cities to channel their religious enthusiasm. Dwight L. Moody's evangelical influence on William Smith and his business colleagues at the College Free Church in Glasgow's West End can certainly be detected after the 1874 campaign in the city. This is not to agree with those who claim that it was Moody who actually inspired Smith to start The Boys' Brigade, but there is no doubt that the progress of youth work in Glasgow owed a great deal to revivalist encouragement of social work among the young. Indirectly, the building of the North Woodside Mission, the birthplace of The Boys' Brigade, by its wealthy Free Church patron owed much to the inspiration of Dwight Moody's preaching, even if the actual idea of building mission churches in the tenement areas of Glasgow preceded the evangelist's visit.[4]

It was in this atmosphere that there emerged various religious organizations aimed primarily at children or the young, foreshadowing the coming of The Boys' Brigade in the 1880s. By far the earliest and most influential was the Sunday School movement begun by the evangelical Robert Raikes in Gloucester a century earlier, with the intention of teaching the poor to read the Bible. By the 1880s the Sunday Schools, in contrast to the Churches, were reaching about three children out of four, almost all of them from the working classes, and were maintaining an attendance rate of two-thirds. In the Sunday Schools the emphasis in the late Victorian period was on religious instruction, play and general education, rather than on the three R's, the need for which was by then fairly well met by the compulsory elementary schools established by the 1870 Education Act. Despite their impressive attendance figures, however, the Sunday Schools were finding by the 1880s that they were losing their members at around the age of twelve or thirteen — in other words at the time most children left elementary school. At this age most boys felt they were too grown-up for the Sunday School, since they would soon become independent wage earners contributing to the family income. And once state educational provision had to a great extent removed the learning function from the Sunday Schools, there remained the difficulties caused by an often unruly membership with no incentive to listen to the teacher. As William Smith recalled in an interview given to the *Boys' Own Paper* in 1898:

> In [Sunday] School they too often came to amuse themselves, and the whole effort of the teacher was spent in keeping order, in quelling riots, subduing irrelevant remarks, minimizing attacks upon the person, and protecting his Sunday hat from destruction. The boys would not listen for two consecutive minutes. What was to be done?

As will be seen in the next chapter, William Smith, himself a harrassed Sabbath School teacher, was to provide his own, very unusual, solution.[5]

As early as 1844 the Young Men's Christian Association had been established to 'influence religious young men to spread the Redeemer's Kingdom amongst those by whom they are surrounded'. Its outlook was strongly evangelical, although presented as a nondenominational, missionary auxiliary to the various Churches. The ideas of its founder, George Williams, a former apprentice draper and Sunday School teacher, became steadily more influential as the century progressed, and by the time The Boys' Brigade was started the Y.M.C.A had a total membership of over 80,000. In 1872 it is known that William Smith had joined the Y.M.C.A. in Glasgow, and by 1874 he had started a Young Men's Society, closely modelled on the Y.M.C.A., at the College Free Church referred to earlier. The success of the Y.M.C.A. in Glasgow and other Victorian cities highlighted the absence of a Church organization catering for the mid-adolescent years, for most boys left Sunday School in their early teens before they were old enough to join the more senior organization at seventeen. It was primarily to bridge this gap that William Smith invented The Boys' Brigade.[6]

The Band of Hope Union also owed much to the impact of evangelical Christianity on Victorian religious life. Inaugurated in Leeds in 1847, and inspired by the work of Jabez Tunnicliffe, a local Baptist minister, and Mrs Anne Jane Carlile, an Irish woman who had been an active prison visitor, it had been launched out of the temperance movement and concentrated on rearing children in sobriety rather than on reclaiming their parents. The term 'Band of Hope' was originally used solely to denote the children's section of the Leeds Temperance Society, but the name was copied by many other temperance and church organizations and given to their juvenile temperance groups. It was nondenominational but largely confined to the Protestant Churches, and the title 'Band of Hope' came to be used as a generic term for all such groups, regardless of their church or secular sponsorship. The informal and cheerful mood of Band of Hope meetings, famous for their teetotal pledge taking, led to rapid expansion. Later there were to be links in particular areas with B.B. companies — the Wesleyan Methodist Band of Hope, for example, was the basis for the 1st Witney B.B. Company in Oxfordshire. William Smith himself took a temperance rather than a total abstinence line, but B.B. members were expected — if not constitutionally bound — to be total abstainers. The B.B. Executive was even to publish a pledge card 'for use in cases where it is felt that this is the best means of promoting habits of Temperance among the Boys'.[7]

Band of Hope meetings were to some extent imitated by the Salvation Army's junior departments, which followed in the same militant evangelical tradition. The Salvation Army's Christian military crusade, a ·variant of late Methodist revivalism, started in 1878 at the time of a wave of jingoist feeling inspired by the Russian-Turkish 'war-scare' in Britain. General William Booth, the founder of the Salvation Army, broke new ground in moving away from the more 'respectable' elements in Victorian religion. His approach was to use regular street meetings, bands, processions and military titles to reach the outcast populations of the urban slums. The methods employed by the Salvation Army often met with official and public resistance, culminating in the numerous English south-coast riots directed against them in the early 1880s by publican-organized 'Skeleton Armies'. Despite such opposition, the Salvationists quickly made their influence felt on organized religion. In 1882, with the backing of the Church of England, Prebendary Wilson Carlile founded the Church Army on the same militant principles. The ability to communicate with the most deprived sections of the working-class community and the combination of social work and Christian mission which the Salvation Army espoused was not to be lost on the more orthodox Churches of Victorian Britain. By the time of the appearance of The Boys' Brigade, it is apparent that religion in uniform was fast becoming an acceptable feature of late Victorian society. Similarly, the revival of the Roman Catholic Church in England in the mid-nineteenth century and, in particular, the leadership of ex-Anglican Cardinal Henry Manning, brought the working classes and their social problems much more within the compass of that Church's care and attention. That the Catholic Church was ready to respond to the ideas of William Smith can be seen by their own Catholic Boys' Brigade, started in 1896 in a dockland parish of southeast London.[8]

The seemingly intellectual and 'joyless' Protestant tendency to identify serious religion with the study of scripture had long militated against any attempt to reach the non-literate population. However, new spiritual life was injected into this somewhat dry approach by the emergence of the evangelical and Tractarian movements in the late eighteenth and early nineteenth centuries. The Oxford or Tractarian movement of the 1830s and 1840s emphasized tradition and ceremonial and was passionately High Church, many of its leaders becoming converts to Rome, but it also identified with social causes in the industrial cities and broadened the appeal of the Established Church, particularly among romantic young undergraduates. Under the leadership of the Rev. Thomas Chalmers, an evangelical movement had also begun within the Established (Presbyterian) Church of Scotland. This culminated in 1843 in the 'Disruption', when the Church of Scotland split over issues of patronage and the appointment of ministers, and the seceding group formed the Free Church of Scotland. In 1874, under the influence of Moody and Sankey's evangelical crusade, William Smith took the step of abandoning the Church of Scotland, in which he had been brought up, to join the Free Church in the West End of Glasgow, where his uncle was already an elder. (The two Churches were not reunited until 1929.) Middle and upper-class philanthropists and businessmen, such as those found at the College Free Church in Glasgow's West End, supported the various temperance and abstinence societies in their cities, and patronized such interdenominational evangelical movements as the Y.M.C.A. and the Band of Hope.

As the nineteenth century advanced, any new organization directed at the adolescent was likely to be influenced by a further development in Victorian religious thinking, the concept of 'Christian manliness'. Dr Thomas Arnold, the early Victorian headmaster of Rugby, is widely known as the primary exponent of athletic manliness among boys through his school reforms, but he was also a notably intellectual and zealous Christian. It was really his admirer, Thomas Hughes, the author of *Tom Brown's Schooldays* (1857) and an enthusiastic Volunteer officer, who helped to bring into being a public-school ethos which upheld the moral and physical value of 'masculine' team games as opposed to 'effeminate' and intellectual scholarship. The cult of character and manliness which the public schools fostered in the second half of the nineteenth century placed an increasing emphasis on athleticism and high spirits rather than on academic work and spiritual piety, and combined this with a fundamental belief in the superiority of the British race. Thus the pronounced aim of William Smith to create a sentiment in the B.B. which would make the members proud of their own company can be seen as an attempt to extend the upper-class value of 'esprit de corps' to boys less fortunate than their public-school counterparts. 'It also seemed to us that by associating Christianity with all that was most noble and manly in a boy's sight,' explained Smith in 1888,

> we would be going a long way to disabuse his mind of the idea that there is anything effeminate or weak about Christianity; an idea that is far too widespread among Boys, as no one who has anything to do with them can have failed to see.

Ideas of 'muscular Christianity' were also spread by the boys' fiction of G.A. Henty, an Honorary Vice-President of The Boys' Brigade, whose boy-heroes were the personification of the English public-school belief in the virtues of manliness and character. The qualities associated with Christian manliness were thus handed down the social scale via organizations like The Boys' Brigade, through books, magazines and Sunday School prizes, and also via the lessons taught and the history textbooks used in the new compulsory state schools.[9]

Another historical development which assisted in the emergence of The Boys' Brigade and certainly lent it social respectability during the late Victorian period was the growing connection between religion and the military in Britain, already instanced above in the form of the Salvation Army. The growth of what might be termed Christian militarism, evident since the Crimea and the Indian Mutiny in mid-Victorian times, owed a great deal to religious literature using the stories of evangelical generals to create the image of the Christian soldier as hero. The reputation of soldiers such as Sir Henry Havelock, an evangelical Baptist general who died during the Mutiny, or General Charles Gordon, the martyr-hero of Khartoum, did much to make the military structure of the B.B. more socially acceptable to the late Victorians. Years of peace and relative stability, with the exception of frequent small-scale colonial wars, had served to soften unfavourable Nonconformist views of the Army, and soldiers were now seen as harmless providers of colour and pageantry. A flood of adventure stories, often set in the further outposts of the British Empire, appeared in popular penny magazines like the *Boys' Own Paper*. Such stories accustomed their youthful readership to the professional military image, and the use of military technology, ranks and titles were to prove fashionable elements in many youth organizations. In one sense, therefore, the drilling, parades and route marches of The Boys' Brigade represented the traditions and forms of the Army and Volunteers transferred to an adolescent environment, with soldier-hero figures like Lord Roberts of Kandahar giving encouragement and lending their names as Honorary Vice-

Presidents. On the other hand, the B.B. was not an organization that deliberately set out to popularize the idea of military service among the people in
general, although given the preponderant militarism and nationalism in
British society during the B.B.'s first decades, it may have had this effect.[10]

During the 1880s and 1890s in Britain, leisure as a major consumer industry
came of age — exemplified by the expansion of the commercial music hall —
and found its most noisy customers among those young men who, without
family responsibilities, were becoming independent of their own parents and
had sufficient income to lead an active social life. The growing concern among
late Victorian adults about the activities of the young in British cities was due
as much to their increased visibility as to their expanding numbers. Demographic factors, especially lower infantile mortality and birth rates, are also
significant in helping to explain why the condition and prospects of city
children and adolescents were a central element in the debate concerning how
to improve urban living conditions. Yet to view the emergence of a separate
adolescent age group purely as a result of the educational and demographic
changes in British society would be to miss the point that youths were now
also better off and could afford to spend their hard-earned pennies on music
halls, boys' magazines and football matches. It was a persistent belief of
Victorian middle-class reformers and youth workers that commercial forms of
leisure acted as a morally corrupting influence on the young, and that this
could only be combatted by the provision of alternative, morally healthy,
church-related recreational outlets. Thus it was claimed that the discipline and
obedience inculcated by the B.B. 'method' would not only prevent adolescent
'lawlessness' but also offer a counter attraction to the 'low' music halls and
public houses frequented by young men. Whatever, in fact, the young spent
their money on, they caused concern in those who saw in the recent emergence of 'adolescence' a social force which they neither liked nor understood.

The age group we would now describe as adolescents or teenagers first came
to be seen as a distinct category, with their own peculiar problems of physical
and social adjustment, between the years 1880 and 1914. The new discipline of
psychology had singled them out as an autonomous group for investigation
by the 1890s when the most effective definition of adolescence as an independent age category between childhood and adulthood was put forward by G.
Stanley Hall, one of the major figures in early American educational psychology. In Britain until late in the nineteenth century the idea of a discontinuity
between the child and the adult was largely a luxury reserved for the upper
and middle classes, and one of the social effects of the mid-Victorian 'reform'
of the public schools has been seen as the 'invention' of adolescence. For
middle and upper-class boys now went to preparatory and public schools,
followed often by university, thus prolonging the transition to manhood.
Such youths passed as schoolboys at an age when most of their less privileged
contemporaries had been in employment for some years. Middle and upper-
class youths thus experienced an extended adolescence or self-conscious
boyhood, which was celebrated in boys' magazines like the *Boys' Own Paper*
and *The Captain*. Among the working classes, on the other hand, the line
between childhood and adolescence was marked, for the sons of the skilled, by
the transition between elementary and secondary education at the age of
thirteen or fourteen; this came at an even earlier age for the sons of the
unskilled who often left school at eleven or twelve. Thus the nature of
adolescence and the timing of its emergence tended to be different between
social classes and within those classes themselves.[11]

The recognition of adolescence as a social 'problem' in the late nineteenth and early twentieth centuries in Britain was directly related to economic changes, such as the expansion of 'boy labour' occupations in all the major commercial centres. At this time, concern for the employment prospects of the adolescent was to be as pronounced among middle-class reformers as the attention given by them to the existence of child labour in the early nineteenth century. Thus those who had formerly been horrified at the large numbers of children roaming the streets or performing manual factory tasks were, by the late Victorian period, worried about juvenile delinquency or the 'problem' of boy labour — i.e., the recruitment of large numbers of adolescents into short-term unskilled jobs with no prospects. Charles Booth, the pioneer social investigator, singled out the London demand for boy labour in the late nineteenth century as a special characteristic of the city's economy. From whatever motive, social, economic or religious, the adolescent years came to be seen as a problem in themselves. Youth ceased to be merely a prelude to adulthood and youth work was no longer seen as just an adjunct of charity or missionary work with adults. Adolescence became a recognized stage of life which had to be dealt with and controlled by the 'respectable' church-going adult. Thus the youth movements of this period were often expressly formed to deal with the so-called 'problem' of youth, especially the problem of the adolescent who was not amenable to religious or social teaching. Attention was being drawn to the adolescent in the 1880s, particularly in the large conurbations, both by the established authorities, who wanted to regulate his behaviour, and by the Christian community, who were concerned for his spiritual and moral guidance. This new awareness of the problem of adolescence does much to identify the historical context within which William Smith created The Boys' Brigade.[12]

Hence the remarkable proliferation of organizations and voluntary activities for the young between 1880 and 1914 — Brigades, Scouts, Clubs, Cadets — is itself a strong indication of the emerging preoccupation with the question of adolescence. In many British cities, the attempt to come to terms with this problem was made through the agencies and methods of evangelical Christianity and the forms of military training. For it was to deal with, and retain within the Church, this adolescent age group that The Boys' Brigade was first established. The prevailing mood and the social, economic and religious circumstances of late Victorian Britain were propitious, in other words, and all that was needed was the right man to come along and fuse these various elements in the historical fabric together. Thus our first chapter will look at William Smith and the origins of The Boys' Brigade in Glasgow, the coming together of the man and the idea.

CHAPTER 1

'THE MAN AND THE IDEA'

William Smith and the Origins of
The Boys' Brigade in Glasgow

ON THE EVENING of Thursday, 4 October 1883, a young Glasgow Sunday School teacher stood in his Free Church Mission Hall awaiting the response to his new idea for the Christian development of adolescent boys. At 8 o'clock, as the doors opened, twenty-eight boys from the Mission Sunday School surged into the Hall. Three nights were allowed for recruiting, and this brought in thirty-one more boys from the North Woodside area of the city. They were a disorderly group, between twelve and seventeen years of age. Some were curious; some were bent on mischief; and some had little else to do. A few left but most stayed, and The Boys' Brigade — the first voluntary uniformed youth organization — came into being. The young man was called William Smith; but who was he and how did the idea emerge?

William Alexander Smith was born on 27 October 1854 some 300 miles from Glasgow at Pennyland House on the outskirts of Thurso. His home overlooked Dunnet Head, the most northerly point on the British mainland. Until he was fourteen years old, he lived and was educated in Thurso, a small Caithness town with a population of around 3,000. William was one of a family of four: his younger brothers Donald and David eventually took up farming in South Africa and Australia respectively, before predeceasing their elder brother; his young sister Kate later moved to Glasgow in the footsteps of her brother and died a few months after him in 1914. Not surprisingly, in an area where the Army provided one of the few alternatives to crofting, the family followed a tradition of military service. Smith's father, David, had been an ensign in the 7th Dragoon Guards during the Kaffir War of 1849-50, and on his return to Caithness he joined the Volunteer Artillery Corps, reaching the rank of major. Smith's grandfather, William, had been commissioned to the 78th Highland Regiment of Foot (formerly the 'Ross-shire Buffs') in 1810, becoming adjutant in 1813 and lieutenant in 1814, then fighting in the Flanders campaigns of 1814-15. The impact of the family's military history on Smith must have been considerable and provided a foundation for his subsequent involvement in the Volunteer movement.[1]

Although statutory provision of education was still some way off, William Smith attended the traditional Scottish parish school, the Miller Institution, later to be known as Thurso Academy. Little is known of his academic record, although Robert Campbell, a childhood friend, mentioned his love of outdoor activities, in particular the game of shinty. Subsequent eulogies of Smith must be treated with caution but it would seem reasonable to accept the opinion of W.R.O. Campbell, one of the Thurso Academy pupils, that he was 'a general favourite amongst us'. In 1868 the pattern of life changed abruptly for William Smith at thirteen when his father, a director of the Labuan Coal Company, died of 'effusion on the brain' following a fever on 6 January at Swatow in China. The widowed Harriet Smith moved with her family into the town of Thurso and accepted the offer of her brother, Alexander Fraser, a Glasgow merchant, to take William into his home and business in Glasgow. Alex Fraser, an evangelical Free Church man, was a wholesale dealer in clothing and shawls, dealing principally with the South American market. Living with his three sisters at 28 Hamilton Park Terrace on the edge of the prosperous West End burgh of Hillhead, Fraser operated a successful business with premises in Princes Square, off fashionable Buchanan Street, and a summer home at Callander near the Trossachs. William and his family spent the summer of 1868 in Callander then, in November, when his mother, brothers and sister returned to Thurso, he remained behind in Glasgow with his uncle and aunts. What sort of environment would this now fourteen-year-old boy have found himself in when he first came to live in the city which, fifteen years later, was to give birth to The Boys' Brigade?[2]

By the late nineteenth century, Glasgow had grown to be the second city of the Empire with a population outstripping that of any other provincial city in the United Kingdom. It was essentially a Liberal city, represented by M.P.s from the middle-class Protestant group of radical free traders whose commercial and manufacturing enterprise had taken the city to its pre-eminent position. With a dependence on textiles, iron and heavy engineering, the city was the centre of industry and commerce in the West of Scotland. The growth in importance of the Clyde and its shipbuilding combined with the success of the traditional industries to give Glasgow entrepreneurs a vibrant confidence dented only by rare setbacks, such as the collapse of the City of Glasgow Bank in 1878. The city was held to be one of the most aggressively efficient in the Europe of this period, and the all-pervading Liberal, Nonconformist influence gave support to the social philanthropy of the merchants and manufacturers which was to make itself felt in the new era of youth work. The same evangelical influence permeated the local corridors of power and, combined with ruthless business efficiency, resulted in 'a Corporation which looks on the Imperial Parliament as a means of registering its decrees'.[3]

Although Glasgow could boast of an unequalled layout of parks and recreational grounds, and an excellent transport system, it suffered critical housing problems. The densely populated city had grown rapidly, but remained compact, having little or no suburban sprawl. Overcrowded housing — more than thirty per cent of the population had only one room to live and sleep in — had its consequential health problems, particularly in the age group which was later to provide the B.B. with its first recruits. By the late nineteenth century, the trend in social segregation in many British cities during the Victorian period was evident, with the factories and workforce of Glasgow being concentrated, by and large, in the centre and the East End, and the middle classes and their businesses edging westwards. The particular geographical characteristics of Glasgow are important in this context and made the provision of 'missionary' work simpler. As the city expanded, new artisan housing areas were located in close proximity to middle and upper-class areas. The growth of the West End, where The Boys' Brigade was initially to establish itself, took an irregular shape about two miles in length from east to west and varying in width from 400 yards to one mile. This resulted in a genteel residential area such as Hillhead (where William Smith and many of his colleagues lived) being sandwiched between the working-class suburbs of Partick and Maryhill. Domestic mission work could be carried out at only a short distance from the parent congregation. The need and scope for such mission work was becoming more apparent with the increasing number of young people — ten per cent of the male population in 1883 were between ten and fourteen years old. Prominent industrialists and philanthropists, such as Sir William Collins the publisher and Michael Connal of the shipbuilding family, were leading the way in this work and were to be strong supporters of The Boys' Brigade. Evangelical groups such as the 'Association for Promoting the Religious and Social Improvement of the City' had men like these in their membership — one of whom was William Smith's uncle, Alexander Fraser.

During his first year in Glasgow, William Smith familiarized himself with his uncle's warehouse, and at the same time took classes at Burns' and Sutherland's private school. In 1869 he entered full time into his uncle's business, living at Hamilton Park Terrace in winter and in lodgings during the summer months while the rest of the family migrated to the country. He settled down to the routine of middle-class business life in the city, attending Y.M.C.A. lectures, sailing trips and soirées, but a growing estrangement from his uncle led to his departure from Hamilton Park Terrace and his uncle's business in 1878 to establish the exporting firm of Smith, Smith and Company with his brother Donald, who had arrived in Glasgow in 1873. William's mother arrived from Thurso to look after her son's new home in nearby Kersland Terrace until his marriage six years later. In 1881 James G. Findlay, a friend and colleague, entered into partnership with him to form the firm Smith, Findlay and Company, dealing in a variety of shawls, plaids and tartans for export. Local descriptions, in 1888, indicate a prosperous business which, by then, Smith had left to become full-time Secretary of The Boys' Brigade. James G. Findlay was later to become General Manager of the Irrawady Flotilla Company in Rangoon. The severing of business ties with his uncle extended to their personal relationship and was to persist until their reconciliation in 1895. A major factor in Alexander Fraser's disapproval of his nephew's way of life, other than the alleged reluctance of Fraser to accept his nephew's modern ideas and business efficiency, was the latter's enlistment in the 1st Lanark Rifle Volunteers, a move which ran counter to Fraser's strongly held pacifist views. The influence of the Volunteer movement on the foundation and early development of The Boys' Brigade was to prove considerable, and so it is appropriate here to give a brief mention of its origins and nature.[4]

The Volunteer Force had been formed in 1859 with the military objective of providing some form of defence in the event of invasion at a time of British weakness. The likely perpetrators of such an offence were regarded as the French under Napoleon III. Victorian anxiety about invasion increased with the application of steam power to ships, thus making the Channel less of a barrier than formerly. Any study of the Volunteer movement, however, will demonstrate that men enlisted for social as well as military reasons, and in some ways the movement might be regarded as a military expression of the Victorian spirit of self-help. Apart from the contribution to the nation's defence, the movement offered opportunities for middle class and working class alike, providing for the former a pleasant and gratifying way of occupying increased leisure time, and for the latter, social and recreational activities otherwise denied them. For the nation it might provide a method of instilling into the younger generation the values of discipline, obedience and esprit de corps which were to be later extended to the adolescent members of The Boys' Brigade movement. Volunteering had 'made men less idle and dissipated and more respectful to authority', and members had now forsaken the dancing saloons and billiard rooms to 'give their days to shoot and evenings to drill and find pleasure in music and chorus singing'.[5]

The Volunteer movement was particularly strong in Scotland, and Glasgow was no exception. Most regiments consisted of companies formed by businesses and professions, led by a strong upper middle-class group such as existed in the city. With the 1st Lanark Rifle Volunteers drawing from the prosperous West End business population and with William Smith's family tradition of Volunteering in Caithness, it was perhaps inevitable that the young businessman now living in Hillhead should enlist. The 1st Lanark Rifle Volunteers included companies originally established for procurators and lawyers, accountants, stockbrokers and actuaries, bankers and clerks, as well as for particular businesses such as Messrs. Wylie and Lochhead of Buchanan Street and J. & W. Campbell and Company of Ingram Street, and the leading shipping companies. The Regiment could later boast of a number of national figures, including two future Prime Ministers — Campbell-Bannerman and Bonar Law — and Jimmy Maxton, future Chairman of the Independent Labour Party. 'Volunteering was an enthusiastic business.'[6]

William Smith enlisted in the 1st Lanark Rifle Volunteers in 1874 and was quickly promoted to lance corporal and then to sergeant in 1876. Commissioned as a second lieutenant in 'L' Company in 1877, he became a full lieutenant in April 1881 before resigning owing to pressure of business in December 1881. He rejoined 'C' Company in 1884 and reached the rank of lieutenant colonel before his retiral in 1908. Thereafter, until his death, he was accorded the rank of honorary colonel, remaining, as the regimental journal in 1895 had put it, 'one of the most popular officers in the Regiment'. The view held by the Regiment that it was the Volunteer movement which was responsible for the emergence of The Boys' Brigade is, in itself, an overstatement, but indicates the attitude of the officers of the 1st L.R.V. at this time, two of whom — James Carfrae Alston and John Roxburgh — were to become Presidents of The Boys' Brigade during its first fifty years.[7]

While still living with his uncle and working in his business, Smith, in the early 1870s, took the first steps in involving himself in the religious life of the city. Living in Alexander Fraser's household, he would have become familiar with the work and ideas of the Glasgow churchmen and philanthropists — work which was gaining in momentum and of which some mention must be made in any analysis of the B.B.'s origins. The religious complexion of late nineteenth-century Glasgow provides the canvas on which the emergence of The Boys' Brigade can be sketched, and an understanding of it helps to explain the initial success of the movement. The new organization was to be interdenominational, and its origins do not lie solely, or even mainly, within the established Church of Scotland. The first ten companies were formed in association with Nonconformist congregations and, indeed, after five years of existence there were more companies connected with Dissenting congregations than with the established Churches of Scotland and England. Of some relevance to the future of the B.B. in Scotland was the 'Disruption' in the Scottish Church of 1843, which followed a century of secessions and unions and brought into being the Free Church as a rival denomination to the Church of Scotland. In Glasgow, a city with thirty-one religious denominations meeting in 331 churches or halls, the strength of religious feeling was clearly visible. The three principal Protestant denominations (Church of Scotland, Free Church and United Presbyterian Church) were fairly evenly represented in the city in the 1880s, and the period is marked by an increase in church building and mission work.

With a more liberal ecclesiastical government (following the Patronage Act of 1874), the Church of Scotland built twenty-six new churches in the city between 1871 and 1880. Free Church growth emulated that of the Church of Scotland by duplicating the latter's expansion in every geographical area possible. Increased church-building did not, however, attract a commensurate increase in members or finance. Seen in this context, the initial encouragement of The Boys' Brigade within the Free Church is not surprising. The aggressive evangelical approach, characteristic of the Free Church in its missionary work, would readily embrace a new organization which might recruit or retain young people in membership. Amongst its office bearers were many of the city merchants and politicians who were to extend their philanthropy to supporting The Boys' Brigade. While smaller than the Free Church, the United Presbyterian Church was better endowed. Liberal in temperament and theology, it had in its 'gathered congregations' many of those industrialists who patronized the charitable work of the city. With its main strength in the cities and in the Scottish industrial belt, the United Presbyterian Church, like its fellow Nonconformists, was suitably located to adopt the new organization. As the city expanded westwards, impressive buildings were constructed in the newly populated areas from where missions could be sent and youth work organized.

Both the geographical structure of Glasgow and the competitive outreach of the major religious denominations facilitated the extension of missionary work. By the 1860s this effort was being supplemented by the charitable and social reform work of evangelical associations such as the Glasgow City Mission. The range of evangelical work intertwined with the missions of the Churches and, to a varying degree, the temperance and reform movements. Glasgow, like other major cities, had suffered from the Industrial Revolution's side effect of greatly increased alcoholic consumption. The temperance movement, which had originated in the Maryhill district of the city in 1829 under Robert Kettle, cotton manufacturer and friend of Thomas Chalmers (the Free Church leader), evolved into the Scottish Temperance League in 1844. The Glasgow Abstainers Union was active, and the Band of Hope had 650 juvenile societies in Scotland by 1870. This activity mirrored the growing national concern with prevention at an early age, as evidenced in the growth of the British League of Juvenile Abstainers, formed in 1847. A more aggressive approach towards temperance was taken in the city by the various evangelical groups. The Grove Street Home Mission, adjacent to the residential West End, complained bitterly that, whereas an application for a licence in the Hillhead area, with a population of 9,000, had been withdrawn in face of opposition to 'a thing so dreadful', in the area around the Mission there were seventy-three public houses. One working man asked despairingly: 'Why don't you West End people deliver us from the curse as well as yourselves?' The Boys' Brigade, originating in this area, was not to promote abstinence actively, but worked alongside various groups to encourage temperance. William Smith, for example, did not lend his encouragement to pledge-taking by boys, but always emphasized the benefits of moderation. Some companies were, however, to be formed by abstinence societies, for example in Wick and Port Glasgow.[8]

As the century progressed, an increasing awareness of the need to channel part of this social and religious missionary effort towards the adolescent population is demonstrated in the various pamphlets, statements and organi-

Sir William Alexander Smith (1854-1914),
Founder of The Boys' Brigade.

Pennyland House, near Thurso on the north coast of Scotland — the birthplace of William Smith.

Portrait of William Smith taken in April 1880, when he was 25. By this time he had left his uncle's firm and set up his own business.

The Mounted Detachment of the 1st Lanarkshire Rifle Volunteers in the early 1900s. Major William Smith, commander of the Detachment, is second from the left in the front row.

The North Woodside Mission Hall in the West End of Glasgow, where Smith founded the 1st Company of The Boys' Brigade on 4 October 1883.

The original officers and sergeants of the 1st Glasgow Company in 1885-86. Smith is standing on the right, and to his left are his lieutenants, James and John Hill. The rifle was introduced for drilling purposes, and could not be used as a firearm. The model shown here had a metal barrel and spring action, but had no connection between barrel and trigger.

zational reports of the time. This awareness assisted the new agencies leading the way in work with young people — the age group who were 'in a large measure lost to the Church'. One major agency was the Glasgow Y.M.C.A. which, by the 1880s, had developed from a relatively small organization with a spiritual objective to an extensive and flourishing association with 180 branches and over 7,000 members. The Y.M.C.A. emblem, a triangle, denotes fitness of body, mind and spirit, and the wider spectrum of activity (which included evening classes, athletic clubs and a range of extramural activities) was in evidence when William Smith and his colleagues were leading their own congregational Young Men's Societies and Sunday Schools. He himself joined the Glasgow Y.M.C.A. in the autumn of 1872.[9]

Some associations operated within a well-defined local area. In 1848 the Spoutmouth Young Men's Institute had been formed in a densely populated area of the city's East End by Sir Michael Connal, Chairman of the Glasgow School Board from 1874 to 1885. The Buchanan Instifition, of a similar nature, was promoted by Connal, Sir William Collins and James Campbell in the Calton and Bridgeton areas, and introduced bugle bands and 'single stick drill' — an interesting portent of what was to come. As an auxiliary to churches of all denominations, the Grove Street Home Mission Institute had been founded on the western side of the city in 1858. The successful methods of the Institute, with strong emphasis on the 'Boys' Department', would not be lost on future Brigade leaders. (The work of the Institute continues today under the title 'The Grove Christian Centre'.) By the time The Boys' Brigade had been formed, further specialized work and organizations for the adolescent were in evidence. William Quarrier, an evangelical Baptist better known for his orphans' homes, had formed Working Boys' Brigades in the 1860s — Shoe-black Brigade, News Brigade and Parcels Brigade — with distinctive uniforms and access to residential accommodation and educational or recreational facilities. Quarrier was supported again by the same families of Liberal Dissenters later to be associated with William Smith — J. Campbell White (later Lord Overtoun), chemical manufacturer; William A. Campbell, ware-house owner (later Campbells, Stewart and MacDonald); Robert Binnie, builder; W.S. Blackie, publisher; and the Coats family of cotton-thread manu-facturing fame in Paisley. In looking at the origins of The Boys' Brigade, the influence of the local movements cannot be accurately measured. However, they were undoubtedly important in creating the environment within which William Smith and the early Brigade leaders were to work. There was one particular organization, in this context, which has received little attention from historians but whose influence cannot be ignored — the Glasgow Foundry Boys' Religious Society.

During the formative years of The Boys Brigade, the Glasgow Foundry Boys' Religious Society was at its peak and many of the early Brigade leaders were associated with it. There is no documentary evidence that William Smith was a member (although this is claimed by the Society) but he would, undoubted-ly, be closely aware of its work. The origins of the Society lie not in the missionary zeal of the middle and upper-class philanthropists of nineteenth-century Glasgow, but in the compassion of a working-class girl, Mary Ann Clough. As the Industrial Revolution reached its zenith, a large number of iron foundries were sited on the banks of the Forth and Clyde Canal, in the north of Glasgow. To assist the moulders, many boys were employed from the ages of ten to twelve, and, thrown in among the rough-and-ready foundry workers at an impressionable age, they would quickly assume the habits and manners of their adult colleagues. It was fear of this which motivated the young factory girl to obtain the use of a room in the foundry where she was employed to hold Sunday afternoon meetings for around fifty boys. When she emigrated to New Zealand in 1862 it seemed that this small pocket of missionary effort would disappear. However, in 1865 the work was taken up by four Glasgow businessmen — William Hunter, William Martin, James Hunter and Alexander Mackeith — and the Glasgow Foundry Boys' Religious Society was officially launched in the Cowcaddens area of the city. The organization, supported by familiar city figures, experienced a rapid growth, reaching a peak of membership in 1886 with over 16,000 boys (and girls) and almost 2,000 leaders. Thereafter its strength slowly declined until World War I, after which a sharper decline was suffered, although it remains active in a few areas of the city today. By the early 1870s the Society had expanded beyond Glasgow to forty-four towns in Scotland and six in England where it was designated the '—— Working Boys' and Girls' Religious Society'. These local groups were instrumental in establishing some of the earlier Brigade companies.[10]

The Foundry Boys' Religious Society was concerned with the same age range as that with which The Boys' Brigade was about to deal, and organized itself in four areas — religious, educational, social reform and provident. The formation of evening classes, savings banks and excursions followed what was becoming a familiar pattern, but of greater relevance, and influence, for The Boys' Brigade was the introduction of drill. By obtaining the services of local Volunteers (from the 1st Lanark Artillery) the methods of the Society looked forward to those of The Boys' Brigade. A cheap uniform, consisting of cap, belt and haversack, was provided and was in use for a few years from 1865 onwards. The influence of the Society on later uniformed youth organizations has not generally been recognized for the likely reason that the promotion of drill and uniform was short-lived. By 1870, drill classes and uniform had all but disappeared as more emphasis was placed on education and recreation. In the same year, girls were admitted. The decline of the Foundry Boys is in marked contrast to the rapid development of The Boys' Brigade over the same period. With improvement in education and alternative leisure pursuits, together with a decline in evangelical zeal, the Society might be expected to show a diminution in strength. An inference by J. Campbell White that many Churches were less than enthusiastic indicates an underlying reason why B.B. companies with their obligatory link to a church or mission could better establish themselves in the longer term. The Brigade and the Scouts, with a purely male membership, were also to develop activities more attuned to the inclinations of the adolescent in the early twentieth century. As the B.B established itself, however, many aspects of the Foundry Boys' work and philosophy can be discerned. The similar age grouping, use of drill, religious basis, encouragement of temperance and development of outdoor activities provided a link which was strengthened by the welcome given by the Society to the Brigade idea in 1883.

The influence of this atmosphere on the young William Smith must have been considerable. In 1874, when he was twenty years old, his religious beliefs were further deepened. This was the year of Moody and Sankey's evangelical revivalist campaign, and Smith's diary records one of its few entries in red ink: '12/2/74. Heard Moody and Sankey for the first time'. An indication of the impression the American evangelists made on Smith can be deduced from the fact that three further entries in his diary record the major Glasgow meetings of D.L. Moody. Moody and Sankey's Scottish campaign in 1873-74 had a considerable impact on Scottish religious life, and nowhere was this impact stronger than in Glasgow where they preached to gatherings of 5,000 time and again. This evangelical revival initially affected the middle classes and provided a strong stimulus to the social and philanthropic work already begun in the city. The missionary agencies were infused with fresh religious spirit as a result of the significant success of the evangelists. Young middle-class business and professional men, such as Henry Drummond and Campbell-White, who were later to be associated with The Boys' Brigade, communicated directly with Moody and followed him in his campaigns, enthusiastically taking the revivalist message back to their particular church congregations.[11]

As well as strengthening and directing William Smith's religious convictions, the Moody and Sankey campaign provided further support for the establishment of The Boys' Brigade by stimulating the social and missionary outreach of the city's churches. One of Moody's most devoted followers was the Rev. George Reith (father of Lord Reith, first Director-General of the B.B.C.), the young minister of the College Free Church where Alexander Fraser and his family were members. William Clow, Reith's biographer, recounts the euphoria when Moody came to Glasgow and, in particular, the effect on the large congregation of the College Free Church, whose office bearers, it was said, could form a quorum should 'the Chamber of Commerce be summoned to meet within the Session Room of the Church':

> Many of the younger members of his congregation such as William A. Campbell and William Smith received a fresh baptism and responded to their young Minister's voice and his appeal with a fearless confession.

The expansion of missionary work was to prove particularly significant in the North Woodside area of Glasgow where, immediately following the evangelical campaigns, the College Free Church established the mission later to become the home of the first company of The Boys' Brigade. Extension work in other towns and cities in Scotland received a similar stimulus from visits by Moody, preceded, and in some cases followed, by supporters such as Drummond who consolidated the message. It may be no coincidence that the provincial centres where this type of organization was carried out, mainly Stirling, Perth, Dundee and Aberdeen, were among the first to establish B.B. companies. Moody, residing with friends in the Mull of Kintyre, did a substantial amount of work in Cambeltown, and it is interesting to note that this small west-coast town had, after five years of Boys' Brigade development, more companies than any other Scottish town or city apart from Glasgow, Edinburgh and Ayr.[12]

Smith's diaries relate that, after hearing Moody and Sankey for the first time on 12 February 1874 and attending subsequent meetings, he formally joined the College Free Church on 12 April 1874, thus switching from the Church of Scotland within which he had been raised to his uncle's Free Church denomination. In September 1874 he and James Findlay called on the Rev. George Reith with a view to establishing a Young Men's Society. This was subsequently formed as the Woodside Morning Branch of the Y.M.C.A., and Findlay and Smith were joined in the leadership of the Society by two brothers, James and John Hill, who were to be officers in the 1st Glasgow Company, and James Moffat, whose later translations of the Old and New Testaments were to become world famous. Smith remained a member of the

Society, becoming President of its evening meetings, until the North Woodside B.B. Bible Class was formed.

It is unlikely that Smith himself would have maintained that he had an actual conversion during the campaigns of Moody and Sankey, as he in later years consistently doubted the value of spontaneous pledges and never encouraged the boys in his charge to risk the subsequent dangers of disillusionment. The feeling engendered, however, led directly to his involvement in the Young Men's Society and to Sunday School work at the College Free Church, followed by his subsequent move over to the North Woodside Mission Sunday School as a teacher and then Secretary. Smith was held in high regard in his church congregation as an able and conscientious young man, and the qualities discerned by Dr Herbert Gray, the assistant minister, no doubt led to his being directed towards North Woodside:

> From the very first I was impressed by his amazing capacity for detail . . . He was very strict but also very kindly and understanding . . . He seldom talked religion, he practised it.

North Woodside Mission promoted an extensive programme of religious club and charitable activities throughout the week for the benefit of the surrounding population. It was into this busy programme that The Boys' Brigade was inserted after 1883, initially each Thursday evening at 8 p.m.[13]

The mission activity which led directly to the establishment of The Boys' Brigade was that of the Sunday Schools. The maintenance of class order was in many instances extremely difficult and was not proving any more manageable now that compulsory elementary education was taking over much of the *raison d'être* of the Sunday School movement. Allied to this difficulty of fulfilling the object of the Sunday School was the failure to retain the older children until they were able to join the Y.M.C.A. or other church young men's society at seventeen. Smith, at the North Woodside Mission, came face to face with the problem of filling this gap between early and late teens. In his direct involvement with it he was also grappling with the week-by-week difficulties of controlling Sunday School boys, and in 1883 he vigorously sought a solution.

In the summer of 1883 William Smith put the idea to the Rev. George Reith and his office bearers at the College Free Church that Sunday School boys aged twelve and over should be formed into a brigade. Although the proposal to introduce week-night activities within a framework of military discipline caused anxiety in some minds, Smith and his colleagues, the Hill brothers, were allowed to proceed, and on 4 October of that year held the first meeting of an organization whose remarkable development could scarcely have been envisaged. In preparation for the inauguration of the movement, the initial format and regulations had been carefully planned. Having decided on the title 'The Boys' Brigade', the organization's Object was defined as:

> The advancement of Christ's Kingdom among Boys and the promotion of habits of Reverence, Discipline, Self-respect and all that tends towards a true Christian manliness.

The text of this Object has remained the same for a century, with the addition of the word 'Obedience' in 1893. The design for a crest was agreed as the now familiar anchor, on which was enscribed the motto 'Sure and Stedfast' (taken from Hebrews, 6:19 — 'Hope we have as an anchor of the soul, both sure and stedfast.'). The Biblical spelling of 'stedfast' has been retained. These words and the symbol were to become emblematic in many features of the work of The Boys' Brigade, as highlighted in the organization's most popular hymn:

> We have an anchor that keeps the soul
> Stedfast and sure while the billows roll.

Fifty-nine boys joined initially, probably for a variety of reasons, not least of which would be the likelihood of further amusement at the expense of the Sunday School leaders. However, the application of strict discipline (no one was allowed to 'fall-in' if even a minute late) brought some surprising results and confirmed Smith's view that boys liked strictness and discipline as long as it was fair. At first, all the boys were connected with the Mission, but soon other Sunday School lads in the area were attracted.

It is often assumed that The Boys' Brigade was formed to 'take the slum kids off the streets' and in many areas of our inner cities it was to do exactly this, but not at the outset. The 1st Glasgow Company catered for the sons of 'good' artisan and working-class families in an area which contained property much superior to that of the overcrowded city centre. Analysis of census returns demonstrates that the boys in the 1st Glasgow came mostly from the families of skilled workers. A sample of twenty-four boys enrolled in the second session of the Company shows a breakdown of social class by father's occupation as follows:

Table 1   1st Glasgow Company Social Classes, 1884-85

Professional Middle Class = 0	0%
White Collar/Lower Middle Class = 3	12.5%
Skilled Working Class = 14	58.3%
Unskilled Working Class = 3	12.5%
Deceased by time of census = 4	16.6%
Total = 24	99.9%

Of the twenty-four boys taken in this sample eleven had commenced employment at the date of enrolment in the Company and held the following jobs:

Joiner	Engine Fitter
Cabinetmaker	Warehouseman
Lithographer	Joiner's Apprentice (2)
Sewing Needle Groover	Clerk
Blacksmith	Ticket Writer

The early growth of The Boys' Brigade was to be centred mainly in this kind of environment before expanding to take in boys from a broader social range in the urban areas. In smaller towns and rural districts a wider social coverage, both at boy and leader level, was to be more obvious from the outset.[14]

The company was divided into six groups or squads, each one led by a 'non-commissioned officer' (NCO). In December 1883, an examination for promotion to NCO was held amongst all the boys aged over fourteen in which a practical drill test was followed by a written examination for the top twelve. Marks for conduct and character were added, after which the first six NCOs were selected — two sergeants, two corporals and two lance corporals. Company rules were formulated and printed on the annual membership cards. The company completed a successful first session with an inspection and display on 24 March 1884, followed, three days later, by a 'soirée', or concert, illustrating the cultural nature of some company activities. At the beginning of the second session, 1884-85, The Boys' Brigade, as yet, consisted of just one company. However, by January 1885 the first indications that it might extend further were evident from the other Glasgow Churches. The 2nd Glasgow Company was formed in connection with the Berkeley Street United Presbyterian Church Mission in North Street, near Charing Cross, Glasgow, an area not dissimilar to North Woodside. J.B. Couper, later to become Liberal M.P. for the Maryhill district of Glasgow, was the instigator, despite some initial reservations on the part of the parent church. Couper was a recruit in the 1st Lanark Rifle Volunteers and a leader of the Glasgow Foundry Boys' Religious Society in the Anderston area. When he called on Smith to collect a Volunteer prize for shooting, the two men spoke of their common interests and the experiment at North Woodside. It was in such a way that Smith's ideas percolated through the West End area of Glasgow where many of the early Glasgow companies were to emerge.

As Smith realized the potential of the movement he had begun, he called a meeting of those involved in the two existing companies, together with other interested youth workers (J.B. Hill, J.R. Hill, J.S. Couper, J.B. Couper, F.P.R. Ferguson, W. Nicholl and E.W. Hamlen). On 26 January 1885 the meeting agreed to designate itself as the 'Council of The Boys' Brigade'. A constitution was drawn up and it was confirmed that a company requesting registration required to be connected to a church or other religious body. Thereafter, the Brigade advanced dramatically and by the time the newly formed Council had held its first annual meeting on 12 October 1885, fifteen companies had been enrolled, twelve in Glasgow and three in Edinburgh. In Glasgow, the success of Smith's ideas led to the establishment of companies by all denominations, with the Nonconformists predominant. The 3rd Glasgow Company was associated with the Adelaide Place Baptist Church at the St. Clair Street Mission Hall, giving the first three companies a denominational spectrum (Free Church, U.P. Church and Baptist). The 3rd Glasgow, however, failed to survive the opposition in the Deacons' Court of the parent church, which could not sanction the continuance of 'anything that tends to foster a warlike spirit in boys'. All twelve of these Glasgow companies in 1885 were located in the West End of the city and all had a connection with the Volunteer movement. The 16th Glasgow Company was the first to be formed in the East End of the city, following which the geographical distribution widened. The early companies were, in the main, established by prosperous churches, many of whom had missions in adjoining working-class areas. In March 1885 the Brigade idea was planted further afield with the formation of the 1st Edinburgh Company at Stockbridge United Free Church. A second company at St. Stephen's Free Church was founded in September 1885 but proved to be short-lived.[15]

Initially, the officers of the first companies were drawn from a more elevated social background than that of the boys they commanded. Most leaders were Volunteer officers, perhaps businessmen, who were involved in church or mission work among young people. Alexander Martin, a young officer under Smith in the 1st Glasgow Company, recalled that the staff were 'gentlemen', as might be expected of the College Free Church. An analysis of the leaders of the first thirty companies gives some indication of their background. Of a total of 409 officers enrolled in the period to 1900, fifty-one per cent had been leaders in Sunday Schools or other religious organizations, and sixty-two per cent had been in the Army or Volunteer movement. Of the first twenty Glasgow companies, twelve had captains in the 1st Lanark Rifle Volunteers, living in the city's West End. Of the remainder, one had been in the regular Army, and the other seven, who were to resign or retire by 1889, were succeeded by men with Volunteer experience. There is no doubt that the 1st Glasgow Company, and many of the early companies to be formed throughout the country, can be identified with a leadership which was predominantly middle-class, catering for a membership which was not. At an early stage, however, as the movement spread across a wider social spectrum, the gap between members and leaders narrowed, and the composition of the 1st Glasgow Company and other similar companies can no longer be taken as the rule but rather as the exception. If we have to identify a 'typical' early company captain, we might well point to a relatively young man of 'respectable' working-class or lower middle-class background, who had been in the Volunteers, and had been or still was a Sunday School teacher.[16]

Why did these officers so willingly give such substantial time and effort to the new movement? Many were already involved with other voluntary work, and the extension of a Sunday activity to cover much of the week must, presumably, have stretched capacities to the limit. Although only a few of the multitude of leaders during the period from 1883 to 1914 have left their ideas in print, and of these the national leaders like Smith are predominant, we can gauge from the records of local companies and the memories of 'old boys' the wide concern for the adolescent and the satisfaction gained in providing for his spiritual and recreational needs. Henry Drummond, before the end of the nineteenth century, had seen clearly that 'The Boys' Brigade would have been worth starting, were it only for the sake of the young men who act as its officers.'

At local level, these officers are unlikely to have developed ideas on the founding of a permanent system of training for the youth of the nation. It is more likely that theirs was a spontaneous reaction to a particular local need. The increasing reputation of the Brigade idea for the efficient use of leisure time to achieve spiritual ends was readily carried to areas where parents, Sunday School teachers and local leaders were willing to apply Smith's method of Christian training to their own particular adolescent population. Officers, despite a possible wish to preserve the existing social order through guidance and control, entered into a major commitment which was fundamentally religious. To become leaders they had to be church members; to remain as leaders they would require religious conviction and a genuine concern for their members. The great majority of these men possessed a social conscience which incorporated both humanitarianism and strong Christian faith.

When the Council met in October 1885, the potential of the new movement had already been recognized. The success of the 1st Glasgow Company had been consolidated and Smith could report that, of fifty-five boys on the roll the previous session, fifty-one remained, and movement of the older boys from the Brigade into the Y.M.C.A. or church young men's societies had begun. The Council elected J. Carfrae Alston, Captain of the 5th Glasgow Company, as first President of The Boys' Brigade. Alston was an influential tobacco merchant, a founder Volunteer and a leading member of the Renfield Free Church congregation. It is a reflection on the character of William Smith that he preferred to take the less illustrious, but infinitely more difficult, office of Secretary. John Lammie, Captain of the 6th Glasgow Company (Newton Place,

Partick) was elected Brigade Treasurer. In the third session, 1885-86, a Brigade Executive was formed consisting of eight members — the President, Secretary, Treasurer and five others: Reverend W. Haldane, Captain of the 1st Manchester Company; J.A.S. Arthur, Captain of the 1st London Company; W. Nicholl, Captain of the 4th Glasgow Company; A.S. Paterson, Captain of the 1st Edinburgh Company; and A. Robertson, Captain of the 3rd Edinburgh Company. Three distinct administrative units were established — (1) the Company, (2) the Battalion and (3) the Brigade. A further unit — the District — was interposed between (2) and (3) in 1913 to assist the more isolated companies and coordinate activities over a wider area.

The company was and is the basic unit, being a detachment of boys connected with a particular church or religious meeting place which has a local designation numbered according to order of formation. The company was placed under the command of a captain assisted by lieutenants, these being the only military ranks used by the adult leaders. A battalion could be formed wherever three or more companies existed in any town or district (in 1889 the requirement was increased to six), with all the enrolled officers forming a battalion council for the management of their own affairs. The term 'Brigade' embraced the whole organization, and this was administered by an Executive Committee between annual meetings of the Brigade Council. Initially Council consisted of company captains or their deputies, the Executive, chaplains and, from 1921, long-serving lieutenants, for it was not until 1952 that all officers were allowed to attend, with one vote for each company to be cast by the captain. Any church, Sunday School, or other group wishing to establish a company received the appropriate literature from a battalion secretary or Brigade Headquarters. Thereafter sanction had to be obtained from the church or other Christian organization and six meetings of the boys take place before formal application for enrolment could be made. Extensive advice emanated from Headquarters and enrolment of a company was not confirmed until a visit by a member of the battalion executive had been carried out. The estimated cost of establishing a company of fifty boys was calculated by Brigade Headquarters in the 1880s as being £3 15s. 5d. net (£3.77p) taking into account the sale of uniform items and an annual subscription of one shilling (5p).

The leaders of the organization might have been expected, with their Volunteer background of full and in many cases flamboyant uniforms, to transmit a similar style to The Boys' Brigade. The uniform adopted, however, was simple and inexpensive. The most junior rank of private had a forage cap (with a chin strap added later) having two rows of eighth-inch white braid and the company number at the front, a white linen haversack, and a leather waist belt with the B.B. crest on the buckle. Lance corporals and corporals wore the same uniform as a private, with the addition of a one barred chevron for the former and a two barred chevron for the latter, worn on the right arm. The sergeant's uniform consisted of a cap with a straight peak, two rows of quarter-inch white braid and the company number. In addition to the haversack and waist belt, sergeants wore a shoulder belt with a pouch at the back, and a three barred chevron. In 1898, the staff sergeant's uniform represented more of a break from the junior ranks with an adaptation of a field service cap, having one row of narrow braid around the top edge and an Anchor badge. Staff sergeants did not wear a haversack or belt but had a four barred chevron and carried a short brown military cane.

The uniform has not changed dramatically in the last hundred years. The forage or 'pillbox' cap remained in use until 1970-71 when it was replaced by a field service style of hat in blue terylene and cotton. The white haversack is now purely decorative rather than functional — in the early years it was used to carry small rations on 'Field Days'. In the first session, officers wore no uniform other than a red rossette in their jacket buttonhole. Thereafter regulation uniform consisted of a glengarry cap with crest, and a navy blue or other dark-coloured suit with tan gloves and a short brown military cane. The boys' uniform was deliberately designed as inexpensive, to be worn over a boy's ordinary clothes, and with a cap price of five pence payable by the membership it was within reach of most. Smith was adamant, however, that financial distress should not prevent membership and held that 'there should be no consideration to induce a Boy to stay away'. The accent was placed on cleanliness and neatness as far as a boy's appearance would permit.[18]

It had often been assumed that the B.B. uniform was taken directly from the Volunteers, but this assumption disintegrates on closer scrutiny. The Volunteers invariably used full uniform clothing, an idea specifically rejected by The Boys' Brigade. The items of uniform (or accoutrements) can be traced to similar parts of some Lanark Volunteer uniforms, but the model for the Brigade was likely to have been the uniform of the Glasgow Foundry Boys' Religious Society. There exists a photographic line block dated 1865 (unfortunately of too poor a quality to reproduce satisfactorily here) showing a Foundry Boy in a uniform of pillbox cap and white shoulder strap and belt worn over normal clothing — almost a replica of the later B.B. uniform. The new organization, effectively constituted, uniformed and led, was now set to launch itself upon the wider world.[19]

The major contributing factors in the shaping of the B.B. are now more clearly identified. The national problem of influencing the adolescent and retaining the Sunday School child through to possible membership of a church or young men's organization was brought more clearly into focus in Glasgow in an environment of competitive Church denominations and extensive evangelical and philanthropic activity. Religious agencies were promoting a greater awareness of the loss of the adolescent boy and girl not only to the Churches but to the desirable control of established authority, particularly during a period in the nation's history when rapid social and economic development was producing an acute anxiety as to the attitude, principles and possible actions of the educated and enfranchised future generation. It was in this environment that William Smith, moving in the company of the middle-class Glasgow philanthropists who were so eager to promote social outreach in the city, became familiar with the ideas and activities of organizations such as the Glasgow Foundry Boys' Religious Society. The impact of Moody and Sankey both strengthened his personal convictions and inspired the extension of the mission work with which he was to become involved. Faced with the common disciplinary problem of many Sunday School teachers, Smith was able to ally knowledge and love of the Volunteer movement and all its peripheral activities with his evangelical work in an attempt to solve what, for him, was a local problem in the Mission of the College Free Church. His unique fitness for such a task has been indicated by the various references from contemporaries. A fellow teacher in the North Woodside Sunday School remarked in retrospect that William Smith

could see a boy through and through. He knew the difficulties of mind and body that beset the life of a boy entering upon the adolescent period. He knew the tremendous pull that was being exercised on the boy's imagination and desires and of the vital need of having that led into a healthy environment. He placed himself alongside the boy and consciously passed onto him the help and guidance he most needed . . . His was a manly, robust religion which found expression in the common ground of every day life.[20]

CHAPTER 2

'TOWARDS A TRUE CHRISTIAN MANLINESS'

The Boys' Brigade in Britain, 1883 to 1900

THE BOYS' BRIGADE, now firmly established in Glasgow, was reaching the ears of others, not only in Scotland, but across the nation. Companies sprang up rapidly, both in the major cities and in small towns and rural areas. By 1890 there were 15,000 boys in membership, and on the tenth anniversary of the movement this figure stood at 26,000. Further promotion and expansion gave a total home and overseas membership of 75,000 at the turn of the century. The explanation for this dramatic progress lies in the social and historical conditions already described and in the attraction to boys, leaders and churches of Smith's ideas on boyhood. His observant study of adolescent nature, its 'gang' instincts and its potential when given, in his own phrase, an esprit de corps, predates the voluminous theories of later behavioral scientists. Smith appealed to the military *and* to the spiritual mind and to the many early leaders who would lay claim to both. The fusion of the ideals of the public school, the Volunteer regiment and Christian boyhood gave many philanthropists and mission members a tangible way of reaching those they were trying to help. Smith's crystallization of the adolescent problem made many look in his direction:

> It was the conviction that Boys were too important a part of the world to be slumped along with the rest of humanity and treated in the general mass that led to the formation of The Boys' Brigade. It was the consciousness that the old methods, however admirable, were not sufficient, that we wanted something that would appeal to the Boys, as Boys, something that would awaken in them that *esprit de corps* which a soldier feels for his regiment.[1]

When the movement proved successful in Glasgow, various channels of communication spread its philosophy into all regions of the country. There was recommendation by word of mouth, from both clerical and lay supporters. There was an increasing supply of information through the press, religious journals, Sunday School bulletins and Brigade publications, while there was also promotion by the various local Volunteer units. In Scotland, rapid growth was experienced from a combination of these forces and, in the five years from 1883, 206 companies were established (see Table 1, p.47). In many medium-sized towns the formation of a company by one denomination could quickly be followed by a second denomination, the Free Church usually taking the lead in the early years. Although this might imply a certain competitiveness, companies were often formed by a combination of Churches. In the small North Ayrshire town of Beith, for example, an application for enrolment was made jointly by the Church of Scotland, Free Church, United Presbyterian Churches (2), Evangelical Mission and Beith Mission School, emphasizing the interdenominational characteristics of the movement. As a result, three companies were formed with 150 boys in the first session. This enabled a battalion to be established — all in a small town of under 5,000 inhabitants. John Lennox, the junior minister of the U.P. Church,

Table 1:   *The B.B. in Scotland, 1883-1888*

Town	No. of Companies 1883-1888	Town	No. of Companies 1883-1888
Glasgow	93	Hawick	1
Edinburgh	17	Bonhill	1
Ayr	6	Cambusbarron	1
Campbeltown	4	Polmont	1
Aberdeen	3	Wick	1
Kilmarnock	3	North Berwick	1
Leith	3	Newhaven	1
Beith	3	Coatbridge	1
Perth	2	Port Glasgow	1
Hamilton	2	New Craighall	1
Dundee	2	Preston Kirk	1
Greenock	2	Alloa	1
Galashiels	2	Airdrie	1
Cambuslang	2	Braehead	1
Stirling	2	Galston	1
Alexandria	2	Forfar	1
Rutherglen	2	Peebles	1
Dumbarton	2	Tranent	1
Grantown-on-Spey	2	Brechin	1
Pollockshaws	2	Renton	1
Arbroath	2	Helensburgh	1
Bellshill	2	Grangemouth	1
Baillieston	2	Innellan	1
Dunoon	1	Newarthill	1
Uddingston	1	Larbert	1
Blantyre	1	Renfrew	1
Bannockburn	1	Burntisland	1
Paisley	1	Dunbar	1
Portobello	1	Fauldhouse	1
Inverness	1	Tarbert	1
Bridge of Weir	1	New Kilpatrick	1
Busby	1	Elgin	1
Johnstone	1	Kirkcaldy	1
Abercorn	1		

assumed the captaincy of the third company and expressed little surprise at the Brigade's popularity as 'wherever he went he heard people talking of The Boys' Brigade'.[2]

Apart from people talking of the Brigade, the voluminous correspondence of William Smith carried his ideas into other fertile areas. Enquiries from the Northeast led to the establishment of the movement in Aberdeen and Dundee where captains of Sunday School and Volunteer background organized the development. By 1888 companies had been established from Campbeltown in the West to Dunbar in the East; from Wick in the North to Galashiels in the Borders. It quickly became obvious that the B.B. was not to be purely an urban movement. In places such as Grantown-on-Spey (with less than 1,500 inhabitants) more than one company could be sustained, provided adequate leadership was available. Existing Working Boys' Societies, as in Hawick and Perth, often assisted in this respect by forming companies under their own auspices. In November 1885 the first English companies were formed in

London, Manchester, Armitage Bridge near Huddersfield, and Penzance. The movement quickly spread among both Anglicans and Nonconformists. Although Church of England extension work had not kept pace with the shifts in population, the prevalent evangelism, encouraged by Archbishop Benson (1883-1896), had created a mood more receptive to The Boys' Brigade. With the Nonconformist Churches having, together, as many active members as the Anglicans, the arrival on the scene of an organization able to direct the young into the Church required close attention by all groups. In London, the Presbyterian connection was strong as a result of the Brigade idea being carried to the metropolis by emigrant Scots. The first company at Pembroke Road Sabbath School in Kilburn was led by James Arthur, a friend of William Smith and a prominent member of St. John's Wood Presbyterian Church.

Table 2:   The B.B. in England, 1883-1888

Town	No. of Companies 1883-1888	Town	No. of Companies 1883-1888
London	14	Marple Bridge	1
Oxford	7	Spennymoor	1
Liverpool	3	Enfield	1
Hartlepool	3	Armitage Bridge	1
Plymouth	3	Penzance	1
Manchester	3	Chatham	1
Jarrow	3	Birkenhead	1
Newcastle	2	South Shields	1
Berwick	2	Tynemouth	1
Bristol	2	Dorchester	1
Jersey	2	Nottingham	1

From Table 2 it will be seen that the strongest area outside London in the first few years was Oxford. This strength, however, was illusory as all seven companies were to be disbanded within four years. The companies were staffed, in the main, by members of the University and located in several of the Oxford Colleges. James Hill of the 1st Glasgow Company was the leading light, following a move south. Other urban areas in England quickly followed the lead of London, with battalions being formed in Liverpool, Manchester, Plymouth, Sheffield, Nottingham and Bristol. In many cities, a request was made for Smith or a member of the Brigade Executive to visit the area. This happened in Liverpool, where there was also some thought given to 'going it alone' as an autonomous organization. However, the leaders were persuaded otherwise. Before the formation of the Church Lads' Brigade, there were occasional suggestions of independent units but little came of them. 'Have already received a letter from Wellingborough regarding proposed Congregational Boys' Brigade!' Smith wrote to the Brigade President in 1886, 'These Englishmen! Quite as friendly however as the Liverpool idea.'[3]

In the first ten years, the strongest areas in England were the North, the Southwest and London. Development was not consistent in the cities and varied from the steady, unwavering progress of Bristol and Sheffield to the more erratic advance of Plymouth and Manchester. An explanation of growth in The Boys' Brigade cannot be sought, therefore, in national economic or social trends; rather it is to be found in local circumstances. In Plymouth the resignation of leaders for business reasons (carrying their ideas with them to

Portsmouth, Weston-super-Mare and Bournemouth, for example), did not lead immediately to adequate replacements. In Manchester, the first three companies collapsed within a few years before progressive development took place under the enthusiastic guidance of C.E.B. Russell, first Battalion Secretary. Russell and F.P. Gibbon were vigorous promoters of the boys' club movement and in 1893 had established the strong 5th Manchester Company at the Heyrod Street Lads' Club in the Ancoats district of the city. Both men, having led the way in the Manchester area, went on to serve the Brigade at national level. Russell's ideas and publications on social reform among adolescents took him beyond The Boys' Brigade and boys' clubs. After serving on the Brigade Executive during his most active period in the movement (1894-1906), his services were much in demand by the Government. He was appointed H.M. Chief Inspector of Reformatories and Industrial Schools in 1913, and was first Chairman of the Juvenile Organizations Committee, sponsored by the Home Office in 1916. Excessive pressure of work in the interests of youth led to his death the following year. Gibbon, likewise, gave his energetic services to the movement nationally, while remaining within its confines. He was editor of the *Boys' Brigade Gazette* from 1928 to 1937, during which period he completed his reliable, if less than penetrating biography of William Smith.

In the stronger of the battalions already mentioned, the Church of England companies overshadowed their Nonconformist counterparts (except in London), although the Nonconformists were predominant over the country as a whole in taking a lead, having fifty-three per cent of the companies in England and Wales and sixty-three per cent of the companies in Scotland. It may be that the Church of England parishes were better able to maintain the existence of a company by supplying new leaders where necessary. Nonconformists, with a greater proportion of Volunteers in their ranks, and much initial enthusiasm, may have met with less response in cases where the founding Volunteer Brigade officers did not have automatic successors of similar background within their own congregations.

Church of England support and links with the boys' club movement were much in evidence in Nottingham, a city which was to become a stronghold of The Boys' Brigade and the Boys' Life Brigade. The city's traditional concern for adolescents and its love of sport combined well and a number of companies were formed jointly with boys' clubs. The first company was established by the former Trent Bridge cricketer Johnny Dixon. The 2nd Nottingham Company, formed at St. James' Church of England by the boys' club leader Oliver Hind, was for many years the largest company in the Brigade, with an incredible strength of 350 boys. Hind went on to become President of Nottingham Battalion and an influential member of the Brigade Executive from 1906 to 1913, by which time the company had a farm for boys in Nova Scotia.[4]

The importance for Boys' Brigade development of support by the clergy and prominent local citizens is nowhere better illustrated than in Carlisle. In 1889 a company was formed in connection with Warwick Road Presbyterian Church but collapsed for lack of support. However, when The Boys' Brigade was re-established in 1891 there was considerable encouragement from the clergy and laity. The local authority promoted recreational activities with the award of grants and facilities, and a strong lead was given by the Diocese, half of the Church of England companies being captained by their chaplains. The Bishop of Carlisle was an ardent supporter of the Brigade and normally presided at the frequent battalion demonstrations which took place in the 1890s. On one such occasion, when William Smith was the guest speaker, the Bishop told his clergy in no uncertain terms that:

> It had given him pleasure to show his appreciation of the way in which many of the young clergy were putting their energies into this movement. Young clergy were apt to fritter away their time catering for the amusement of the people but in a movement of this kind their services were well spent and he heartily thanked them for the enthusiastic way they were seeking to promote The Boys' Brigade.[5]

The strong hold of the Brigade in the north of England gave it a wide cross-section of membership, with an outreach which went far beyond the 'respectable' Sunday School or church congregation. In Sheffield some boys were 'of the very poorest', and in Liverpool the clergy were convinced that:

> The Brigade gets hold of a class of lads our Sunday School and other organizations have failed to reach and not only humanizes but Christianizes them too, in the truest and highest sense.

This mirrored the situation in Glasgow, where within a short time a wider social range than is evident in the earliest companies was being recruited. When questioned in 1902 by the Royal Commission on Physical Training in Scotland, Thomas Cuthbertson spoke of the 'boys from all classes' in the organization. While admitting the difficulty of reaching more of the 'lowest stratum of boy life', Cuthbertson drew from his own experience in the Broomielaw area of Glasgow, where he had enrolled the sons of quarry labourers, 'men of very irregular occupation and irregular habits'.[6]

C.E.B. Russell continually cautioned against overlooking 'the rough and tumble, dirty urchin', who was more in need of help than the 'easier managed, better dressed, better brought-up boys'. Russell's views on the dangers of a company becoming 'too respectable' were given wide publicity through the *Gazette* (December 1901) but class consciousness could not be completely eliminated from some of the church congregations with which The Boys' Brigade was associated. The Captain of the 2nd Arbroath Company in Scotland was forced to disband his small company in 1889, reporting that they

> had not enough boys in their own Mission and made up a Company with boys of persons who were regular members of other Churches and who did not care to be classed as Mission children.

Such instances are not frequently recorded, but the tendency would undoubtedly exist to concern oneself with the less troublesome material. When the 4th Aberdeen Company was formed in 1888, the overwhelming response of 200 applications had to be dealt with and 'first those with dirty faces were asked to go'. Russell's own company, the 5th Manchester, tried to give a better lead by having a wide range of schoolboys *and* pupil teachers, unemployed cart-boys *and* apprentice skilled tradesmen.[7]

In the first decade of The Boys' Brigade, the ideas gaining currency in Scotland and England were rapidly transmitted to Wales and Ireland. In Wales, The Boys' Brigade took root firstly in Newport, where George Reynolds, a local draper who had worked in Glasgow and had taught at the North Woodside Mission Sunday School, formed a company in 1887 at Havelock Street Presbyterian Church. By 1893 the movement had spread to Swansea, Cardiff, Abergavenny, Merthyr Vale, Pontymister, Rhyl and Tredegar. The Nonconformist influence was strong, with the Calvinistic Methodists, the Baptists and the Wesleyan Methodists taking the lead. This is not surprising in an area where Nonconformists outnumbered Anglicans by two to one and the recurring evangelical revivals produced an environment receptive to the Brigade idea.

A similar situation prevailed in the north of Ireland, although the first company was formed in 1888 at Charlotte Street Mission Hall, attached to the St. Mary Magdalene Episcopal Church of Ireland, Belfast. It was inevitable that The Boys' Brigade should establish itself in the North of a united Ireland where the influence of Scots ancestry and Presbyterianism was strong. The driving force of the organization for many years in Ireland was William McVicker and his family. McVicker was superintendent of the Charlotte Street Mission Sunday School of St. Mary Magdalene Church and, following an article published by the London Religious Tract Society on Smith's success, he visited Glasgow to discuss the possibility of extending the movement to Ireland. Despite initial difficulties in establishing the Brigade in an area suspicious of all things military, and where there was no Volunteer force, McVicker persisted and by 1893 there were eighteen companies in the Belfast Battalion and a presence in ten provincial towns. William McVicker, the director of a firm of hardware merchants, went on to captain the 1st Belfast Company for thirty-six years, until his death in 1925. With his friend the Rev. R.H.S. Cooper of the 1st Whitehouse (later 31st Belfast) Company, he led the strong Belfast Battalion in the influential role it was to play in the sustained development of the organization.

In the united Ireland of this time, Dublin followed the lead of the north when William Gibson, curate of St. Matthias Church, visited Belfast and returned to form the 1st Dublin Company. By 1893 the city could boast twenty-one companies, most of which were connected with the Church of Ireland. The English influence was confined to the capital of this over-whelmingly Catholic country, and there was little development of the Brigade 'beyond the pale'. In contrast, the strength of The Boys' Brigade in Northern Ireland has been maintained in relation to numbers in the rest of the United Kingdom. The strong support of the Presbyterian Churches, in the long term, outweighed the lack of Volunteer influence and has allowed the promotion of a vigorous and extensive range of companies and activities in often difficult circumstances.

After ten years of the new movement, 673 companies remained in existence out of the 919 which had been formed in the British Isles. England and Wales accounted for fifty-two per cent of the membership, with Scotland taking up thirty-seven per cent and Ireland eleven per cent. Although the story is one of success and rapid development, it will be seen from these figures that some twenty-five per cent of companies formed had to disband at an early date. How can this be explained? What made for a successful Boys' Brigade company and where might it be found? The pattern of success was certainly not uniform within a region. In Scotland, for example, Glasgow maintained a strong survival rate, as did Aberdeen, Dundee and Paisley in the urban sphere. Edinburgh, however, presented a less confident picture with an alarmingly high failure rate before the turn of the century. By 1893 only twenty-three of the forty-one companies established remained in existence.

In a sense, the environment of Edinburgh provided several interacting factors which were detrimental to relatively weak Brigade companies. As a centre of administration, banking and law, Edinburgh was exceptional among cities of comparable size for the proportion of its population engaged in non-manual occupations. Many of the early Brigade leaders came from these professional middle-class groupings, and the 1891 Census Enumerators Books show that, of a sample of forty-six persons listed as B.B. officers, only twenty-eight could be traced at their last address, indicating movement either within the city or to another area; the Census also shows that twenty of those twenty-eight lived in a household with at least one servant. An analysis of the first thirty Edinburgh companies confirms the difficulty of finding replacements for young captains who had probably completed their studies or professional apprenticeships and left home. For the sons of wealthy parents with a strong church connection, The Boys' Brigade was possibly only a transient interest, or even an obligation. With working-class leaders a permanent commitment in one area was more likely. An analysis of boys enrolled in the Edinburgh Battalion between 1887 and 1900 indicates that the wavering in strength of the actual number of companies was not of necessity related to a reduction in boy strength. Battalion records confirm that the major problem was that of retaining leaders or of recruiting their successors. The relative weakness of the Volunteer movement in Edinburgh, in addition to the nature of the city's population and the less strongly evangelical atmosphere, contributed to this early instability.[8]

In England there were similar disparities among the regions, but of a less extreme nature. The particular circumstances of Oxford and the early stutterings in Manchester contrast with the almost unbroken progress of Bristol and Sheffield. In Bristol, with the highest number of boys enrolled outside the metropolis, the attributes of success rather than those of failure can be discerned. A city of comparable size to Edinburgh, Bristol was more akin to Glasgow in character — hence possibly its success in having the best company survival rate in England during the early years. Although no longer the second city of England, having been overshadowed by the urban creations of the Industrial Revolution, Bristol displayed a commercial and religious vigour which produced the kind of Nonconformist philanthropists, such as J.J. Usher (of brewing fame) and T. Thornton Wills (tobacco merchant), who were to be actively involved in the promotion and development of The Boys' Brigade. With a high level of mission activity and a strong Volunteer tradition, Bristol provided the background of philanthropy, social outreach and military experience ideal for the establishment of a Boys' Brigade company. As in Glasgow, the movement began in a relatively prosperous artisan area at the Wye Congregational Chapel, Clifton. However, there was a rapid development into the poorer areas and a wide spectrum of the city was covered by sixteen companies between 1888 and 1893.

Although records show which Boys' Brigade companies survived for any length of time and which disbanded at an early date, it is more difficult to analyse the losses in boys from within each company. The overall Brigade strength increased numerically each session, thus disguising to some extent the natural existence of a degree of loss. There was a numerical wastage through removal from the area, attendance at work or evening classes, and misconduct. The difficulty of boys working long hours is frequently referred to, and many companies with a high proportion of boys over school age suffered as a consequence. In 1889 the 1st Penicuik Company lost eight boys, five of whom were mere privates in rank, in the Mauricewood coal mine disaster. In Hawick the problem was that of evening classes, and one company was put at risk with boys leaving to attend 'night-school'. The 1st Aston Manor Company, one of the first companies in the Birmingham area (and later to be redesignated the 1st Birmingham Company), recorded details of all boys who left their roll early between 1896 and 1912. Of the seventy-five for whom a valid reason can be ascertained, twenty-seven per cent were unable to get away from work, six per cent claimed poverty, eight per cent ill health, and eleven per cent died. Others moved from the area, joined the Armed Forces, or were dismissed for misconduct. Lack of attendance through pressure of work might be expected in this proportion in many areas, but adolescent employment would diminish with the increasingly protective legislation of successive Governments concerning hours of work, and also with the raising of the school leaving age. While loss through leaving the area might remain a constant factor, the twenty-five per cent loss through a combination of death, ill health and poverty can only be regarded as a depressing and deplorable feature of pre-1914 social conditions, although admittedly this particular company was drawn from the poorer end of the social spectrum.[9]

The rapid development of The Boys' Brigade during the first ten years of its existence continued through to the end of the nineteenth century. Glasgow led the field with ninety-one companies, followed by London with eighty-three companies. The largest battalions thereafter were Liverpool (thirty-two), Dublin (thirty-one), Manchester (thirty), Edinburgh (twenty-nine) and Belfast (twenty-six). This development led to essential changes in Brigade organization. The administrative machine, devised to carry out a limited function in Glasgow, was now called upon to oversee a widening network of units and activities. In 1894, Headquarters moved from 68 Bath Street to 162 Buchanan Street, Glasgow. A branch of Headquarters was opened in London under the control of the Rev. G.L. Harding, appointed Assistant Brigade Secretary in the session 1894-95.

The most important administrative innovation for the future of the B.B. had occurred some years earlier, when William Smith was appointed the first full-time Secretary. In the initial years, lack of funding had precluded such a possibility, but by 1887 the development of the organization had demonstrated the need for a full-time appointment. Smith voiced his concern to Carfrae Alston, the Brigade President, which resulted in an appeal. Such was the response that in April 1888 a trust was formed to administer funds donated by prominent Scottish businessmen, giving a salary of £350 per annum to Smith 'as long as he holds office as Secretary'. The principal subscribers were, in fact, many of those philanthropists already mentioned for their work in the Glasgow area — John Templeton, James Stevenson, J. Campbell-White, William and James Campbell, Sir William Collins, Carfrae Alston, J.G.A. Baird, and the Coats family. There were thirty-eight other contributors making a single payment. Again they consisted of well-known Scots, including Sir John Neilson Cuthbertson, Chairman of the Glasgow School Board; John Stephen, shipbuilder; David McBrayne, shipowner; Henry Drummond; and Henry Campbell-Bannerman, the future Prime Minister. The support of these men enabled William Smith to withdraw from his business and devote himself full-time to the B.B. We cannot estimate the sacrifice this would have involved. Although no records of his firm survive, contemporary opinion indicated a business capacity which Smith's competence and effectiveness in Brigade affairs would lead us to assume. It is unlikely that he was improving his financial prospects by accepting £350 per annum. Smith's full-time appointment illustrates the substantial support the Brigade was receiving not only from the Churches but from important lay spheres — a major factor in its rapid development.[10]

On 5 March 1884 William Smith had married Amelia Pearson Sutherland, daughter of a former Presbyterian Chaplain to the Army at Gibraltar. They had first met in 1872 and had entered into a lengthy engagement, primarily at the request of Amelia's parents. Setting up home at 4 Ann Street (now Southpark Avenue), Hillhead, close to Glasgow University, Amelia Smith, called 'Pearcie' by her husband, readily supported her husband's activities at the North Woodside Mission. A particular feature of her work for the company was the extensive entertaining carried out for the boys. Mrs Smith's drawing-room tea parties with lavish home baking for each company squad in turn made quite an impression. This reversal of normal mission and fellowship work — whereby the homes of the poor were visited — was something of an innovation, but it was highly successful and, by all accounts, highly appreciated. In 1889 the Smiths' first son, George Stanley, was born, and in 1891 their second son, Douglas Pearson. Amelia Smith's sympathy with and involvement in her husband's life work was a source of great strength both to him and the movement. We can presume a ready acquiescence on her part when Smith later gave up his business interests. Tragedy struck, however, in 1898 when Amelia died, aged forty-two. The Smith household was thereafter managed by Kate Smith, William's sister, and the family moved round the corner to 12 Hillsborough Terrace (now Bower Street), Hillhead.

In the session 1888-89, the Earl of Aberdeen accepted office as Honorary President and was responsible for a vigorous promotion of the movement both in the United Kingdom and in Canada, where he became Governor General. In 1897, the Duke of York, later King George V, became Patron. By 1900 an impressive array of top educational, military and religious figures featured as Honorary Vice-Presidents, lending prestige and publicity to the organization. The involvement of educationalists, both from the schools (Sir John Neilson Cuthbertson) and from the universities (the Principals of Aberdeen and Glasgow, and the Masters of the Oxford and Cambridge Colleges), was particularly far-seeing. Principal Caird of Glasgow University highlighted the usefulness of Establishment support both by his public appearances and by the encouragement given to his divinity students who, in later years, would be responsible for the adoption or otherwise of the B.B. in their parishes. The interest of politicians was also readily obtained — a feature which has continued to this day. The Brigade idea was promoted both nationally and locally. George Isaacs, Minister of Labour in the post-World War II Government, maintained that he owed more to his B.B. captain in Clerkenwell than to any other influence in his life. At the same time, the Lord Mayor of London in 1897, J.D. Davies, was captain of a company in another part of the city.[11]

The increasing interest of the local and national press gave the movement added publicity. Its own publications were widely distributed and commented upon by the press. In 1889 the *Boys' Brigade Gazette* was introduced as a bimonthly magazine for officers and, in 1895, the *B.B.*, a monthly magazine for boys, began publication. The *Gazette*, published continuously from 1889 to the present day, has proved an effective means of communication. William Smith, with a small committee to assist him, was the magazine's first editor. In the early issues there were no illustrations and, at a cost of one shilling (five pence) per dozen, Brigade Headquarters were able to send six copies free to each company. Despite two World Wars, the *Gazette* has never missed an issue, and prominent editors such as F.P. Gibbon (1928-37), J. Harold Early (1937-42), R.S. Peacock (1942-47) and T.C.F. Sharman (1954-73) have given the journal its reputation for readability. Under the present editorship of David White the style and size of the *Gazette* have been modernized and it is now issued to every officer in the Brigade (but no longer free!).

The Brigade's greatest propagandist was Professor Henry Drummond of the Free Church College, whose active promotion of the movement, both at home and on his extensive travels overseas, earned him the title 'Apostle of The Boys' Brigade'. Drummond's great ability was his effective communication with all ages and classes. At one level, he preached the Brigade idea to the Establishment in association with his close friend Lord Aberdeen, Brigade Honorary President. At another level he was a prolific writer of material for the boys. His straightforward advice and racy storytelling put him on the same wavelength as his audience:

> Boys, if you are going to be Christians, be Christians as Boys and not as your grandmothers . . . if you cannot read your Bible by the hour as your grandmother can or delight in meetings as she can, don't think you are necessarily a bad Boy. When you are your grandmother's age you will have your grandmother's kind of religion. Meanwhile be a Christian as a Boy.

Very few of the movement's exponents could aspire to Drummond's level of activity or experience, but the combined efforts of clerical, lay and Volunteer supporters and the writings of the Honorary Vice-Presidents such as G.A. Henty and Drummond proved extremely effective in terms of recruitment.[12]

But what was being promoted? The rapid development of the movement is better understood in terms of what it meant to its members. The basis of the organization, and its success, lay in what the boys actually did. The range of activities which were quickly developed by The Boys' Brigade presented new and undoubtedly attractive horizons for many of the adolescents in membership and answered any criticism that it was an organization blinkered by drill and Bible instruction. The spiritual basis of the movement was, at the same time, maintained, and many of the sports and educational classes on offer were seen to promote the basic aim of 'Christian manliness'.

In a sense, this extension of Brigade work mirrored the increasing support and encouragement given to recreation by both Church and State. The Protestant ethic of self-improvement in the mid and late nineteenth century had influenced many in the 'rational' use of leisure time, and the link of 'muscular Christianity' with physical health had encouraged the transfer of the public-school ethos of organized games and team spirit to other classes. Such a transfer of upper-class values to the less privileged was a part of the missionary impulse out of which many Boys' Brigade companies originated. What must be borne in mind, however, is that the Brigade was applying these ideas in the last two decades of the nineteenth century, predating their general implementation at adolescent level in the twentieth century. State schooling did not seriously venture into the area of leisure activities during the late Victorian period. At the time of the formation of The Boys' Brigade the provision of organized games or athletics was very much the preserve of the public school, with its available space and facilities. The Boys' Brigade, therefore, found itself in the vanguard of the promotion of these sporting activities and was already offering what the Churches were realizing should be offered (and what the State may have liked to, but could not, offer). Brigade involvement with modern leisure activities which were otherwise outside the reach of most of its working-class members also widened the catchment group from which the Churches might eventually draw membership. At the same time, a range of activities which would improve the physical and mental quality of British youth was welcomed by the lay Establishment:

> these will form the future British people and upon their condition and capacity will depend not only the happiness of our own country but also the influence of our Empire in the world.

The range of activities covered, broadly, the spiritual, the educational or cultural, and the physical.[13]

Together with Bible Class, the most regular meeting was to be the weekly 'parade night', which initially concentrated on military drill. Many recollections from members in the pre-1914 period emphasize that drill was actually enjoyed. William Sharpe, a boy in the 31st London Company before the turn of the century, recorded that he

> liked the drill — I took to it and my shoulders are still square. We *did* like it . . . I honestly think it was that which taught me to walk upright. I never had anything to do with the Army or other drill.

Henry Drummond, in a much cited address to Harvard University students, remarked perceptively on the value of drill in dealing with unruly lads:

> Call these Boys 'boys' which they are and ask them to sit up in a Sunday class and no power on earth will make them do it, but put a fivepenny cap on them and call them 'soldiers', which they are not, and you can order them about till midnight.

Perhaps this is why there were no eyebrows raised at the first Annual Inspection of the 1st Glasgow Company when the captain put the boys through eighteen separate drill movements lasting almost one and a half hours! Dummy rifles were used by most companies when drilling, but aversion to their use after World War I caused them to be abandoned by many, and to be finally abolished by 1926. The culmination of the session's parade nights was, and is, the Annual Inspection and Display, held normally in the spring and, in the early years, involving a guest of honour of military background. Battalion inspections and parades soon followed and gave the movement an opportunity of presenting itself to a wider public.[14]

Although The Boys' Brigade had basically been formed to provide week-night activities for Sunday School lads, separate Brigade Bible Classes were soon to be formed in most companies. Bible Class normally commenced at 9.30 a.m. or 10 a.m. An earlier start or a service exceeding an hour was frowned upon by Smith who was not surprised, on one occasion, at

> the Boys not liking the idea of having Bible Class at 8 a.m. on Sunday. We could never get our Boys out so early as many of them work late on Saturday night.

Responsibility for the Christian education of The Boys' Brigade members lay, as it still does, with the church or religious organization to which each company was connected. The Brigade might advise on format or possible syllabuses, but the religious teaching imparted to the boys necessarily reflected the spiritual values and interpretation of their leaders and their denominational background. There was much liaison, however, among the denominations on parades, battalion services, Christian education examinations, missionary support, and suchlike activities. How far this coming together of different Protestant groups at adolescent level had a consequential effect on l ter Church unions is an interesting conjecture.[15]

Having c tered for the 'twin pillars' of religion and discipline, companies thereafter in.roduced a varying range of leisure activities designed to meet the social needs of the boys, yet within the framework of the movement's philosophy. The formation of a company band was an activity readily promoted by leaders of military experience and just as readily participated in by boys in an age when martial music and parades were never far from public view. The impact of the bands taking part in a battalion parade comes across most vividly in ex-Staff Sergeant Charles Hovel's memories of a London B.B. parade over fifty years ago:

> ... we heard sounds we'd never heard before, it was quite stirring, and looking away to a bend in the road, we could see an enormous crowd coming into view. At first it was masses of local kids, but then as they came on and swirled past us I was enchanted. This was, although I knew nothing of such things, a Battalion Parade of The Boys' Brigade. There were the 101st with their French type E-Flat Bugles, there were the 77th London with their enormous Brass Band, Captain Cave Allan's 1st London in their pride with their Silver Band, and rank after rank, hundreds of Brigaders — band box smart and marching in unison. As they passed the 6th London Bugle Band was playing, side drums playing as one, bass drum sticks cutting swathes in the air and look at him again — glory be — its one of my schoolmates — old Pocock, and he's got a great white leopard skin under his leather overall and the opened jawed head is resting on the back of his shoulders showing frightful fangs. The following Tuesday I enrolled.[16]

In 1885 the first band was formed by the 1st Glasgow Company, instructed by an ex-band sergeant of the Regular Army. This was a sixteen-man flute band and it paved the way for the steady growth of this popular activity. Two years later there were 35 bands functioning — 2 bugle, 4 brass, 25 drum and fife, and 4 pipe — and by 1914 a total of 868, involving thousands of boys. Although at first the band, with its separate roll cards, was something of a separate entity within the company, the tendency soon died out and the band, with a recommended strength of not more than one-third of the company, assumed the role it has maintained to this day. As well as playing on parade nights and at Sunday services, bands were soon in demand in the community at large, playing at concerts, excursions, flower shows and the like. Proficiency badges and company prizes put a competitive edge on the activity, and the early enthusiasm remains, as can be observed at the National and Scottish Band Contests where large numbers of top-class bands of all types compete. The mix of bands has changed over the years, with the bugle band remaining the most popular. The introduction of the three-valved trumpet bugle, bell lyra, timpani and other instruments (perhaps with the influence of American marching bands) has given a new style of approach to B.B. band work. A wider range of music, formation marching, and the gradual change from high to low-pitch instruments (allowing bugle and brass bands to play together) have given rise to some new and exciting 'show bands' of great attraction to boys, but not always wholeheartedly accepted as suitable by some leaders. To the working-class boy of the late nineteenth century the opportunity of learning how to play a musical instrument and to participate in an otherwise adult or middle-class activity was one to be seized. The enthusiasm for company and battalion bands has not waned and the role The Boys' Brigade has played this century in encouraging band music among young people has to be recognized.

The educational or extramural type of classes introduced by The Boys' Brigade followed the philosophy of the late nineteenth-century voluntary agencies in imparting knowledge and values to the young. The Brigade Executive encouraged the provision of 'good literature, elementary science and technical classes'. In addition:

Fretwork, metal-work, wood carving and carpentry will always prove attractive to boys and may be made a means by which the boys can help the Company funds.

Local Education Authorities gave assistance, enabling vocational classes in reading, shorthand and technical subjects to be offered on other evenings. Class work was sometimes adapted to local needs as in the 212th Glasgow Company at Kelvinhaugh, where a cobbling class repaired footwear desperately needed by some of the boys. This particular company, led by Sandy Martin of 1st Glasgow Company fame, was not purely concerned with functional classes, however, and their musical enthusiasm and ability was directed into the formation of a company orchestra. The weekly parade night was now expanded to include class work such as first aid, or 'Ambulance' as it was then called. In the twentieth century the range of classes was to be greatly widened in accordance with the times and incorporated in a comprehensive badge structure. Awards for physical and educational attainment were structured in stages and grouped to allow for the eventual goal of the King's Badge, introduced in 1913.[17]

The 'club room' was a great attraction to boys and often provided a welcome contrast to an overcrowded home or the dubious attractions of the street corner. The idea was promoted by William Smith himself, following the success of its introduction in the 1st Glasgow Company:

> The officers had long been conscious of the demoralizing effect upon the boys of hanging about at night, for want of any better place to go. They accordingly made application to the Deacons' Court and were cordially granted the sole use of a large room in the Mission Buildings. This room is now brightly and tastefully, though plainly, furnished; is supplied with games, papers and attractive periodicals and books and is open every night in the week. It really forms the 'home' of the Company and very pleasing it is to drop in of an evening and find the boys taking full advantage of it, some sitting quietly reading, others playing games and others sitting around the fire discussing matters in which they may be interested.

The idea was taken up by many companies, although the peaceful scene depicted by Smith is not borne out elsewhere. The experience of the 26th Edinburgh Company, who also had an orchestra on their club nights, was perhaps more typical:

> We are occasionally treated to a musical 'turn' by Jock Stewart who plays on his wooden crackers, the noise of which annoys the boys studying a game of draughts.

Some companies with restricted accommodation operated their clubs on a Saturday evening, while others went to some lengths to have the facility available on each free evening. This often meant a purpose-built room in more prosperous areas or the lease or gift of premises for conversion. The magnificent premises of the 1st St. Andrews Company provided a workshop, reading room and recreation room open each week night from 6.30 to 9 p.m., whereas the 86th Glasgow Company leased an empty shop in Eglinton Street and equipped it with books, games and a small billiards table.[18]

Physical training and games have always been a major feature of Brigade activities — a feature which has retained its prominent place in the company programme. The promotion of athletics and games by 'muscular Christians' followed the recent formation of national and professional associations in football, rugby, cricket and tennis, and extended what had hitherto been a public-school activity to a wider social spectrum. Officers hoped that, in addition to the physical benefits to be obtained, the public-school ideal of esprit de corps could be brought to the boys of the Brigade in another format.

Smith with his first wife Amelia (sitting),
his sons Stanley (with Smith) and Douglas,
and Smith's sister Kate.

1st Glasgow Company, THE Boys' Brigade

SUMMER CAMP,

At AUCHENLOCHAN, TIGHNABRUAICH, KYLES OF BUTE (one of the most beautiful spots on the West Coast)

From *FRIDAY Morning, 13th JULY, till FRIDAY, 20th JULY, 1888.*

(GLASGOW FAIR WEEK.)

The 1st South Essex Company leaving Leytonstone at 4 a.m. for camp at Bognor in 1904.

The first camps were held indoors, but by the 1890s many companies were using bell tents.

Three scenes from the 1896 camp of the 9th and 32nd Glasgow Companies at Strachur on Loch Fyne. The doghouse was not a normal method of discipline.

*Boating was an important camp activity in the early years. Here the
1st Glasgow Company sets off from the Auchenlochan Jetty in 1909.*

*Members of the 1st South Essex Company (and dog)
pull ashore their boat at their first camp in 1904.*

The 1st Nottingham Company relaxing in the hay in 1889.

*The 14th West Kent (Bexleyheath) Company at Herne Bay in 1907.
The Boys' Brigade taught many boys to swim,
and swimming galas soon became a popular event.*

*Music has always played a prominent part in the activities of the B.B.
This is the band of the 1st Glasgow in the 1890s.*

*The football team of the 1st Birmingham in 1911. Many boys first joined
the B.B. for the chance to play in competitive B.B. league football.*

Almost all companies acquired equipment and instructors to allow the introduction of physical training as a major Brigade activity. This was quickly extended to participation in organized sport at company and battalion level. The formation of football leagues gave this sport the predominance which it has retained, although not all leaders were enthusiastic: the 1st Blackburn (Lancs.) Company failed because the captain 'would not allow a Football Club — which is a curse and not a blessing'.[19]

Generally, however, sport was enthusiastically adopted and, in some instances, boys joined a company primarily for the benefit of playing football before becoming involved in other, more fundamental, activities. The Rev. Donald English, President of the Methodist Conference in 1978-79 recalled being one such person:

> I owe so much to The Boys Brigade . . . I first joined the 10th North West Durham (Consett) Company because they needed an outside right in the football team . . . Although I joined the B.B. to play football, I soon discovered that there was a great deal more . . . There was a process going on in my own thinking which reached a conclusion when I was invited to read a lesson at an Enrolment Service . . . that really made me think very deeply about my standing before God.

Football has continued to be a popular and successful activity, with many boys working their way through company and battalion teams to enter the junior and senior professional ranks. The highly organized structure of competitive B.B. football has provided the national teams in the British Isles throughout this century with many of their more talented and dedicated players. A number of distinguished players in the most recent Scotland World Cup teams began their football careers in the B.B.[20]

Cricket followed as a popular sport in the Brigade, adopted more extensively in England than in Scotland or Ireland. When played in midsummer outside the normal company session, the leaders maintained a discreet level of supervision and, as with football, formed competitive leagues. It is also worthy of note that the 76th Glasgow Company introduced basketball, a relatively unknown sport in Britain, to The Boys' Brigade, while the introduction of swimming at an early stage allowed as high a level of participation as possible (unlike team games) and became well established by the end of the 1880s. Arrangements were made with local authorities in many areas for concessionary entry charges to the public baths. Pass cards at a penny each were issued in Glasgow and Carlisle and copied later in other cities. Company swimming clubs and battalion galas reflected the increasing popularity of the sport among boys and leaders. In the pre-World War I period other sports such as cycling and athletics were introduced as Brigade recreational activities widened. The trend has continued with more 'modern' sports such as sailing, skiing, hill walking, table tennis, and badminton taking their place in the overall programme.

While the wholehearted adoption of games by the Brigade reflected, to some extent, the tradition of the public school in attempting to instil character and teamwork, the introduction of camping as a major activity was more of an innovation and helped to sow the seeds of one of the most popular recreational pastimes of the twentieth century. Although some organizations had provided holiday breaks, and many Brigade leaders would have had experience of military camps, the introduction of widespread, organized camping for adolescents was something completely new in late nineteenth-century life. This activity, which was to be taken up some twenty years later by the Boy

Scouts and subsequently by the ordinary family, was introduced into the Brigade programme at an early date and quickly established itself as a prominent feature:

> The good results of the camps are remarkable. Not only do the boys benefit in health and physique — and even a week's sunshine will bring colour to the cheeks and brightness to the eyes — but still more noticeable is the effect of a well conducted camp on their characters. No better method could be devised for teaching the boys the duty of sinking the wishes of the individual in the common-weal, for inculcating the true spirit of comradeship, and for putting into practice these principles of manly Christianity for the advancement of which the Brigade exists.

While to many leaders camp represented social conditioning in a recreational environment, to the boys it meant a break from family restraints or urban squalor. To them it was a major annual event, to be saved for and eagerly anticipated.[21]

The first B.B. camp was held by the 1st Glasgow Company in July 1886 at Tighnabruaich in the scenic Kyles of Bute in Argyllshire. Camps were not under canvas at first and halls or barns were often used. The 1st Glasgow Company were given the local hall at Auchenlochan, Tighnabruaich. The 1st Belfast Company refurbished a grain store to house the many and well-known camps at Killough, County Down, where the 'whole village' would turn out to 'see the young warriors'. Very soon, however, canvas camps at company or battalion level were in vogue — some running for fifty years and more on the same site. The Whitecliff Bay and other sites on the Isle of Wight, pioneered by Roger Peacock as London Secretary, are a good example. There was careful preparation for each camp, with instructions and a programme being issued to each boy prior to the summer holiday. In order to subsidize the cost, donations were received from prominent members of the church congregation and community, covering possibly half the expense.[22]

The 1st Glasgow camp fund provided 'Rations, Kit Bags, Camp Beds, Pillows, Knives, Forks, Spoons and Soap and a four-oared boat for each squad'. Each boy brought a Bible and a hymn book, double blanket, extra suit and cap, change of underclothing, socks, towels, hair brush, and swimming wear. A fishing line was also recommended. Daily orders were posted up and the following programme at Tighnabruiach set out the basic timetable for daily activities:

Reveille	6.30 a.m.
Morning Prayers	6.45 a.m.
Bathing Parade	7.00 a.m.
(Bathing Optional)	
First Breakfast Bugle	8.15 a.m.
Breakfast	8.30 a.m.
Inspection of Camp	9.30 a.m.
Full dress Parade	9.45 a.m.
(Parade will take shape of an expedition by the boats or otherwise, to some desirable place in the neighbourhood.)	
First Dinner Bugle	1.15 p.m.
Dinner	1.30 p.m.
(The afternoon will generally be free for cricket, games, rambling over the hills or whatever the boys may desire.)	
First Tea Bugle	6.15 p.m.
Tea	6.30 p.m.
Fishing Parade (Boats)	7.00 p.m.

(Fishing Competition between the Camp Squads may be held.)
Evening Prayers   9.30 p.m.
Tattoo   9.45 p.m.
Lights Out   10.00 p.m.[23]

Programmes varied in detail in different areas. In some camps the standing orders and programme were run on strict military lines. At West Kent Battalion camps, discipline was enforced in accordance with the Queen's Regulations 'so far as they can reasonably apply to the B.B.', and it was stipulated that 'the key note of the Camp should be absolute and cheerful obedience'. The insertion of company drill into the programme at 7.30 a.m. might, therefore, come as no surprise. In most other camps, and increasingly so as the modern era dawned, there was more concern with recreation, sport and fun, while retaining a degree of military precision. The attraction of the programme to working-class city boys is obvious. Regardless of the attainment or otherwise of the idealistic aims of some leaders and supporters, the fairly full programme provided at camp would have given many of the boys a memorable and enjoyable break from routine. The non-commissioned officers among the boys were given particular responsibility for maintaining order in each tent or dormitory area and were requested to ensure that the younger boys were not 'teased or made unhappy through the thoughtlessness of older boys'. With an NCO in charge of each squad of boys, a continuously competitive atmosphere was encouraged to maintain interest and standards. The extensive preparations carried out by the 1st Witney Company for its pre-1914 camps on the Isle of Wight included a private notice to NCOs on their responsibilities, including the 'tone' of their tent and 'offences against good taste'.[24]

The standard programme required major alteration on a Sunday to allow for a church parade and service. Some companies arranged for church attendance both morning and evening, and the *Christian Leader*, reporting on the first B.B. camp, carefully emphasized the Presbyterian cooperation at Tighnabruaich, with the company attending the Church of Scotland in the morning and the Free Church in the evening. A successful camp also required extensive preparation on the part of the captain and his staff. Brigade handbooks for camping gave comprehensive guidance and have been frequently revised over the years. Some diaries of William Smith have been preserved illustrating the work involved in organizing finances, equipment, travelling arrangements and accommodation. The formulation of a programme for each day and the hospitality to be given to parents and friends visiting the camp were given meticulous attention by William Smith, and there is little doubt that his own company camps repaid this detailed organization with a success commensurate with the results of his work in other spheres.

One item in the preparation for camp which necessitated considerable thought was that of food. The calculation of provisions and the formulation of menus were not dealt with casually, and the diaries detail all aspects of 'camp kitchen'. A typical daily menu might be:

Tuesday, 19th July 1892
7.30 a.m.   Breakfast   —   Porridge, Milk
                                 Bread, Rolls, Butter
                                 Fried Ham
                                 Coffee
12.30 p.m.   Dinner   —   Beefsteak Pies and Potatoes
                                 Bread, Semolina Pudding and Milk

5.00 p.m.	Tea	—	Bread, Scones, Butter and Jam
			Biscuits
10.00 p.m.		—	Biscuits and Cocoa.

The main course in the middle of the day varied with each menu and, on certain days, took the form of a packed lunch taken on expedition or 'in the boats'. The standard of cooking is not normally referred to in official publications and may have varied considerably from company to company depending upon whether or not a professional cook accompanied the officers and boys. The 1st Blackheath Company, from South London, took the problem in their stride and gave hints on camp meals in their company magazine:

> If the tea is a bit strong, down with it and say nothing; If the duff [plum pudding] is a bit heavy, ditto; a game of football afterwards will soon put that straight!

Fortunately those members of the company proficient in 'Ambulance' formed a first-aid team which might, we suppose, deal with any emergencies following this sort of advice.[25]

It was a general rule that food should be 'good and plentiful', with professional cooking (rather than by groups of boys themselves) ensuring a greater benefit. The Captain of the 5th Dublin Company was adamant on this point:

> I insist on quality: many of our Boys who are out at work from early morning only get a square mid-day meal on Sundays and for their sakes, there must be plenty . . .

The transportation of cooking, sleeping and sport equipment might be accompanied by less essential items. The 22nd Paisley Company arranged for the carriage of a full-sized piano from Sherwood Church, Paisley, to Kilchattan Bay on the Island of Bute, presumably being convinced of the value to the company of this expense. The result of all this care and trouble appears to have been well-appreciated, judging by the glowing memories which have been documented. Lavish praise of camping could, of course, be tempered with more realistic accounts of the less happy times: the 58th Glasgow Company's problem in 1904 with 'myriads of midges which made numerous attacks during the evenings'; the 4th and 5th Glasgow Companies' trouble with a sleepwalker, resulting in the 'big toe of the boy on his right acting as a tether-peg'; or the Yeovil and District Camp in 1903 at Weymouth where 'our tents were soaked, the mess tent was a quagmire, the wind blew a hurricane and the rain descended in torrents'. Such unfortunate features of camp life are relegated into semi-obscurity, however, when minds are cast back to the many and varied incidents which former Brigade members most vividly recollect. The extensive reporting of camp activities indicates the prominence given to this feature of Brigade life. The experience gained was to be used by later uniformed youth movements such as the Boy Scouts and Boys' Life Brigade. It is a matter of conjecture as to how far the twentieth-century fascination for camping holidays can be attributed to the pioneering role of The Boys' Brigade in this area of adolescent leisure activity.[26]

Although camping was the major annual outdoor activity of the Brigade, daily excursions and 'field days' proved a great novelty with the boys from towns and cities. A day trip to Pinner by the 31st London Company from London's East End made a strong impression on the young William Sharpe:

> We didn't see so many green fields and great green spaces in the East-End of London . . . I'd never been out on such a treat or an expedition like that before . . . it was a rarity to me and a great many other boys my own age.

The 1st Hamilton Company in Lanarkshire has retained several handwritten essays of a high literary standard which describe, with obvious relish, the annual excursion of 1888 to Lanark. The full-day outing was organized in detail. The morning consisted of a mock battle in true military style and, following a light lunch, the afternoon was given over to various sports and 'athletic games'. A camp-style dinner rounded off the proceedings and, on return to Hamilton at 8 p.m., prizes were presented before the boys dispersed 'delighted with our day's enjoyment'. Such an outing provided an opportunity for the public to see a company in a more informal atmosphere:

> A lot of people took a good look at us, and they seemed to be well pleased with what they saw of us . . . at Lanark . . . a crowd of men and boys had gathered round us, all anxious to know who we were and where we came from.

These various Brigade activities by no means form a comprehensive list. There was an early extension of outdoor activities, and 'scouting' was shortly to be introduced — some years before the actual Boy Scouts came into being. Development was continual, as it is today, with involvement in such programmes as the Duke of Edinburgh's Award Scheme (see Chapter 7).[27]

What motivated the Brigade in the development of all these activities? Was the promotion of sport, bands and educational classes a further means of social control? There were many supporters of the Brigade who regarded the total range of its work with one view: the inculcation of standards to which the rising generation should be encouraged to adhere for the preservation of the existing moral and social fabric of society, and for the defence of the Empire. It is likely that the desire to maintain social order and stability was an important factor in the motives of some leaders, but there is a danger in confusing this with a genuinely felt awareness of social need. In local companies, attractive weekday activities, many of which had been experienced at adult level in the Volunteers, encouraged the translation of Sunday theorizing into practice. That this may have represented an imposition of 'bourgeois' values is unlikely to have disturbed (or even influenced) most of those boys enthusiastically engaged in a competitive football match on a Saturday afternoon. During this early period, the leadership was being drawn from an increasingly broad social spectrum, and, in the minds of this widening leadership, the range of popular activities provided gave the boys opportunities otherwise denied them, and gave their leaders a greater possibility of success in their aim — as well as a great deal of pleasure in its implementation. As far as the boys themselves were concerned, the activities in which they might participate were attractive to them: in short, they *enjoyed* what they were doing.

Before 1900 it became evident that the significance of The Boys' Brigade for the youth of the nation was not to lie solely within its own organization and methods. The pioneering role of the Brigade as the first uniformed youth movement was demonstrated by the formation of others springing from the ideas of William Smith — movements ranging from the short-lived Catholic Boys' Brigade to the international and multiracial Scouts.

The first to follow the lead of The Boys' Brigade was an Anglican organization, the Church Lads' Brigade, the first company of which was established at St. Andrew's Church, Fulham, London in 1891. The founder of the C.L.B. was Walter Mallock Gee, an ex-Volunteer officer and Secretary of the Junior Branch of the Church of England Temperance Society. Gee's enthusiasm for the temperance ideal and the need to teach 'the lads of the Church on distinctly

Church lines' led him to form a separate but similar organization, against the advice of Smith and his colleagues. Despite the interdenominational nature of the B.B. and the successful Church of England companies in membership, a second organization was thus formed and, regardless of occasional friction, progressed in cooperation with the original Brigade.[28]

By 1893, the C.L.B. had spread throughout England and Wales, although making no headway north of the Border, and had a membership of 8,000 boys. The organization survived, ironically, a breakaway movement within the Church of England when the London Diocesan Church Lads' Brigade was set up in the metropolis on teetotal lines and worked in association with the C.L.B. until amalgamation in 1919. The patronage and support of clerical and military leaders for the C.L.B. was quickly obtained. The agreement of the Archbishop of Canterbury in 1893 to become Vice-Patron of the B.B., however, upset the more rigid C.L.B. leaders:

> They must feel downcast and disheartened that he who should be our leader in this work gives the great weight of his name to an organization which treats the doctrine of the Church, the Wesleyan and the Calvinistic Methodists as being of equal value in the training of our youth.[29]

The C.L.B. proved to be the strongest of the Brigades deriving from the original organization but it was to suffer decline during the interwar years following its identification with military training and the defence of an Empire which was soon to be dismantled. Affiliation to the Army Cadet movement from 1911 until 1936 (see Chapter 4) emphasized their position. The organization continues to this day, being combined with the Church Girls' Brigade, and is particularly prominent in the Northwest of England. There are some 15,000 members in England and Wales and a few units in South Africa and the West Indies.

The Jewish Lads' Brigade, while always to be much smaller than the B.B. or C.L.B., was a further development of the Brigade idea. It was initially directed to the problems of the social adjustment of Jewish immigrant lads living in the East End of London. Colonel Albert Edward Goldsmid began the movement in 1895 with the help of the Maccabean Society. Many leading Anglo-Jewish philanthropists directed their attention to the inculcation of 'orderliness and honour' in the younger members of the Jewish community. Although based initially in the East End of London, the J.L.B. quickly spread into the provinces, following the dispersal of the Jewish community. B.B. methods and ideas were adopted in the main, but with a distinctive uniform and a more imposing array of military titles. By 1914 the organization had built an impressive headquarters at Camperdown House in London and had extended its membership to 4,000. After affiliation to the Royal Fusiliers as an Army Cadet Battalion, recruitment to the services in 1914 was high, as were the subsequent casualties sustained. Like its Anglican counterpart, the J.L.B. was to suffer from adverse public opinion in the postwar period. The organization endures today, however, alongside the more recent Jewish Girls' Brigade, and maintains the tradition of uniformed Jewish youth work, but far removed from its original purpose.[30]

The least known of the organizations to derive from the B.B. was the Catholic Boys' Brigade. The C.B.B. was started in September 1896 at the Dockland Students' Institute — a boys' club in Bermondsey — and drew largely from the unskilled Irish Catholic labouring classes in the dockland areas of southeast London. The problem of retaining Catholic youths in a close relationship with their Church gave the C.B.B. the same object as its Church of England counterpart. Military training and a mixture of recreational and educational activities aimed at holding the boys until they were of age to join the Catholic Young Men's Society or similar organization. The movement was founded by the Rev. Father Felix Segesser, parish priest at Bermondsey until 1905, by which time the Catholic Boys' Brigade had established itself strongly in London. The movement spread to Ireland and other parts of England, giving a membership in 1906 of 8,000. There is no trace of the Catholic Boys' Brigade after 1927. It is quite feasible that the remaining companies were absorbed into Catholic Boys' Guilds, which had become increasingly popular, or into the Scout movement as Catholic Scout Groups. Cardinal Bourne, Roman Catholic Primate from 1901 to 1935, was an enthusiastic supporter of the Boy Scouts, although President of the C.B.B., and may well have been instrumental in the winding up of the Brigade and the transference of the boys to Scouting or boys' club work.

The three Brigades which followed The Boys' Brigade before the end of the nineteenth century were less insistent on their non-military objective and gave the impression, however valid, of sacrificing some of their religious ideals for a stronger display of patriotism and militarism. Accordingly they suffered in the postwar pacifist backlash to a much greater extent than the original Boys' Brigade. The J.L.B. and C.L.B. have survived in a less substantial form, while the C.B.B. has completely disappeared. The last of the male Brigades to be formed as a direct consequence of The Boys' Brigade had no such difficulties in that its position was made quite clear from the outset.

The Boys' Life Brigade was founded in 1899 as a non-military boys' organization working along very similar lines to The Boys' Brigade. As the founder John Brown Paton said:

> We don't intend our Brigade, in any sense, to be a rival to The Boys' Brigade. I would rather call it a complement to it — in this sense that while The Boys' Brigade is hindered by the objection which many people take to its military organization and associations, the new Brigade will meet those who desire to have boys secure the advantages of the discipline and so on of The Boys' Brigade free from the objections I have named. Personally I do not object to the military forms of The Boys' Brigade but it is useless to ignore the fact that many people do.

John Brown Paton, a Scot from Newmilns in Ayrshire but who had lived most of his life in England, was a Congregational minister, recently retired as Principal of the Nottingham Congregational Institute. He was an admirer of William Smith and the methods of The Boys' Brigade. Paton's organization evolved out of the apprehension of many Churches, particularly in the Nonconformist sphere, at the paramilitary forms of the other Brigades. The Boys' Life Brigade was to be an integral part of the Nonconformist National Sunday School Union, more so than the B.B., and the control and staffing of the organization reflected this influence. The stated object of the movement, however, departed little from that of the original Brigade.[31]

The emphasis was on life saving (from fire and water) as a substitute for military drill, and the teaching of swimming was fundamental. The organization had its greatest strength in the Nonconformist Churches, particularly the Methodist Church where, within ten years, there were over 3,000 officers and boys. The movement spread throughout the country and by 1914 there were over 15,000 boys and 1,500 officers in 405 companies. The B.L.B. uniform closely resembled that of The Boys' Brigade, with an alternative blue full-dress uniform available. While never reaching the strength of the original Brigade, the B.L.B. maintained its position by rigorously opposing affiliation to the Government's Cadet Scheme. This philosophy similarly precluded any early amalgamation with The Boys' Brigade, with its sporadic use of dummy rifles. These derivative organizations have one common feature in that they were designed exclusively for a male membership. The Boys' Brigade, however, was to inspire the revolutionary idea in late Victorian Britain of uniformed organizations for girls. Brigades for young women began with three distinct groups, following the ideas of the B.B. and the B.L.B. The first was formed in Dublin in 1893. Calling itself the Girls' Brigade, it provided weekday evening activities for Sunday School girls in the Irish Protestant Churches. The movement remained small and restricted to Ireland. It was to be overshadowed by the Girls' Guildry, with its more closely parallel development to that of The Boys' Brigade.

The founder in 1900 of the Girls' Guildry, Dr William Francis Somerville, was a medical practitioner and Free Church member in Glasgow. Living close to William Smith in Hillhead, he was likewise influenced by Moody and Sankey and, not surprisingly, took up the captaincy of the 28th Glasgow Company of the B.B. in the Anderston Free Church Mission, where his father was minister. He saw in his work the possibilities of extending the Brigade idea to girls:

> For the girls and women of the leisured class it offered something new and constructive; for the girl who lived in a tenement, worked long hours in a factory and had no knowledge beyond that of mean streets, it was a way into a large place.

The Guildry spread throughout Scotland but did not extend to England and Wales to any great extent. As the Guildry mirrored the B.B. in Scotland so the third organization, the Girls' Life Brigade, was to mirror the B.L.B. in England and Wales.[32]

The Girls' Life Brigade, founded in 1902, closely followed the pattern of the B.L.B. and was vigorously promoted on temperance lines by the National Sunday School Union, thereby establishing itself predominantly in Nonconformist congregations. By 1914 the Guildry and the Girls' Life Brigade each had some 4,000 members. In 1965 the two organizations amalgamated with the Girls' Brigade of Ireland to form the Girls' Brigade. Since the amalgamation, membership has continually increased, and currently stands at around 180,000 in the United Kingdom and overseas.

Thus, as the new century dawned, The Boys' Brigade had spread throughout the nation and was already established overseas, with a wide range of activities and the enthusiastic support of the community. It was both providing the ideas for new derivative organizations and impressing the pre-existing workers and groups in the field. Dr Barnardo wrote to William Smith in 1891:

> To my mind (and I have had some experience in these matters) no finer, no wiser, no better method was ever discovered, to lay hold of lads of the class your Brigade influences and to bring them under Christian oversight. I congratulate you, and all those concerned, in the magnificent results which our Heavenly Father has allowed you to realize in so short a time.[33]

CHAPTER 3

'OUR COMRADES BEYOND THE SEAS'

The Boys' Brigade Overseas, 1887 to 1914

IN OCTOBER 1906 William Smith sent an official New Year's greeting to The Boys' Brigade of Australia. 'It is a great stimulus to us in the old country,' he wrote, 'to know that there are thousands of our comrades beyond the seas enrolling in The Boys' Brigade, and helping to keep the flag flying for all that is good in Boyhood and Manhood.' There were then, indeed, very good grounds for continuing optimism concerning the expansion of the 'Work Overseas'. Increasingly since the 1890s Brigade Headquarters had been struggling to take a close interest in this somewhat unexpected and haphazard phenomenon of overseas expansion. The knowledge of what was happening beyond Britain's shores was achieved mainly through the reports of unpaid B.B. emissaries abroad or through an increasingly important (and burdensome) correspondence with overseas secretaries and officers. Control and contact were, however, mainly informal, since the demands of expansion at home were so many. With the turn of the century, however, the pace of overseas expansion still showed no sign of abating. By November 1903 there were 802 registered (and known) companies, 2,400 officers and 36,000 boys outside the United Kingdom on every continent. By November 1907 the comparable figures had risen to 933 companies, 2,500 officers and 45,000 boys. Over this four-year period alone the claimed overseas share of total world membership rose from just under forty per cent to just over forty-three per cent. At Brigade Council in Edinburgh in October 1907 the Brigade President, J. Carfrae Alston, confidently affirmed that 'colour is no bar to [the Brigade's] spirit and methods,' and local conditions shape themselves to promote its great object'.[1]

But, as neither Smith nor Alston could possibly foresee, the Brigade overseas would soon be rudely beset by some of the common problems facing Britain's declining Empire. The Brigade overseas had already weathered with difficulty the initial shocks of the 'late momentous war' in South Africa. In that country itself the effects were severely disruptive. But, with the increasing alarms over Austro-German designs and expansion, Brigade organization ultimately proved too weak in most dominions and colonies to withstand the calls for juvenile military training and preparedness made by their own and Imperial politicians. 'Local conditions' then — to use Alston's own words — worked against the movement's survival. Whereas in Britain the Brigade was successfully able to confront those forces bent upon the complete militarization of uniformed youth groups (see Chapter 4), overseas it mostly succumbed before similar local demands. In the U.S.A., where it was initially very strong indeed, the Brigade also went into decline. In the British Empire it was decimated.

Given the considerable geographical variations (and consequent vast differences in local circumstances of Boys' Brigade work around the world) it is difficult to attempt more than passing analyses in some countries and territories of the movement's responses to the changing conditions during this

Indian summer of British Imperialism. Australia and New Zealand, for instance, had only recently become fully self-governing. The main concerns of their governments included the problems of small populations and an almost utter dependence on Britain for seaborne defence in the face of German or (it was feared) Russian and Japanese expansion. Canada and Australia still had vast natural resources to exploit and territories to open up. Human and capital resources were scarce. In these three white dominions there was, it is true, considerable interest taken in the welfare of the younger generation, and particularly in any new experiments in child philanthrophy and youth work. In Britain the dominions were often seen as potential hosts for deprived emigrant youths. The Boys' Brigade, widely promoted abroad as an experiment in religious welfare work, was indeed also viewed by many in the U.S.A., Canada and Australia as a model movement for social work among deprived boys. By others it was simply interpreted as an organization for boys to act as soldiers in training. Consequently the Brigade overseas took some turns and paths far removed from William Smith's original concepts.

Between the Brigade's foundation in 1883 and the First World War there was still a strong tide of British emigration running to North America, the Antipodes, and parts of Africa. Strong personal (particularly family) and business links existed between Britain and the colonies and dominions. In their commercial, investment, professional, trade and Church connections with the Empire, Scotsmen were particularly prominent. In consequence 'B.B. men' (particularly single ones) might easily find themselves settled permanently or as transients in many parts of the Empire. As ambassadors from home with a knowledge of new and successful methods in boys' work, they very often found, given some measure of personal tact, a willing local following. But, as we shall see, although B.B. emigrants were many, those who had the leisure, tact or inclination to start and sustain B.B. companies were few in numbers. Although Glasgow B.B. Headquarters gave their blessing to these emigrants, supporting them through reports and exhortations in the *B.B. Gazette*, there was very little tangible help available to the overseas Brigade pioneers. There was, too, little or no local B.B. literature, and Brigade infrastructures were often very rudimentary indeed. The margins for misunderstanding and deviation, and even for conflict with local customs and mores — including those of the English-speaking dominions and the U.S.A. — were in consequence large. Whereas a strong Brigade tradition and tightly bonding esprit de corps had evolved relatively quickly in Britain, it was to take several generations after the First World War before this was achieved in more than a handful of B.B. countries and centres outside Britain. To those trained in the movement, B.B. tradition was strong. The B.B. man arriving in the colonies often found that his hosts did not share this view quite so enthusiastically. It was not unknown for there to arise instances of resentment and conflict between the local Brigade and the migrant B.B. expert. This remained a fact of B.B. life overseas until well after the Second World War, when many overseas councils had eventually cemented their own traditions.

As we shall see, the B.B. did reach some very remote and seemingly unlikely places before 1914. It was active well before World War I in isolated centres on the Indian subcontinent (including Ceylon), on mainland China and in Hong Kong, and in Burma and Japan. The movement's expansion throughout Africa was extensive, and it grew to a respectable size in the Caribbean and some contiguous South and Central American territories. In such places traders, administrators (both government and business) and in particular missionaries were at the forefront of moves to establish B.B. companies. During this first period of Brigade development overseas — a very tenuous and provisional one — there appeared only the first glimmerings of that Brigade missionary fervour which was to sweep the British colonies after World War I. Before 1914 the B.B. missionary commitment consisted mainly of providing financial support to the professional missionaries, for their evangelical, medical, agricultural and related work in the field. Only much later did the movement awaken fully to its own potential for extension among non-European, non-white boys. The early success of the Brigade in the racially mixed Caribbean and parts of Africa before 1914 was a useful pointer to the boom of the 1930s (see Chapter 6).

William Smith we know was an able administrator. Undoubtedly his persuasiveness, especially as a writer, contributed greatly to overseas expansion. He was, too, able to win over others to spread the message, literally, abroad. They included influential colonial and Imperial administrators, ministers of religion, and professional men. Among two of the most successful B.B. propagandists were Smith's close friends Professor Henry Drummond and John Campbell Gordon, first Marquis of Aberdeen and Temair (Lord Aberdeen), who was Governor General of Canada from 1893 to 1898. The Brigade in Australia, Canada and the U.S.A. owed these two a great deal. Drummond was an extraordinarily gifted and popular lecturer and writer, who enthusiastically espoused Smith's B.B. cause. His influence was seminal overseas in the 1890s.[2]

Apart from the obvious proselytizers and emigrants, there were also those local officers who caught the B.B. vision from reading their own or imported church magazines, newspapers and other literature, the novelty of the Brigade in the 1880s and 1890s being widely reported in the press. Many Sunday School teachers and ministers eagerly embraced it as the answer to their 'boys' work' problems. Finding success with their own local endeavours, the more literate often reported on their B.B. work, usually offering to pass on further information to enquirers. When he was able to locate or hear from such men, Smith promptly appointed them, their successes proven, as local and unpaid B.B. agents, secretaries or 'correspondents'. It was a relatively cheap way of passing the message on. In Australia, Sutherland Sinclair became Australian Secretary, and in Canada the Rev. T.F. Fotheringham, T.W. Nisbet and Captain (later Major) F.V. Longstaff all served the Canadian B.B. movement in succession as secretaries before 1914. By the 1890s Smith had found several willing correspondents and organizers in the U.S.A. He was later assisted in assessing overseas conditions by B.B. globe-trotters from Scotland and England. Between 1901 and 1904 three highly-placed Brigade men, travelling privately and on business, reported regularly on the B.B. overseas. In 1902-3 James W. Hannan, Vice-President of the West London Battalion, visited India, Ceylon and Australia. In 1903 Thomas W. Cuthbertson, the Brigade Treasurer and editor of the *B.B. Gazette*, reached India to inspect the 1st Darjeeling, and visited Burma to see the 1st Rangoon. The following year the Brigade President, H. Carfrae Alston, got as far as New Zealand. Unlike Robert Baden-Powell, who travelled the world a decade later to visit his burgeoning Boy Scout movement, William Smith travelled little overseas, with the exception of two triumphal visits to Canada and the U.S.A. in 1895 and 1907. Yet he maintained as close and personal a knowledge of distant events as the relatively slow mails and his informal, largely voluntary, correspondents' network would allow. Rarely in the first twenty years or so of overseas extension did Smith attempt any autocratic control. He was not, indeed, the Imperial centralist and autocrat in youth work organization that Badeń-Powell subsequently became. Only towards the end of his life, as many overseas officers succumbed to the demands of a militarized Brigade movement in the dominions, did Smith attempt to exercise any preemptive right to do more than tactfully offer advice. By then it was too late: the Brigade overseas had foundered.[3]

The Boys' Brigade, however, was certainly not completely immune from the more extreme jingoism and religious-Imperial sentimentality and fervour of late Victorian and early Edwardian Britain. In the *B.B. Gazette* of June 1902, for instance, 'Mark Thyme' presented an allegorical religious vision of the movement as a force in the British Empire marching under 'The Symbol of the Union Jack'. But Smith's encouragement to colonial, dominion and foreign B.B. officers was usually sober and pragmatic, benevolent rather than bellicose. Viewed from some parts of the Empire itself the B.B. was undoubtedly seen by a few as — to borrow John Barry's words of 1904 — a 'Factor in Imperial Unity'. Many politicians, theologians, free-traders, academics and scientists at this period were striving to engender through round-table conferences and consultations a spirit of unity throughout the whole English-speaking world. Addressing Brigade Council in 1902 on the thorny issue of moving B.B. Headquarters to London, the Rev. J.H. Morrison Rose argued that the movement 'had become more than national; it had become Imperial'. With his talk of 'Imperial Unity', John Barry, a Scotsman, had presciently and succinctly expressed the essentially cooperative and democratic spirit of the Brigade. In 1904 he foretold that:

> . . . some day we shall be able to have a Meeting of Council at which not only one but several Colonial Officers will be present, when not only countries under the Union Jack, but countries under other flags as well, will be represented in what will be an International Council . . .[4]

History was to prove Barry correct, but not in Smith's lifetime nor in this first period of international growth of The Boys' Brigade. Whatever the vision, the resources, organization, experience and expertise for international cooperation on the scale required were lacking in the Brigade movement. The Empire, too, was not ready, willing or able to respond so early. Its security, so badly shaken by the South African War of 1899-1901, was rocked again in 1914. Some countries, like Australia and New Zealand, still had to 'come of age' fighting Europe's wars, at Gallipoli, on the Somme and elsewhere. Their governments' commitment was first and foremost to a youth coerced into military uniform. Smith, the Founder, was certainly highly respected outside Britain, but even his influence could not overcome 'local conditions' overseas. At home he had started early enough and was already firmly established as the recognized leader of uniformed boys' work by the time the War Office cast covetous eyes on the various brigades. He did not therefore easily abandon his religious principles for the sake of changing sentiment and opportunity. Abroad, however, although he found some support for resisting militarization of the Brigade, the movement, even in its strongest centres, proved unable to resist the first tempting offers of incorporation into military Cadet systems. Where it did — and the cases were isolated and rare — the cudgel of legislation soon defeated most B.B. work. Between 1908 and 1920 Smith's rivals — if that is the word — in international youth work (principally the Boy Scout movement) were better able to adapt themselves to the prevailing winds of fashion. The lessons of the pre-1914 years remained, however, deeply engrained on the Brigade psyche.

Historians of religion and youth work in the nineteenth century have already shown that there existed close spiritual and personal links between Dwight L. Moody, the popular American travelling evangelist, and his British admirers, including Lord Aberdeen, Henry Drummond, W.A. Smith, and their Scottish circle. 'Moody and his friends', notes Kathleen Heasman, 'were responsible for giving a definite objective to the scattered threads of evangelical work for boys and girls and in helping to direct such work along lines which would meet the various needs of young people.' It was this same strong evangelical network, this shared willingness to experiment, which gave an early impetus to the expansion of Boys' Brigade work outside Britain in the late 1880s and in the 1890s. After 1886-87 the movement spread overseas, as Henry Drummond put it, with 'all the violence of an epidemic'.[5]

Although the first B.B. company formed in the U.S.A. was in St. Louis, Missouri, in 1887, the epicentre of the movement in that country was California. The Rev. John Quincy Adams commenced the 1st San Francisco Company at the Westminster Presbyterian Church in August 1889. Carefully following the Glasgow example, Adams had fifty companies operating in California and the West Coast by 1892. As first United States B.B. President from 1890, based in San Francisco, he willingly held 'power by consent from the parent body in Great Britain'. Very soon enquiries flooded in from all over North America and even from Honolulu. By 1891-92 reported membership was 3,000 among seventy-five companies. But California's remoteness from the main centres of industrial America soon eclipsed its ability to retain the national leadership. Two further divisions were established, a Central one in Chicago (where the B.B. commenced in 1890) and an Eastern one at Jamaica Plains, Massachusetts. Diffusion proved the prelude to an unwelcome and uncontrolled diversity. From 1892 two magazines began to appear, the *Boys' Brigade Bulletin* in California, and an Eastern rival, the *Boys' Brigade Courier*, in Cincinnati. For the moment, however, the leaders of the infant and rapidly spreading movement retained a loyalty to the magazine that inspired them most, the *Boys' Brigade Gazette*. Words of commendation from Glasgow were their encouragement and even hints of caution from the same source were mostly heeded. In San Francisco B.B. work remained for a time very traditional, if recognizably American: a regular battalion camp, combined competitive activities, the Bible Class, and, in 1892, a mass evangelistic rally attracting 4,000 boys and 1,000 adults. Ministers wrote enthusiastically about the new boys' work from all over the U.S.A.:

> During the three years of its history [reported Adams in 1892] the 1st San Francisco Company Boys' Brigade has been such a power along all lines of our church work as has no other of our Societies. To cite only one result, thirty Boys have come from its ranks into full membership.

In the same year union was achieved with the Boys' Army, a similar organization run by the Rev. Howard H. Russell in Chicago. But, inevitably in so vast and diverse a country, deviation from Smith's original methods and some divisive competition arose in the 1890s.[6]

In New York a Baptist Boys' Brigade started about 1893, allegedly to counter 'the many mistakes of the Scottish movement'. Already the Methodists had their similarly constituted Epworth Guards and, as Henry Drummond found on his visit to the East and Midwest in 1893, there was 'a tendency to run to gold braid, white gloves, cocked hats and feathers'. In 1893 the influential Cincinnati Brigade leader Dr Charles B. Morrell published a simple official American *Handbook of The Boys' Brigade*, outlining, with certain obvious concessions to American styles in military dress and social organization, a programme and structure based firmly on the British model. By 1893 there were an estimated 14,000 boys in 220 or more United States companies. But by then Glasgow had given up the unequal task of registering companies in the U.S.A. Henceforth national records in that country remained chaotic and statistics erred annually on the inflationary side. Critics, moreover, carried or wrote messages of disquiet to Britain: the American movement was 'too elaborate', 'too military', and was rapidly removing itself from the Churches and catering overwhelmingly for 'the better classes'. Adams sprung to its defence, citing their 'complex problems' and the size of their country, and stating that there was 'an overwhelming work thrust upon us'. In 1894 certain 'Chicago area clergymen carried out a coup' and, wresting the movement from its West Coast founders, set up the United Boys' Brigades of America (U.B.B.A.) with 524 known companies and a Midwest 'national' headquarters in Chicago. As one American historian of boys' work notes, the U.B.B.A. henceforth became in its publications 'more narrowly military, and the leaders embarked upon an unsuccessful hunt for a prestigous general to lend them his name'. Increasingly the national leadership became more remote from the companies and local officers. A hierarchical rule-by-convention gradually set in, and the U.B.B.A. became year-by-year more militarized and less Church-based. In 1894 the Chicago national meeting endorsed the setting up of 'regimental formations' above the battalions. The already long-standing debate on boys' age limits between nine and twenty-one years went unresolved. By 1894 the U.B.B.A. proclaimed a membership of 16,000 boys with another 16,000 in associate and affiliate organizations.[7]

Smith and his British Executive, although viewing the American trends with disquiet, continued faithfully to report developments in the U.S.A. The Founder did seem to favour, it is true, those accounts which emphasized traditional activities like camping and the simple pronouncement of Christian virtues throughout the movement. Whilst visiting Canada in February 1895 he deviated for one day to inspect boys in Boston, finding there a zeal amongst American officers for the essentials of the Object 'scarcely . . . equalled by any of our Home Battalions'. But, for the next twelve years, he had to watch the U.B.B.A., variously accoutred and attired, wax and wane in the major population centres of the U.S.A. Its national organization, although increasingly elaborate, was weak, since companies were prone to favour battalion, regimental and state affiliations more than national ones. Drilling and manoeuvring in complex military fashion failed to retain boys, and high costs of membership and uniform precluded many working-class or immigrant boys from joining. The U.B.B.A. largely lost touch with its roots in Scotland and with Smith's concept of a boys' movement centred strongly in the Churches and Sunday Schools. The rank structure and uniforms became progressively more elaborate and the movement aped the military more and more. Contemporary photographs of U.B.B.A. encampments and activities are very reminiscent of Yankee manoeuvres in the 1860s.[8]

In 1901, reflecting the maxim that money and industry speak loudest, the U.B.B.A. national command moved to Pittsburgh under a new Commander-in-Chief, General H.P. Bope, formerly a stenographer and now a steel magnate in the great Carnegie Steel Company. With an appropriate rod of iron, Bope, after personally eliminating the U.B.B.A. Chicago debts, revitalized the movement in the industrial East. In 1902, after the failure of the earlier *Knapsack* (1894-96), the *Brigade Boy* was commenced as the official U.B.B.A. bulletin under the remarkable Rev. Joseph H. Cudlipp of Lancaster, Pennsylvania. In August and September 1905 he led a small contingent of boys and officers to Britain, visiting all parts of the kingdom to study Brigade methods and funding. Warm and personable, he won British hearts and deeply admired the ability of Smith's followers to reach boys poorer than those joining the American movement:

> I was much impressed with the fact that with your sixpence or shilling entrance fee and two shilling uniform, you are reaching the street arab, the 'scape', as we would call him, or the 'hooligan', as you have it. I am aware that many Companies are formed of the better and more fortunate class of Boys, but on the whole you reach more factory hands, message Boys and (saddest of all social conditions) Boy breadwinners. This is well. Here and there we are reaching the street Boy, but as a rule we are more apt to get the school Boy and those of the better classes. It goes to prove that in proper hands The Boys' Brigade can be adapted to Boys of all conditions.

Soon afterwards Smith himself received an invitation to tour the U.S.A. with his wife.[9]

From May to June 1907 Smith triumphantly visited New York, Boston, Philadelphia, Washington — meeting President Theodore Roosevelt, 'an awfully nice sort and strong supporter of B.B.' — Baltimore, Pittsburgh and, further west, Chicago (the only disappointment on this exhausting itinerary because of poor turnouts) and St. Louis. Smith was deeply impressed by the bearing and attitude of the American boy. His advice to the enthusiastic but curiously diverse and militarized U.B.B.A. was courteous but unchanged. They must strengthen Church relations, organize a strong and efficient national office, and operate under a proper constitution. The U.B.B.A. should also adhere strictly to prescribed age-limits, strive for 'simplicity and uniformity in dress', scale down titles, and reduce the costs of membership to the boy. Smith did not advocate strict adherence in all matters to the U.K. model: such a goal was clearly un-American. But the leaders of the U.B.B.A., although largely sympathetic, could muster neither the will nor the strength for reform before 1914. Smith's standing as Founder was unchallenged in the U.S.A., but his low-key diffident Scottish pragmatism lacked the charisma or drive to leave a permanent impression on his friendly and enthusiastic hosts, most of whom still continued to relish playing the soldier. Individuals, it is true, like S.F. Shattuck of Neenash-Menasha, Wisconsin, and Joseph Cudlipp, now active in Baltimore, were brave enough after 1910 to run, and sometimes even equip, their units along British lines, but they remained the exception rather than the rule (see Chapter 6).[10]

The U.S.A., vast, pluralistic, and industrially and demographically dynamic, lacked, as Smith put it, men of permanent 'social influence' at the head of its U.B.B.A. affairs. Altruism and philanthrophy in U.B.B.A. circles were of a different magnitude and bent than those similar virtues amongst B.B. men in Britain or Canada. In the latter country Smith's direct influence was stronger and his methods better understood. Indeed he had the men, the means and, he supposed, the influence, to ensure they were.

Canada's Brigade founder, the Rev. Thomas Francis Fotheringham, an Ontario-born Presbyterian, made sure that the movement was initially kept under the influence of the main denominations, the Sabbath Schools, and Glasgow Headquarters. Fotheringham started the first Canadian B.B. company at St. John Presbyterian Church, St. John, New Brunswick, where he had ministered since 1883. Widely respected through the Dominion as a Christian educator, he used his many travelling opportunities to promote the Brigade and the Young Peoples' Society of Christian Endeavour. From 1891 Fotheringham presided over a Provisional Executive for B.B. Canada, and in 1892 inaugurated the St. John Battalion with seven companies. By the end of that year the movement had spread with eighteen companies to Nova Scotia, Ontario and Quebec. Fotheringham, fully supported by Smith, brooked no deviation from the latter's precepts and practices. Yet he remained staunchly Canadian and Imperial in his outlook. He told the U.K. movement that:

> You regard us as 'Colonists' . . . we regard ourselves as part of the same Empire. Most of us decline to be expatriated because we happen to be born a six days' sail from 'the tight little Island', and cannot see that our cousins who did not leave 'home' are any more British than ourselves.

Part of their unity, as Canadian officers soon found, was in defending their new experiment from the 'invectives . . . of the Peace Society', a defence which the *B.B. Gazette* in Britain willingly espoused on behalf of all North Americans: 'Long may the two Flags [the Stars and Stripes and the Union Jack] blend their folds in shielding the Boys of Greater America.' In September 1893 Lord Aberdeen, Honorary President of the Brigade in Britain, arrived as Governor General of Canada, determined to lend his considerable influence to the B.B. movement.[11]

No strangers to Canada since an earlier visit in 1890-91, Aberdeen and his consort, Ishbel Maria (née Marjoribanks) did much during their viceroyship of 1893-98 to unify sectarian and nationalist feelings across the sprawling Dominion. As strong liberals with a 'sincere interest in social welfare', however, their stay in Ottawa was not without its troubles politically. Favouring liberal forces — they were close to the Quebec Liberal Wilfred Laurier (Prime Minister, 1896-1911) — the Aberdeens brought with them strong memories of the socioreligious fervour of their London and Scottish days at the heart of the Moody-Drummond circle, the milieu from which The Boys' Brigade had directly sprung. 'Our dear friend', Henry Drummond, was often their intimate confidant in Ottawa and elsewhere during his North American tours. In her revealing private *Canadian Journal* (published in 1960) Ishbel Aberdeen gives valuable insights into the viceregal promotion of religion and welfare in Canada, and of Aberdeen's social and religious orchestration of William Smith's highly successful whirlwind tour of 1895. In January 1894, for example, the Aberdeens intervened directly to initiate an enquiry into youth employment in Ottawa, intending to 'induce as many Churches as possible to form Companies', and to open recreation clubrooms for the many aimless 'boys whose avocations take them into the streets'. They offered the 'smart young fellows' in their household staff for the projects and hoped that young local civil servants would officer and manage the new enterprises. By July 1894 three companies (two Episcopalian and one Presbyterian) were operating in Ottawa.[12]

Aberdeen needed little prompting from either Glasgow or Canada to invite Smith to the Dominion. Although asked in 1893-94, the Founder did not cross the Atlantic until February 1895. By then the task of controlling the rapidly expanding Brigade had become herculean. Under Fotheringham's interim B.B. organizational arrangements J.W. Cassidy in St. John, New Brunswick, was looking after the Maritime Provinces and Quebec, and T.W. Nisbet in Sarnia, Ontario, was responsible for Ontario and 'everything West' — over 3,000 miles. By 1893-94 the Brigade had reached Manitoba (Winnipeg and Glenboro), Saskatchewan (Regina), and British Columbia (Vancouver and Victoria). In St. John's, Newfoundland, a company was started in 1893, and in the Maritimes, Quebec and Ontario, especially the latter province, expansion was proving rapid. The movement was receiving support from all major Protestant denominations, and companies were affiliated in some centres to the Y.M.C.A., and in New Glasgow (Nova Scotia) even to the influential Women's Christian Temperance Union.[13]

Smith's Canadian tour began publicly on 20 February 1895 with a large representative meeting in Montreal hosted by the Governor General. Travelling by courtesy of the various railroad systems, and sometimes by sleigh, Smith then went east to New Brunswick and Nova Scotia, and thence back to Toronto and from one end of Ontario to the other: Kingston, Sarnia, Niagara Falls and, for some days of conferences and recuperation, to Government House in Ottawa. Everywhere he was fêted and shown the best of B.B. Canada. On 26 March he was again enthusiastically received at a great public meeting in Toronto, where the same day a Canadian B.B. Constitution was ratified and an Executive elected under the presidency of Lord Aberdeen. Thomas Nisbet, already well known for his vigorous promotion of the movement from his $12,000 'Brigade Hall' in Sarnia — lavishly equipped with a gymnasium, showers, a bowling-alley, offices and recreation rooms — was appointed Canadian B.B. Secretary. Dominion Headquarters were moved to Sarnia. In March 1895 a membership of 2,850 (all ranks) was reported from throughout Canada. Within nine months the Canadian B.B. grew to 120 companies with an estimated overall membership of 5,000. No national council with such high hopes and prestige would be formed overseas for many years to come. At the head of Canadian B.B. affairs stood one of Smith's greatest friends and supporters, Lord Aberdeen. The Canadian B.B. Secretary, Nisbet, 'a smart soldierly man . . . a vigorous speaker', was a former member of William Smith's own regiment, the 1st Lanarkshire Rifle Volunteers. The Founder had good reason to believe that the future of B.B. Canada was sound and secure. More so, perhaps, than its counterpart south of the border, the U.B.B.A.[14]

Nisbet made great business and personal sacrifices to accept the position of Canadian Secretary. In the summer of 1895 he attended Brigade Council in Dublin and spent a further two months on deputation work in the Maritimes, Quebec and Ontario. Within five or six years he enrolled, it is estimated, a further 200 Canadian companies and sanctioned the formation of battalions in British Columbia and Montreal (1896), Winnipeg (1897), Hamilton (1898), and in 1900 at Ottawa, Georgian Bay (Ontario), and on Prince Edward Island. Although punctilious in his correspondence, zealous in his promotion of the Brigade, and frugal in his expenditures, Nisbet and his Canadian Headquarters did not secure the loyalty or financial support of the bulk of the country's B.B. companies. Writing to William McVicker in 1946, Frederick Longstaff, for long a perceptive analyst and chronicler of Canadian Brigade history, felt that Aberdeen was so keen on forming new companies that 'he left out the keystone, for he did not look after forming a Dominion Headquarters Staff and fund'. True as that was, the records show that initially Aberdeen did give substantial amounts out of his own pocket towards the cause. Sarnia, however, proved to be too peripheral to the B.B. heartland of Canada which was (and remains) the Greater Toronto region.[15]

In Toronto a battalion was formed in 1893, which in six years grew to 800 members with seventeen companies. At Broadview Avenue Congregational Church the 11th Toronto (formed in 1896) attained a membership of 170 NCOs and boys. Under the remarkably energetic C.J. Atkinson — who became one of North America's best known leaders in boys' work — this company was among the largest in the contemporary B.B. world. At West Toronto Junction the Rev. Charles W. McKim, as Episcopalian rector there, was inspired in 1892 by the B.B. work of his brother Richard. The following year Charles formed his own company for 'newsboys and shoeblacks' in Central Toronto. He later recalled his B.B. career:

> Strange as it may seem I had less trouble in getting those Boys to respond to B.B. ideals than any other Boys I have ever handled. They were real Boys. No soft material in that crowd. They threw themselves fully into whatever they did, work or play. We had a Sunday School for them and they were quite keen on the study of their lessons. They had all seen much of the rougher side of life before I got them. Some had been in jail . . .

In his subsequent ministries in Whitby (Ontario), Winnipeg and Kenora (Ontario), McKim formed successful companies along the well-tried lines. In Toronto, some leaders — notably Atkinson at Broadview Boys' Institute, and those at All Saints Episcopal Church — transferred the traditional B.B. programme into highly successful boys' clubs and institutes pursuing, like their contemporaries in Nottingham and other centres in England, a more secular, muscular programme of gymnastics, sports, athletics, games and other recreations. This sort of evolution in boys' work, building upon the initial B.B. base, occurred contemporaneously in many other parts of the world, including Honolulu (Hawaii) and in certain Australian centres such as Hobart and Sydney. Toronto itself became recognized as one of the leading North American centres for boys' work well into the present century.[16]

Episcopalian ministers were among some of the most active promoters of the traditional B.B. methods in Canada, especially in the West, where migration grew rapidly from the 1890s to the outbreak of the First World War. In Vancouver, British Columbia, the Revs C.C. Owen and A.H. Sovereign laid the foundations for a strong Brigade work after 1908. As Bishop of 'the miserable diocese' of Yukon and Athabasca, Sovereign once went on strike to secure a decent wage for his clergyman and became known as 'one of Canada's most outspoken exponents of social reform'. Moving to the seven-house village of Kitsilano, Vancouver, in 1909, he started an excellent company there and pioneered boys' camping on Lower Mainland British Columbia at Bowen Island, Howe Sound. Before the turn of the century both black and Red Indian boys — the latter notably in Regina — were to be found in Canadian companies.[17]

In the first period of B.B. expansion, despite all the difficulties of isolation and the great distances between them, there were a number of creditably active companies throughout Canada. Between 1895-1900 about 90-100 companies were probably working with a membership of 3,000-4,500. By 1903, however, any pretence at national coordination was gone: the great plan of 1895 was in ruins. From now onwards, reported Longstaff later, many officers followed 'their own bent instead of the Manual' and cohesion was lost except in the bigger provincial centres. In 1904 Glasgow B.B. Headquarters had to reassume responsibility for registering Canadian companies, and up to 1914 sixty were entered on the 'Overseas Register', thirty of them in provinces west of Manitoba. Like many Canadians, old and new, The Boys' Brigade too was 'going west'. That westward movement provided one last chance before 1914 to overhaul the fragmentation and rebuild a national Boys' Brigade presence in Canada. The architect of this venture was the forceful and persistent former Cambridge student Frederick Victor Longstaff, sometime Secretary of the Thames Valley Battalion and member of the London Committee.[18]

Longstaff paid a short visit to Canada in 1903 when he met Thomas Nisbet at Sarnia. In September 1910, close on the heels of Robert Baden-Powell's Canadian section of his world tour of inspection of Boy Scouts, Longstaff arrived in St. John, New Brunswick, 'to investigate the condition [of the Brigade] from the Atlantic to the Pacific'. Everywhere he found B.B. companies transforming themselves into Scout groups: 'The Boy Scout movement', proclaimed some sections of the Canadian press approvingly, 'does not spell militarism . . . It abhors the routine which would convert a man into a machine.' As he moved steadily westwards to British Columbia, Longstaff found a healthier B.B. morale and more lively activity in Winnipeg, Calgary, Edmonton, Vancouver and elsewhere. The secret to success, he concluded, was to adopt the idea of his friend Hugh M. Urquhart (former Captain of the 43rd London) in Winnipeg: to attract a leaven of British-trained Brigade officers to Canada. Back in Britain he reported accordingly to the Brigade Executive, and in 1911 himself emigrated to Victoria, British Columbia, as self-styled Honorary B.B. Organizing Secretary for Canada. In 1911 he issued an 'Annual Report' listing twenty active Canadian companies (only seven of them east of Manitoba) and advocating a Winnipeg-based national headquarters to produce an indigenous Canadian B.B. literature, sell equipment, and promote the movement. Soon afterwards battalions were re-established in Montreal and Winnipeg, and an Officer's Council formed in Calgary. But Longstaff's demands for $500 to launch his national scheme went unheeded on both sides of the Atlantic.[19]

Badgered in London by Longstaff on one of his visits there, Smith and Roger Peacock in March 1913 secured Brigade Executive's confirmation of his appointment as Honorary Organizer for Canada for two years, retrospective to 1 June 1912. Receptive in most respects to the suggestions made to it, but ignorant of many of the Canadian realities, the home movement responded as best it could to Longstaff's pleas and demands. Articles and notices appeared frequently in the B.B. Gazette promoting the virtues of emigration by B.B. officers and boys to Canada, and extolling the need for British citizens to pre-empt American migration into 'the best of Canada': the Prairies and the West. Oliver Hind of Nottingham reported fully in 1912 on his visit to Canada and his experiments in assisting young B.B. men to emigrate. The 2nd Nottingham Company maintained a farm in Nova Scotia to assist in the migration process. The challenges to any British B.B. officer prepared to come and 'adapt . . . to the prevailing conditions' were many. For the right candidates, boys or officers, there was employment enough if they were prepared to work hard out West. With unemployment rife in many parts of Britain, the attractions of a country where 'Boys possess more "wealth" than is good for them, and most of them, born as it were in the saddle, own either a horse or a pony' were great indeed. But A.S. Roberts, Captain of the 83rd London Company, warned in 1907 after a Canadian tour, 'let every Englishman when he migrates to a new country . . . drop his prejudices and adapt himself to the

*These Australian Aboriginal boys are members of the 1st Weipa Company,
founded in 1910 at the Weipa Presbyterian Mission in Queensland.*

*The original 1st and 2nd Sydney Companies, circa 1897-98.
In Australia and New Zealand the Brigade was unable
to resist statutory incorporation into Cadet Schemes
before the First World War.*

The first church parade of the 1st Port Chalmers Company, New Zealand, on 1 December 1901.

The B.B. in Canada initially thrived with the active support of the Earl of Aberdeen, Governor General from 1893 to 1898. Here the 1st Calgary Company braves the cold in the winter of 1912.

In the U.S.A. in the 1890s and 1900s, companies of the United Boys' Brigades of America largely went their own way, developing elaborate uniforms and indulging in a more flamboyant military style.

prevailing conditions'. B.B. officers would find, for instance, that 'in a democratic country [like frontier Canada] where Jack is as good as his neighbour, it
is very hard to instil that amount of respect and discipline into Boys that we
expect and get in the Old Country'. 'Self-reliance, recklessness, and (for want
of a more expressive word) "cheekiness",' reported another British observer
in 1912, 'are prime qualities with a Canadian Boy and nothing daunts him in
their exercise.' True emigrant B.B. officers, claimed an 'old Country officer',
should not be put off by the raw boy material available to him in Canada. It
was their 'plain duty [to endeavour] to do a little in return for the cause which
has meant so much to many of them in the past'.[20]

Longstaff persistently hammered out the same message during his stormy
time as Canadian Organizer. To him William Smith appeared slow in dealing
with his letters and their pleas, demands and suggestions for the B.B. overseas. Longstaff adopted, therefore, a hectoring, sometimes peremptory tone to
get the Brigade Secretary to respond more quickly. Smith *must* encourage not
discourage migrant officers to take up B.B. work *immediately* on arrival abroad.
Many such men seemed 'ashamed' to admit to a B.B. allegiance in Canada and
some were 'apathetic', giving Longstaff the 'idea that they only did B.B. work
at home because they were afraid to do otherwise' — a shrewd comment.
Longstaff also demanded direct contact with the 'Higher Policy' makers of the
home movement, expecting to be put on the Executive mailing list. In April
1914 came the real shock for Smith in this increasingly ungentlemanly barrage.
Under pressure from the Adjutant General in Ottawa, and from some B.B.
companies in Montreal, Calgary and Winnipeg who wanted to borrow army
equipment, Longstaff was in negotiation with the Director of Cadet Services
to ascertain under what conditions the Brigade 'in Canada could enter the
Cadet Service and still retain its essential features'. Not surprisingly, by 1914
the Canadian Army, given the growing threat of war in Europe, was not
indisposed to accommodate the B.B.'s request for special privileges in exchange for willing integration into the Cadets. On 5 May 1914, five days before
his death in London, Sir William Smith wrote a long, sad, tired letter to
Longstaff from Glasgow requiring him to seek the sanction of the Canadian
Executive (there wasn't one) and 'Home Executive' before proceeding further.
He outlined the British experience and successful resistance to the Army
Council's designs and inducements in this matter, warning that 'experience
. . . in South Africa, Australia and New Zealand' showed that acquiescence
spelt 'an end of The Boys' Brigade so far as its main purpose is concerned'.
Smith shrewdly sent copies of his letters to 'the respective Centre Secretaries'
throughout Canada 'for their information and guidance'. In British Columbia
the Brigade largely supported Smith's stand, but the matter never came to a
direct head since Longstaff, Urquhart and others left Canada soon afterwards
to fight their own real war in Europe. Subsequently the B.B. in Canada
languished as a national movement, surviving only in pockets around the
Dominion.[21]

Given more propitious times Longstaff undoubtedly would have succeeded
in rebuilding the Canadian Brigade. As H. Fiddes, an immigrant Captain of
the 5th Vancouver, wrote in a postscript in 1915, Canada needed a Headquarters led by 'a capable man — a man with a broad mind and common sense, a
man who is a hustler and an organizer; one who knows the B.B. work and the
Canadian Boys in particular'. The Scouting movement undoubtedly prospered overseas after 1910 by learning something of the organizational lessons
which the Brigade before 1914 never fully grasped. Already in the 1890s, as the

North American experience demonstrates, the B.B. had grown too vast at home and abroad for Smith, with limited professional help, to manage alone. Longstaff by 1911 was convinced the formula could be devised for B.B. Canada to 'show the B.B. in Australia and South Africa how to organize over vast areas'. But, to ensure success, 'there should be a special officer at Brigade Headquarters, Glasgow, to handle correspondence with Overseas Companies. Why not have a 'Colonial Secretary', Longstaff asked, to receive reports from travelling B.B. officers and to correspond with B.B. centres 'or even a single isolated company'? Longstaff was years ahead of Britain in such thinking. The pertinence of Longstaff's arguments becomes clearer historically if we consider the B.B. experience of countries more remote from Britain than North America. The latter enjoyed at least the aura of Smith's visitations. But in Australia and New Zealand, for instance, the Canadian story finds a number of parallels.[22]

New Zealand, the remotest B.B. outpost until the 1930s, exemplifies the problems of extreme geographical isolation and susceptibility to local pressures. In the 1890s and early 1900s there was, it is true, perhaps no more fertile ground in the Empire for successfully receiving and adapting British liberal experiments in welfare and philanthropy than the colony of New Zealand. It was widely considered as the model state in social and political liberalism. But only a dozen short-lived B.B. companies — there were probably as many more unofficial experiments — are recorded before 1914.

As early as October 1886 an 80-strong Boys' Brigade group was formed for the poorer boys of Christchurch. Although not attached to any particular church, it boasted a simple uniform cap and ran classes useful for gaining lucrative employment as well as a Bible Class. The first conventional B.B. company was raised in May 1887 at St. James' Presbyterian Church, Auckland. Another followed in 1889 at Trinity Presbyterian Church, Timaru. Thereafter only three small centres of B.B. activity are discernible in New Zealand, the first in Otago, an extrovertly Scottish province. In Dunedin, its capital, John Tennant, an 'old boy' of the 1st Glasgow, started in 1891 a short-lived company at St. Andrew's Presbyterian Church, home pulpit of the great reformist anti-sweatshop preacher, the Rev. Rutherford Waddell. In nearby Ravensbourne and Port Chalmers, Otago, two neighbouring companies were started in 1901, soon attaining a combined membership of 130 boys. These units were recruited, however, to the sound of martial exhortations from some local Presbyterian pulpits. Former soldiers in the Second South African War (the Boer War) told the boys of their exploits and experiences. The Ravensbourne and Port Chalmers companies were proudly provided with old government-issue Snider rifles, until it was found that most boys found them too large to handle. In Christchurch three companies formed at the same time in 1902-03 soon folded under strong competition from local Cadet units. In New Zealand's capital, Wellington, two large B.B. companies registered at the Boys' Institute in the early 1890s were 'gazetted as a naval cadet company' in 1896.

New Zealand's Government politicians had listened intently to the warnings coming from Britain about German expansionism and the need for military preparedness. In 1909 all New Zealand males from twelve to twenty-one years of age became subject to the Defence Act regulations concerning weekly military training. Following an official visit by Robert Baden-Powell in 1910 the Act was amended to allow Boy Scouts in New Zealand to coexist with Cadets. In 1912 the regulations concerning twelve to fourteen year olds were repealed. But, so far as the Brigade was concerned, the damage had by then already been done. By 1914 the movement was dead in New Zealand. In the twenty-seven or so years of its fitful existence no known attempt was made to provide outside help or internal assistance to help run a viable national B.B. organization. The country was, moreover, deeply divided over the issue of compulsory military service. In the Churches the B.B. at this earliest period never gained a very secure foothold.[23]

In the six neighbouring colonies of Australia one of the principal preoccupations in the 1890s was with the rapid move towards Federation. In that decade the B.B. became established on largely orthodox lines. But by 1906-07 the movement's commitment to a naval and military training scheme within the Brigade structure was almost irrevocable.

When he set out on his lecture tour of the Australian universities and colleges in 1890, Henry Drummond was concerning himself deeply with the current debate on 'Imperial Federation'. He was also determined on that tour to promote the Brigade officially in Australia. Already in Sydney there was evidence of interest among certain promoters of newsboys' brigades in the mainstream ideas of the B.B. (see Chapter 6). In 1891, as a direct result of Drummond's promotion, a company was started at St. Martin's Church of England in Fitzroy, a suburb of Melbourne, Victoria. Two thousand miles away in Western Australia, in a colony lately made rich as a result of frenetic gold rushes to Coolgardie and Kalgoorlie, the 1st Perth Company was started in 1895. But, hopelessly isolated, it flourished only until the turn of the century. In 1896 Sutherland Sinclair, a staunchly Presbyterian philanthropist from Greenock, near Glasgow, commenced the 1st Sydney at St. Peter's Presbyterian Church, North Sydney. Run according to Smith's precepts, Sinclair's unit became the focal point of Australian B.B. organization. In 1898 Sinclair commenced a regular Brigade column in *Australia Young Folks*, a Christian magazine, and in 1899 became Honorary Australian Secretary to an Australian B.B. Council. By then a dozen units were operating in all four eastern states and in South Australia.

With Australian Federation in 1901 the movement doubled in size. In South Australia the Brigade was adopted officially by the state's Methodist Conference for promotion in its Sabbath Schools. Soon afterwards a battalion was formed in Adelaide, the state capital. From an office supplied for him at the Y.M.C.A. in Sydney, Sinclair sent imported B.B. literature throughout Australia and organized the purchase of locally manufactured equipment. The patronage of the Governor General was also secured. But, isolated by distance and often by strong local state sentiments, many companies failed to report statistics and rarely paid either their fees or bills. Between 1900 and 1903 Sinclair never conceded an official Australian membership over 700 boys. In 1904, disillusioned and declaring a deficit, he handed over his Australian responsibilities to the Victorian Sunday School Union office under A.B. Field in Melbourne. By 1903 two-thirds of the known Australian boy membership of 750 was in Victoria where already the Brigade movement had taken some quite unusual turns. In 1901-02 Warrant Officer Robert ('Gunner') Kearns started a Boys' Naval Brigade (B.N.B.) at Williamstown, a port suburb of Melbourne. The unit was raised in the St. Andrew's Presbyterian Church, Williamstown. It soon proved a popular innovation among the boys of Melbourne. Before 1911 over twenty B.N.B. companies, supported by all denominations from Anglicans to Baptists, sprang up in Victoria, reaching even as far as inland Ballarat.[24]

The rise of the B.N.B. coincided with an Australia-wide debate over the new nation's pathetically limited ability to defend her twelve thousand miles of shoreline. Four million people occupied the peripheries of a continent nearly three million square miles in extent. In 1904 Captain W.R. Cresswell, the new Director of Commonwealth Naval Forces, inherited 'a few odd vessels, hand-me-downs from colonial defences; a thousand men, mostly part-time; and several hundred voluntary cadets, mere playful youngsters'. Many Australians (and New Zealanders) now rightly doubted the Royal Navy's ability or the Imperial Government's willingness to protect their region in the event of a global conflict or even a localized threat. The Boys' Naval Brigade units represented one small response to the new national pride and sentiment. Both state and federal governments — although defence was chiefly the responsibility of the new Commonwealth of Australia — willingly aided and abetted the B.N.B.'s requests for the loan of launches, equipment and training staff. The Naval Depot at Swan Island, Victoria, became for several years the annual venue for the 400-strong summer training camps of the state's B.N.B. units. In 1907 both the Prime Minister, Alfred Deakin, and the Governor General, Lord Northcote, travelled to Swan Island to inspect Captain Cresswell and his boy Naval Cadets, among whom the B.N.B. units now proudly numbered themselves. The B.N.B. became more and more integrated by choice rather than regulation into the Naval Cadet Scheme. Not to be outdone, units of the B.B. in Victoria soon formed themselves into a military battalion. Under the umbrella of A.B. Field as Australian B.B. Secretary, the two sections, naval and military, happily coexisted in Victoria. In 1907 there was a reported membership of 1,350 boys and NCOs and 120 officers in B.B. Australia. In January 1911 all boys over twelve years of age in Australia became subjected to the training provisions of the Defence Act of 1903-10. By then The Boys' Brigade had mostly either ceased to exist independently in Australia or had willingly become fully integrated into the military Cadet Schemes.[25]

The pockets of orthodox B.B. work elsewhere in Australia did not long survive the new Defence Act regulations. In Sydney, Adelaide and Broken Hill (New South Wales) an efficient Boys' Brigade continued a work primarily concerned with social and educational welfare among poor working-class boys (and subsidized by strong local business interests), begun in the late 1880s under the same name. We shall briefly consider the importance of this movement — which was not part of the mainstream B.B. development — below (see Chapter 6). Like the so-called Boys' Brigade Try Societies of Melbourne and Geelong in Victoria, these older institutions had at various times — and not in the name alone — been influenced by William Smith's ideas. Similarly in Tasmania the traditional B.B. company work of the late 1890s and early years of this century gradually evolved into boys' gymnasiums, clubs or institutions.

In 1910 an all-Aboriginal company was formed at the Moravian Mission, Albatross Bay, Cape York Peninsula, North Queensland. Twelve hundred miles further south in the same state B.G. Pattersen, a mining engineer and former close B.B. associate of Sinclair in Sydney, was quietly transforming his 1st Mount Morgan Company (formed for the sons of miners in 1910) into a 'B.B. Scout Troop', which flourished in different guises into the 1920s. In 1913 George Orr, one of W.A. Smith's 'old boys' and lieutenants in 1st Glasgow, started a new and strictly orthodox company in Brisbane. With him the

Brigade in Australia, as will be seen in Chapter 6, entered into a new era.[26]

Just over fifty Brigade companies were formed in the two British colonies and two Boer republics of South Africa between 1889 and 1899. It says much for the B.B. founders in that period that boy membership embraced most races: African, Coloured and European, including 'one Company almost exclusively of Dutch Boys' in the Transvaal. The consistent strength of the movement lay in Cape Colony, particularly in the Cape Town Battalion (formed 1894) — which had 500 members in sixteen units by 1895 — and its outreach work at Port Elizabeth where a battalion was formed in 1897. One of the most influential B.B. leaders of the prewar years in South Africa was the immigrant Rev. John C. Harris who lived in Cape Town from 1892 and from 1898 in Johannesburg in the Transvaal. As Captain of the 1st Cape Town, the famous and efficient 'Black Watch' Company (formed 1892), Harris addressed himself openly from the outset to the racial and social problems he found in South Africa. 'Our aim should be chiefly to reach the poorer and rougher lads, and they are black,' he reported in 1894. 'There is no colour distinction. That I insist on as a *sine qua non*, as I regard a colour line as being disastrous and unchristian.' Outside individual companies, however, local social realities soon impinged upon the views of even the most impartial and dedicated optimists. By 1901 Harris was more at grips with the complexities of South Africa. 'As far as possible', he recorded of the Cape Battalion,

> we ignored 'colour' altogether, for in Cape Town, so bewildering is the variety, it was not possible to classify. As a rule we found it best to allow the white Boys to have Companies for themselves, for, in spite of sentimental theories, we could not advise indiscriminate mixture. I think this colour difficulty has been one of the drawbacks of the Cape Battalion, but it has also tended to intensify the spirit of competition.

In 1895 sixty per cent of the membership in the Cape Battalion was white.[27]

In Natal the movement had commenced fleetingly at Durban and Pietermaritzburg in February 1889. But this early promise was halted by some misidentification of the Brigade with the Volunteers and later, more decisively, by the 'Government system of Cadet Corps in Public Schools [which] seemed to eclipse the Brigade'. A Durban Battalion, established in 1895 with five companies, failed to survive, although a temporary rejuvenation occurred with the influx of refugees from the neighbouring Transvaal during the South African (or Boer) War of 1899-1902. This renaissance, although vigorously pursued in 1901-02 to attract boys away from the Cadets, did not outlast the postwar upheavals and Government regulations. Interestingly, however, in 1891 a cousin of Lord Aberdeen, John H. Moir (formerly Captain of the 1st Aberdeen Company), launched the 1st Umsinga Company at Gordon Memorial Mission, Zululand, northeastern Natal, made up of boys from Zulu and other tribal backgrounds.[28]

During the first period of B.B. expansion the movement did not gain a strong foothold in the Orange Free State. Only half-a-dozen companies were formed there between 1892 and 1905. In the other Boer heartland of the Transvaal, however, a booming mining economy ensured a strong British commerical and technical presence. Both longer-term and migratory personnel were able, therefore, to provide staff and recruits for the Brigade movement. After 1891 a Transvaal Battalion — made up totally of Presbyterian companies — operated briefly in Pretoria. It was revived by J.C. Harris towards the end of the decade, when fourteen companies with a membership of 500 from all Churches were quickly formed. At this period the B.B. gained some support from the Dutch Reformed Church. Contemporaneously a Jewish Lads' Brigade regiment of 150 boys was also raised in the Transvaal. In the years before the Boer War the Transvaal Battalion of The Boys' Brigade secured a measure of support from the State Secretary, F.W. Rietz, and even from President Kruger himself. In the Transvaal there was no compulsory Cadet Force. Yet, as the rift between the Boers and British grew, so too did the sense of insecurity. The Brigade was undoubtedly seen as one way of training boys for military service. The rapid prewar expansion of the B.B. in the Transvaal therefore inevitably brought some peculiar problems. These were not very different from those faced by the U.B.B.A. in the U.S.A. 'Each Captain,' reported one B.B. officer, 'became his own "Manual" and fads and experiments, cockades, feathers and gold lace' abounded.[29]

In October 1899 the Boer Republics invaded Natal. For the first time in its short history one branch of the movement found itself divided, dispersed and disrupted by war. Many dominions and colonies of the Empire rushed to the Imperial summons for help in South Africa. For many a young colonist it offered the first opportunity outside his own shores to experience 'adventure under fire'. Fanned by British and local hysteria, the experience of the South African War struck responsive chords in the dominions. Demands for universal military training for boys and men slowly gained wider support as the new century progressed. The following chapter will show how William Smith, confident of a strong Church-based support, was able to resist overtures from a government eager to swallow up the Brigade. As we have seen, this was never the case in the British dominions overseas. Not only was the B.B. too weak to resist, but it also showed no inclination, except for isolated exceptions, to want to do so. In South Africa the Boer War was the first watershed in Brigade development. In the Transvaal after British annexation a fatal courtship with the new compulsory Cadet Scheme resulted in the movement's extinction. Only in the Cape Battalion did the B.B. retain some of its former glory until 1914.

Throughout the rest of the African continent the movement gained mainly isolated toeholds before 1914. In West Africa several companies were begun in the Gold Coast (now Ghana), achieving particular strength in Presbyterian and mission boarding schools. In nearby Southern Nigeria, Lagos became a Boys' Brigade centre after 1908. Commencing at the Holy Trinity Anglican Church Ebute-Ero, Lagos, the Nigerian movement, catering mainly for African boys, was served by both African and European leaders in the first four companies started between 1908 and 1912. In Nyasaland (now Malawi) a mission-based B.B. company was established in 1910. In British East Africa, a medical missionary from Glasgow, Dr John W. Arthur, started the 1st Kikuyu Company in 1909 at the Church of Scotland Mission, near Nairobi, Kenya. By 1912 three further units were active in the Protectorate, and in 1911-12, a company was started at the Church of Scotland Mission Boys' School in Alexandria, Egypt.[30]

Between 1894 and 1913 fifteen companies are known to have started in Asia and the Indian subcontinent. They included missionary-based companies at Darjeeling (1894) and Jalna (1894), and Y.M.C.A. units at Madras (1903), Allahabad (1904) and Bombay (1904), and at Rangoon, Burma (1902). In 1895 A. O'Dell Figg, late Captain of the 1st Kingston (Dublin) Company, commenced the 1st Colombo Company in Ceylon (now Sri Lanka), which flourished for many years in the Crown Colony at Christ Church, Galle Face, Colombo. In 1902 two more units started, one in Colombo and another in Kandy. By 1909, with the formation of the 4th Ceylon at Wolfendahl Church, Colombo, hopes were briefly entertained for a national B.B. movement in Ceylon. It was not to be. Only in Calcutta — with three companies founded between 1897 and 1902 — did the Brigade grow sufficiently to warrant consideration of some cooperative organizational structure. But competition from local Cadets together with language and social barriers made progress difficult. Whilst most of the Indian and Ceylonese units attempted to reach Asian boys, those formed in Shanghai (Union Church, 1903), Hong Kong (St. Andrews, Kowloon, 1910) and Yokahama, Japan (1905) catered almost exclusively for boys of European or American extraction. In Shanghai the Brigade recruited boys from among ten European nationalities. Although 'making no bar as regards colour' the Shanghai company managed to attract only a few mixed-blood Eurasians. Chinese boys were rarely recruited. Before 1914 there was as yet no clear indication of the remarkable attraction which the movement would prove to ethnic Chinese after the First World War. Although Baden-Powell found The Boys' Brigade in Hong Kong 'trained and dressed as Scouts' during his world tour in 1910, there is no doubt that soon afterwards the 1st Hong Kong, climate permitting, was functioning in all respects like a model British company.[31]

Before 1914 nearly sixty Brigade companies were raised in the British West Indies, British Guiana, British Honduras, Bermuda, Panama and Honduras. The first six recorded West Indian B.B. companies were formed on the Windward Island of St. Vincent in 1892-93. Over seventy per cent of the units formed before 1900 were in Wesleyan-Methodist churches. In the Leeward Islands three companies were active on St. Christopher (St. Kitts) after 1894-95 but the principal growth in the Lesser Antilles was on the southern Windward Islands. Up to 1901 St. Vincent raised ten companies but isolation soon proved the principal enemy to their successful maintenance. By 1893 the Brigade, with two companies, reached Barbados and in 1898, Grenada. Lying only ninety miles north of Trinidad the B.B. in Grenada was soon able to establish close links with that colony. In July 1896 the Trinidad Battalion was formed with a total membership of 210 (all ranks). Within five years B.B. membership doubled with the formation of another half-a-dozen units around the island and on nearby Tobago, a ward of Trinidad. The Trinidad Battalion was strongly supported by its Patron, the Governor, Sir Hubert E.H. Jerningham. Within several years of its foundation a number of minor concessions to the B.B. uniform worn in the colony were wrung from William Smith. In this episode we gain some insight into Smith's colonial B.B. policies. The Trinidad Battalion Secretary, Theodore Tanner, reported in 1897 that:

> The Brigade Executive did not interfere in matters of detail with Colonial Battalions so long as they adhered to the main principles of The Boys' Brigade, as laid down in the Constitution. The Colonial Battalions were in a better position than the Home Executive to judge what modifications in the way of Uniform, and otherwise, might be deemed advisable in view of local circumstances; and whatever changes might be resolved, the Executive relied upon the Colonial authorities keeping the one great purpose consistently before them, and adhering as closely as possible to the methods which experience had shown to be best adapted to attaining the ends in view.

At the same period similar principles were laid before the B.B. in Australia which, not unnaturally, had also sought some concessions to climate in the uniform worn.[32]

On the largest British possession in the West Indies, Jamaica, the B.B. was started in 1894 by the Rev. David Parnther, a Jamaican who had experience of the movement whilst studying in Britain. The 1st Kingston Company proved the forerunner of another eight units in 1894-95. The B.B. suffered a setback in 1899 when the Governor invoked an old law prohibiting negroes from drilling and carrying arms without his authority. Furthermore, Brigade membership was limited to boys under sixteen years of age, and in 1910 the restrictions were made even harsher when the number of officers was limited to no more than three per fifty members. There appeared to be no clear reason for these moves which did, however, severely restrict B.B. expansion in a colony which later was to become one of the principal Brigade centres in the Caribbean.[33]

In South America nine companies arose before 1909 in the sugar and rum colony of British Guiana (now Guyana), with the main activity centred on the capital, Georgetown. In Central America, Belize, the principal town of the timber-rich crown colony of British Honduras (now Belize), was the centre of all prewar Brigade activity. The first company was formed there in 1899 and three more were attempted in 1911-12. At nearby Flowers Bay, on Roatán Island, Honduras, a Baptist company was started by the Rev. John Henderson in 1912. Much earlier, at the free port and railway centre of Colón, Panama (until 1903 in the Republic of Colombia), the movement was commenced in 1894 in the Wesleyan Methodist Church. The following year at the other end of the short interocean railroad, a company was formed in Panama City itself.[34]

By the early 1900s the Brigade idea had been adopted and used in its own national form in other overseas countries. The most successful and enduring early 'transplant' was in Denmark, where the Frivilligt Drenge-Forbund (Voluntary Boys' Organization) has maintained close ties with the original movement since its inception. The F.D.F. originated in Frederiksberg, a prosperous suburb of Copenhagen, comparable with the Hillhead district of Glasgow. The founder of the F.D.F. was Holger Tornöe, a Copenhagen architect, who saw in The Boys' Brigade, as had William Smith, a method of retaining the boys in his Sunday School. The first company was formed in the Sankt Lucas Kirke (St. Luke's Lutheran Church) in 1902, following communication between Tornöe and Smith. Tornöe first came across the Brigade idea through the work of Henry Drummond:

> Then it happened that I took a walk with a dentist who belonged to the congregation. I knew he had been in England so I asked him if there was not among so many voluntary organizations one for boys. At first he said no but then he happened to remember that at home he had a book in Norwegian — a translation of Henry Drummond's *New Light on Old Truth* — with a chapter entitled 'Guttbrigeden — The Boys' Brigade'.[35]

With a company of 102 boys, the F.D.F. developed in a manner very similar to that of The Boys' Brigade in Glasgow. The first three companies were formed within two years in residential Frederiksberg and the surrounding district but by 1905 the first company outside this district had been started, in a more socially mixed area. Within four years the movement had spread to North Jutland at Aalborg and Helsingor, and by 1907 there were twenty companies with 3,000 boys and leaders.

The object of the F.D.F. is 'to confront boys and girls and young people with the Gospel of Jesus Christ', and its aims and methods had much in common with The Boys' Brigade. In 1952 the female parallel organization — the Frivilligt Pige-Forbund — was formed, with the object of developing 'a complete individual' in the Christian sense. Activities in the later twentieth century have inclined more towards orienteering and practical classes (such as boat-building and motor-car maintenance) with a more casual uniform and less rigid regulations on such activities as camping.

The F.D.F. and F.P.F. are constituent organizations of the World Conference of The Boys' Brigade and have been instrumental in a substantial exchange of ideas, company visits and the like with the British Boys' Brigade. The F.D.F., having adopted the ideas of Smith in Denmark, assisted the spread of the Brigade idea to other parts of Scandinavia, although the organizations there are of post-World War II vintage.[36]

By 1908 a 'Gibraltar Boys' Brigade', comprising six companies and 400 boys, was gaining wide approbation in the Colony. Evidence shows that throughout the world there were scores of Smith-inspired experiments in boys' work being tried which never came to official notice.[37]

At Brigade Council in Liverpool in September 1913 the U.B.B.A. submitted a resolution, warmly approved by the Brigade Executive, for an 'International Boys' Brigade Convention' to be held in conjunction with the home Council Meeting. The idea was 'heartily received' and the Brigade Secretary began to contact Brigade authorities all over the world seeking delegates' support to hold the Convention in September 1915. The death of the Founder and the beginning of World War I in 1914 thwarted this major forward thrust in the Brigade's international policies and development. Ideas which had evolved throughout some twenty-five years of cooperative, trial-and-error experimentation in international Boys' Brigade work had to await postwar reconstruction. By then overseas strengths and the responses from the home movement would be very different indeed.[38]

CHAPTER 4

'BOYS, BE STEADY'

The Boys' Brigade in Britain, 1900 to 1919

As THE NEW CENTURY dawned, The Boys' Brigade was expanding at a greater rate than ever before, and at the same time was developing a wider range of activities and interests. In the midst of Boer War euphoria, the membership increased in the first year of the century by 6,000 officers and boys. The strength of the Brigade, in relation to the male population, was greatest in Scotland and Ireland, followed by the Southwest, Wales and the North of England. Membership showed a progressive increase until the organization's Silver Jubilee year of 1908. Significant events, however, were looming on the horizon, which were to give the movement very real challenges: the formation of other organizations, particularly the Boy Scouts; the issue of War Office control in the form of the Government's scheme for Cadet Corps; the death of William Smith in 1914; and, of course, the traumatic effects of World War I. It is these successively disturbing events — which were to determine the future development of the B.B. for the years to come — that will be dealt with in this chapter.

By the time of the 1908 celebrations, the Brigade was becoming accustomed to public prominence. At the 1902 Coronation Review, inspected by the Prince of Wales (the future George V) in Horse Guards Parade, London, 11,000 boys took part, with the 1st Glasgow Company leading The Boys' Brigade, Church Lads' Brigade, Catholic Boys' Brigade and Jewish Lads' Brigade. Lambeth Palace grounds provided a campsite for 1,000 of these boys. This publicity was followed through two years later when the movement's Twenty-first Anniversary was celebrated. There was constant gain and loss. Prior to the Silver Jubilee, Thomas Cuthbertson, Brigade Treasurer and editor of the *Gazette*, died at the age of thirty-five when thrown from his horse. Like his father, John Neilson Cuthbertson, he had been an aggressive advocate of the B.B. idea and method until the end of his life. As for honorary officers, the Duke of York, now Prince of Wales, continued as Patron, and Randall Davidson, Archbishop of Canterbury after Archbishop Temple's death in 1903, readily agreed to become Vice-Patron.

In 1906 William Smith married Hannah Ranken Campbell, a cousin of the Prime Minister, Campbell Bannerman, whose family he had known for many years. The household moved to more spacious accommodation at 13 Belmont Crescent in the West End of Glasgow. Hannah accompanied him on his 1907 visit to the United States and, like his first wife, became deeply involved in Brigade work. Tragedy struck not long after, however, when Smith was widowed for a second time. Aged fifty-one, Hannah Smith was found dead on the morning of 27 July 1907 at Hillside Cottage, Tighnabruaich, near the 1st Glasgow Company campsite. She had been under medication for a nervous ailment, and apparently mistook bottles in the medicine cabinet. Accidental death, by carbolic acid poisoning, was determined.[1]

The Silver Jubilee celebrations themselves, in 1908, gave a substantial boost to the movement and attracted a large measure of publicity. The events included the annual meeting of the Brigade Council in Glasgow, attended by a large number of U.K. and overseas delegates, with representatives from the other uniformed organizations. A review at Queen's Park, Glasgow, was held on 5 September by Prince Arthur of Connaught, providing the largest gathering of boys yet seen in Scotland. This prompted an extensive editorial by the *Glasgow Herald*:

> This extraordinary expansion which naturally obtains prominence in this Jubilee Celebration is perhaps the highest testimony to its [The Boys' Brigade's] usefulness . . . to make useful men, often out of the least promising material, is perhaps the highest service that anyone can render to the state.

The *Herald's* sentiments had been echoed before the Jubilee celebrations began by the citizens of Glasgow, on whose behalf the Lord Provost, Sir William Bisland, made a stirring testimonial to William Smith. A number of influential citizens commissioned Smith's portrait, by Alexander Roche, for the city's Kelvingrove Art Galleries. A replica by Fides Watt was presented to Smith himself and is now a feature of the Glasgow Battalion's Executive Room.[2]

The Jubilee celebrations provided the opportunity for the more prominent supporters of The Boys' Brigade and the great mass of 'old boys' to come together to pay tribute to the somewhat reluctant Smith. The illuminated address presented to him on 4 September 1908 at a large gathering in the St. Andrew's Halls, Glasgow, was signed by a cross-section of those supporters whom Smith had always been keen to involve in the work of the Brigade, comprising:

The Earl of Aberdeen
The Duke of Fife
The Moderator of the General Assembly of the Church of Scotland
The Moderator of the United Free Church Assembly
The Chairman of the Congregational Union
The President of the Wesleyan Methodist Conference
The Moderator of the Presbyterian Church of England
The Bishop of London
The Principal of Aberdeen University
Field Marshall Lord Roberts
The Secretary of State for Scotland
The senior Law Lords of Scotland

While Smith must inwardly have felt some satisfaction at this gathering, outwardly he addressed himself to the large number of 'old boys' to whom he looked for support and example. By 1908, the increasing group of ex-members included, of course, not only those of The Boys' Brigade but of the newer uniformed organizations, and Brigade leaders were gratified by the recognition given to the pioneering movement by the other groups who had gone their own way. This tribute paid by a leader of the Catholic Boys' Brigade was particularly appreciated:

> During the many years I have worked among boys I have never come across any infallible system whereby to hold them absolutely and safeguard them from all the evils that beset their terribly exposed youth; but the nearest to infallibility of all the systems and far, far away beyond all the rest in value, and above all in results, is that of The Boys' Brigade to whose happy conception I owe most of my glowing moments in recent years because of the harvest of good, straight, honourable men it has reaped.

The Jubilee celebrations culminated the following year in the knighthood conferred on William Smith. The news of this was received with great enthusiasm by the 1st Glasgow Company. During the annual camp at Tigh-nabruaich, Smith absented himself for the shortest possible time to receive the honour in London.[3]

Carfrae Alston now retired as Brigade President. He was succeeded by Lord Guthrie, Senator of the College of Justice in Scotland and son of Thomas Guthrie, preacher of Ragged School Union fame. Guthrie was a man of wide interests and many contacts, an accomplished public speaker, and a Boys' Brigade enthusiast. His ten-year term of office gave the organization a valuable figurehead. Guthrie maintained that of all his duties in Church and State, his most important work for the community was as President of the B.B.

One vital sphere for the adolescent boy in which the Brigade took an increasing interest was that of employment and training. The Edwardian years saw an increased focus on the problems of 'boy labour' — youthful recruitment into short-term unskilled work with no prospects. This wide-spread practice, by which boys were exploited for their commercial utility, directly and adversely affected many B.B. members. Others found it a struggle to obtain a job at all on leaving school. The B.B. followed the Y.M.C.A. in its concern — a concern which has again, recently, been to the fore as the recession of the early 1980s affects senior members. Before the turn of the century, the Brigade Executive was aware of informal contact between em-ployers and company captains which led to the placing of boys with local firms. The employer would be attracted to boys receptive to discipline and order, and displaying the smartness and courtesy required by the organiza-tion. The B.B. was only too glad to be helping the boy at a difficult time ensuring, moreover, that he was granted facilities to enable him to participate in all Brigade activities. This informal assistance led to the establishment of employment registers in battalions. The lead had been given in Carlisle in the 1890s and was then streamlined by Glasgow Battalion under the supervision of an Employment Register Committee which advertised the scheme in the press.

Glasgow followed the Carlisle scheme whereby a boy wishing employment completed an application form giving particulars of his age, type of employ-ment desired, wage expected, and the standard he had attained at school. This form was then passed to the company captain who completed a confidential report, giving his opinion as to the boy's character, trustworthiness, industry, punctuality, and so on. He indicated how the boy had served in the company and if any problems had been encountered. The boy's application, together with the company captain's report, were then sent to battalion headquarters and retained on file. An employer wishing to recruit staff would contact the battalion giving details of the vacant position and related wage. The appropri-ate convener would, if possible, send three boys for interview. In Carlisle, the assistance of NCOs was obtained each Monday evening, with a boy providing the communications link between each company and battalion headquarters passing forms and invitations to interviews back and forward. At a later stage employers were charged 2/6d (12½p), reduced subsequently to a shilling, for each application to the battalion. The employment registers or bureaux in Carlisle and Glasgow were followed quickly in other areas before World War I. Publicity was given through the press, Brigade literature and national maga-zines for boys. The schemes did not solve the problem of youth unemployment in the organization but, at least, alleviated the situation in some areas and for some individuals. The danger of leading a boy into a 'blind-alley' job with little potential was realized and cautioned against. Wherever practicable, officers were advised to consult with parents and explain that a lower wage at the outset might be counterbalanced by more favourable career prospects.

As the century progressed, greater initiative was taken by the State and local authorities in the promotion of welfare services for the adolescent. Much was done in liaison with the existing voluntary youth organizations, where a great deal of experience might be called upon. In 1910 the Mansion House Advisory Committee of Associations for Boys was formed under the presidency of the Lord Mayor of London and the chairmanship of Colonel Ford, Commandant of the London Diocesan Church Lads' Brigade. The Committee consisted of representatives of all the youth organizations, the London Chamber of Commerce, and the London Labour Exchange of the Board of Trade. The Committee encouraged membership of the uniformed organizations, and urged coordination and certification. At the same time statistical data were collected 'to aid Government Departments concerned with the physical and industrial wellbeing of the people'. This latter provision was, in a sense, the thin end of the wedge, and the Committee became quickly involved in the possibility of recruiting for the Armed Forces. In 1912, with military officers in attendance, consideration was given to a 'British Boys' Training Corps', stating clearly that the aim was 'military training carried out as a means of producing a boy, from raw material, who is morally, intellectually and physically fit to learn the trade they will teach him which will afterwards turn out a good citizen . . .' A record card was approved for issue to all organizations, to be returned to the Committee, showing the destination of the boy when leaving the company or unit — for example 'joined the Royal Navy, joined Mercantile Marine, joined Territorial Force etc.' The evolution of this Committee into an agency for promoting military reserves overlapped the heart-searching entered into by the Brigade in response to the Government's proposals for incorporating the movement into its Cadet Scheme. The B.B.'s London District Committee reacted uncompromisingly to the statistical return and instructed that the record cards should not be issued.[4]

The attempt by the Government, from 1909 to 1911, to incorporate the B.B. into a national Cadet Force provided the movement with its greatest challenge to date and brought into focus, in traumatic fashion, the question of militarism. The plans of R.B. Haldane, Secretary of State for War in the Liberal Government, to absorb all the uniformed youth movements into a reserve force affiliated to local Territorial Associations demanded the full power of William Smith's nerve and diplomacy to ensure the best interests and reputation of the organization. Of course The Boys' Brigade, with its use of drill and military methods, had always laid itself open to the charge of militarism from some sections of the public. The concern expressed by some of the clergy and laity since 1883 are understandable. The advent of a uniformed youth organization led, in the main, by Volunteer officers was not unconnected with the emergence of the new imperialism of the late 19th century and with an increasing spirit of jingoism. The public hero-worshipped such renowned evangelical generals as Havelock and Gordon and the jingoistic mood of the population had intensified by the end of the century.

The Boys' Brigade gained both supporters and detractors by being, in many senses, a product of the military spirit of its age. But the fundamental *raison d'être* of the movement remained its link with the Sunday Schools and other religious and philanthropic organizations. Smith and his colleagues continually stressed the distinction between the basic objective of the organization and the methods, attractive to boys, used to attain this objective:

> You see drill is not an end in the Brigade, as it is in the Volunteers, but only a *means to an end.*

This philosophy was not always obvious and the Brigade suffered, in some respects, from the patronage of military leaders, whose enthusiasm, transmitted in public statements, did not always follow the accurate emphasis given by Smith and his colleagues. Even Smith's own ideas on the value of military training could easily be misunderstood, if taken out of context, since they were usually tailored to suit a particular audience. 'Although in the Brigade the military training is simply the means to an end,' he told the militarized United Boys' Brigade of America in 1907,

> there can be no doubt that the military training itself is of great value and if ever the boys are called on to take a stand for the defence of the Country, the State would have good cause to thank the Brigade for the military training the boys had obtained.

His strong sense of patriotism and his acknowledged love of the military gave Smith's opponents material to formulate their complaints. The most vociferous opposition came from pacifists who saw The Boys' Brigade as a paramilitary force. The Peace Society organized a campaign during the first ten years of the movement, alleging that it was inculcating a spirit of jingoism in the boys which would blaze up like matchwood and plunge the nation into desperate strife. The Peace Society requested the press in 1890 to print a letter referring to

> this new-born Scottish monster, which claims God and the devil for parents . . . It is unquestionably the master-stroke of Mars, by which Ministers of Christ's Gospel are used as recruiting sergeants for the British Army. What is this but dragging true religion into the gutter of corruption? Be it ours, therefore, in season and out of season, to do our utmost, in the interests of righteousness and peace, to crush this young praying and fighting monster.[5]

A critical issue for The Boys' Brigade during the period up to 1900, as it consolidated itself, was the reaction of these 'Ministers of Christ's Gospel' to the methods employed by the organization. We know of the apprehension of a number of Churches across the denominations, reflecting a division of opinion. In some areas, Brigade leaders would, according to their own views and background, promote the military idea among boys regardless of the philosophy expressed by Brigade Headquarters. In Boston, Lincolnshire, the organization came to an abrupt halt with the disbanding of the 1st Company in 1894 owing to the acting captain's disavowal of the supposedly 'military spirit' fostered by the B.B. The Boys' Rifle Brigade was formed in Leeds, a few years later, when the 6th Leeds Company left the local battalion in protest against the decision that rifles capable of being fired were not to be allowed. On balance, however, there was strong support for Brigade policy from all denominations. The Bishop of Carlisle continually remonstrated against criticism of the B.B. on grounds of alleged militarism and, in the same year as the demise of the 1st Boston Company, he supported the adoption of military drill and discipline as an extremely effective instrument in attaining the B.B. Object, noting that 'boys love anything with a military flavour and they take to it like ducks to water'.[6]

Efforts were made both at national and local level, however, to ensure that accurate appraisals of Brigade methods might be made. Support was received from the religious and the national press, while individual battalions made known their strong distaste for militarism. In 1890, Plymouth Battalion added to its rules the provision that the promotion of the cause of peace was a primary aim, making it clear that it was

> desirable to put an end to the idea that this is a movement trying to inculcate into youth that military spirit which is the bane of Empire.

During the same year, Belfast Battalion amended its rules to prohibit the use of rifles except by special permission of the Executive Committee.[7]

The uniformed youth movements attracted closer attention from the Government and the military authorities following the Boer War (in which military inadequacies had been revealed), and with the emergence of a new fear of German aggression during the following decade. Owing to Baden-Powell's dual role as military and youth leader, the Boy Scouts, formed in 1908, were seen by many ardent militarists as providing a pool of recruitment for the Territorials. The Scout Commissioner for Ireland, Lord Meath, propagated the Imperial idea to schools through the Empire Day Movement, and the Boys' Empire League, formed in 1900 with the enthusiastic support of the military, was intended to strengthen the 'true imperial instinct' in British boys. National Service League members advocating conscription, such as Lord Milner and Lord Roberts, toured the country warning of the dangers of a lack of preparedness. Roberts called for education in patriotism and instruction in habits of 'order, obedience and discipline' as a preliminary to any thorough system of national defence. The possible alignment of such ideas to the basic training provided by The Boys' Brigade was not lost on military and political leaders.

Haldane's Territorial Forces Bill was passed in 1907, although that portion of it which proposed compulsory military training for boys at elementary school was rejected following strong opposition by Ramsay MacDonald and the Labour and radical Liberal M.P.'s in the post-1906 House of Commons. The Cadet movement, which had been seen as a junior preparation for the Volunteers, had been expanded beyond the public-school environment in the 1880s, being linked with working boys' clubs and university settlements. Haldane's general plan was now to absorb all the uniformed youth movements into the State military system, to act as feeders for the newly created Territorial Force. Government proposals were incorporated into the Army Council Cadet Regulations issued in 1910 which invited an application for recognition by the youth organization to the County Territorial Force Association on penalty of forfeiting the military and financial assistance previously on offer from the War Office, including:

1. Permission to camp on Government ground
2. Provision of camp equipment at special rates
3. Instruction and inspection by senior officers
4. Lease or rent of drill halls and other buildings at favourable rates
5. Exemption from part or all of recruits' drill on entry into the Territorial Force[8]

A debate within The Boys' Brigade movement was initiated, with Smith, at the outset, appreciating that 'the ulterior purpose is to strengthen the military forces of the Country'. While throwing the matter open to the movement as a whole, he was quite adamant on the likely conflict with the fundamental religious aims of the movement, deploring the ultimatum to the uniformed organizations. His view, set out at length in correspondence to Roger Peacock, the London Secretary, and to the leaders of the other uniformed organizations, was that what was being proposed was detrimental to both the organizations and the State. An attempt to enlist the aid of the Admiralty and the Territorial Force Association in bringing pressure to bear on Haldane was of no avail. An approach by Lord Guthrie to Haldane produced only the response that, unless recognition was sought, it would be impossible for the War Office 'to hold out any prospect of privileges or facilities being granted to any bodies of boys who have not been recommended for such privileges'. Brigade Headquarters, in September 1910, issued a memorandum to all companies detailing the War Office proposals and the implications for the Brigade. Consideration was invited on the effects of recognition on the boys, the officers, the Churches and related organizations, the funds, and the facilities presently enjoyed. The question was fully discussed at the annual Brigade Council meeting in October 1910 at Brighton, where the prevailing view was that substantial damage would be done to the reputation of The Boys' Brigade as a religious organization should it submit to the ultimatum of the War Office. It was agreed that the opinion of all officers and all churches with which companies were connected be sought before an official decision was taken. In November 1910, by an overwhelming vote, The Boys' Brigade rejected the proposal for official recognition. Eighty-seven per cent of the churches and eighty-eight per cent of parents and supporters similarly disapproved.[9]

The decision taken by The Boys' Brigade, at grass-roots level, confirmed to a great extent its philosophy throughout the previous quarter century — namely that the use of military methods was merely an attractive means towards its religious and social ends. The decision was welcomed by the Churches and, in general, the press, as well as in some local Territorial Forces:

> In Glasgow, the cradle of the Brigade, they understood it perhaps better than those elsewhere and he [Hugh Reid, Chairman of the Meeting] thought that if Mr Haldane applied to the Glasgow Territorial Association for an opinion they would unhesitatingly say that he ought to extend to The Boys' Brigade in every part of the country every encouragement by giving them first of all any equipment they might require and also recognition on all possible occasions by the Army and Territorial Force [applause].

Although Smith had coordinated the B.B. reaction to the War Office with that of the other Brigades, differences of opinion had arisen. Efforts by Walter Gee, Secretary and Founder of the Church Lads' Brigade, to persuade Smith to accept recognition were unsuccessful, and Gee's separate representations to the War Office on behalf of the B.B. were strongly resented and quickly squashed. Smith's conviction that 'we shall come out of this trouble stronger than ever' was fully justified in the light of the contrasting fortunes of the B.B. and the C.L.B. in the aftermath of the First World War. William Smith's clear-sightedness and the movement's overwhelming unity of purpose had withstood the pressures of the Government and others in resisting incorporation into the military machine. The Brigade's fundamental position as a religious organization was confirmed and further challenges could be met with confidence.[10]

A further challenge had, indeed, arisen with the formation of the Boy Scouts in the period 1907-09. The other Brigades which had followed the original movement were working in cooperation with it and remained numerically less strong. However, there now appeared a youth movement which was to outstrip all others in size and geographical spread. What is not always appreciated is that Scouting evolved directly from a B.B. activity and was established in close harmony with the pioneering organization.

The founder of Scouting, Baden-Powell, was an ex-public-school boy of upper middle-class background, and carried with him from his days at Charterhouse a strong assertion of the Scout qualities of honour, loyalty and duty which, together with public-school discipline and a fervent patriotism, so clearly influenced his own career. His army experience in India and Africa, and his particular involvement in military scouting, provided the framework within which his ideas on character training might be incorporated. The siege of Mafeking during the Boer War made Baden-Powell a household name and gave credibility to his subsequent promotion of scouting. An instruction manual drawn up by him at this time — *Aids to Scouting for NCOs and Men* — was the basis of the later guidelines for boys. Following the Boer War, with Baden-Powell in semi-retirement, the climate of popular opinion was favourable to his warnings against the deterioration of the 'British race' and the need for adequate precautions for the survival of the Empire and for defence against German aggression. Baden-Powell combined his imperialism with ideas of woodcraft lore and open-air scouting such as were being promoted by Ernest Thompson Seton, leader of the American youth movement, the Woodcraft Indians. This accorded with the views of many members of the Establishment, such as Meath and Roberts, who were convinced that the military and character training of the rising generation was necessary to avoid a repetition of the fall of the Roman Empire. Baden-Powell admonished British youth:

> And it will largely depend upon you, the younger generation of Britons that are now growing up to be the men of the Empire, don't be disgraced like the young Romans, who lost the Empire of their forefathers by being wishy-washy slackers without any go or patriotism in them. Play up! Each man in his place, and play the game! Your forefathers worked hard, fought hard, and died hard, to make this Empire for you. Don't let them look down from heaven and see you loafing about with your hands in your pockets, doing nothing to keep it up.[11]

In this atmosphere of military preparedness, Baden-Powell's attention was drawn quite naturally to such youth organizations as already existed and, having been appointed a Vice-President of The Boys' Brigade in 1902, he became a close associate of William Smith and involved himself in many Brigade functions. At the London Annual Display in 1903 at the Albert Hall, he appreciated that boys would come eagerly in their thousands to be trained where the training had an attraction for them. Over the next year he took a close look at the operation of The Boys' Brigade throughout the country and concluded that if some form of scout training could be devised in the Brigade it would be very popular. At the same time such training within a youth organization 'would be a strong force behind the Volunteers and the Army'. Following a suggestion by William Smith that Baden-Powell write a manual for B.B. boys on scouting, an early version of *Scouting for Boys* was published in the *B.B. Gazette* in June 1906, and proficiency tests in open-air observation, camping and orienteering were adopted within The Boys' Brigade badge scheme. The 'fleur-de-lys', which was later to become the Scouts' own badge, was the badge awarded. Within a few years, scouting had become an integral activity of The Boys' Brigade, but was considered strictly as one activity within the programme of The Boys' Brigade as a whole. In the B.B. session 1907-08, 414 officers and 4,361 boys were returned as having taken up scouting in one form or another. However, given the widespread public support his ideas were receiving, it is not surprising that Baden-Powell was not totally satisfied with this limited application of his ideas in an organization with somewhat different aims — although the long-term promotion of schemes of a paramilitary flavour for character training may have led him to believe, for some time, that a wide-ranging organization, possibly incorporating the existing Brigades, might be formed to ensure the essential good citizenship and defence needed by the nation.[12]

In 1907 an experimental Boy Scout camp was held on Brownsea Island, Poole Harbour, in Dorset, where methods of instruction were tested. The success of this camp, at which half the boys present came from either the 1st Bournemouth or the 1st Poole B.B. Companies, led Baden-Powell further in his plans for a mass movement. *Scouting for Boys* was published in fortnightly parts from January 1908, by which time Scout patrols within B.B. companies were enjoying a wide popularity. Baden-Powell's promotion campaign had reached many influential adults, particularly of the skilled working class and suburban lower middle class. The movement was to find its greatest support within these groups, who felt much in sympathy with the ideology and practical schemes put forward. For adolescents, the attractions of open-air activity, games, and adventure 'yarns' with a strong flavour of Kipling and Henty were all the more obvious when not directly related to compulsory Sunday School or Bible Class attendance. Emphasis on the secular ideals of 'our Empire' and 'citizenship' rather than on Christian education invited greater mass support.

By September 1908 the popularity of Baden-Powell's ideas had led to the establishment of a National Systems Advisory Committee to register Scout groups and ensure a minimum standard for the selection of scout-masters. The subsequent administration of a badge scheme and the establishment of an organizational structure led, in the following year, to the formation of the Boy Scouts as a separate organization under a Governing Council. Not long after, the remarkable growth of unofficial 'Girl Scouts' was formalized by the introduction of an organization to be called 'The Girl Guides', which had an immediate membership of 8,000. In a sense the new movement, as the sister organization of the Boy Scouts, mirrored the development of the female uniformed Brigades, although becoming very quickly the largest and most widespread uniformed organization for girls. The major problem now arising was that of the relationship of a new organization with existing uniformed youth movements, and in particular with the B.B.

Baden-Powell approached William Smith in 1909 on the possibilities of a single organization, combining The Boys' Brigade and the new surge of Scout patrols. Baden-Powell's argument was that the development of Scouting, outside the organizations such as The Boys' Brigade and the Y.M.C.A. for which the idea was originally intended, had led to the formation of a fresh organization somewhat against the intentions of the Scout leaders:

> I can see nothing more than very partial results if we are all working as separate organizations taking our separate lines.

Baden-Powell moved in this direction by firstly inviting Smith to become a member of the Scout Governing Council. Smith, it would seem, was concerned over the secular nature of the new organization, and the correspondence indicates a courteous but firm reluctance to become closely involved in its governing structure. Baden-Powell's strong desire for Smith's active involvement is evidenced by a further letter to him on Christmas Day 1909:

If leagued as a 'combine' we might tackle the whole mass effectively and really make a nation of God-fearing virile citizens in the next generation.

We all naturally look to you as the leader of the Boy movement — if you decide to help in directing the policy of the Scout movement the other heads will follow suit . . . the possibilities are then enormous . . . the Prince of Wales is in favour of such amalgamation of aims and would I believe become the President of such a Council if formed.

It is not difficult to see the possibilities which Baden-Powell hinted at, should the Brigade and Scout movement have been under communal leadership. Smith appears, however, to have been quite decided in his own mind that — even with the suggestion of Royal involvement as distinct from mere patronage — the sacrifice of the basic aims of the other uniformed organizations to allow for the required compromise was a price that need not be paid:

It seems to me that scouting is an excellent thing as taken up within The Boys' Brigade or other organizations, as an interesting and helpful adjunct to its regular work, but when you take the Boy Scouts as a separate organization and propose to include all the other and senior organizations within an Advisory Council of the Boy Scouts directed by the heads of the other organizations it seems to me that, from both points of view, the thing would be unworkable and would tend to create the very difficulties which you seek to avoid . . . Let me say again how much I value and appreciate all that you have done in so many ways for the interest of The Boys' Brigade and for the good of boys in general and I can only add that this makes me feel all the more regret at having to disappoint you . . .

The decision having been taken, the Boy Scouts moved forward independently and were soon to dwarf the other, older organizations, attaining a membership of over 150,000 in the United Kingdom by 1914. Scouting as a single activity within the B.B. (and the other Brigades) eventually disappeared as other outdoor work, such as 'expedition' and orienteering, was introduced. Contact between the Scouts and The Boys' Brigade has continued at all levels during this century and the cordial relationships established in those early years have been maintained.[13]

Both the Cadet issue and the appearance of the Scouts help to explain the fall in B.B. membership from 63,122 boys in 1909 to 55,819 boys in 1912. Matters were not helped by the withdrawal in 1908 of the paramilitary Bolton B.B. from national membership; they assumed an independent existence and did not rejoin the Lancashire and Cheshire District until over fifty years later. The Brigade Executive formed a special Extension Committee in 1912 and used the thirtieth anniversary of the movement in 1913 as a vehicle for a recruitment campaign. At a cost of around £700, the campaign was called the 'great national extension movement' and every company was asked to enrol a special squad of recruits. A range of glossy, illustrated publicity material and special recruiting bills were produced, and the various religious denominations issued their own literature in conjunction with the Brigade. The campaign had the desired effect and the decrease in strength was brought to a halt after 1912. In the following year the United Kingdom's numbers increased from 55,819 to 59,714. By 1915 there were 63,373 boys on the roll in the United Kingdom, eighty-seven new companies having been formed. The total international strength of staff and boys had been recovered and increased to over 117,000.

Following closely on the 1913 campaign, discussions on amalgamation between the B.B. and the Boys' Life Brigade took place. These discussions highlight in a convincing manner the irreconcilable differences then prevailing between these two Christian Brigade organizations for boys.

> I would hope all the same that if union should not be attainable there could at least be co-operation to the extent of each recognizing that our aims are the same, and showing a feeling of Christian charity and good will towards the other,

wrote William Smith to F.P. Gibbon, in the midst of negotiations which were chiefly remarkable for the absence of such qualities. The real obstacle remained that the Boys' Life Brigade was not actively seeking amalgamation; indeed, the majority of their officers viewed such a move unfavourably owing to the unequivocally military basis of the B.B. William Smith, although receptive to the idea of a conference, had his own doubts as to whether union was possible without the B.B. to some extent abandoning its distinctive military characteristics:

> We frankly accept *military* organization and drill as the basis of our training, and to suggest, as one writer does, that a union could be effected on the basis of The Boys' Brigade consenting to give up its 'military training', is equivalent to suggesting that The Boys' Brigade should cease to be The Boys' Brigade! ... It is the combination of the efficiently military and the earnestly religious that has made The Boys' Brigade what it is, and we must be very careful not to lower our flag whether on one side or the other![14]

A conference attended by representatives of the two organizations was held in January 1914 at Liverpool's Exchange Station Hotel, following which a complete scheme of union was to be jointly drafted and submitted for final approval to every member of the conference before submission to the respective governing bodies of both Brigades. Unfortunately, despite the fact that it was jointly drafted, the more detailed report, when it appeared in proof, gave the impression to the B.L.B. delegates that their movement was to be swallowed up by the B.B. There was also deep concern over the use of dummy rifles by the B.B. On 14 March 1914, therefore, the Administrative Council of the Boys' Life Brigade unanimously rejected the proposed scheme of union, on the entirely predictable grounds that

> while welcoming all possible co-operation, this Council regrets that it cannot agree to the proposed scheme of union, because it does not provide for the elimination of the model rifle.[15]

In his reply, Smith pointed out that the grounds on which the Boys' Life Brigade Council had thrown out the proposed union were already before them at Liverpool, where it was made clear that the use of the dummy rifle by any Boys' Brigade company was quite optional and a matter to be decided by the individual church with which the company was connected. After what was interpreted as the success of the Liverpool Conference, the decision to abandon the negotiations for union taken by the B.L.B. Council caused some disappointment in The Boys' Brigade. If nothing else, the events clarified that amalgamation would only become practical politics when The Boys' Brigade, as one B.L.B. Commissioner succinctly put it, 'decided to abandon the gun'. When this took place a decade later, the much-anticipated consummation of the 1914 meeting at last became a genuine possibility.

The Boys' Brigade was dealt a heavy blow in 1914 with the death of its Founder and Secretary in his sixtieth year. On 6 May 1914 William Smith travelled to London for the Annual Demonstration in the Albert Hall the following day.

On 8 May he attended a meeting of the Brigade Executive in the London Office, where he was taken ill and admitted to St. Bartholomew's Hospital. Without regaining consciousness, he died of a cerebral haemorrhage on Sunday, 10 May 1914. Stunned by the loss of its Founder, who had so deeply involved himself in the growth and development of the movement throughout the thirty-one years of its existence, the Brigade prepared an appropriate memorial tribute with an impressive service in St. Paul's Cathedral on 15 May, attended by the leaders of all the uniformed youth organizations and other religious and secular representatives. A telegram of sympathy from the King to the Brigade President, Lord Guthrie, on the day of Smith's death was followed by many further tributes.

Following the service at St. Paul's, William Smith's body was taken with great ceremony and emotion from London to Glasgow for the funeral service in the College and Kelvingrove United Free Church. As the overnight London-Glasgow train sped through Rugby, the stillness of the night was broken by the sad notes of the 'Last Post' sounded by a detachment of the 2nd Rugby Company, 'who had waited long hours through the night to sound farewell to our beloved Chief'. Following the service, taken by Dr Reith, Chaplain of the 1st Glasgow Company since its formation, a massive funeral procession accompanied the cortege through the West End of Glasgow to the Western Necropolis, along a route familiar to Smith, on that day lined with an estimated 164,000 people. Arthur Jackson recalled, as a young officer, attending on behalf of Leeds Battalion:

> The whole of Glasgow seemed to turn out. The people were eight and nine deep on both sides of the footpath . . . every B.B. boy in Glasgow was provided with a carnation and they dropped this carnation into the grave and it was absolutely chock-a-block with flowers. But we filed past and then the buglers sounded the last post and we returned home, a very disconsolate, miserable crowd of officers, because we almost thought our world had come to an end.

This great feeling of loss was echoed by Arthur Reid, the first boy in the Brigade to gain the King's Badge. He was Colour Sergeant of the 1st Glasgow Company in 1914 — the number one boy in the Company and the first boy to be told of the Founder's death. Some sixty years later, he could recall the impact of the loss, simply and vividly — 'I cried bitterly.'[16]

Tributes to Sir William Smith, at the many memorial services held immediately after the funeral, were as numerous as might be expected. At a service for 4,000 members of the organization in the St. Andrew's Halls, Glasgow, Lord Guthrie, Brigade President, quietly led the praise:

> Sir William Smith was a man of great shrewdness and excellent business capacity: he had a grasp of principles along with infinite capacity for details; but he could not cut and parry with the broad sword of Mr Asquith or thrust with the rapier of Mr Balfour. He was a calm, lucid, convincing speaker and he wrote well; but he had not the silver tongued eloquence or the splendid written style of Lord Rosebery . . . but I venture to say that he originated and successfully developed directly and indirectly a work infinitely more important than the generality of the business of Parliament . . . it was left to Sir William Smith to spell the word Boy.[17]

A detailed appraisal of William Smith is superfluous here, bearing in mind that his ideas and attitude were so consistently aligned with those of the organization he led and influenced. In any reference to The Boys' Brigade or its Founder, by journalists or historians, the impression is often given of a rather austere disciplinarian: a Christian gentleman, certainly, but from a puritanical Scottish Free Church background, exhibiting a rigidity of personality and a lack of emotion. Photographs of William Smith do little to counteract this impression, and his strict adherence to regulations and good order create a formidable, perhaps not very attractive image in modern eyes. Having left little record of his personal thoughts and opinions, Smith has not given historians an abundance of material with which to correct this impression. However, from unearthed personal correspondence and diaries, and from the memories of 'old boys', we can see behind the stern image a leader and friend of boys, whose qualities of warmth, thoughtfulness and compassion would have been required to a great degree for the work he undertook to be carried out successfully.

William Smith's uncompromising attitude towards Government, his non-interfering advice to The Boys' Brigade in other countries, and his consistent relationships with his colleagues and boys cannot but attract recognition for his significant and often unacknowledged achievement in the development of voluntary youth organizations. It is a measure of his influence and personality that the leader of the Church Lads' Brigade, with whom relations were somewhat strained, could remark in 1894:

> But I must confess, to me the whole room was filled with one personality, and it was that of Mr W.A. Smith who was on the platform. I could not help thinking, without in the least belittling the noble deeds of those heroes of whom Archdeacon Farrar so eloquently discoursed, that probably for the highest good of the English-speaking race the founder of the Brigade system was far and away the greater hero of any of whom mention had been made that evening.

As a temporary measure H. Arnold Wilson, the enthusiastic Brigade Treasurer, was appointed Acting Brigade Secretary. Colonel Sir John Roxburgh, a wealthy shipowner, took over as Treasurer and until August 1914 Stanley Smith remained Assistant Secretary, when his brother Douglas replaced him, until he too obtained a commission. F.P. Gibbon undertook to be 'Brigade Travelling Representative'.[18]

In August 1914 an even greater blow fell. The First World War marked the end of an era, not only for The Boys' Brigade but also for the nation as a whole. For the first time Britain was engaged in a total war that would in the end completely transform its social and political life. Many companies were at camp when war broke out and, as a result, suddenly found themselves without officers, because a large number were called away to report to their Army or Territorial Units. (During the first year of the War, about 100,000 officers and ex-members of The Boys' Brigade joined the Armed Forces.) Other companies found their camp sites and tents quickly taken over by the military, while transport home from the coastal areas often proved unexpectedly difficult.

In the heady early months of the War, countless Brigade officers swelled the ranks of Army volunteers, many quickly being promoted to be NCOs, officers and drill instructors. A great number joined units composed almost entirely of Boys' Brigade recruits. In Oxfordshire, for example, about forty young men enlisted with J. Harold Early in the 4th Battalion (Territorial) of the Oxfordshire and Bucks Light Infantry, most of them 'old boys' from the 1st Witney Company, of which Early was Captain. In due course, as Sergeant Early, he went with them to France, having declined a commission because that would have meant separation from his Witney group. It was only when The Boys' Brigade recruits eventually became scattered by sickness, injuries and death that he accepted a commission. In 1917, as Lieutenant Early, he was severely wounded and invalided home.[19]

Why should these young men have been so eager to enlist? Primarily, in a religious culture of Christian manliness which tended to dismiss concern for the physical sufferings of war as so much 'mawkish sentimentality', it needed very little to send a young man to war. This was particularly so before the advent of trench warfare and conscription, when so little was known of the unpleasant side of war. In notes for a Bible Class, Smith himself wrote:

> It always seems to me curious that while we admit the principle that in the moral sphere of the individual life there can be no progress without stress and conflict, we are apt to shut our eyes to the fact that in the life of a nation the same principle holds good, and that no nation ever yet attained to true greatness or influence in the world without going through the training and discipline of war . . . No one could desire war for its own sake, but may there not be a danger that our natural horror of war may lead us into an undue emphasizing of the merely physical side of the sufferings entailed by war. There is a certain mawkish sentimentality abroad which tends to magnify the physical at the expense of the spiritual . . .

That the Founder of The Boys' Brigade was not himself immune to currently fashionable social Darwinist ideas in the years immediately preceding the outbreak of war should come as no great surprise; even leaders of men are liable to be influenced by the surrounding social culture in which they live. As a movement, The Boys' Brigade may have helped to popularize the idea of military service among the population generally, although one cannot necessarily infer from this that The Boys' Brigade helped pave the way for the recruiting drives of the First World War.[20]

Already, before 1914 was out, the fighting was being referred to as 'The Great War', and the Brigade — in answer to the question 'How Can I Help My Country?' — was suggesting 'Will You Join The Boys' Home Reserve Force?' Boys were urged to be steady, kind and helpful in the home, for:

> Shouting and waving little flags may be fun but it isn't business. Men are dying under that flag. This war is a big, terrible business, and we all have to see it through. Boys, be steady.

They were further encouraged to help their country by assisting their mothers, not grumbling at plain food served them because of rising prices, doing without some little treat and performing some odd job instead. Soon even greater mobilization of B.B. boys was to be required on the home front: collecting wastepaper, acting as messengers and orderlies, sounding the 'all clear' signal, acting as ambulance squads, and participating in numerous flag days.[21]

As an organization loyal to King and Country, the Brigade was certainly eager — within certain constraints — to show positive evidence of its willingness to help. According to Arnold Wilson's memorandum of 27 August 1914:

> The Executive was anxious, as far as possible, to safeguard the non-military character of the Brigade, as Church authorities might deprecate the use of our Organization in performing what might be deemed semi-military duties, but they feel that, under the very exceptional circumstances, the danger of any misconception is remote. We, as a nation, are out to fight against military despotism. It is a war against war.

Companies were thus recommended by the Executive to assist in Red Cross work, orderly work in hospitals and war fund collections, to act as cyclist messengers, and to assist the Civil Authorities generally. On the immediate outbreak of war, several local military and police authorities declined the use of the adolescent volunteers so patriotically offered by the Executive, but as the War went on, year after year, their services became more highly appreciated. A special badge was issued to every boy in the Brigade who gave a total of not less than one hundred hours of voluntary and unpaid service — performed out of school and business hours — in connection with the War; up to April 1918, 2,650 badges had been won. Large numbers of boys collected waste paper, bottles and old metal for the Prince of Wales Fund and other funds. In October 1915, the first Red Cross Day in Scotland was organized entirely by the Glasgow Battalion and other Boys' Brigade centres throughout Scotland, raising over £1,500. Because of the Zeppelin air raids on London, Boys' Brigade orderlies and messengers were regularly supplied at police stations and certified raid shelters, together with orderly buglers to sound the 'all clear' signal.[22]

Perhaps the most worthwhile fund-raising project undertaken by the movement in wartime was the provision and maintenance of two large recreation huts, one at Rouen and the other at Edinburgh, for serving soldiers and sailors. An appeal was made in March 1915 for a Rest and Refreshment Hut, at an estimated cost of £450, to be run in cooperation with the Y.M.C.A. for the benefit of the troops generally and for ex-B.B. servicemen in particular. The response was magnificent. With characteristic enthusiasm, the B.B. had raised £2,820 by November 1916, thus providing for the building of one large double hut at Rouen (costing £1,000) and another in Edinburgh — where so many men passed on their way to and from France. Brigade staff must have felt that the end result was well worth all the bureaucratic headaches over passports and permits for the canteen staff sent out to Rouen.

A surviving leaflet advertising the Rest and Refreshment Hut on the Mound, Princes Street, Edinbugh, to 'soldiers and sailors passing through' invites them to take advantage of the Hut, open day and night, and offers breakfast, tea or supper at very reasonable rates, a free wash and brush up, sleeping accommodation or a 'shake-down' on the floor, blankets provided for a 1d., hot baths — plunge 3d., spray 2d. — and a free cloakroom for left luggage. In Rouen, The Boys' Brigade Recreation Hut, close to the front line, was large enough to accommodate a thousand men at a time, and was well provided with games, papers, magazines, a billiard room and a canteen. It was managed and staffed by Boys' Brigade officers and was intended to be as similar as possible to the club rooms which so many companies ran. There is no question that the value of the Hut to the ex-Boys' Brigade member was even greater than to the troops in general. 'At a time when the fierce and cruel temptations of a large camp are making themselves felt, it is no small Service to remind Old Boys of the things that they were once taught in "The Old Company",' wrote George Barclay on 5 October 1915 in a report to Peacock:

> I cannot refrain from saying that the men as a whole seem amazingly responsive to any religious teaching. I would almost be inclined to say definitely that never in all our nation's history has there been a large section of the Community as accessible and receptive as the men of the Expeditionary Force seem to be today.[23]

Roger Peacock had other bureaucratic difficulties to contend with at home. The unwelcome opportunity provided by the death of the Founder and the

Prior to the formation of the Boy Scouts in 1908, scouting was already established as an activity within The Boys' Brigade. These boys are scouts of the 6th Enfield Company of the B.B.

Smith (on the left) and Baden-Powell at an inspection of the Glasgow Division of Boy Scouts in March 1911.

*The funeral procession of Sir William Alexander Smith on 16 May 1914
climbs towards Glasgow's Western Necropolis. Smith's death
was hastened by overwork in the service of the movement he founded.*

*Members of the 'B.B. Battalion' of the 16th Highland Light Infantry
cheerfully prepare to set off for France.
In 1916 the Battalion lost over 500 men on the Somme.*

During the First World War, the B.B. raised the money for recreation
huts for servicemen at Rouen (above) and Edinburgh (below).

The Cadet uniform adopted by those companies of the B.B. which chose to affiliate with the Cadet Scheme from 1917 to 1924.

1917 saw the formation of the first junior branch of the B.B., known initially as The Boy Reserves. The uniform was nautically inspired, with sailor's cap, navy-blue jersey, and shorts.

administrative void this had left behind led, in 1914 and 1915, to several proposals for the reorganization of the Brigade, including the possible transfer of the national Headquarters from Glasgow to London. In 1895 the Brigade Executive had appointed an Assistant Brigade Secretary resident in London, and in 1901 even went so far as to recommend the transfer of Headquarters to the capital, only to have their proposal defeated by that year's Council meeting held in Glasgow. Then in 1902 a London Office, with its own full-time Secretary, Roger Peacock, was established at 34 Paternoster Row, under the shadow of St. Paul's Cathedral in the City of London. The office accommodation consisted of a room for the Secretary, a larger room as general office for a book-keeper, two clerks and a shorthand typist — all male — and a small room for stores. Several important national negotiations were conducted out of this London Office, including meetings with the War Office in the prewar years over the issue of official recognition as Cadets. It was also argued by the pro-London lobby that the recruitment of the Brigade in the Anglican Church, which offered as rich a field for extension as all the other denominations put together, was greatly handicapped at this time because of the idea prevalent among English clergy that while the national Headquarters were in Glasgow, the Brigade must be mainly a Scottish and therefore — in their eyes — a Nonconformist or Presbyterian movement. In the South it was generally held that this impression would be largely removed and the original high ideal of interdenominationalism better served with the Headquarters removed to London — the capital of the Empire. Thus at the annual meeting of the Brigade's London Council on 16 November 1914 it was unanimously moved that Headquarters should be transferred to London, as opposed to adopting the Executive's proposal for two Headquarters Committees, one sitting in Glasgow and one in London, each with its own Secretary.

However, the reorganization scheme which was eventually submitted for the approval of the Brigade Executive proposed a Southern Committee, consisting of members of the Executive in England and Wales, and a Northern Committee, of Scottish and Irish Executive members, each appointed annually to deal with general administration in their own areas, subject to the policy control of the full Executive meeting thrice-yearly as before. This scheme received the official sanction of the Brigade Council meeting at Sheffield in September 1915, thus formally dissolving the old Headquarters Committee in Glasgow — where it had resided for over thirty years — and giving two official Brigade addresses, one in London and the other in Glasgow. Stanley Smith was appointed as Northern Secretary, but in his absence on active service his brother, Douglas, acted for him. Roger Peacock became the Southern Secretary, until he too was sent on active service as an officer in the Royal Army Service Corps. Of the two Committees, Peacock later wrote:

> This arrangement disregarded the elementary fact that the work did not divide itself naturally between the nations, but in the main was common to the whole movement. As a consequence there was a tendency to re-enact the Battles of Bannockburn and Flodden in alternate rotation.

Hence a scheme which was originally meant to provide merely a wartime 'temporary expedient which cannot be looked upon as a final settlement' endured for some fourteen years, despite its inconvenience and 'unnecessarily cumbersome' machinery.[24]

On the other side of the English Channel, away from the internecine struggles of the committee room and the conference table, the relentless stalemate of trench warfare had settled down into a murderous routine, merely reinforced by offensives such as that on the Somme in July 1916. Numerous ex-Brigade members from both the London and Glasgow areas were present at the Somme battles. In Glasgow it is well known that the 16th Battalion of the Highland Light Infantry — known as The Boys' Brigade Battalion — was formed almost entirely from ex-members in the city, and led by David Laidlaw, Glasgow Battalion Treasurer. However, The Boys' Brigade had difficulty in getting official recognition from the H.L.I. for this special battalion (like many in 1914 formed from 'Old Pals' groups with a common institutional or work-place background), and even threatened to offer it to the Cameron Highlanders — not traditionally a Glasgow regiment. Eventually, all was smoothed over and the three Glasgow units were taken over by the Highland Light Infantry. The 16th Battalion of the H.L.I. was decimated at the Somme, listing over 500 men killed. 'Nobly indeed have those formerly connected with The Boys' Brigade movement rallied to the flag,' wrote the *Glasgow Post* ecstatically on 7 March 1915, continuing:

> They are to be found in every part of Britain's wide Empire . . . Never will it be said that men who were connected with The Boys's Brigade movement throughout the length and breadth of the United Kingdom and Ireland funked in the hour of Britain's need.[25]

Another 'B.B.' unit was 'D' Company of the 13th Battalion of the Rifle Brigade. On 12 September 1914 over a hundred 'old boys' from the London area assembled at Horse Guards Parade where they took the King's shilling, and left next day from Waterloo Station for Winchester Barracks. R.E. Thompson, who when war broke out was in camp with the 2nd Enfield Company, remembers 'D' Company sustaining many casualties on the way up to the front line trenches in the Somme offensive, then receiving instructions that the Battalion was to 'go over the top' on the following morning, early in July. This order was cancelled without warning and the troops stayed in their trenches all day under continuous shelling, the casualty list growing until, at 8.15 that evening, word was passed along the line that the Battalion would launch an attack on the German trenches in half an hour. Rum was issued to all the troops, who stood waiting with chinstraps of steel helmets pulled taut and gas masks on the 'alert'. At last the C.O.'s whistle gave the signal to go over in three waves towards the enemy with 'D' and 'A' Companies leading the way:

> Shells were busting all round, the shrapnel descending like rain, the high explosive crashing and spouting up great black fountains of earth, while hidden machine guns by the dozen poured out their pitiless streams of lead. The advancing lines of khaki were now being thinned at every yard, but the gaps filled up quickly and the dauntless survivors pressed on until at last they battered their way into the German front line . . .

This assault turned out to be a costly mistake because fresh orders to cancel the attack yet again never reached the men. This single battalion, with no support or covering fire, advanced alone towards the German lines:

> We went over in three lines and eventually got into the German trenches and bombed our way in and along the trenches, and after being there for about three quarters of an hour the word came to us that we had to return to our front line trenches as the attack had been cancelled.

So the Colonel gave the order to retire and all those remaining alive had to retreat through a second inferno, having no choice but to leave behind the bodies of the dead and wounded.[26]

W.H.A. Monckton, late of the 38th London Company, took part in the same assault and vividly remembers the German mortars shelling the ground in front of the trenches with shrapnel reminiscent of a hailstorm. 'Well, after all, we were told to go over the top and you either have to go or be shot for cowardice,' he remembers bluntly:

> So I'd had this nasty smack in the trench and then I had a shrapnel ball went through my arm just below the elbow joint . . . and my brother, when he came to see me in the hospital, said: 'Did you pick it up?' You imagine trying to sort that out in a battle! Anyway, the next time I was hit in the chest and that knocked all the wind out of me, just like a blow with a pick. And I thought, 'This is your number, you're up.' Anyway, I found I was still alive.

Squad leader Monckton, on being wounded, received two stripes and took over the burial of the scores of Tyneside Scottish dead. Their bodies — some with their rifles still wearing bolt covers — were thrown into a huge crater which became one vast tomb. When the 13th Battalion, to which the ex-Boys' Brigade contingent belonged, was fully mustered the next day after being scattered throughout the night — some sleeping in craters with the dead — only about half of the 800 actual fighting men were left alive, some eight or ten of them ex-Brigade boys. When the Battalion had returned from its terrible experience, there doubtless came to the mind of each survivor a lasting impression of the true significance of modern warfare which had led to the futile sacrifice of so many young lives.[27]

From 1916 to 1917 the Brigade wrestled with its conscience once again over the issue of seeking recognition by County Territorial Associations as part of the nation's Cadet organization. The unexpected duration of the War had revived this as a patriotic proposition, if only in order to protect The Boys' Brigade from the competition of Cadet battalions conducted on secular lines which were being recruited by the military. 'It is generally realized that the position today is very different from that of 1910, when the question was first raised,' proclaimed an Executive circular of 10 March 1917 which sought to ascertain the opinion of company captains on this issue, 'and it is evident that there is a widespread and growing opinion throughout the Brigade in favour of recognition.' Feeling was strong among several Manchester companies that this circular, in taking a plebiscite of companies, struck at the very root of Brigade principles in which military drill had never been more than a means to a primarily religious and voluntary end. They asked that consideration of linking the movement to County Territorial Associations, and thus indirectly to the War Office, should be postponed until after the War was over, in order to avoid 'the permanent fostering of a military spirit upon the youth of the future'. After all, the War was ostensibly being fought to suppress Prussian militarism. It was also suggested that if a national system of compulsory Cadet training was introduced after the War, The Boys' Brigade would be in a stronger position if it could negotiate in complete independence as a voluntary organization, rather than if it were already attached in some way to the Army Council. A similar attitude to the Executive's circular was taken by the Captain of the 1st Hamilton Company, which actually maintained strong links with its local Territorial Force Association:

> It seems to me that by adopting this scheme it would only go to foster the spirit of

militarism which this almost world-wide war is being waged to eradicate. Your circular indicates that it is likely that military training for boys after the War will be general, but I am of the opinion that this diabolical conflict will have taught the civilized world the absurdity of war, and should be the means of formulating in the minds of legislators some scheme whereby all war will be avoided in future.

This reply also pointed out that there was no guarantee that, despite recognition, the military authorities might not, after a time, impose regulations unpopular with the Brigade — an eventuality which in 1924 led to the Executive decision not to allow companies to continue as recognized Cadet units.[28]

Despite these adverse opinions, over half the companies polled voted in favour of recognition as Cadets (twenty-nine per cent failed to make any reply, fifty-three per cent voted in favour and eighteen per cent against). With these replies before them, the Executive were of the opinion that, while they did not warrant a recommendation that the Brigade as a whole should become Cadets, the desire for recognition was so widespread (660 companies) that individual companies should be allowed to apply for Cadet recognition by the Territorials — without in any way damaging their position within the Brigade. Not only were the Brigade Executive sympathetic towards recognition, but in the patriotic climate of wartime, and fortified with the precedent already set by the Church Lads' Brigade, support for such a proposal was predictably much stronger among the Brigade as a whole than seven years earlier. 'The question the Brigade has had to solve,' as Acting Brigade Secretary Colonel Sir John Roxburgh put it to an Executive meeting in 1918,

> is whether they were likely to do more good by maintaining a protest against the cadet movement from outside, or by associating themselves with it, and trying to influence it from within.[29]

In order to protect the Brigade from military competition, it was arranged that where local companies of The Boys' Brigade and other boys' organizations were willing to be officially recognized, special Cadet battalions would not be formed in that area, and the Army Council would agree to refrain from interfering with the spiritual side or with the appointment of officers. In fact, by January 1919 only about 311 companies or thirty-one per cent of the B.B. total had actually accepted official recognition by their local C.T.A.'s and, of these, only sixty-three had actually adopted a khaki uniform. Since total boy numbers in The Boys' Brigade fell from about 60,000 in 1914 to 43,000 in 1919, it must be left open to some doubt whether by allowing companies to enrol as Cadets, the Brigade actually succeeded in attracting those who might otherwise have joined secular Cadet units. In 1917, by allowing individual companies to accept recognition, the B.B. not only exacerbated its potential differences with the Boys' Life Brigade — to whom Cadet training was anathema — but also created an unfortunate link with the State's military machine which, in a different climate of public opinion before the War, William Smith himself had astutely avoided.

The year in which Boys' Brigade companies were first allowed to accept individual recognition as Cadets also saw the creation of the first junior branch of the movement, the Boy Reserves. For several years there had been an increasing number of boys under twelve joining Boys' Brigade companies without proper authorization, and so the need for a separate organization had become increasingly apparent. Since 1916 Scouting had established the Wolf Cubs for the under-twelves, modelled on the animal characters in Kipling's

Jungle Books; and, because of the absence on war service of many of the more responsible Boys' Brigade officers, there had also sprung into existence various unacknowledged B.B. 'Cadet Corps' offering the rudiments of training to boys under twelve, with their own adaptations of The Boys' Brigade uniform. A number of resolutions were accordingly put before the Brigade Executive to lower the age limit in The Boys' Brigade in order to accommodate these younger boys.

At the Executive meeting held in Carlisle on 26 January 1917 a different resolution was on the agenda: a proposal by the Plymouth Battalion for the setting up of a separate 'Junior Corps' for boys under twelve. Since this met with some approval from the members present, it was delegated to F.C. Carey Longmore to draw up a scheme and bring solid proposals before the next Executive. Longmore, or 'Carey', was a professional surveyor, a small, almost delicate man, with an impish sense of humour that by unbalancing his opponent allowed his serious intentions full play. As Captain of the 1st Warley Company in Essex, and a member of the Executive, he urged that if a junior organization could be successfully sponsored, officers would have a viable alternative to the unofficial units and a solution to the recruitment of under-age boys into the Brigade. Moreover, a great reserve of potential Boys' Brigade enlistment would be created and trained along lines suited to their particular age group, while the wartime falling off in Sunday School attendance could be arrested by the simple expedient of making it compulsory in a junior organization.

In the *Gazette* of April 1917 a letter was printed from Carey Longmore asking for ideas to be submitted that could be incorporated into the new junior organization, and at the Brigade Executive meeting held at Windermere on 18 May 1917 a plan was drawn up for submission to the next Brigade Council meeting. Douglas Pearson Smith, Acting Secretary at the Brigade Office in George Square, Glasgow, cooperated with Carey Longmore in drawing up the original scheme until late in 1917, when he left to join the Royal Naval Air Service. Someone on the Executive proposed that, as Carey Longmore was its founder, the new organization should be known colloquially as 'Carey's Chickens', but eventually the name 'Boy Reserves' was chosen. (In 1917 the term 'Reserve' had taken on a new meaning — Regimental Reserve Battalions in the Army consisted of untrained youths.) At the Brigade Council meeting in Manchester on 15 September 1917 Carey Longmore proposed a motion for the formation of an official junior organization; the motion was seconded by Douglas and, after some discussion, carried by a large majority.

The Object of the Boy Reserves, for nine to twelve year olds, was 'the advancement of Christ's Kingdom among Boys and the training of suitable recruits for The Boys' Brigade'. The uniform was deliberately nautical, consisting of a sailor's cap, navy blue jersey and shorts. Use of the naval salute and petty officer titles for the equivalent to The Boys' Brigade NCOs further distinguished the Boy Reserves from the more military image of The Boys' Brigade. Each unit was known as a section, and until the 1920s all the leaders were men. Sunday School attendance showed a marked increase in churches which adopted the Boy Reserves, and boys under twelve soon disappeared from the ranks of The Boys' Brigade. While the programme followed had to be distinguished from that of the more senior organization, it is perhaps surprising that in the first Boy Reserve Manual, published in 1918, there were detailed thirty different forms of drill and only ten possible children's games. By the time of the second edition, published in 1923, there were thirty-four different games, and drill had been reduced to a bare minimum. Lady leaders, or honorary instructors as they were then called, had made their presence felt by the early 1920s and were to become an important element in Brigade leadership. From 1925 to 1928 Miss Dora Webb of Northampton was appointed by the Executive as the first and only lady demonstrator in the Boy Reserves and in that capacity extensively travelled throughout the British Isles.[30]

Clearly, as the events narrated here show, the First World War saw several important changes and adjustments in the organization and development of The Boys' Brigade. Although many companies were compelled to close during the War years, and by 1919 membership was some 20,000 down on 1914, The Boys' Brigade was not daunted and, once the Armistice came, quickly set to work to rebuild its strength. Soon the losses were more than replaced, and during the interwar years the Brigade was to experience a remarkable revival, which will be examined in the next chapter.

CHAPTER 5

'ALL YOUR STRENGTH IS IN YOUR UNION'

The Boys' Brigade in Britain, 1919 to 1939

THE BOYS' BRIGADE had come through the First World War with much of its leadership and organization intact, based upon the makeshift tripartite structure of Executive and Northern and Southern Committees. Hence the problem of postwar reconstruction was to become largely a financial one. Nonetheless, at the company, battalion and district levels, many officers had been killed, companies had closed down or accepted recognition as Cadet units, and membership was 20,000 down on the figure for 1914. Lord Guthrie, who had played a prominent part as Brigade President throughout the difficult War years, retired from his onerous post in 1919 and handed over to Colonel Sir John Roxburgh, a long-serving Vice-President, and an old friend and fellow officer of the Founder in the Glasgow Volunteers. Roxburgh, a leading Glasgow businessman of the old school, remained President for fourteen years, taking office when Boys' Brigade strength had been reduced by the War to its lowest figure for years, and serving until the Jubilee Year, shortly after which membership reached its peak. It is, in fact, the unexpectedly rapid rate of Boys' Brigade expansion between the Wars in Britain — proportionately higher than that of any other uniformed youth movement — that this chapter sets out to explain and to place in its proper historical context.

In the immediate aftermath of the First World War, The Boys' Brigade was sorely stricken financially, with many sources of income drying up, particularly donations and subscriptions (although even today investment income, grants and donations are only sixteen per cent of total B.B. income). So the timely suggestion was made by the Southern Secretary, Roger Peacock, that the boy membership should be encouraged to raise money through collections among parents and friends. After much discussion this proposal was approved by a majority of the Executive. Peacock's idea was that the boys in every company should be asked to collect money annually during one particular week — the famous 'B.B. Week' — by means of collecting cards; the sum raised was to be divided equally between the Brigade General Fund and their own company funds. When the idea went before the Brigade Council at Dundee on 10 September 1921, the Captain of the 5th Motherwell Company objected that a better scheme than that of collecting cards (which raised the demeaning possibility of door-to-door collections) might be found, and moved that the matter be remitted to the Executive for further consideration. In this he was supported by the President of the Glasgow Battalion, W.E. Scott, who believed not only that the proposed scheme would be placing temptation in the way of the boys but also that they ought not to put the responsibility for financing the Brigade onto their youthful shoulders. Leaving aside the question of method, however, there was a general agreement at Council on the need for holding a 'B.B. Week', but this was not enough to prevent the motion for a remit being carried. Not surprisingly, the Southern Committee — led by Peacock — feeling that the opposition to their idea had come almost entirely from Scotland, thereupon added to 'the world's successful acts of rebellion' by launching it solely for England and Wales. When the total money collected during the last week in November 1921 was announced as £2,855 the possibilities of the original plan were more than realized and the opposition effectively silenced.

'B.B. Week' proved to be the financial salvation of the movement in the early 1920s for, although the greater part was retained by the companies themselves, the share sent to Headquarters was always sufficient to enable the Executive to undertake many otherwise impracticable but necessary projects. In 1922 the whole Brigade took part in 'B.B. Week' and £4,697 was raised; this upward trend continued almost without a break, until 1978 saw the record total of £320,955 being collected by companies (see Appendix 6). So if the First World War left The Boys' Brigade on the verge of bankruptcy, the 'B.B. Week' scheme pioneered by Roger Peacock ushered in an era of unexpected financial stability that enabled both individual companies and the movement in general to meet the new and difficult financial conditions of the postwar years with some confidence. 'B.B. Week' continued as an integral part of The Boys' Brigade's fund-raising activities, taking place during the week ending the last Saturday in November. Over the years sponsored activities with sponsor cards replaced the original collecting cards, and fund-raising moved towards working or doing something for the cash solicited. As the originator of the idea put it, 'our faith in the B.B. Boy — not to mention his Officer — justifies our confidence that B.B. Week still has a long and triumphant ascent before it'.[1]

The Boys' Brigade, as the economic historian might interpret it, had consistently shown itself stronger in the home of the 'old' declining heavy engineering, shipbuilding and textile industries — the Northeast, lowland Scotland, and Northern Ireland — rather than in the areas of the 'new' expanding consumer industries of the interwar period — the Midlands, London, and the Southeast of England. Hence, in common with other voluntary youth organizations, The Boys' Brigade was to experience difficulties in recruiting from outside its traditional strongholds, difficulties that could only be overcome by vigorous campaigning and positive leadership. However, from 480 companies and 20,314 boys at the end of May 1919 to the year ending 31 May 1934, The Boys' Brigade in England and Wales had accumulated 1,662 companies and 54,854 adolescent boys (although since this fell to an average of 50,000 boys in the succeeding years, the 1933 Jubilee celebrations were obviously a contributory factor). Significantly, when The Boys' Brigade amalgamated with the Boys' Life Brigade in 1926, it inherited over 18,000 English boys who came largely from the 'new' industrial regions of the Southeast and Midlands. This accession of numbers meant that England and Wales leapt from 45.6 per cent of total boy membership to 57.5 per cent, whereas Scotland and Ireland declined from 54.3 per cent to 42.4 per cent of U.K. boy strength on union. The cities with the largest battalions in this period are detailed in Table 1 (p.121).[2]

In the Northeast of England and in South Wales, one difficulty obstructing expansion was that in the Nonconformist mining valleys antimilitarism was sometimes an effective barrier to the spread of The Boys' Brigade as a result of parental reaction to memories of the carnage of the First World War. In some areas of the Northeast, for example, Church youth movements in uniform were in danger of being seen as recruiting agencies for the Army — 'an insidious way of instilling militarism into the lads'. The Church Lads' Bri-

Table 1: *B.B. Battalion Strength in 1927 after Union (1926)*

Battalion	Companies	Boys
Glasgow	242	11,256
Manchester	90	3,161
South London*	78	2,747
Sheffield	75	2,184
Belfast	57	2,151
Aberdeen	55	2,138

*In 1892 London was sub-divided into North, South and West London Battalions, and a few years later the City and East London Battalion was created.

gade, in contrast to The Boys' Brigade, was to experience a steady decline in numbers during the interwar period, largely owing to a failure to ride out this same public mood of antimilitarism, since until 1936 they were firmly attached to the Army Cadet Force and mostly wore khaki uniform. 'Almost immediately after the war, there was an anti-everything feeling going abroad and particularly was this feeling directed against any organization what [sic] was considered militaristic,' writes the 1930 historian of the St. Mary, Lewisham, Company of the Church Lads' Brigade:

> . . . with the result that, although many lads desired to join, they were prevented by parents, who imagined the Church Lads' Brigade synonymous with militarism. From 1919 to 1924, the Company undoubtedly passed through a very difficult period. Numbers were steadily declining . . . After the war came the forming of the League of Nations and with it came the desire for peace and a misunderstanding of the word 'militarism'. The general cry of public opinion was 'down with militarism'. A good number of clergy pandered to this opinion, and in consequence, more companies were compelled to close down.

The Boys' Brigade, on the other hand, was able to overcome the hostility which any British organization in uniform that marched and drilled provoked in a period of widespread antimilitarism and pacifism. It managed this by a series of astute policy decisions that served to defuse latent Nonconformist fears that the military means might overtake the religious ends of the movement. Thus in 1924 the Boys' Brigade Executive determined, in the face of only minimal resistance, to cut all remaining ties with the War Office Cadet Scheme and, eventually, to discard the dummy rifle used for drill purposes. These concessions to Nonconformist feeling and contemporary opinion made an eventual merger between The Boys' Brigade and the Boys' Life Brigade much more probable, as the following outline of events will attempt to demonstrate.[3]

Early in 1923 it had been officially announced by the War Office that government financial support given to the Cadet Force, in the form of capitation grants awarded annually to each cadet and the use of Army camp equipment, was to be withdrawn in consequence of antimilitarist pressures and the need to reduce Army expenditure. The Advisory Council of Brigade Cadets, representing more than half the total Cadet Force, protested by pointing out that the public-school Officer Training Corps were unaffected by these cuts, but to little avail. At a meeting of The Boys' Brigade Executive on 21 January 1923, Roger Peacock expressed the view that, given the need for national economies in the wake of the recommendations of Sir Eric Geddes' 1922 Economy Committee, there was little prospect of the decision to withdraw the grant being reversed, and it was therefore agreed to concentrate efforts upon securing the free use of military camp equipment for their cadets. A further blow was still to come, for Army Council Instruction 583 of September 1923 set out to reorganize the Cadet Force on an entirely military basis, requiring affiliation to, and administration by, local Territorial units; this would place the autonomy of B.B. Cadet units as Brigade companies in serious jeopardy. The Executive agreed to inform the War Office that The Boys' Brigade was unable to accept the new regulations requiring affiliation to Territorial or Regular Army Battalions and that, consequently, if these more restrictive Army Council regulations were adhered to, no units of the Brigade could remain in the Cadet Force. Thus, when a draft of the new Cadet regulations was finally put before the B.B. Executive on 10 May 1924, it was unanimously agreed, after some discussion, that it was no longer desirable for The Boys' Brigade to participate in the Cadet Force and that the necessary steps be taken to withdraw all individual Cadet units. When these units ceased to belong in 1924, it is probable that there were only some 15,000 B.B. cadets in all, or roughly a quarter of the total B.B. membership at that time. The effect of their withdrawal on the Cadet Force, however, led to a marked reduction in overall cadet numbers until the outbreak of the Second World War.[4]

At the same Executive meeting which determined on pulling out of the Cadets, it was also reported that resolutions had been passed by several battalions in favour of discarding the dummy rifle used for drill purposes which, in the past, had been a bone of contention among the Nonconformist Churchmen both inside and outside the Brigade. A lengthy discussion took place in which the general view was expressed that the Executive should announce a definite policy upon the issue, and the following resolution was drafted accordingly:

> The Boys' Brigade Executive, while believing that the rifle has a certain value for drill purposes, are of the opinion that the time has now come when its use is detrimental to the extension of The Boys' Brigade and should be discontinued. They therefore request all Companies that still use the rifle to consider the question of its disuse, and they recommend from the close of the present session its use in competitions and combined parades should be discontinued. The Executive have decided to prohibit its use in new Companies.

Executive member C.L. Beckett, a Birmingham engineer, proposed to move a resolution before Council in Bristol that a date be fixed after which the use of the dummy rifle be ended. But it was felt that it should be made clear to Council that this resolution was not being made on behalf of the Executive and it was left open to its members to speak as they thought fit.[5]

At the close of the 1922-23 session only thirty-seven per cent of B.B. companies still used the rifle for drill practice, so the argument for discarding it, as outlined in the June 1924 *B.B. Gazette*, was not expected to be seriously challenged. Nonetheless, some vocal protest was made against the Executive's resolution at the Council held in Bristol from 5 to 8 September 1924, but, unfortunately, the most earnest and sincere speaker in favour of retention, S.W. Cuff, Captain of the 1st Barnet, was both a slow and largely inaudible speaker who — owing to the poor acoustics of the hall — received a rather impatient reception from the officers in the rear seats. There were frequent appeals to 'speak up' and to 'get to the point', as Cuff read laboriously from a formidable bundle of manuscript and, although the Chairman several times called for silence, he eventually had to give way to the next speaker. 'Wearied with the strain of war', Cuff soundlessly declaimed,

> a section of our nation can see nought but evil in all things military, and seeks to

sweep away all traces of a soldier's calling, and unless a firm stand is made, not only rifles, but military drill, military titles, and with them the great idea of our Founder will be destroyed, and The Boys' Brigade become a set of Juvenile Church Clubs. I do not deny that this increasing anti-militaristic spirit may become so strong as to render Boys's Brigade work, as we have known and loved it, impossible . . .

In reply, Stanley Smith, then Northern Secretary, spoke of attending literally hundreds of meetings all over the country where he had consistently found that the one lay and clerical objection preventing the formation of new companies was that The Boys' Brigade still sanctioned the use of model rifles. Even in districts where the rifle was not actually in use, the mere fact that it was sanctioned was sufficient for its retention to do incalculable harm to the development and extension of the movement. J.H. Early, Captain of the 1st Witney, then moved an amendment that the time limit after which the use of the rifle be discontinued be fixed at twelve months and, in an unexpectedly overwhelming vote against retention, this was carried by nearly three hundred votes to five. The debate provided striking evidence of the value of preparing a case clearly and concisely at Council, for most of those intending to vote against Beckett's comparatively mild resolution had now voted for Early's far more drastic amendment.[6]

An amendment to what was now the substantive resolution was proposed on behalf of the Executive that 'the date on which such a period of twelve months shall commence be referred to the Executive to fix, provided they find by a referendum that a majority of companies favour the decision of this Council that the use of the Rifle shall cease'. J.H. Early having accepted the amendment, his resolution with this addition was put to Council and carried with only one vote against. The result of the referendum, as announced at the January 1925 Executive meeting in Sheffield, was 917 companies for the Council resolution, 228 against and 230 not voting; in other words, two-thirds of companies were for the resolution to abandon the use of the rifle. The Executive therefore decided to fix a time limit after which this should take place, commencing on 1 June 1925 and finishing on 31 May 1926, after which no company of The Boys' Brigade would be allowed to use the rifle for any purpose whatsoever. Thus, in a matter of months, The Boys' Brigade had successfully managed to remove all the remaining obstacles to their amalgamation with the Boys' Life Brigade: they were no longer linked to the War Office through the Cadet Force and they had agreed to abandon the use of the model rifle. Nevertheless, tortuous negotiations were still to take place before their eventual coming together with 'the prospect of a great increase in our strength for service to the Christian Church and the Boyhood of our land', and it is to these negotiations which we must now turn.[7]

The ultimate lack of success of the first initiative to bring the two sides together to discuss union in Liverpool during January 1914 has already been recounted. A second attempt was made after the War by Sir Arthur Haworth, ex-President of the Congregational Union, and Sir George Croydon Marks, Chairman of the Sunday School Union's Council, who called together a conference in Manchester from 27 to 28 February 1920, consisting of representatives of the two Brigades and observers from the Nonconformist Churches. This conference reaffirmed the findings of its predecessor that the existence of the two Brigades was confusing and that the work could be done more effectively by a united body. However, on 13 March 1920 the Boys' Life Brigade Administrative Council — which corresponded to the B.B. Executive — again rejected the compromise proposals put forward, 'whilst the use of the

model rifle is continued, and the Cadet scheme remains under the control of
the War Office'. Clearly, 1924 was a much more propitious year in which to
renew attempts at amalgamation given that The Boys' Brigade was preparing
to overcome these two major obstacles, but it was still to be two long years
before final agreement was reached on the circumstances surrounding union.[8]

The revival of interest in amalgamation between the two Brigades occurred
as the outcome of a Conference for Workers Amongst Boys held under the
Presidency of College Principal A.H. Angus at Westhill, Birmingham, during
Easter 1924. Speakers from both Brigades were present, as were some of the
secretaries of Young Peoples' Departments in the English Nonconformist
Churches who, being aware of the harm done by the competition between the
two rival Brigades, suggested that yet another attempt to come together
should be made. A preliminary meeting was held informally between the
senior members of both Brigades in Glasgow on 21 June 1924 during the
World's Sunday School Convention. The Boys' Life Brigade felt that a united
new movement, 'with a fresh appeal, a wider vision, and larger outlook,
would be more effective than the present system in challenging the boyhood
of Britain for Jesus Christ'; whereas The Boys' Brigade, disregarding all the
rhetoric, simply expected to absorb their long-standing rival. 'I feel that a great
deal of the language used is pure eyewash,' Arnold Wilson informed Principal
Angus on 17 July 1924, ' "the fresh appeal", "the wider vision", "the larger
outlook", etc.' The Boys' Brigade evidently felt aggrieved by the attitude of
their competitor that unity should not simply be on the basis of the mere
fusion of the two Brigades or the absorption of one by the other:

> . . . it does seem rather ridiculous that an organization [the B.L.B.] which has
> practically lived on borrowing its ideas from us, that is about a quarter our strength
> in numbers and a long way from a quarter our strength in efficiency, and,
> according to their own balance sheet, is in very poor financial condition to say the
> least of it compared with the splendid position in which we stand, should be trying
> to dictate a policy to us, and evidently plans to get together all the representatives
> of the Young People's Societies [sic] in order to talk them over to their point of
> view.[9]

To place these allegations in some perspective, the strength of the two
Brigades in the last session before amalgamation was roughly as follows:

| Boys' Brigade | 60,000 | Boy Reserves | 19,000 |
| Boys' Life Brigade | 21,000 | The Lifeboys | 8,500 |

The relative strength of the two Brigades has also to be seen at the regional
level: in London, for example, the Boys' Life Brigade had 141 companies and
3,975 boys and The Boys' Brigade had 97 companies and 4,430 boys, in
Sheffield the Boys' Life Brigade had 57 companies and 1,668 boys, while The
Boys' Brigade had only 21 companies and 702 boys. In many English cities, in
other words, the Boys' Life Brigade was still a flourishing movement, even if
its overall totals were easily diminished in comparison to the more robust
Boys' Brigade figures. Meanwhile, the negotiations dragged on behind closed
doors, hindered by the absence until early 1925 of an agreed time limit for the
abandonment of the model rifle by B.B. companies. F.P. Gibbon, soon to
become editor of the *B.B. Gazette*, attributed less than honourable motives to
the Boys' Life Brigade for their generally evasive tactics but, since he was
himself so well versed in the subtler arts of committee intrigue, he tended
perhaps to overestimate the duplicity of his opponents:

> Quite clearly, the majority of The Boys' Life Brigade higher ranks don't want to

come into an organization in which efficiency and the taking part by practically all Officers in the religious teaching — the Bible Class especially — are put before the glitter and show and the noise of bugles. Formerly they had an excuse plausible to the ignorant, even if petty to the expert — the rifle. They could always put that forward as the excuse for disunion. The ground is now cut from under their feet — or, at any rate, it's precarious footing now . . .

It is just as I expected from my dealing with them. They are not straight. They won't unite with us if they can possibly help it, and they are afraid of giving a straight refusal lest the Boy Department Secretaries [sic] should feel bound to pronounce publicly against them, and so put them in the wrong with the Churches and the Sunday School Union.[10]

The major breakthrough in the negotiations came on 7 November 1925 when a further joint conference was held in London between nine delegates from each Brigade, with John Roxburgh, B.B. President, in the chair. With a time limit now fixed for the abandonment by The Boys' Brigade of the model rifle, it was found that the prospects for union had suddenly become much brighter than heretofore. After lengthy discussion, a preliminary agreement on union was hammered out and passed unanimously, then a Joint Sub-Committee of three members from each Brigade was appointed to draw up a more detailed scheme of union. One of the major sticking-points proved to be the use of the term 'military organization and drill' in Article Three of The Boys' Brigade Constitution, but this was eventually replaced as a concession by the more anodyne 'company organization and company drill'. Thus on 13 March 1926, the Boys' Life Brigade Administrative Council, meeting at Swanick, approved the draft scheme of union, following a lengthy speech by Birmingham High Court Judge D.L. Finnemore, who offered 'convincing argument of the benefit which the work amongst boys will derive from the fusion of the two organizations'. In April, representatives of the B.B.'s Boy Reserves and the B.L.B.'s Lifeboys met to arrange details affecting the union of their respective junior organizations as the Life Boys. A few days later, the Joint Sub-Committee met in conference the secretaries of the Young People's Departments who promised their full support for a combined youth movement. Next, a memorandum dated 21 May 1926 and authorized by the B.B. Executive was sent to all members of Brigade Council with a full outline of the proposed terms of union since, as certain constitutional changes were involved, the entire scheme had to receive a two-thirds majority of their votes. 'Should it fail to do so all prospects of union, it is feared, will vanish, at any rate for this generation,' the memorandum solemnly declared, 'the present competition and rivalry will continue in an aggravated form, and the principal sufferers will be the Boys, for whose good we exist, and for whom many of us have spent the best years of our lives.' In the event, such fears were to prove groundless. In a packed hall at Brigade Council in Brighton on 4 September 1926, Arnold Wilson moved on behalf of the Executive that Council approve and adopt the scheme of union as contained in the memorandum. With only one exception, the members rose to their feet to record their votes in favour.[11]

'It is idle to pretend that we do not miss our old happy family relationships as they were,' wrote Arnold S. Clark, a former B.L.B. Commissioner, to his fellow officers in January 1927,

> but we are now in the transitional period, before we have had time to settle down . . . If still in your mind there lingers any feeling that these old Boys' Brigade Officers are not ready to co-operate with us in every possible way, please take my very definite assurance to the contrary.

During this 'transitional period', before the two elements in the united body had become indistinguishable, there were many constitutional and battalion arrangements to be amicably settled, such as designating new battalions and their boundaries and coordinating rules of competitions within districts. The *B.B. Gazette* did not gloss over the problems:

> And now a difficult and thorny path lies before us. It would be cowardly and wrong to shut our eyes to the fact that there are difficulties and even dangers in the way. The adjustments that will have to be made in brigade, battalion and company affairs may produce heart-burning on both sides unless tackled, in the finest spirit of service, with complete setting aside of self.

For, as this account has indicated, the merger between the B.B. and the B.L.B. had only come about after some protracted and often acrimonious negotiations that had gone on intermittently since before the First World War, and it would have been overly sanguine to expect these differences of opinion and practice to disappear overnight. Yet, as Roger Peacock pointed out, in the long run Hiawatha's good advice prevailed:

> All your strength is in your union,
> All your danger is in discord,
> Therefore be at peace henceforward,
> And as brothers live together.[12]

The year following union with the B.L.B., 1927, saw the B.B. increase its strength from 27,000 to 45,000 in England and Wales — well over half of the total U.K. figure — although union made little difference to numbers in Scotland. The Brigade President, Colonel Sir John Roxburgh, directed a letter to captains of companies conveying a resolution of Brigade Council which announced that this was to be 'the year of Crusade for increased efficiency and extended effort'. To this end, it was suggested that every battalion should appoint a strong 'Crusade Committee' to tackle the question of company efficiency, endeavour to get new companies formed, and arrange for the training of newly secured officers.

The Boys' Brigade had issued a striking booklet entitled *The Boys' Brigade as an Auxiliary of the Church of England* in 1923 which conveys the general thrust of their energetic recruiting campaign within the Anglican Church. This campaign was so successful that by 1937 The Boys' Brigade had well over twice the number of companies active in England and Wales as the Church Lads' Brigade — their Church of England counterpart. However, it should be pointed out that, in the session 1935-36, of the 135 new companies enrolled in England and Wales, over forty per cent were Methodist, and the share of Congregationalist, Baptist and Anglican denominations was only about fifteen per cent each. Whatever success The Boys' Brigade's campaign had within the Anglican Church was largely due to the particular attractions of the B.B. as outlined in the booklet. It advised that clergy and Sunday School workers, before deciding upon any organization for their boys, should note that of the uniformed youth movements The Boys' Brigade was the least expensive, the freest from red tape and unnecessary military trappings, the most interdenominational, and the most successful at bringing boys together for systematic religious instruction ('in particular . . . compare the state of the Bible Classes in each organization, for this is surely the most convincing of tests').

Less attractively, the booklet is unable to avoid the adoption of a patronizing tone towards its potential juvenile recruits, which strongly suggests both the class-divided nature of British society in the 1920s and a calculating appeal to the public-school ethos of much of the Anglican clergy. The training in drill and discipline given in The Boys' Brigade, we are constantly told, is the best substitute there is for 'the public school spirit' which working-class boys have no chance of acquiring:

> The trouble with the working-class Boy — splendid fellow though he is in many ways — is that he has not learnt at school to 'play up, and play the game'. He is a rank individualist half his time, and one of a flock of sheep the other half. Discipline and *esprit de corps* are what he needs, wisely combined with individual training and strengthening of character, so that he may make the best of himself and do the most good for others.

Not only does this reflect the prevalent middle-class fear of a supposed combination of selfish individualism and communal solidarity among the working class, it also suggests that the clerical and Brigade leadership of this era was both a product of and nostalgic for the public-school ideology of an earlier, prewar generation. The booklet's reasons for advocating 'real' discipline as a method of training are equally vulnerable to modern charges of attempting to enforce 'social control':

> An organization may dispense with Discipline when it appeals mainly to a different and more docile class of Boys — the Boy from a 'respectable' home outside the crowded areas; the Boy who is well provided with outdoor and indoor games at school and at home; and whose parents are better able, and as a rule more inclined, to supply religious, moral and educational instruction. But with the average type of Boy of the working-class districts, Discipline is essential before instruction can be given; and this is where The Boys' Brigade system scores.[13]

The accession of strength following amalgamation between The Boys' Brigade and the Boys' Life Brigade accentuated the need for better accommodation to cope with the newly reorganized movement, although The Boys' Brigade's London Office at Paternoster Row and the Glasgow Office in George Square had served them well for decades. In London, suitable premises on a first-class site were eventually found overlooking Westminster Abbey, on the first floor of a former hotel at Abbey House, Victoria Street, Westminster (a new building now occupies the site). Following a simple service of dedication jointly conducted by Bishop Taylor Smith and Dr Scott Lidgett a fortnight previously, the offices were formally declared open on 6 April 1927 by the primly Victorian Tory Home Secretary Sir W. Joynson-Hicks, later Lord Brentford. In comparison to Paternoster Row, the accommodation at Abbey House was truly palatial, being well-equipped for offices and the issue of supplies and equipment. A largely junior staff had, with the absorption of three members from the Boys' Life Brigade, risen to fifteen and included Tom Sharman, a familiar member of staff in London for half a century. Meanwhile, in Glasgow, moves were afoot to move from the offices occupied since 1909 at 30 George Square to premises at 168 Bath Street which had been purchased by the Glasgow Battalion for entry as from 1 April 1930. (At the time of writing, this address is still occupied by the Brigade in Glasgow.)

Notwithstanding these changes of address, the strongest feeling to emerge from the 1929 report of the Organization and Administration Committee, a sub-committee of the Brigade Executive, was that someone was needed to act as overall head of the Brigade's administration — Northern and Southern Secretaries were not accountable to the Brigade Secretary — and that the then current method of management by the Executive, through the Northern and Southern Committees and their respective Secretaries, was both 'wasteful' and 'cumbersome'. 'It tends to great delay and robs the Secretariat of initiative and responsibility . . .' They therefore recommended the radical solution that the Northern and Southern Committee structure set up in 1915 be abandoned, thus eliminating the posts of Northern and Southern Secretaries, and that the Brigade Secretary should make his Headquarters in London — a course which Stanley Smith, Secretary since 1925, himself favoured. The Brigade office in Glasgow would be retained, however, with a reduced staff moving to the new premises in Bath Street. The Committee felt that since England and Wales offered incomparably the larger field for extension and recruitment, it would make sense to concentrate the work of Headquarters in the capital city. That this was not a point of view shared by all the officers of the Brigade in Scotland and Ireland is indicated by the resignation from the Executive of G.W. Shannon, a Dublin barrister, in protest at the transfer of the Brigade Secretariat to London.[14]

The Executive resolutions for Brigade Council in September 1930 nonetheless recommended by a large majority that there should be two Brigade offices, in London and Glasgow, with the Secretary making his Headquarters in the former. Roger Peacock, ex-Southern Secretary, and Edward Cooke, ex-B.L.B. Secretary, were to be designated Deputy Brigade Secretaries and installed to assist Stanley Smith at Abbey House. Andrew McPherson, Secretary of the Glasgow Battalion, was to become Assistant Secretary for Scotland and Ireland. Despite some acrimony over the apparent demotion — more apparent than real — of the Glasgow Office and the transferral of the Brigade Secretariat to London, the ensuing reorganization went forward fairly harmoniously. Hence in the autumn of 1930 Stanley Smith belatedly took up his position as Secretary of The Boys' Brigade at Abbey House in London which, forty-seven years after the movement had been started by his father, now became the national and international Headquarters for the entire movement. The transferral certainly involved a major uprooting for Stanley Smith, including the wrench of having to pass on the Captaincy of the 1st Glasgow Company to his brother Douglas; however, most summers continued to see him at their Portavadie camp and, of course, residence in London brought its own compensations for a clubbable man like the Brigade Secretary.

The Boys' Brigade was now entering into its most successful and self-confident years, highlighted by the massive 1933 Golden Jubilee Celebrations held in Glasgow. By general agreement this period has come to be seen as the 'Golden Age' of the organization's history. Before going on to look at the events of the Jubilee in more detail, something should be said of the circumstances in which the movement found itself during this decade. Social trends in British society were leading towards a general relaxation of the regimentation and subordination to adult authority which The Boys' Brigade method, if unimaginatively practiced, could have been seen to represent. Such tendencies in the field of adolescent leisure showed themselves most clearly in the boys' club movement which, in the 1930s, began to rival the uniformed youth organizations — Scouts, Brigades, Cadets — for the allegiance of working-class adolescents in large cities. In terms of their ability to recruit new members, the boys' club movement was probably the most successful youth organization during the interwar period in Britain, doubling its membership during the 1930s alone to around 126,500 in 1,400 affiliated clubs. The Scouts and Guides — after a period of slow but unspectacular growth — appeared to have stabilized their membership at around 200,000 each after 1935, and The Boys' Brigade to have peaked at the figure of over 96,000 adolescent boys in 1934. Boys' clubs, of course, required no uniform, had no church affiliation, and did not expect attendance at religious services or the ability to perform military drill. The success of voluntary youth organizations in appealing to boys over fourteen varied considerably, not only between organizations but also from area to area. By 1938, the National Association of Boys' Clubs, with an estimated fifty per cent of its members over fourteen, and The Boys' Brigade, with the proportion of those between fourteen and eighteen at seventy-two per cent, were the most successful of the major voluntary groups in this respect; while the Boy Scouts and Rovers, with only thirty-nine per cent of their members between fourteen and nineteen, appear to have been the least successful. The Church Lads' Brigade, the Jewish Lads' Brigade and the Cadet Force all suffered from a sharply declining membership between the Wars — the last-named falling by over seventy per cent in numbers between 1918 and 1930. To put all these figures for membership of youth organizations in some perspective, it should be mentioned that in 1934 the Carnegie U.K. Trust collected data for fourteen to eighteen-year-old boys from some 253 towns, representing about eighty-five per cent of the boy population in this age group, and found that only a mere twenty-one per cent of them were members of a youth organization *of any kind*.[15]

The 1930s were also marked in leisure terms by the increasing popularity among the young of hiking and rambling, and also by the related and dramatic growth of the Youth Hostels Association. Whereas the 1931 Y.H.A. Handbook claimed only 16,000 members, throughout the 1930s membership rose at a rate of approximately 10,000 every year, until by the outbreak of the Second World War it had reached over 100,000. The 'keep-fit' boom became almost a national mania — as will be seen from the 1937 Festival of Youth in which The Boys' Brigade played an important part — with far more people going in for walking, cycling, sunbathing and all kinds of sports, epitomizing a faith in fresh air and healthy, physical exercise as an antidote to the often depressing economic climate. Organizations such as the Women's League of Health and Beauty, which had 16,000 members by 1939, did much to popularize the new cult. The small English 'woodcraft' groups that flourished during the interwar years — the Order of Woodcraft Chivalry, the Kibbo Kift Kindred, and the Woodcraft Folk — were equally representative of this fashionable trend towards the vigorous outdoor life, while also offering coeducational, non-religious and non-military alternatives to the more established Church youth movements which had emerged during the late Victorian period. Yet the greater competition which all these different forms of leisure activity represented does not seem to have had any appreciable effect in slowing down Boys' Brigade recruitment, at least not until after the Second World War. However, there is no doubt that even before the outbreak of war the Church youth organizations found it increasingly difficult to come to terms with a rapidly changing social and cultural environment.

Like many pre-1914 youth movements, The Boys' Brigade began to enter a defensive stage of self-preservation and self-congratulation during the 1930s. At times this encouraged the adoption of an almost incurably conservative and hierarchical pose in their attitude towards contemporary British society — a society in which materialism, pacifism and an apparent lack of patriotism were much more in evidence than in the late Victorian Scotland into which the movement had been born. That the Church Brigades stood out against what they saw as the dangers of increased cinema attendance, gambling, drinking and juvenile smoking cannot seriously be doubted. Total abstinence was recommended in the contemporary Officer's Manual as a condition of Boys' Brigade membership (boys were urged to sign a pledge), and smoking was forbidden in uniform, in camp and at all Brigade meetings, while great stress was laid in all Brigade handbooks on smartness, cleanliness and punctuality. One B.B. captain, making a declamatory appeal to 'traditional' values which in 1924 he saw as being undermined by mass leisure and anti-militarism, claimed:

> In the pseudo-pacificism now popular we are faced by a great danger that our nation may lose its ideals, and our youth grow up caring nought for the military virtues of sacrifice, discipline [and] hardihood — soaked in the soft luxury of the cinema and the glittering excitement of the sweep-stake. Against these at present we offer a life of duty, effort, drill. Every Boys' Brigade Officer knows how hard it is to keep Boys from sinking into the former, but also that there are still many Boys of grit who appreciate the latter, and who will be profoundly disgusted if The Boys' Brigade becomes 'soft'.

The new electric greyhound racing which came to the fore during the interwar years was, like the commercial cinema, condemned by The Boys' Brigade Executive in 1928 for demoralizing boys and seriously threatening the youth of the nation. 'So say all B.B. Officers, and especially those who have been in the ranks as Boys, and have experienced the temptations which beset a lad in office and workshop, and in his hours of leisure,' confirmed F.P. Gibbon's pamphlet *Sportsmen or Mugs?*, written to deter boys from the 'national curse' of betting and gambling:

> . . . so say thousands of men whose lives have been wrecked and who have been dragged down into the depths of misery because, at your age, when they had bright hopes of becoming honourable, useful and happy citizens, they did not realize what a Mug's Game gambling was.

At their best, such evangelical moral strictures may have served their function as a much-needed deterrent while, at their worst, attitudes such as these contributed to a certain social arrogance which bolstered a number of Church-appointed youth leaders in their role as moral arbiters of young people's leisure activities.[16]

Owing to its association in the popular mind with a currently unfashionable 'militarism', The Boys' Brigade also found itself out of step with that vocal section of public opinion in the 1930s — the pacifist movement. What has been loosely termed 'pacifism' gained most political weight in Britain between the start of the Manchurian Crisis in 1931 and the outbreak of the Italo-Ethiopian War in 1935. A remarkable leaflet was issued by Brigade Headquarters around 1930 entitled *The Torch of Peace*, which contained a Tom Curr frontispiece of the Unknown Warrior handing on the torch to two boys in Brigade uniform. The leaflet is worth citing in some detail for the light it sheds on the Brigade's ambivalence towards the growing support for pacifist sentiments in England and elsewhere:

> The Boys' Brigade stands for Peace. It fosters the international spirit, it encourages the study of the League of Nations, and so helps youth to visualize the world of their day leagued against the horror and wickedness of war. Yet there are still some people who think that The Boys' Brigade is military, if not even militarist, and they

Up to 1925-26, some companies drilled and paraded with dummy rifles. The abandonment of the rifle eased the path towards union with the Boys' Life Brigade in 1926.

The 1st Horsham Company of the Boys' Life Brigade prior to amalgamation with the B.B. The B.L.B. was founded in 1899 with an emphasis on lifesaving in place of military drill.

At the 1933 Jubilee Review in Queen's Park, Glasgow,
seventeen battalions of the B.B. paraded behind the 1st Glasgow Company,
while a massed pipe band of 637 pipers played 'Highland Laddie'.

The 1933 Jubilee Conventicle held in Hampden Park football ground,
Glasgow, attracted 130,000 people to the ground,
while another 100,000 were unable to gain entry.
This was the largest open-air service ever held in Britain.

Over Forth Bridge

Cheers at Belfast

The Start at Lowestoft

Midnight at Banbury Cross

*In 1935 to celebrate the Silver Jubilee of George V the B.B.
organized a marathon relay run of 2,300 miles from the extremities of
the British Isles, converging on London with a message for the King.
These pictures are from the Brigade's souvenir booklet.*

*At the 1937 Festival of Youth at the Empire Stadium in Wembley,
the B.B. gave the largest massed physical training display
ever staged in Britain.*

(*Central Press Photos Ltd.*)

point to our drill and marching, our ranks, our saluting, our discipline, even to our uniforms, bands and colours. Here, they say, you copy the army and, therefore, you must have a similar purpose and objective. This is the old fallacy of confusing the ends and the means.

Military forms of organization and a strict system of discipline were justified on the grounds of producing 'esprit de corps' and enabling large numbers of boys to be controlled and trained, 'without undue fuss and worry'. Since the League of Nations Union reached its peak of membership in 1931 when over 406,000 subscriptions were collected by local branches, The Boys' Brigade was anxious in this leaflet to draw attention to the fact that on the first Sunday in February company Bible Classes were to have a special lesson on the League and its work for peace. (It should also be noted that a B.B. Certificate was given for passing an examination on the League.) In conclusion the leaflet claimed:

> No organization in the world is keener on Peace than The Boys' Brigade. To-day the field is set between arrogant and narrow nationalism and Christian internationalism. With the Boys of to-day will lie the decision of world politics to-morrow, and the Brigade Boy, while dearly loving his own country, will learn to extend that love to all his fellow-citizens and stewards in God's Kingdom on earth. He holds aloft the Torch of Peace.

Whilst there is little doubt, in the final analysis, that the flowering of Christian pacifism in the 1930s was an integral part of British liberal Protestant culture, it should also be remembered that The Boys' Brigade emerged in the Glasgow of the 1880s from an evangelical culture of Christian militarism whose pedigree can be traced back to the same liberal Protestant sources.[17]

The Brigade managed to overcome the obstacles to its continued survival in an era of pacifism and anti-militarism and was to be at its most self-confident and expansive during the 1933 Golden Jubilee Celebrations held in Glasgow, the birthplace of the movement half a century earlier. If it is, perhaps, rather self-congratulatory that the biggest 'event' in the history of The Boys' Brigade between the two World Wars should be its own Jubilee, there is little doubt that the sheer numbers involved made this a milestone in youth work. Thus, while some details of the Executive's preparations for 1933 had varied, it was always intended that a boys' camp should be held to which two boys from every company in the Brigade would be invited to represent their comrades. This was also the year during which William H. McVicker, the full-time Honorary Secretary of the Belfast Battalion and son of the founder of the 1st Belfast Company, was invited by the Executive to come to Brigade Headquarters in London and take up the position of Secretary for the B.B. Overseas and for the Life Boys — an appointment which was to be of far-reaching significance for the development of the movement.

The Jubilee Celebrations were to take place in Glasgow from 8-11 September 1933, and the principal events, in addition to the Brigade Council meeting, were to include a reception for visiting officers on the Friday; a massed Review and Display, followed by a dinner and social gathering for officers, on the Saturday; a great Church Parade and open-air service or 'Conventicle' on the Sunday; and, to round off the long weekend, an excursion by special steamers for officers and boys on the Firth of Clyde on the Monday. The boys, encamped in their thousands just outside Glasgow at Dechmont, near Cambuslang, were to take part in the Saturday Review and Sunday's Church Parade — both of which were to be the largest ever seen in the history of The

Boys' Brigade. They paid 15/- (75p) each for four days and three nights with ar extra 4/6d. (23p) for each additional night, which included transport, meals entertainment and the Monday steamer excursion. Like many other 'old boys present on that historic weekend, ex-Staff Sergeant Charles Hovell of the 147th London Company claims that he will never forget the experience of being chosen to represent his company at Dechmont Camp. 'What a sight, I believe it was 2,500 lads from all over the world under canvas,' he recalls, '. . . line upor line of bell-tents, with at one end of each line the most enormous marquee I could ever imagine, [it] seemed as big as Buckingham Palace.' This was the dining and communal tent for each of the seventeen lines of 400 bell tents. The officers were billeted at Jordanhill College, outside the city centre, where because of the overcrowding, there was no room for beds and they slept or straw mattresses on the floor — all heads turned in line towards the wall.[18]

Bright and early on the Saturday morning of 9 September 1933, the fiftieth Annual Meeting of Brigade Council was held at Jordanhill College, with the much respected Colonel Sir John Roxburgh in the chair for the last time; the only item of business, apart from the adoption of the Annual Report, was the Executive's report to Council on the 'old boy' question. In the afternoon, the Brigade's impressive Jubilee Review took place at the Queen's Park Recreation Ground, near the Victoria Infirmary, where the inspecting officer was Prince George, later the Duke of Kent. 32,520 boys and officers were on parade with over 50,000 spectators crammed into the ground. Admission at the gate was 1/- (5p) standing, grandstand 5/- (25p) and car park 2/6d. (12½p) — 'Field glasses useful'. 'There were busy scenes in the Stations and streets before the Review began and by three o'clock there was a vast concourse of people on the slopes of the Queen's Park Recreation Ground, where for many years the Annual reviews of the Glasgow Battalion had been held,' ran the commentary of the Jubilee film. 'From every direction long columns of Boys continued to arrive until it seemed as if the huge field would hold no more.'

Leaving his car, H.R.H. Prince George stepped forward from the saluting base to acknowledge the Royal Salute from the seventeen battalions drawn up on parade, led by the 1st Glasgow. The National Anthem crashed forth from the massed brass bands in which hundreds of boys were playing. The massed pipe bands of the Glasgow Battalion almost formed a battalion in themselves as they marched along, and one policeman observed, 'What for do they have English horses to head the pipes?' After driving round the ranks, Prince George returned to the saluting base for the march past, 'and for three-quarters of an hour this great army of healthy happy Boyhood goes swinging past to the music of the bands. On they come, English, Scottish, Irish, Welsh and Boys from distant lands, all proud of The Boys' Brigade and the high ideals it stands for.' Aerial photographs taken during this occasion survive to give a vivid impression of the vast assembly gathered together on the Review Ground in honour of the Jubilee. 'Officers and Boys of The Boys' Brigade, this has been a great day in the history of the movement you represent,' ran Prince George's speech as scripted by the Brigade Secretary:

> I congratulate you on your march past, the displays, the playing of your bands and the march of a thousand pipers. I know many of you have come long distances to be present at the Review, and I am sure you must think it has been worthwhile to play your part in this historic event.[19]

That same evening, the 'Lady Visitors' were the guests of the Glasgow Area Life Boy Council at the Grand Hotel, and the officers were entertained to dinner in St. Andrew's Halls by the Glasgow Battalion. Members of Brigade

Council were initiated into the mysteries of 'piping in the haggis' and the English officers present bravely partook of this traditional Scottish dish. Arthur Jackson, an officer in the 4th Leeds Company, believes that as a result he was taken ill with severe enteritis and subsequently to his great chagrin missed the Sunday morning Church Parade. The splendid dinner was followed by the Jubilee Meeting at which the retiring President, Colonel Roxburgh, made the public announcement of the willingness of the Earl of Home, father of the future Prime Minister, to become his successor. There followed a short programme of special gymnastic displays and living friezes by the Glasgow Battalion teams and a speech in appreciation of The Boys' Brigade by Sir John Gilmour, Home Secretary in the National Government. In defending the afternoon's Review against charges of having a 'warlike tinge', he said:

> Those of us who have taken part in war, the South African War and the Great War, would not say that we desire to encourage what is sometimes called a military spirit. Discipline? Yes! Responsibility? Yes! But not necessarily a military spirit . . . I can assure you that the members of this National Government, men drawn from all sections of the community, realize that in such Movements as yours lies a great part of the strength, vitality and energy of our race . . .

Next, the sealed casket, containing the message from the boys of 1933 to those of 1983 and some mementos of the Jubilee, was brought from the camp at Dechmont by a guard of honour and handed over for safe-keeping until the Centenary. 'We, the Boys of 1933, on our Jubilee, give into your keeping this Casket, which contains a Message to those who follow us', said Sergeant Cameron G. Hizzey of the 1st Glasgow in a clear voice. 'We ask that you and your successors keep unbroken these seals until the Casket is delivered to those appointed to break them in the year 1983, on the Centenary of The Boys' Brigade.' (Of the six NCOs who signed the scroll only two are still alive at the time of writing.) After the Jubilee Celebrations were over, the casket was handed over for safe-keeping to the Museum and Art Galleries Department of the Glasgow Corporation.[20]

Sunday morning services and a meeting of the Brigade Executive at Jordanhill College followed the next day, for those who had recovered in time from the previous evening's haggis, and a 'Drumhead Service' was held at the Dechmont Camp attended by the Lord Provost of Glasgow. In the afternoon, there took place another memorable highlight of the Jubilee Celebrations: the spectacular 'Conventicle' held at Hampden Park, Mount Florida, the ground of Queen's Park Football Club. This was a vast open-air service of thanksgiving, conducted by the Moderator of the Church of Scotland and broadcast by microphone, which was attended by some 130,000 boys, 'old boys' and friends, with at least another 100,000 unable to get into the ground. 'As Companies will not be allowed to break-off inside the Ground, O.C. Companies must make necessary arrangements for Boys to relieve themselves before reaching Hampden Park,' the *Notes for Officers* sensibly warned. 'The Committee hopes that Officers will encourage hearty singing [and] ensure that the utmost reverence and discipline is preserved throughout the service.' The choice of the word 'Conventicle' derived from the simple religious meetings held secretly by the Scottish Covenanters in the seventeenth century 'under the canopy of heaven'. Whereas in the 1640s the Scottish Covenanters tried repeatedly without success to export their religious 'revolution' to England, The Boys' Brigade had peacefully invaded south of the Border without attempting to impose Presbyterian reforms on the recalcitrant English.[21]

The Conventicle at Hampden Park — not to be repeated until the 1954 Council in Glasgow — was probably the largest open-air service ever held in Scotland, taking place in probably the second largest enclosure in the world at that time. It stood in Boys' Brigade terms for 'Devotion to an Ideal', whereas the Review had represented 'Drill and Discipline' incarnate. 'For several hours beforehand the streets were congested with Boys and men accompanied by their friends and tens of thousands of Old Boys marched in orderly columns from the centre of the city,' recounts the official film commentary:

> Hampden Park is the largest football arena in Great Britain but it could not nearly accommodate all who wanted to attend this service. Long before the Service began the gates had to be closed . . . The Glasgow transport officials say that the crowds far exceeded the attendance at any international football match. Such a gathering was a tribute to the high place The Boys' Brigade holds in the hearts of the people of Glasgow.

Thousands of people who were unable to get tickets were locked outside the ground and made violent attempts to break down the gates. The Moderator, poet-preacher the Right Rev. Dr Lauchlan McLean Watt, entered the pulpit, and after the Colours had been deposited ceremonially on the drums, conducted the singing of psalms, the reading of the Sermon on the Mount, and gave an address based on The Boys' Brigade motto, Hebrews 6:19. 'No one who was present on this day will ever forget the sight of this vast throng,' as one report put it. 'The volume of praise which arose as they sang the old Scottish Psalms was heard miles away.' If the Conventicle represented the climax to this weekend of celebration and thanksgiving, the seal was not set until the Devotional Service was held for officers that evening in St. Andrew's Hall. 'The most uniformly alive Christian congregation I have ever worshipped with,' was how the Rev. George F. MacLeod afterwards described his impression of the officers who took part in this service which, apart from the setting alight of the 'Fire of Friendship' beacon at Dechmont Camp, concluded Jubilee Sunday.[22]

Although the pageantry of this most momentous weekend in the history of The Boys' Brigade was now over, the celebrations continued with the steamer excursion on Monday 11 September 1933 for both officers and boys. Two specially chartered turbine steamers, the *Duchess of Hamilton* and the *Queen Mary*, were filled with visiting officers and friends, while two more, the *Duchess of Argyll* and the *Jupiter*, were crowded with boys from the Dechmont Camp. The boys went by special trains direct from Kirkhill Station to Wemyss Bay and then sailed across to the Isle of Bute and through the Kyles of Bute, whereas the officers took the more traditional route to the island by sailing from either Broomielaw or Bridge Wharf in Glasgow down the Clyde. Eric Chapman, then a Lieutenant in the 4th Plymouth Company, remembers passing the 'great rusty hulk' of what was to become the Cunarder *Queen Mary* in John Brown's silent, empty shipyard in Clydebank — a significant memory of the Depression in Scotland, for when work was resumed it was taken as a sign of recovery. Passing Dumbarton Rock, the attention of the officers' steamers was drawn to the great banner of welcome put up by the 1st Dumbarton Company on the face of the cliff. On approaching the Kyles of Bute, the excursion vessels began to keel over a little when the officers' and the boys' steamers passed each other going in opposite directions and everybody rushed to the side to exchange cheers of greeting. Similarly, when the steamers passed the little island of Eilean Bhuide (Yellow Isle) in the Kyles, near Colintraive, the boats keeled over again in response to the boys of the 1st Rothesay Company who had put up a big greetings banner and then let off rockets. Another welcome came further through the Kyles from the 1st Kyles of Bute Company at Auchenlochan Pier, which was crowded with children given a school holiday in the Brigade's honour. (This was, of course, the site of the first ever Boys' Brigade camp held in 1886 by William Smith and the 1st Glasgow.) Lunch was supplied on board the steamers and the time went by happily enough with singing and attempts at Highland dancing, until in mid-afternoon Wemyss Bay was reached once more, where all the excursionists disembarked to the strains of 'Auld Lang Syne' followed by 'Abide with Me' — returning to the city's Central Station by five special trains and thence homewards. Thus the 1933 Jubilee Celebrations were at last officially over and, as the Moderator put it appropriately in his address to the Coventicle, 'The little boat launched prayerfully in Glasgow fifty years since has become a fleet freighted with all good'.[23]

The further consolidation of The Boys' Brigade in the aftermath of the 1933 Jubilee took place against a much more sombre international background, in which the seeds of another world war were already planted with the accession to power in Germany of Hitler and the Nazis. In a speech delivered on 24 October 1936 to the second annual dinner of the Wolverhampton Battalion, the Brigade President, the Earl of Home, made these gathering tensions clear when he pointed out to the assembled officers that

> ... something was desperately wrong with the world at the present time, and other countries were looking towards England to give them the right lead. England was doing this, but it was a godsend that in this country were old members of The Boys' Brigade, the Scouts, and other youth organizations, who had kept their heads. These men had never allowed themselves to be 'rattled', and others, fortunately following their example, had not become 'rattled' either. He was convinced that the future of the country depended, to a great extent, on its boys and girls.

The contemporary instability of European politics was exemplified by the German reoccupation of the Rhineland's demilitarized zone in March 1936 and the outbreak of the Spanish Civil War in July of that year. At home, the economy was showing some signs of recovery, and in the General Election of November 1935, the National Government kept enough coalition support to give them a majority of 247 M.P.'s over all the opposition parties combined, with Stanley Baldwin effortlessly taking over from Ramsay MacDonald as Prime Minister. In general, this was a period of gradual but steady improvement in the British economy, except for the so-called 'distressed areas' of South Wales, the Northeast and Northwest, and the industrial areas of lowland Scotland. Such depressed regions spoilt the picture of economic recovery painted by the National Government, and it was this economic contrast between the 'modest advance' in living standards for the majority and the poverty of a substantial minority which provided the basis for the historically misleading image of the 'hungry thirties'.[24]

The first week-long Brigade residential Officers' Training School was held during the week 2 to 9 June 1934 at 'Bolobo', a country house near Edgware named after a Baptist mission station in the Belgian Congo. The course attracted twenty-one students and eight staff instructors and became the forerunner of a regular annual event. In November 1934 a bill, the Depressed Areas (Development and Improvement) Bill, was introduced at Westminster to provide, among other things, for the appointment of unpaid Commissioners — one for England and Wales and one for Scotland — to initiate and assist measures for the 'economic development and social improvement of the depressed areas', a phrase the House of Lords squeamishly changed to 'special areas'. A grant of £2 million was provided which allowed the Commissioners to allocate money to local authorities, but this was clearly inadequate in areas where, for example, there was little local finance to provide full-time youth workers and few appropriate bodies to help start improvement schemes. One of the voluntary bodies to which the Commissioners for the Special Areas gave assistance in 1935 was the National Council of Social Service (N.C.S.S.) which, in turn, made money available to The Boys' Brigade and other national youth organizations to help finance projects which would assist youth in the 'distressed areas'. Dennis Webb, then on the Brigade Executive, remembers Stanley Smith pulling out the crucial letter from the N.C.S.S. while they were travelling up to a meeting together by train. The Brigade's Annual Report for the session 1934-35 summarized these developments:

> The Government Commissioners for the officially scheduled 'Special Areas' . . . where industrial depression is particularly acute, have, by means of grants, enabled the Executive to do much to alleviate the difficulties under which B.B. Companies in these districts have had to carry on their work. With the guidance of active local Committees and suitable Boys' Brigade organizers assistance has been given towards the training of Officers, increased camping facilities, and the provision of premises and equipment. Many suspended Companies have been revived and new ones started and, what is more, Officers and Boys have been given new hope and fresh enthusiasm to go forward and overcome the apathy and depression which are the outcome of prolonged industrial distress.[25]

Indirectly, then, The Boys' Brigade — for the first time in its history — was in receipt of Government financial aid, so providing the unprecedented opportunity of administering State funds to encourage further expansion, in particular among the coalfield towns worst hit by the Depression. A Brigade Development Committee was set up by the Executive, chaired by Farrar Vickers from Leeds and with Stanley Smith as Secretary, with the responsibility for overseeing the distribution of these funds (totalling £1,800 during 1935 alone) by linking up Headquarters in London with the Brigade authorities in the 'special areas', 'as it might think best for increasing its personnel or for making small grants in aid of equipment or other needs that are holding back the extension of its work'. Further, as a result initially of the N.C.S.S. grant, the Brigade was able to pay the salaries of its first full-time Organizing Secretaries — forerunners of the Field Officers — in the 'special areas' of Northumberland and Durham, and Monmouthshire, South Wales. The Brigade's Development Committee was convinced that there was a vast field ripe for extension on the Northeast coast. At the Tyne Valley Battalion Council meeting held on 18 February 1935, the long-serving Battalion Chairman, Dr Alfred Swindale, captain of three 'pit-village' companies, gave details of how the district grant for Brigade extension was to be spent locally on camping facilities, training courses, assistance for new companies, hiring of local halls, and various other schemes for increasing local company membership. Grants of up to £5,500 (a large sum in those days) were also made available from 1935 to 1937 by the Commissioner for the Scottish 'special area' to stimulate and extend the work of the Brigade in the industrial belt of West-Central Scotland.[26]

The Brigade received another well-merited windfall in March 1935 when the

King George's Jubilee Trust was set up as a permanent commemoration of twenty-five years of George V's reign. The aim of the Trust was to 'advance the physical, mental and spiritual welfare of boys and girls, particularly during that difficult period in their lives from the time they leave school up to the age of eighteen'. When the Trust was inaugurated, it was suggested that its immediate work should be to assist and extend the work of the already existing and proven voluntary youth organizations, because their long experience already provided a firm structure on which to build. This cautiousness meant that organizations like the ten-year-old Woodcraft Folk, which lacked the reassuring solidity and social respectability of the Scouts and the Brigades, did not benefit from the Trust. During the first three years of its existence, the Trust spent £100,000 annually, and by 1950 grants totalling approximately £750,000 had been made, although by the latter date the amount being distributed among youth organizations had declined to about £80,000 a year. In 1938, with the aid of a generous grant from the Trust, James Jack was appointed full-time Brigade Training Officer for Scotland and Ireland and S.E. Barnes was made Training Officer for England and Wales, working from Abbey House. Stanley Smith, asked by the Trust as to where the need for development was greatest in The Boys' Brigade, cited in reply the following areas: parts of the country where there were new housing estates, the 'special areas', London and the Home Counties (rapidly increasing in population in the 1930s), and the populous districts of Lancashire and the West Riding of Yorkshire. 'The interest in boys' work which has been aroused by the formation of King George's Jubilee Trust made the time opportune for Battalions to inaugurate extension work,' a Development Committee Report concluded, 'and it was felt that every effort should be made to awaken all Battalions to a new interest in development.' Further Government encouragement was forthcoming in 1937 from the Physical Training and Recreation Act which provided grants for P.T. classes in schools and for the development of playing fields, summer camps, and recreation or youth centres. The National Fitness Council set up by the Act financed a full-time P.T. Organiser for the B.B., but it has to be said of it that 'never was so much spent by so few with so little result', and it was dissolved two years later on the outbreak of war. Nonetheless, the Act was passed with the good intention of encouraging both local authority and voluntary initiatives that would contribute towards raising the level of national fitness. Unfortunately, however, it made little impact in the areas where help was needed most.[27]

That The Boys' Brigade possessed a strong flair for attracting public attention in the 1930s has already been exemplified by their own Golden Jubilee Celebrations in Glasgow. This was to be followed in 1935 by the 'Jubilee Run', and in 1937 by their participation in the Festival of Youth. To begin with, let us look at the Brigade's involvement in King George V's Silver Jubilee, remembering that he was the Brigade Patron from 1897 (when Duke of York) until his death in 1936. In the mid 1930s, celebrations such as took place for the King's Jubilee were unprecedented for a reign of a mere twenty-five years, and some critics saw in it merely another stunt by the National Government to restore its lost popularity. Yet these critics were soon forgotten amidst the pageantry in London and the provinces, in the dominions and the outposts of Empire, which paid homage to the King in processions, church services and military reviews. The institution of monarchy had never seemed stronger in Britain, and the wearer of the Crown himself never more popular, but within two years the old King had died and his successor, Edward VIII, had abdicated, as the country moved towards a numb acceptance of the certainty of war. The King's Silver Jubilee in 1935 was, therefore, a moment for retrospection, for commemoration of the quarter century of King George's reign, only to be surpassed forty-two years later when his granddaughter was Queen. 'In times of trouble, when thrones had tottered and decent governments crumbled, the King was unchanging, a reassurance of the solidity and continuity of things,' as Charles Loch Mowat's magisterial history puts it. 'Time had made him the father of his people, the father of the peoples of the empire.' It is hardly surprising in such an atmosphere that a loyal organization such as The Boys' Brigade should heed Stanley Smith's plea for a participatory event in honour of their Patron during Jubilee year.[28]

The initial suggestion for The Boys' Brigade to put on a Silver Jubilee Run came from Dennis Webb, who had joined the Executive in 1932 to represent the West Midland District. 'I thought of something like a Run with a Message to the King in celebration of the Jubilee,' he explained in an interview, 'to be carried by Boys from the various extremities of Britain and conveyed by relays of runners [so that] as many Boys as possible could take part.' The general plan was that a pair of B.B. relay runners were to escort a boy, the holder of a B.B. King's Badge, carrying a message held aloft in a silver baton surmounted by the Brigade crest. The message would be read to the assembled crowds in market squares or on town hall steps by the local mayor and then transmitted on to another message-bearer for the next, approximately four-mile, lap of the journey. The Brigade's message to the King would thus be carried from hand to hand across the length and breadth of Britain and read out at each relay point, sometimes in the middle of the night. It was also planned that the arrival of the final bearers and their escorts at the Royal Albert Hall in London should be carefully synchronized, so that they could all deliver their messages personally to the Duke of York (the future George VI). Starting points for the Jubilee Run were selected at John O'Groats, Land's End, Londonderry, Neath, and Lowestoft, so that in all 2,309 miles would have to be transversed by nearly as many runners, all of which required careful organization by the Brigade and readily forthcoming local cooperation.[29]

Over two weeks after the first bearers had set off, the runners converged on London and the Albert Hall, where a Boys' Brigade Jubilee Display was in progress, 'poised in expectancy waiting for the great moment to arrive'. The first message-bearer handed his baton to the Duke of York on 16 May 1935 to cheers from the crowd, the same performance being repeated for the other four messages to the King. Thus ended the Jubilee 'Marathon Run'. As the Souvenir Booklet put it with pardonable use of hyperbole:

> . . . not since the days of Ancient Greece had there been anything to equal this enterprise. Light of heart and fleet of foot, these Boys would carry the Message by day and night through crowded cities, along country lanes, over highland and moorland, to their beloved Sovereign.

Certainly, it is apparent that well-coordinated and well-organized events such as this helped to draw considerable and welcome national attention to The Boys' Brigade through the extensive press coverage and photo-publicity which they received. In a less confident era of Brigade development similar 'Runs', undertaken for the Festival of Britain in 1951 and for the Headquarters' Appeal Fund in 1961, simply did not receive the same media coverage as the Jubilee Run.[30]

Two years after the Jubilee Run, as part of the 1937 Festival of Youth, The

Boys' Brigade were to give the largest massed physical training display ever staged in Britain, at the Empire Stadium in Wembley. In the same year that Parliament passed the Physical Training and Recreation Act, it can be seen that such a rally not only drew public attention to the work of voluntary youth organizations but also demonstrated what was already being done by them in developing the national physique. This was not the only inference to be drawn, unfortunately, for there was a genuine fear in some quarters that the aim of physical training was to train youth for war. 'Scaremongers declare that their fears are proved because the Physical Training Bill and the Rearmament programme have been produced simultaneously; they speak as if physical training were some new-fangled craze,' the Festival Programme complained plaintively:

> The truth is that the present 'drive' towards national fitness is simply the outcome of the work of Government Departments, voluntary organizations and individuals during the last thirty or more years. The Central Council of Recreative Physical Training, which during the past two years has done much to extend physical recreation all over the country, was formed some time before there was any talk of launching the Rearmament programme.

Besides providing an opportunity for the various youth movements present to celebrate the Coronation, the genuine interest in the Festival was to assist the King George Jubilee Trust financially, enliven public interest in organized youth activities, and stimulate the desire for physical fitness and healthy recreation. The Festival was organized by the British Sports and Games Association in conjunction with the Central Council of Recreative Physical Training, with the aim that the work displayed would be demonstrative of the work performed by the Jubilee Trust, which received the proceeds of the Festival.[31]

On 3 July 1937, under a blue sky and in brilliant sunshine, the opening display item at the Festival was provided by The Boys' Brigade. 'Headed by the finest B.B. Massed Band the writer has ever heard, more than 800 Boys, all over fourteen, drawn from the London District, marched into the arena with a style and precision that called forth loud applause from the vast assembly of spectators,' reported the *Gazette*. This huge Boys' Brigade display team completely filled the Wembley arena, performing firstly a training tableau and then a series of exercises to music, producing 'the marvellous effect of the co-ordinated rhythm of hundreds of healthy Boys . . .' The Brigade certainly merited the applause it received for this display, considering that adequate rehearsal, under the supervision of Brigade P.T. Organizer Major F.W. Stevens, had only been made possible by means of gramophone records. The Brigade also provided a representative detachment for the march past the King and Queen, and, together with other boys' organizations, took part in the gymnastic games item. The Brigade Secretary, Stanley Smith, was presented to the newly crowned King George VI and Queen Elizabeth and the little Princesses before they left the stadium, and was told by the King that the Brigade's physical training item was 'splendid'. At a similar rally of Scottish youth held at Murrayfield, Edinburgh, on 8 July 1937, over 6,000 boys from all parts of Scotland attended to represent The Boys' Brigade. The many spectators and families who travelled long distances to these rallies must have felt proud of their sons' performances. Certainly, the B.B.'s prominent part in the Festival of Youth, unrivalled by that of any other youth organization, was a triumphant vindication of the worth of Brigade training methods.[32]

Under the umbrella of Government orthodoxy, as the preceding pages have indicated, tentative attempts were made by the State during the 1930s to assist in local youth work, using financial instruments which would have been anathema not long before. The Boys' Brigade undoubtedly benefited from such Government policies, but neither grants to finance voluntary youth work in the 'special areas' nor the national drive towards physical fitness can wholly explain the movement's conspicuous growth during these years. The lead in 'development' given by a strong Executive Committee — consisting of men like J.H. Early, Charles Widlake, Farrar Vickers, Dr Alfred Swindale, John Chalmers and Dennis Webb — provided a contribution of equal importance to the Brigade's expansion during the Depression years. Ex-servicemen returning to Brigade work after the First World War did a great deal to boost leadership recruitment, and membership of Boys' Brigade officers in the Territorial Army was maintained at a consistently high level throughout the interwar period. The effect of all this was that, after an initial drop in 1919 to 43,000 boys, the Brigade showed a steady increase in numbers from 1921 onwards, reaching well over 60,000 even before amalgamation with the Boys' Life Brigade, which brought their total boy figure (excluding Life Boys) to 78,000, and culminating in 1934 when the movement reached its highest point at 96,000 total U.K. boy membership.

As Brigade Secretary, Stanley Smith — in office for fourteen years by the outbreak of the Second World War — contributed to these figures by providing inspired leadership and by making it his business to travel the British Isles to be present at company and battalion inspections on an almost constant basis. The service of the hundreds of anonymous voluntary officers at the local level who gave up their leisure to help extend and sustain the growth achieved during this period should also be remembered. All of these factors help to explain why The Boys' Brigade had more boys and companies in the mid 1930s than at any time before or since in its history, but each taken alone is inadequate to account for the fact that the Brigade increased its boy membership at a faster rate proportionally than any other uniformed British youth movement between the Wars.

CHAPTER 6

'WE WILL CARRY ON'

The Boys' Brigade Overseas, 1914 to 1945

SIR WILLIAM SMITH, as we have seen, died convinced that the movement he founded had compromised its position too readily in some countries of the British Empire, particularly in the dominions, and certainly in the U.S.A. After 1914 the home movement was naturally more concerned with problems of wartime survival and reorganization than with overseas development. In the 1920s the efforts to reconstruct and negotiate union with the Boys' Life Brigade, together with other changes, absorbed much energy on the home front, to the continued detriment, we must conclude, of a coordinated forward-thinking international Brigade policy. At the Glasgow Battalion Review of May 1917, no less an Imperial personage than Sir Joseph Ward, ex-Premier of New Zealand, made it plain in his address to the B.B. sergeants that in his country the Cadet Training Scheme in schools was achieving all that 'The Boys' Brigade were engaged in' in Britain. In the Annual Report of 1919-20 the optimistic hope was expressed that 'we shall no doubt soon regain at least our prewar position'. But throughout the 1920s, despite renewed prosperity in most dominions, in the majority of formerly strong Brigade countries this was not to be. Only with the onset of the Great Depression did a sometimes quite spectacular revival take place in the white dominions and elsewhere overseas. In the face of this renewed momentum the Brigade Executive, still the controlling body for all work throughout the Empire and overseas (except for the officially-styled 'brother movements' of the U.S.A. and Denmark), was forced to adopt a positive, directing stance towards its branches abroad in order to avoid the old prewar problems. This policy became clearer after the Golden Jubilee in 1933 when William McVicker was appointed Overseas Secretary. In the 1930s The Boys' Brigade demonstrated that it had learned well the lessons of 1890-1914.[1]

In the 1930s The Boys' Brigade became so well established in many places that the vicissitudes of the Second World War actually had a strengthening effect on the movement's morale and organization, if not necessarily on the numbers retained. In the Antipodes the arrival of Japanese forces at the 'front door', so to speak, after their cataclysmic attack on Pearl Harbour in December 1941 only temporarily halted the already steady growth in New Zealand and some parts of Australia. 'We will carry on' was the brave message from a beleaguered Singapore in 1942. Even the leaner 1920s held strong clues to this growth and the eventual emergence of independent national Boys' Brigade Councils. Throughout that decade certain companies survived to form the base for revival, and new units arose in countries and regions where the movement had formerly been weak or nonexistent. Among the latter were New Zealand, the South Pacific and Asia. All these successes foretold a new and more vigorous internationalism in Brigade affairs. The success rested mainly upon a firm adherence, actively pursued from London throughout the

1930s, to William Smith's original methods. Posthumously the Founder's influence became more potent overseas than during his lifetime.

Outside Britain itself there were fewer more successful representatives of Smith's actual practical B.B. philosophies than his own former First Lieutenant in the 1st Glasgow, George Orr. Founder Captain of the 1st Brisbane Company at the inner-suburb of Red Hill (Ithaca Presbyterian Church) in March 1913, Orr had grown up in a humble working-class home in North Woodside Road, Glasgow, directly opposite the pioneer B.B. Company. Losing his father early in life he joined the 1st Glasgow in 1887. Ill-disciplined and 'a little savage', Orr, according to 1st Glasgow legend, caused the hall-keeper at North Woodside Mission to remark that he 'wad pizzen the hale squad' if allowed into the ranks. But, in that finest of B.B. schools, Orr was firmly taken in hand by the man he came to revere. In 1890-91 he rose to staff-sergeant and became for nineteen years one of Smith's most able lieutenants, being entrusted with the company leadership during Smith's travels to Canada and the U.S.A. Excelling as gymnast and bandsman, Orr also attended the first B.B. camps at Tighnabruaich and Auchenlochan, and became an excellent Bible Class teacher. Whilst qualifying as a master plumber Orr developed his own modest business. In 1911 he visited the Scottish National Exhibition in Glasgow and was attracted by the call for sanitary plumbers and tradesmen to emigrate to Queensland, Australia, where public works were being rapidly extended, especially around Brisbane. In 1912, carrying Smith's written testimonial to his 'great capacity for training the Boys', Orr emigrated to Queensland with his family and one employee, Archie McDonald, an ex-sergeant of the 1st Glasgow.[2]

Appointed an elder at Ithaca in 1914, Orr remained absolutely undeterred by the unfavourable official attitude towards non-Cadet uniformed organizations in Australia. Most certainly fully briefed by Smith, Orr may also have read the depressing reports coming from that most intelligent observer of Australian youth affairs, B.G. Pattersen. Pattersen ('Banjo' to his friends) we have already encountered as the jaunty, determined Captain of the 1st Mount Morgan B.B.-Scout Company in mid-Queensland. 'He would need to be a very optimistic Officer', Pattersen had told the Brigade world in 1911, 'who would undertake to work a B.B. Company on home lines in the face of . . . the most excellent scheme of Junior Cadet training adopted by the Commonwealth [i.e. Australian Federal] Government.' But with true Scots determination, Orr launched his new 1st Brisbane Company with William Smith's full B.B. programme: drill (with rifles), Bible Class, band, 'Ambulance', signalling, gymnastics, camping, and strict discipline. His home was, like Smith's, thrown open for NCOs' and squad teas. In 1915 he even presented two 'King's Men' to Glasgow, only to have the application disallowed because, technically, the service of the two candidates during the company's foundation year, 1913, was not recognized at Headquarters. Fittingly, Orr's first residence in Paddington, Brisbane, was named 'Woodside'. The announcement of his company's registration appeared in the 'Memorial Number' of the B.B. Gazette in June 1914, an issue devoted almost completely to the death and funeral of the 'Chief', William Alexander Smith. As Britain mourned that event, 12,000 miles away Orr led his new company in tribute to the Founder who had made him the man he was and whose ideas would make hundreds of Queensland boys proud to belong to an organization bearing the name 'The Boys' Brigade', especially when, twenty years later, worried men tried to take that name from them. The annals of the 1st Brisbane, a company still in existence, show that on that day of mourning the sturdy, determined Glaswegian plumber wept unashamedly.[3]

Parading fifty-four strong in 1915, the War notwithstanding, the 1st Brisbane grew apace. In that year Major Pendlebury of the Queensland Military Command declared himself 'astounded' at the company's bearing and standards. For years afterwards Orr, shrewdly aware of the effect, invariably invited inspecting officers from the local military to review his company. By 1919-20 a separate drill hall was constructed for the 1st Brisbane alongside its parent church. 'Banjo' Pattersen, although totally unimpressed with Orr's performance as an Australian bushman camper, confessed, after visiting Brisbane, that Orr had 'altered everything — he proved that a company *could* be run on perfectly orthodox lines'. In 1922 Major-General Bruche declared after an inspection that 'never in forty years of his military experience had he seen a higher standard of correctness and smartness amongst cadets' than that presented by the Brisbane Company. By 1914 it had 144 members (all ranks) and, becoming the subject of considerable viceregal and wider attention, was acknowledged as 'one of the finest Boys' institutions in the Metropolis [of Brisbane]'. Yet it was destined to exist in almost complete isolation in Australia throughout the 1920s. Brigade work did start intermittently in Perth and Fremantle (Western Australia), and Pattersen established a second B.B.-Scout unit in Rockhampton, Queensland. Some churches and groups in Queensland tried to imitate Orr's work, but most such experiments collapsed. Working from Richmond Baptist Church in Adelaide, Albert Green, generously supported by his old company, the 37th London in Balham, accomplished a most effective work among the poorer boys of the city's inner suburbs. But in 1932-33, with many boys undernourished and Green unemployed himself, the 1st Adelaide was grossly undermined by a minister's obdurate design to limit membership to 'Baptist Boys' alone. True to the Brigade tradition, Green closed his company rather than submit to shortsighted denominationalism.[4]

Orr died in 1929, not living to see the ultimate revival of the movement in his adopted country. Rightly described as 'a pointer to the Founder', Orr left a legacy which was continued vigorously by his 'old boys', and one which could not go for ever without successful emulation. In 1929 the 1st Sydney Company commenced in Glebe Presbyterian Church, New South Wales. This initiated in Sydney the recommencement of a work based directly on the Brisbane example. In the same year, inspired by B.B. immigrants from New Zealand, the Brigade was restarted in Melbourne, Victoria. The scene was thus set in Australia for enduring renewal in the 1930s.[5]

The 1st Brisbane was a conspicuously successful B.B. Company by any standards throughout the 1920s. Why, we might ask, did the movement therefore not revive more quickly in Australia? Orr, it must be admitted, did remain somewhat parochial and insular, proving to be no great 'extension man'. But the social causes of Brigade stagnation were many and complex. After the First World War, the ANZAC troops from Australia and New Zealand, having lost nearly 80,000 dead in the Imperial cause, returned home to grateful peoples. Increasingly, however, many Australians felt that their debts to the mother country had been adequately repaid. After the rude interruption of the War, people wanted to get back to the more positive tasks of building a nation, and settling and taming a harsh but supposedly limitless continent. Occupied with their new short-lived 'booms', many people had little time for a seemingly militaristic movement like The Boys' Brigade. Scouting, with its new emphasis on peaceful reconstruction and great brotherly international jamborees, satisfied the temporary Australian revulsion against militarism. The League of Nations euphoria, the revival of romantic utopianism, and the new international pacifism, so actively espoused in the postwar Scouting movement, were widely welcomed, especially among the increasingly prosperous skilled working class and lower middle class in Australia and the other dominions. Scouting, therefore, grew. Many churches and their leaders in Australia were still suspicious of the way in which The Boys' Brigade had so easily been militarized a decade before (see Chapter 3). (In New Zealand, few Church leaders fully shared these suspicions, since the Brigade, militarized or otherwise, had never been so prominent there before World War I.) Subsequent history has shown that in the influential and populous state of Victoria, where the militarization of The Boys' Brigade had been swiftest and strongest, the movement would never gain the per capita 'popularity' as a proportion of the population of its more vigorous branches in New South Wales, Queensland or Western Australia.[6]

The 1920s also witnessed the climax of a development on the Chinese mainland which captured the imagination of the B.B. world, and eventually spilled over into the colony of Singapore. The advent of ethnic Chinese into The Boys' Brigade was to prove one of its major and enduring success stories overseas.

In 1915, then only twenty-five years of age, the Rev. A. Guthrie Gamble, a former student at Cambridge with Donald Finnemore (future B.L.B. then B.B. leader) and sometime Captain of the 6th Cambridge Company, went to South China as a missionary of the Presbyterian Church of England to run a mission school at Swatow (subsequently renamed Shantou). Firmly convinced that the B.B. method was relevant to Chinese boys, he soon commenced the 1st Swatow Company, securing its registration in August 1917. Very soon two more companies were operating at Wukingfu and Shanghang, and in 1920-21 a South China Battalion of seven companies and 650 boys was formed. Gamble overcame initial Chinese prejudice against foreign institutions — a prejudice scarcely surprising in the light of a century of European interference and intervention — by running the Brigade along strictly orthodox lines. 'Loyalty and discipline' were virtues especially coveted by the mercantile Chinese of Swatow and district. Many southern Chinese had forged strong family and commercial links with emigrant groups in the thriving Chinese communities in the Straits Settlements (now Singapore and Malaysia), the Philippines and Java. In due time The Boys' Brigade Institute in Swatow, established and built with funds raised by the South China Auxiliary formed in Britain after Gamble's furlough lecture tour in 1923-24, attracted the sons of many of those widely dispersed emigrant families. The Swatow Brigade's reputation was widely known throughout the trading settlements of Southeast Asia. A well-trained B.B. Red Cross unit operated in Swatow itself and was frequently called out to assist at emergencies following one of the many natural disasters, principally typhoons, floods and earthquakes, to which the region is prone. The movement soon earned a special place in the affections of the local people who flocked, 50,000 strong, to the annual half-day demonstrations, dazzlingly efficient affairs of drill and all forms of physical recreation carried out in a carnival atmosphere. The B.B. Anchor became known locally as 'The sign of love in action'.[7]

By the mid-1920s, however, deteriorating civil and political unrest throughout China threatened to disrupt the B.B. work in Swatow. Canton's declaration of independence from the Republic of China in 1921, the election of Sun Yat-sen as President and his death in 1925, and the swift revival, with Russian help, of his Kuomintang (Nationalist) party all led to an intensifying of the unrest. Some Nationalists deeply resented Russian domination in Chinese affairs and this led to war with the Communists. The Southern forces of Chiang Kai-shek took Peking and in 1927 established a government in Nanking to oppose the Communists based in Wuhan. In 1928 Chiang Kai-shek was declared President in the Nationalist Government, although its authority was partial and precarious in the north and south. In Swatow and environs the Christian Church and The Boys' Brigade operated in the late 1920s by grace and favour of the local Communist administration.

After his return from Britain Gamble found the 1st Swatow Company under his Chinese lieutenants as steady and active as ever. By 1925-26 a deeper indigenization of Brigade work had taken place. The end of the B.B. session in May 1926 saw the 'first rumblings [of] persecution' around Swatow:

> In the succeeding months, when anti-foreign feeling ran high [reported Gamble], the Boys behaved magnificently. They have yielded to none in true patriotism, but they have refused to be stampeded into senseless vituperation of foreigners, and the relations between us have never been better. In the face of considerable personal risk, and — from the Boys' point of view still harder to bear — much scorn and ridicule, they have borne abundant witness to the strength of the bond that unites us in the great brotherhood of the B.B.

In September 1926 the Brigade Council telegraphed its sympathy to Swatow. Two months later the city came 'entirely under Bolshevik control', and 'the anti-foreign agitation' developed into 'a fierce anti-Christian campaign'. The Boys' Brigade was 'singled out for an onslaught of particular vigour and venom . . . our headquarters were looted, roll-books and records were destroyed, and worse violence threatened unless the Company dispersed within two days'. The order was ignored and no absentee was recorded from the weekly parades. But a price was exacted when the first lieutenant was arrested and thrown with 'some fifty criminals' into a 'filthy cell . . . amid indescribable filth'. In December the abolition of the B.B. Bible Class was decreed. 'If we refused we were to be regarded as criminals and outcasts. We could give but one reply — that the terms were impossible. The B.B. stood for Christ, and to surrender on that point would be to surrender its soul.'[8]

The B.B. hall now came under constant surveillance; boys were violently handled and 'mob attacks' became more frequent. The odds and pressures were too great and by early 1927 parades ceased temporarily and the boys gathered daily 'in little groups' at Gamble's house for solace. In that first year of overt persecution Gamble baptized many boys but could accept only forty per cent of the hundred recruits applying to join the Company. By 1927-28 a 'reign of terror' prevailed in South China: thousands of deaths by torture, including two boys of 8th South China Company and a parent of 1st Swatow; the 'martyrdom' of Church ministers and officials; and many other acts of personal and corporate violence. The B.B. Institute frequently served as a refuge, and on several occasions even came under fire. During 1928 no parade was abandoned and forty-five boys received baptism. By 1929 even the most heroic stoicism could resist no longer, and Gamble wisely closed 1st Swatow, South China's only surviving unit. Soon afterwards foreigners were ejected from the region.

Gamble returned to Britain to a lifetime of Brigade service as Captain of the 6th London Company in Bayswater. The spirit of Swatow was revived, as we shall see, very soon afterwards in Singapore. The stories of these dramatic years in 'revolutionary China' stunned the home movement in Britain and the Brigade world generally, becoming the material for many a Bible Class talk and the 'inspiration' of stories respun for Sunday Schools and other young people, in which, it must be said, fancy sometimes eschewed fact. More soberly — but certainly mindful of the effect — the Brigade Executive published in 1929 a twopenny sixteen-page pamphlet entitled *A Record of Heroism: The Story of The Boys' Brigade in China*, retelling in Gamble's own words (some already published in the *B.B. Gazette*) the story of Swatow. In so doing, it missed — with very good if naive intent — one of the prime lessons of the South China years: the ability of indigenous non-European populations to adopt and internalize the Brigade movement. In patronizingly offering 'financial assistance to new Companies enrolled in a foreign Mission Station *under the charge of a qualified European*' [my italics], Brigade Executive demonstrated how conservative in reality was its attitude towards overseas expansion during the 1920s and early 1930s.[9]

Certainly *one* strength of Brigade expansion overseas at this formative period lay in the missionary support given to charismatic individuals, mostly Europeans, and to missionary causes and societies prepared to further the B.B. method. But Gamble's Swatow story, whilst inspiring many during the drab and depressed 1930s, had its real sequel and significance in the Brigade's rise and survival in that ultimately vulnerable pivot of British Far Eastern fortunes: Singapore. The significance was, of course, that the Chinese embraced the movement *in their own way*. Europeans certainly provided initial and then sometimes joint leadership, but in all countries, in all situations, the revival and survival of The Boys' Brigade depended ultimately upon the local officers' ability to adapt, develop and eventually to govern the movement along lines suitable and acceptable to their particular circumstances. And these circumstances became increasingly more stressful and volatile from the 1930s onwards as Britain's direct Imperial influence and strength slowly waned. That fact became just as real in Britain's remaining colonies as in her white dominions: the withdrawal, whether sudden and violent, or discreet and sedate, ultimately affected them all. In considering Boys' Brigade history from this period we must bear this decline in Imperial power constantly in mind. The general overseas revival, started in the 1930s, provided the curtain-raiser for the increasingly autonomous international Brigade development of the 1950s, 1960s and later. Paradoxically, the Second World War acted as either a stimulus or a temporary block on this natural evolution depending upon where one lived in the Empire. Those furthest away, like Australia and New Zealand, tended to be the first to act with greater freedom and less routine reference to London. After the Second World War, however, even they appealed to Britain to supply full-time B.B. professional training organizers at their own expense (see Chapter 8).

Repeating the caution about the dangers of generalizing across so wide a spectrum of Brigade developments internationally, we can now consider the overseas history up to 1945 from two generally distinct standpoints. The first, the predominant but by no means exclusive British view of priorities for overseas extension in the 1920s and 1930s, was that of missionary-supported Brigade work mostly in colonial situations. The second was that of the 'autonomous' and largely locally inspired revivals in the dominions. Simply put, Gamble's experience in Swatow exemplifies the former and George Orr's in Australia the latter. Both developments merged in the late 1930s to put greater pressure on the Brigade in Britain to expand its overseas extension programme in the field. The male midwife at the birth (in some cases the rebirth) of the Brigade in most overseas territories after 1933 was the Overseas Secretary, William McVicker, 'the father of the B.B. International'. McVicker calculated himself that the number of overseas companies grew from 76 in 1930 to 444 in 1951 when he at last visited Australia and New Zealand.[10]

In 1926 the Rev. William J. Mellor, whose work in Nigeria in the 1930s became as well-known to British, especially Methodist, companies as that of Gamble's in Swatow a decade before, founded the 1st Shagamu Company, Ijebu Province, at the Methodist Mission there. The Brigade already had a strong presence in nearby Lagos and environs, building upon the work started there before the First World War. As Manager of Methodist Schools and Superintendent Minister, Mellor became Captain and Senior Chaplain to all Methodist B.B. and Life Boy units. There were at least ten such sections, teams or companies registered throughout the province under the title of 1st Ijebu. All lieutenants-in-charge and chaplains of the constituent sections gave allegiance to Mellor. In September 1933 he and William H. Mann (Captain of the 1st Lagos Company) attended the Jubilee Brigade Council in Glasgow and reported a movement of 850 officers and boys in Nigeria. Centred mainly in the long-established Methodist and Church Missionary Society stations and the B.B.-funded clinics and hospitals, the movement had already reached far beyond Lagos, Ibadan and Ijebu Province to Kano and Kaduna in the Moslem North, and extension into the Eastern Region soon followed. From 1933-34 Mellor, supported by Mann as secretary, assumed the chairmanship of a newly constituted all-Nigeria Executive Committee. Within two years the work had spread southeast to Calabar and Port Harcourt.

In other parts of British West Africa the Brigade restarted somewhat fitfully in the 1920s and 1930s. In the Gold Coast (now Ghana) most activity was in Greater Accra and the Eastern Regions, and in Sierra Leone the movement maintained a rather precarious presence at the U.M.C. Mission at Gbangema. In 1936 two new companies were formed in Freetown, Sierra Leone. Nigeria, however, would henceforth remain the leader in Brigade developments in West Africa.[11]

Mellor proved a most shrewd and persuasive promoter in Britain of the West African Brigade cause. In 1933 he took with him Sgt. David Fasanya of the 1st Ijebu Shagamu Section to attend the Jubilee festivities, and while in Britain he raised sufficient funds, including a grant from Brigade Executive, to take 'a typical B.B. lad with no special privileges or training but immensely keen on the Brigade and on foreign missions' back to Nigeria with him. The chosen candidate was the unemployed artisan Albert Griffiths of the 5th North Staffordshire Company. Many factors contributed to a strong revival of British missionary-awareness in the late 1930s: informal missionary gossip and lobbying at Brigade Councils; the enthusiasm of McVicker and his strong missionary-minded circle, including the hardworking denominational B.B. missionary secretaries; and, above all, the renewed Imperial challenges of the 1933 Jubilee and the 1937 Coronation of King George VI, which brought another stream of overseas B.B. visitors, both officers and boys, to Britain. At the Leeds Council of September 1936, overseas reports of the visits of a bevy of Brigade notables to Canada, India, Singapore, New Zealand and South Africa were curtailed only by the time guillotine. The following November, Irish officers (from both Eire and Northern Ireland) met at B.B. House in Belfast to consider 'a thrilling address' from C.F. Beckett of Dublin entitled 'The B.B. Overseas, its challenge to us at home'. They resolved 'to do more to help our coloured brothers — whether in Africa, India or elsewhere'. As a result of this meeting, the Irish Methodist companies inaugurated a systematic visitation by selected officers of all their Bible Classes to promote the cause. Ireland, indeed, was to prove a consistent stronghold of B.B. missionaries and interest in overseas work, and from 1929 to 1951 the Dublin Shield for drill and athletics (provided by the Dublin Battalion) was competed for eagerly by many Nigerian companies.[12]

No more clear proof of British missionary interest in and commitment to the 'African rewakening' could be given than the near fatal visit of the Brigade Secretary, Stanley Smith, to Sierra Leone and Nigeria in October and November 1936. It was a gruelling, demanding odyssey, reminiscent of his father's tours of Canada and the U.S.A. in 1895 and 1907. Everywhere he went, Smith was feted by chiefs, British Residents, B.B. missionaries and B.B. privates, and shown, almost ad nauseam, the movement at work. After a brief call at Freetown, the Brigade Secretary spent the first eleven days of his tour in Lagos and Ijebu Province inspecting what was then the core region of B.B. strength in Nigeria. From there he motored to Ibadan and Abeokuta, and on 4 November left by train northwards on 'a long unpleasant journey in great heat' across the Niger to Kaduna. Visiting all the principal B.B. clinics and centres of the North — at Zaria, Shikka, Angwa Chefu and Gangara, and the Life Boy Dispensary at Chafe — Smith was deeply moved by the compassion and relevance of the B.B.-funded medical missionary work in that part of Nigeria. 'At Maska I saw the B.B. Hospital in operation, and the African orderly took a short service, attended not only by patients but by many others interested in the Bible lesson.' Smith then penetrated further north to Kano which had a company, en route finding it 'a wonderful experience to be greeted so warmly in these Moslem villages because I represent the B.B. and The Life Boys'. Shortly afterwards Smith was struck down by a severe and persistent 'blood infection', and made his way painfully and slowly northwards by rail to Enugu in the Eastern Region. Several car trips, with pauses for treatment, took him to the European Hospital at Onitsha, where his planned visits to Calabar and Port Harcourt were wisely cancelled. Barely fit to travel, Smith left Calabar on board the *Abosso* on 16 November 1936, calling at Lagos and Freetown once more before the welcome steam back to Plymouth and immediate dispatch to Glasgow and a nursing home early in December. His long winter convalescence of 1936-37, followed immediately by the demanding Coronation celebrations, convinced Brigade Executive, meeting at Windermere in May 1937, to place 'Empire and Overseas' extension in the hands of a new 'Overseas Committee' serviced by the ubiquitous and capable McVicker. Henceforth McVicker was to become the British Brigade's principal traveller to distant lands.[13]

In June 1936, much to the movement's delight, William Mellor's fifteen years of missionary and youth work in Western Nigeria were recognized locally by his ceremonial installation before a crowd of many thousands at Shagamu as 'Ashiwaju Muleoruwa' ('Leader of the People') of Ijebu Remo. The vision of Mellor and Mann and the gruelling journey of Stanley Smith both bore fruit. By 1940 the Brigade in Sierra Leone was 260 strong (all ranks) with eight companies comprising the Freetown Officers' Council. The movement found particular acceptance among the highly religious Creole majority in the population. Over the same period the Nigerian movement grew to just over 1,400 (all ranks including Life Boys), spread among twenty-four companies. In Northern Nigeria the Rev. F.B. Whale of the Sudan Interior Mission guided a steady growth, but the main strength remained in the Western Region under Mellor and Mann. Already, however, the groundwork was being laid in Nigeria, with the training of indigenous Nigerians, for the phenomenal growth which gave that country soon after the Second World War the largest B.B. membership of any country outside Britain. Mellor's visionary planning is seen again in this development. For thirty-one years he used the Brigade 'to evangelize our youth', and graduates from his companies took the movement's message and methods throughout the country. One influential co-worker with Mellor was W.G.T. Lawson, Captain of the 3rd Lagos, who inspired the Rt. Rev. I.O.S. Okunsanya with the B.B. idea whilst he was curate of St. Jude's Ebutte-Metta. Another African to start with Mellor in 1926 and, like Okunsanya, to remain active in Brigade leadership was the noted educationalist, Chief E. Oye Sofudu.[14]

Few other African countries outside the Union of South Africa developed such strong B.B. infrastructures as Nigeria and Sierra Leone before the Second World War. In the Bechuanaland Protectorate (now Botswana) the London Missionary Society had promoted two companies at Molepolole since the mid-1920s. Soon afterwards, units were started at Kafue and Serowe and later at Ngami 'on the edge of the Kalahari desert, with the nearest B.B. Company distant ten weeks by ox-waggon'. At Serowe under the Rev. J.H.L. Burns, sometime secretary of the Brigade in the Protectorate, the movement (including the Life Boy Team started in 1930) grew to 270 boys before the War. One important feature of the work at Serowe was the support given by the royal family of Chief Tshekedi. Writing of his experience at Serowe in 1934 Burns noted:

> At first I was doubtful if B.B. methods would meet the needs of African Boys, but after nine years' experience I have found that, with certain modifications, they do. Only, one has to give oneself freely to the work. The more one gives himself [sic] to it the more attached does he become to his Company and the richer are the results . . . One great encouragement in the work has been the loyal support of Companies in the old country.

The experience was similar in the pioneer company of Uganda raised in 1933 in connection with the Church Missionary Society work at Kigezi High School, Kabale, by the Rev. William W. Orpwood (an 'old boy' of 4th West Middlesex). Orpwood drew upon both African and European officers, one among the latter being their bandmaster, the Rev. (later Bishop) Lawrence Barham. The influence of this fine unit was not lost, for in future years the rapid national growth of the Brigade in Uganda began in Kigezi.[15]

In neighbouring Kenya Colony the long-established work of Dr J.W. Arthur of the 1st Kikuyu Company at the Scottish Mission School was reorganized on his retirement in 1937 after thirty years work among the Kikuyu people. No longer was membership of the Company 'semi-compulsory' within the Mission School, and, under the captaincy of Dr Andrew Shaw, the connection was transferred to the 'Church of the Torch' in Kikuyu. Notwithstanding these changes, the boy membership remained consistently high until the War. Even more isolated than any of these African mainland B.B. units were the island companies on Madeira (started in 1930) and on Mauritius (St. Andrews

Church of Scotland), the latter founded by the Rev. R. Mackinnon in 1937. Before 1939-40 the Brigade had also spread to Tanganyika (now Tanzania — 1st Sikonge, Moravian Church), the Sudan (1st Kajo Kaji, C.M.S. Mission), and again to Nyasaland (now Malawi). Since the revival of Brigade work in the Union of South Africa belongs more particularly to the similar shared experiences of the other dominions, we shall briefly consider it in that context below.[16]

In Nigeria and other parts of Africa the Brigade's support for medical missionary work had earned for it a special place in the esteem of local populations. In India, where the rigidity of internal social and caste barriers, let alone those between Europeans and Indians, had already proven inimical to the movement's progress in Calcutta and elsewhere before the First World War, several isolated attempts were made in the 1920s to sustain B.B. companies. In 1923 the Baptist Mission at Barisal on the Ganges Delta in East Bengal (now Bangladesh) started a short-lived company. In 1927 the 1st Calcutta Company was raised at the Union Congregational Church, and this was followed in 1928 by the formation of the 1st Dichpalli, at the Wesleyan Leper Mission Hospital, ten miles south of Nizamabad (Indur) in what was then the princely state of Hyderabad. During the 1930s the two companies of Dichpalli (the second was registered in March 1932) gained increasing support from Methodist companies in Great Britain. Dichpalli, indeed, became widely known in the medical and missionary worlds as a successful centre for the humane and scientific treatment (and in many cases the cure) of that age-old scourge, leprosy.[17]

With strong support from British and Indian authorities the Dichpalli Leprosy Hospital had opened in 1915 as a direct result of the vision of two Scottish missionaries. They were George Kerr and his talented wife Dr Isabel Kerr (née Gunn), a medical graduate of Aberdeen University. George Kerr publicly proclaimed the aims of the settlement at its very commencement:

> While there will be Christian teaching, there will be no restriction of caste or creed. Moslem and Hindu are welcome no less than Christian. The supreme purpose in view is to care for the leper and to save others from a constant menacing danger; and it befits Indians of all faiths to help their suffering fellow-countrymen.

In 1921 a newly developed treatment — intramuscular injection of a non-irritant chemical extract from the oil of the native Indian chaulmoogra tree — was introduced at Dichpalli, thereby revolutionizing patient attitudes and prospects.[18]

Brigade work started at Dichpalli as the direct result of the arrival of Sister Ruth Witney, a missionary nurse, who commenced a Girls' Life Brigade company there. Soon afterwards the 1st Dichpalli Company of The Boys' Brigade (registered in London on 2 January 1928) started under the captaincy of the settlement's headmaster, B.J. Yesucharanam (literally 'The Feet of Jesus'), followed four years later by the 2nd Dichpalli under the leadership of Pandiri Daniel. For many years nursing and other missionaries provided secretarial services for the three Brigade companies at Dichpalli. It became commonplace for Girls' Life Brigade and Boys' Brigade members at the settlement to undertake many activities together, including camps and outings. With the improved medical treatment, B.B. units increasingly served only short-term members — two to three years — since, once cured, patients left the hospital. But the work reached most of the younger male patients — one to two hundred on average. Enthusiasm was high and the boys' 'cheerful

The 1st Swatow Company keeping fit some time in the 1920s.
The B.B. in South China was forced to close down in 1929
after the Communists had taken control of the area.

The 1st Dichpalli Company in 1940.
The Company was recruited by missionary staff
from boys at the Dichpalli Leprosy Hospital in Hyderabad,
and lasted longer than any other B.B. work on the Indian subcontinent.

Among the islands of the Pacific, the Brigade has had a great success.
These are the NCOs of the 1st Arawa Company on the Cook Islands in 1939.

*A B.B. company at the Mampong Akwapim School Mission
in the Gold Coast (now Ghana), circa 1920.*

*In 1940 the B.B. in New Zealand held a Dominion Camp at Waikanae,
near Wellington, to celebrate the centenary of
New Zealand's formal adherence to the British Crown.*

(The Evening Post, Wellington)

The 1st Riga Company, Latvia, in camp in 1930. This Company was inherited from the Boys' Life Brigade, and seceded to the Boy Scouts in 1935, five years before the Russian invasion.

By 1945 the United Boys' Brigades of America showed no signs of wishing to dispense with elaborate uniforms, although by this time their numbers were much diminished.

activity' provided 'a welcome counterblast to the full apathetic leper mentality'. The example of the G.L.B. girls and the B.B. boys

> . . . inspired acts of personal service and dedication to Jesus Christ, fostered the
> ideals of village service, and the breaking down of caste barriers . . . The Brigade
> also made a significant contribution to the social life of Dichpalli.[19]

Nor was this mere missionary propaganda from the field for home consumption. In 1936 J. Harold Early, Captain of the 1st Witney Company
(Oxfordshire), Chairman of the Life Boy Committee and a member of the
Brigade Executive, visited Dichpalli whilst on a world tour. He went to
Dichpalli with the express purpose of turning the first sods for a new Brigade
hall — subscribed for by home companies — as part of the new complex of
buildings arising in the leper settlement. Here was a high-placed Brigade
emissary able to confirm at first hand the well reported enthusiasm, effectiveness and orthodoxy — combined with Indian adaptations — of the B.B. in
Dichpalli. Great events in the year there were 'B.B. Week' and the annual
camp, sometimes held at Indalwai, only ten bullock-cart miles away, in the
forest. At these camps 'Boys of differing caste sat down side by side, and,
having thanked God for their food, shared the fellowship of the meal.' As one
missionary sister reported, 'It is due entirely to the influence of the Brigade
that such a remarkable step forward has been made by the boys.' Such reports
further fanned the missionary fervour of the Methodist Brigade officers in
Britain. In 1938 an agreement was reached with the Methodist Missionary
Society for Methodist companies and teams to raise money annually towards
the eventual goal of total support for the Dichpalli hospital work (then costing
the Methodist Mission £1,400 per annum). The same year Dermott Monahan
published his book, *The Lepers of Dichpalli*, recounting the work of the Brigade
and of the medical-missionaries, and giving a great boost to further active B.B.
interest in the venture. In 1944 a Life Boy Team was started at Dichpalli and in
1945 nearly £1,250 was raised from home companies for the work, so that
finances for staff 'came almost entirely from The Boys' Brigade Branch of the
Methodist Missionary Society'. Throughout World War II, B.B. men, whether
garrisoned nearby as troops or among those few who actually went to
Dichpalli as missionaries and doctors, sustained home interest in the leprosy
hospital.[20]

With Independence in 1947, however, the whole Indian subcontinent —
India, Pakistan and Ceylon (Sri Lanka) — was thrust into a new and long-
delayed stage of sociopolitical evolution. Hyderabad, with its Moslem prince
and predominantly Hindu population, was not immune from the unrest and
the sometimes painful readjustments. Already with the War and then with
Independence, the Brigade in Dichpalli had slowly begun to dwindle and, by
the early 1940s, the only other B.B. company in India — in Bombay (formed in
1937) — had disappeared. In 1946 a Colombo company was formed at St.
Luke's Church, Borella, under Ceylonese (Sri-Lankan) leadership, but it too
soon waned. By the end of the early 1950s the Brigade movement was no more
in the Indian subcontinent. Dichpalli, unashamedly Christian, had provided
one important focus for the British Brigade's missionary zeal of the 1930s and
1940s. Both the medical and missionary purposes had, indeed, been admirably furthered. However, among the ancient cultures and religions of India, so
difficult for the Christian Gospel to reach en masse, it is perhaps not surprising that permanence is scarcely ever achieved except in practical matters by
the Christian missionary. Dichpalli demonstrated once more the possibility of

racial harmony and partnership in the running of Brigade companies in an environment where the primary concern had been the welfare and humane treatment of all, regardless of caste or creed.[21]

With strong missionary support the Brigade also became established before the Second World War in what was, even then, still rather romantically known as the 'South Seas'. Since 1823, when the Rev. John Williams landed on Rarotonga in the Cook Islands, the London Missionary Society (L.M.S.) had developed Polynesia and, later, Papua New Guinea as particular spheres of activity. As the European powers, particularly Imperial Germany, scrambled somewhat belatedly for the last remnants of 'Empire' in the South Pacific towards the close of the nineteenth century, Australia and New Zealand had already been long enough settled by Europeans to lay strong claim to 'spheres of influence' and even to claim territories in the region. The eventual result of these claims was that both countries inherited certain British as well as some former German territories before and after the First World War. Inevitably, as national Brigade structures were re-established permanently in New Zealand and then in Australia, so the responsibilities for B.B. extension in the neighbouring Pacific were, in time, deliberately passed to them from the Brigade Executive and Overseas Committee in Britain.

The first B.B. Company in Papua (southern New Guinea) commenced with forty-five boys under the Rev. J.H. Homes ('Homu') at the L.M.S. station, Orokolo, in 1899-1900. Homes had pioneered the Mission's work in the north of the Gulf of Papua in the 1890s, and in 1905 he handed the Orokolo station over to the newly arrived Rev. Reginald Bartlett, a graduate of Western College, Plymouth, and a former B.B. boy and officer in Bristol. 'Bati', as he became known in Papua, proved a most unconventional and down-to-earth missionary, beloved by all in a difficult locality. Homes had insisted that each B.B. boy 'support himself entirely by his own industry, apart from food' and had maintained an 'entire isolation from relatives and the life of their villages . . . [to avoid] the degradation and heathenism of their people'. Such a regime did not greatly appeal to the fun-loving, personable 'Bati', who formed 'the first and only Band in New Guinea' and made his B.B. Papuans the pride of that whole remote district. Bartlett left New Guinea in 1912, returning to Europe to distinguish himself (gaining the O.B.E.) as a wartime chaplain in France.[22]

Popular and much in demand on deputation work in postwar Britain, Bartlett was sent in 1929 with his wife, Alice Mary ('Bati Vaine'), to a troubled Western Samoa, then a mandated territory of New Zealand. There as principal of the L.M.S. College at Malua on the island of Upolu, he played a not insignificant part in achieving a great measure of reconciliation between a sometimes vacillating New Zealand local administration and the unofficial opposition, the popular Samoan movement, or 'Mau'. Bartlett found the Samoans fiercely loyal to the Church and the L.M.S., and his standing in the territory was very high indeed on his departure in 1931. Within eight years he was back again at Malua, and the following year he started the 1st Samoa (Malua) B.B. Company. Bartlett correctly foretold that the movement would eventually capture the imagination of Samoan and other Polynesian boys and could provide in Samoa a much-needed outlet for the graduates (mostly young pastors) of Malua. Reformed by his successor the Rev. E.J. Edwards, the Malua Company, strategically placed and strictly run, became the forerunner of many units throughout both Eastern and Western Samoa, and also in other parts of Polynesia. Bartlett in his 'retirement' in Britain continued to be a staunch advocate of the Brigade:

> All Theological Colleges should put The B.B. on their syllabus, so that Ministers would go out trained. Such training would cut more ice than some of the stuff which is administered.[23]

The main centre for Polynesian expansion was, however, the principal island of the Cook Group, Rarotonga. Arriving there as an L.M.S. missionary in 1933, the Rev. Robert Lye Challis — 'Salesa' to the Islanders — was greatly distressed by the poor social conditions among the young Cook Islanders. In February 1933 he started the 1st Rarotonga Company at Avarua with a Polynesian staff, including one Ringiao, the *Vaa* or ceremonial orator of the High Chief. Having long assimilated Christianity into their culture, Cook Islanders now embraced the Brigade enthusiastically, and by 1936 three more companies were operating with 200 boys in the villages of Aorangi, Ngatongira and Titikaveka on Rarotonga. Challis, a former member of the 13th South Essex Company, was registered as Captain of all the far-flung Cook Island companies, servicing those of Rarotonga on his bicycle. The Cook Group of nine atolls and six high volcanic islands extends over 750 miles of ocean. As a missionary Challis was called upon to visit most of them. In his absence the Brigade continued under its Polynesian lieutenants, although Challis remained the organizer, training officer and chief inspiration. The movement quickly gained support from all sections of society, including Government — the Cook Islands were a New Zealand territory — and influential Polynesian leaders. In Britain much help in kind and finances came from Congregational companies, and the ever generous Dublin Battalion gave 'a handsome Drill Shield'.[24]

The Second World War and subsequent Japanese incursions into the Pacific brought an extension in Brigade responsibilities and activities. At the Cook Island Administration's request Challis trained B.B. boys for a coastwatching service, and he also sent Tariu Teaia, a student pastor and lieutenant of the 3rd Rarotonga, to form companies on other islands, including Mangaia, Mauke, Atiu and Aitutaki. By 1942 the membership reached 600 and in October 1943 Tariu 'was ordained to the work of The Boys' Brigade'. At war-torn Abbey House McVicker shrewdly saw a way to promote this faraway missionary growth. 'New Zealand', he told the influential President of the Brigade in that country, Frederick Scott Miller, 'might undertake the responsibility of meeting salary and expenses of a Maori B.B. Agent to work under the Rev. R.L. Challis in the Cook Islands.' Writing the same day to the B.B. Dominion Secretary, Roland Hill, McVicker thought that 'such a missionary B.B. project might strongly appeal to the B.B. in New Zealand, as the Cook Islands are administered by the Dominion politically'. Only £100, he added, would be required. B.B. New Zealand rose eagerly to the challenge and responsibility of 'a special Missionary & Mission [of] its "very own"'. At the price of several letters and some adroit planning McVicker had shifted the onus for Pacific extension to the New Zealand B.B. In 1944 Tariu moved to Auckland to gain more B.B. experience, serving as pastor there among the immigrant Cook Islanders working on war projects. The War brought many Island Polynesians to New Zealand, the start of a major immigration. Tariu eventually became Captain of the 6th Auckland Company, an appointment hailed by McVicker as an example of wartime 'B.B. lease-lend'. With a somewhat naive understanding of New Zealand, although with remarkable prescience of B.B. and Church development, McVicker asked:

Is this the first instance of a dark-skinned member of one of the younger Churches taking charge of a B.B. Company of white Boys in a white [sic] country? May it not be the forerunner of further exchanges as the World Church becomes more of a reality?[25]

Eventually the multilingual Challis, destined to become 'Papa Challis' or 'The Father' to thousands of Island people, was called to minister to the Pacific Islanders in New Zealand, and later spearheaded B.B. extension into the South Pacific under the auspices of The Boys' Brigade in New Zealand. The significance for B.B. history of McVicker's partial transference of Pacific extension responsibility to New Zealand as early as 1944 lay in the willingness with which Brigade Executive now appeared ready to confer responsibility on well-established overseas Councils for the oversight of Brigade affairs beyond their own shores. Not only would it release resources in Britain for the home movement's postwar ventures but it also heralded the eventual autonomy of those countries accepting such responsibilities.[26]

As the dominion least affected by the clash between compulsory government military training for boys and a pre-existing B.B. movement, New Zealand was the first to revive its national Brigade structures in the early 1930s. The rebirth of the movement occurred autonomously and almost by accident in the mid-1920s.

Otago and Southland, New Zealand's pre-eminently 'Scottish' provinces, were initially the scene of the revival. At Caversham Baptist Church, Dunedin, Horace Grocott, a retired New Zealand missionary from the High Andes of Bolivia, took up the challenge from two dozen boys in his church to form a club in 1924 which he called the 'B.B.B.' — the Baptist Boys' Brigade:

> The group was very military minded. It created ranks from corporals to generals. It had a comb band, and it sang, it drilled, it marched. It held mimic camp-fire gatherings, with the lights off. It told spooky yarns with a strong religious flavour. Its numbers grew to sixty. Then it uniformed itself in grey with skyblue facings.

Grocott, recognized by many as the 'Founder' for the second enduring phase of the B.B. in New Zealand, claimed no foreknowledge of a wider Brigade movement. Soon, however, he obtained some Boys' Life Brigade literature — being particularly impressed with Donald Finnemore's writings — and promptly sought affiliation in London for his Dunedin 'B.B.B.'. With union of the B.B. and the B.L.B. in 1926, however, Edward Cooke, former Secretary of the B.L.B. and now inter alia in charge of 'Overseas Affairs' in the unified movement, steered them into The Boys' Brigade as the 1st Dunedin Company. 'We were convinced', recalled Grocott in 1960, 'that The Boys' Brigade movement was something which the Evangelical Churches had long been groping for in the interests of their teenage Boys.' In 1928 his friend and former co-missionary, the Rev. Harry Hogg, started the 1st Winton Company in Southland, and the movement, judiciously guided by Cooke from London, grew apace. With the establishment of two more Dunedin companies, an Officers' Council was formed there in 1927-28 which began to issue the *N.Z. Brigade Boy* in 1929 as a magazine for the South Island, and eventually for the whole of New Zealand. Grocott was appointed honorary Dominion Secretary and, encouraged by London, engineered the formation — not without some opposition — of a B.B. Dominion Council in 1931-32 at the annual South Island camp at Waikouaiti, near Dunedin. The previous year Southland companies had grown strong enough to constitute themselves as the Southland Battalion.[27]

After 1930 the movement spread rapidly via Wellington to the North Island, reaching Auckland in 1931. One architect of the phenomenal growth in the 1930s was Roland Hill, Dominion Secretary since the formation of the National Council, who travelled up and down the country enthusing leaders and Churches, and ran a small office and depot initially from his bedroom in a Wellington suburb. Hill's ideas were almost a generation ahead of their time in B.B. and Life Boy work, and his reward was to see the movement grow by 1939 to 2,300 boys in 110 companies and nearly 1,100 Life Boys in 62 teams. Battalions and groups sprang up in all the cities, main centres and smaller towns of New Zealand and, even during the austere Antipodean Depression years, there was no falling off in the enthusiasm or growth. In 1937-38 alone, 71 new companies were formed, and in 1940-41 a Dominion Camp was held at Waikanae, near Wellington, attracting 950 members to celebrate the centennial of New Zealand's formal adherence to the British Crown. Although the Second World War, especially in the Pacific theatre, took officers away on military service, the B.B. growth flagged only temporarily, so that by 1944 there were 145 companies (3,015 boys) and 82 teams (1,640 boys). With strong Church, Government and viceregal support The Boys' Brigade in New Zealand had already by then earned respect and recognition at home and abroad as an innovative leader in youth work and Brigade affairs.[28]

In a small cohesive country, especially with the Scouting movement facing internal problems in the 1920s and 1930s, the Brigade had decisive advantages. Native-born New Zealanders responded eagerly to the new movement, although some inexperienced enthusiasm in the early days was tempered in a positive fashion by the contribution made by immigrant officers such as F. Scott Miller (formerly of 1st Glasgow) in Wellington and James Clarke (formerly of Wolverhampton) in Southland. Hill, unemployed when he first arrived in New Zealand from England, threw himself might and main into a B.B. arena that was both manageable and receptive. Fiercely pro-British in most matters, New Zealanders were nonetheless distant enough geographically to accept the desired elements but ignore the impossible in adapting the Brigade to their country. Their deep-rooted indigenous Bible Class movement in all Churches, for instance, remained unassailable, even to the 'assaults' of official B.B. visitors like R.A.S. Mason, and the British B.B. Bible Class pattern rarely caught on in New Zealand. Indeed, the clashes when individuals tried to overturn the status quo could sometimes be painful. On the other hand, New Zealand's well-established secondary school system, with its traditions, uniformed formality and orderliness, together with its generally high retention rates to the upper forms, nicely complemented the B.B. in that country throughout the 1930s, 1940s and beyond. By the early 1930s the New Zealand Brigade had adopted a full uniform based upon that of most schoolboys. The movement also got underway just as 'war boom' babies were attaining Life Boy and Brigade age and just as the insecurities of the Depression encouraged their parents to enroll them for the kind of programme the Brigade could offer. In the late 1930s a number of all-Maori companies — a cause predictably dear to McVicker, even at so great a distance — were formed in the North Island. The more familiar pattern in New Zealand, enhanced by the recent migration of rural Maoris to the cities, is for most companies and teams to be racially mixed.[29]

Inevitably the renaissance of The Boys' Brigade in New Zealand attracted the attention of those dreaming of the same in neighbouring Australia. But the major expansion did not take place there until the late 1930s. More urgently, the embryo Brigade movement in New South Wales (and later in South Australia) had first in the mid-1930s to resolve the difficult question of what name it could operate under. Since the 1880s and 1890s two successful organizations, originally newsboys' clubs, had functioned in Sydney and Adelaide under the name 'The Boys' Brigade'. With strong business and initial Church support, they were both clearly influenced at an early stage by William Smith's ideas, but grew later into strong non-sectarian inner-city clubs for working-class boys, acquiring their own premises, full-time workers, and influential supporters. They provided a strong focus for social welfare and concern during the depression of the 1890s, and grew vigorously throughout and beyond World War I. They outlived the rise and demise of the mainline Brigade movement of 1890-1914, whose fortunes we have examined earlier (see Chapter 3). In the 1920s the Sydney-based organization was legally incorporated in New South Wales as 'The Boys' Brigade', and similar steps were taken in South Australia. By the early 1930s, however, three mainline Church-sponsored B.B. companies were operating in Sydney. Following innocent publicity of the work of the mainline companies, the Boys' Brigade Incorporated (the former newsboys' organization) instructed its solicitors to challenge the public use of the name by these companies, firmly requiring an abandonment of the same to avoid 'damage' and 'the diversion of gifts' intended for its own long-established work.[30]

This legal hot potato was swiftly sent to Abbey House in London, and in 1934 the Brigade Executive, meeting in Oxford, decided to require all companies in New South Wales to register as units of 'The British Empire Boys' Brigade' (B.E.B.B.). In Sydney the existing mainline companies readily agreed to this compromise, whereupon the Boys' Brigade Incorporated also required that the new name be adopted *throughout* Australia. In March 1935 McVicker, as Overseas Secretary, conveyed this as Brigade Executive's final decision to all B.B. companies in Australia. From Queensland and Victoria the reaction was swift and uncompromising. 'Quite frankly', wrote Robert H. Tait, George Orr's successor as Captain of the 1st Brisbane, 'without wishing to embarrass the Brigade Executive, we have no intention of changing our title.' He continued that it would be a sacrilege to do so, a disgrace to Smith's and Orr's legacy and memory. Australian states were, in most respects, legally autonomous: the writ of one did not run automatically in another. 'This attempt by Sydney people generally to dictate to the other States in the Commonwealth is no new thing and has frequently been the cause of dissension in Australia-wide organizations.' Robert Hunter Tait, a canny public servant, a product of 1st Brisbane and a Queenslander to boot, led the opposition to the 'dictation' from London and Sydney. Only in South Australia and New South Wales did the curious 'British Empire Boys' Brigade' name survive for another thirty or forty years. It caused endless embarrassment as an Imperial legacy which outlived even the Australian Brigade's formal independence from Britain in 1958. It remained a matter not resolved until the adoption of the name 'The Boys' Brigade Australia' at the fifth Australian Council in Canberra in 1971. Tait ensured that no further assault could be made on the name 'The Boys' Brigade' in Queensland by registering the movement there as a foreign company. In other states and territories outside New South Wales and South Australia similar safeguards were taken, but in most it was never a problem. The major difficulty in future years was in the populous state of New South Wales where the B.B. was (and still is) a relatively strong movement.[31]

Although saddled with the title 'The British Empire Boys' Brigade' after 1935, the Brigade movement in Sydney soon expanded sufficiently to form the first Australian B.B. battalion since before the First World War, and by 1939 it was seventeen companies strong. By 1942 over thirty companies had been registered in New South Wales, the majority in the capital of Sydney. The acknowledged leader in this revival was Robert McEwan, Captain of the 3rd Sydney Company at Haberfield, a young emigrant engineer from Northumberland, where he had gained invaluable experience in the Boys' Life Brigade. Wartime conditions in Australia required the manufacture of some badges and other equipment locally, and for many companies, both in Australia and New Zealand, necessity became the mother of invention. In 1942 McEwan purchased a property privately at Macquarie Fields south of Sydney, starting on it 'Camp Plessey' which in time became a major national and local home of The Boys' Brigade in Australia. In 1944 the 50th Sydney Company was registered and the Battalion was already showing signs of dividing into more localized groupings. In Newcastle, north of Sydney, an Officers' Council was started early in the War, and already in New South Wales many units were providing boys to act as air-raid wardens and as civil defence volunteers. In no other Australian state was this extraordinary growth matched during the Second World War, although the movement made significant gains in Melbourne (Officers' Council, 1940) and some advance in Brisbane and Adelaide. The real expansion occurred outside Sydney only in the postwar years, when the Overseas Committee in London appointed McEwan as its official honorary Brigade Organizer for Australia.[32]

In Canada and South Africa, where isolated companies had existed continuously since the First World War, Brigade development more closely paralleled that in Australia than that in New Zealand. As in post-Jubilee Britain, the B.B. growth from 1934-36 onwards was quite remarkable. Canada in the 1920s had several consistent yet dispersed B.B. strongholds: 2nd Winnipeg (founded 1908), formerly under Hugh M. Urquhart at Elmwood Presbyterian Church, and the companies of British Columbia, particularly those of the Greater Vancouver area, of which the most successful was 1st Point Grey (later 1st Vancouver), founded in 1920 at Marpole Methodist Church under A. MacGillivray. These ranked with the 1st Brisbane as among the most outstanding overseas companies of the period. In Ontario the great revival was portended in Windsor where five units were operating before 1933-34. The prewar leap forward was centred, however, in Toronto and other Ontario cities (notably Hamilton and London), and in Montreal. In Winnipeg it occurred between 1937-40. Between 1929 and 1944 just over 120 companies were registered in Canada through Abbey House.[33]

In 1936 the Brigade Treasurer, H. Arnold Wilson, visited Toronto to find a highly efficient Battalion of 770 (all ranks), fifteen of whose companies had been enrolled over the previous eighteen months. In 1978 J. Howard Richardson recalled the successful efforts of Wilson in Montreal to entice leaders of boys' work in the Canadian Churches away from the Trail Ranger and Tuxis movement, a brand of Christian Woodcraft Scouting led by the prominent Canadian boys' worker, Taylor Statten. The B.B. revival in Montreal took place in 1936-38 fanned, as elsewhere in Canada, by the enthusiasm with which ex-B.B. immigrants greeted the second coming of the movement to Canada. In these two years sixteen companies arose in Montreal. By 1943 thirty-four had been registered in Toronto, where two former Glasgow officers, Jack A. Gair and T.A. McGregor, led the advance. In London William McVicker, whose persuausive pen sent reams of advice and encouragement across the Atlantic, watched the Eastern renaissance with extreme interest, as did the doughty, evergreen Frederick V. Longstaff, former Canadian Secretary, from his home in Victoria, British Columbia. McVicker was after all the embodiment of international policies suggested by Longstaff as long ago as 1911. In 1937 the Governor General, Lord Tweedsmuir (better known as the novelist John Buchan), became Canadian patron. In May of that year 105 Canadian officers met on the occasion of the third Annual Review of the Toronto Battalion to constitute the second Dominion Council of The Boys' Brigade.[34]

'There was', wrote Longstaff, who had hurried east to represent the British Columbian and Winnipeg companies at that 'epoch-making assembly',

> a wonderful fraternization and tightening of bonds . . . Many of the Junior officers heard Senior officers exchanging reminiscences of the times they were in the ranks of a Company in Scotland, England, Ireland and Canada.

Behind it all were the 'suggestions' and steady hand of McVicker, whose counsel prevailed when a simple constitution and an all-Canada Executive and Council were established under Jack Gair's dynamic presidency. In October and November 1938 McVicker came in person to Montreal, Ottawa, Toronto, Hamilton, London, Windsor and Winnipeg to marvel at first hand over the resurrected Canadian movement. Such accomplishments, he wrote, 'I doubt have ever been equalled at home, except perhaps in the early pioneer days of B.B. . . . The B.B. in Canada has definitely arrived.'

But had it? Gair's travel and enthusiasm certainly worked wonders before the War. Vancouver, Montreal, London, Hamilton and Windsor rose to achieve battalion status, and by 1940-41 over eighty companies and thirty-five teams were reaching over 3,000 Canadian boys. In 1940 Canadians, with native hospitality, made ready to receive, if required, Brigade evacuees from war-harrassed Britain, and many ex-B.B. servicemen from both countries enjoyed Brigade hospitality on both sides of the Atlantic as their wartime callings took them away from home. By 1943-44, however, the expanding bubble had burst: the exodus of officer manpower to war, and the absence of cohesion normally provided by a full-time secretariat, led to disharmony and fragmentation. In short, Canada's 'bigness' had triumphed again. The movement did not die, but in 1944 its membership was scarcely half that of 1941.[35]

Howard Richardson, who trained thousands of B.B. boys in Montreal, consistently maintained that the Brigade in Canada also suffered from too strong an overdose of B.B. tradition from Britain, especially Scotland. Though frequently wearing the kilt with his B.B. uniform, he remained first and foremost a Canadian. Richardson, whose international Brigade contacts reached to every point of the globe in his fifty years of B.B. work in Canada, held strong views on the heavy-handed attitude of many British B.B. officers towards his country. There were in his opinion too many 'raps on the knuckles' administered by British officers or Britons-away-from-home against those B.B. Canadians who went, however mildly, 'against Grandma's will', i.e. against British B.B. lore and practices. Even McVicker, it seems, did not encourage that essential Canadianization of the movement, so necessary if it were to take deep root locally. When Air Cadet programmes began in Canada in the 1940s many boys preferred to join in rather than remain loyal to the B.B. In Francophone and ethnically mixed Quebec, Richardson was at the heartland of Canada's modern dilemmas and complexities. There were also those who maintained that Canada, unlike the more distant dominions of Australia and New Zealand, was too close to Britain politically, culturally and geographically to develop its own B.B. traditions. Arguably this has remained consistently true for the movement in Canada.[36]

In South Africa after 1914, the main strength of the movement remained amongst the companies of Cape Province. Several units survived strongly through the 1920s until a general revival took place in the mid-1930s. Prominent among these were the 2nd Cape Town (Wynberg) and 3rd Cape Town (Strand) Companies, which provided the bases for an important B.B. growth in the Methodist churches of the Cape. Whilst some temporary advance was made at Paarl amongst the Congregational churches in the late 1920s (four companies by 1932-33), developments in the same denomination at Port Elizabeth soon outstripped this. By 1934-35 Port Elizabeth, traditionally a B.B. stronghold, had momentarily overtaken even the Cape Town district in its growth and development. In that year the South African membership (all ranks) stood at 780 in fourteen companies all of which, except the 1st Pietermaritzburg (Natal), were in Cape Province. Work in the Transvaal (principally in Pretoria and Johannesburg) remained fitful and sporadic until after the mid-1930s.[37]

In May 1936 the Cape Peninsula Officers' Council was formed with six companies under the presidency of the Rev. William Mason of Cape Town, who had striven hard since the First World War to bring some unity among the somewhat independent-minded B.B. units of the Cape Province. At the same time the Port Elizabeth Officers' Council was also constituted, and for the first time since the First World War local administration of the South African Brigade movement was on a sound footing. In Cape Province, B.B. work until the Second World War was almost exclusively amongst — to use the South African expression — 'coloured' boys, i.e. those of Asian and mixed race. By June 1937 the movement around Cape Town had almost doubled to a membership of some 600 in eleven companies (not including two Life Boy teams), thus resulting in the formation of a Cape Peninsula Battalion. In 1936 Robert J. Mitchell of Edinburgh commenced a new Johannesburg company at St. Stephen's Presbyterian Church, inaugurating a new B.B. growth amongst white boys of the Transvaal. Within three years the Rand Officer's Council was working, and by the early 1940s membership in the Transvaal rose steeply to over 300 boys. McVicker's visit in the summer of 1939 to B.B. units in Cape Province, Natal and on the Rand resulted in a new spurt of South African growth. By 1939-40 the reported membership stood at nearly 1,550 (all ranks) in thirty-two companies, and five Life Boy teams with just over a hundred boys. Although leadership shortages were experienced as officers left for the War, the work in South Africa, particularly in the Transvaal, gained strong Government support and prospered accordingly. As in the other dominions (except perhaps Canada) the Brigade in South Africa emerged from the Second World War on balance with greater strength and morale than it had experienced during the interwar years.[38]

Brigade work in the British West Indies and Central America between the Wars never attained the same prominence, except in Jamaica and British Honduras (now Belize), as it had before 1914. Between 1927 and 1943 about thirty new companies were registered in the region: two-thirds of them in Jamaica; three in the Bahamas (including the Turks Islands); four in British

Honduras (of which three were in Belize, the capital); and the remainder on St. Kitts and the Dutch possession of St. Eustatius in the Leeward Islands, in Colon (Panama Canal Zone), and at Essequebo, Diamond and Hopetown in British Guiana (now Guyana). In the former stronghold of Trinidad only the 1st Trinidad lasted until the early 1930s. By 1934-35 total membership in the Caribbean stood at just under 450 (all ranks). In May 1937 a contingent of four boys and two officers from two of the three very strong and active Belize companies (where membership was over 180) travelled with local Church Lads' Brigade members to attend the Coronation celebrations in Britain. They were cordially and hospitably received throughout Britain and spent some time as guests of the Manchester Battalion in camp at Llanbedrog, North Wales. Soon afterwards a Belize Officers' Council was formed and the movement broke new ground with the formation of the 1st Haiti Company in the Methodist Church at Cape Haitian, Republic of Haiti.[39]

The major growth on Jamaica took place after 1937-38; by 1940, when a Jamaica Officers' Council was formed, the membership (all ranks) had risen to over 400 amongst eleven companies. By 1944 the movement had also grown sufficiently in British Guiana to permit the formation of an Officers' Council, based in Georgetown. During the War a steady growth in the Caribbean was to leave the movement ripe for postwar extension work supported by British enterprise. In Jamaica the labours of H.D.McD. Messam as General Secretary and President for over thirty years and C.A. Adams as his Presidential successor set the scene locally for the subsequent emergence of a strong B.B. movement on the island.[40]

In the U.S.A. the story of the United Boys' Brigade of America (U.B.B.A.) between the Wars was a continuing one of strenuous but unfruitful efforts to simplify all round and set up a viable national office to bring cohesion among scattered and heavily localized independent companies, battalions and regiments. America's entry into the First World War, when nearly 580 officers of the movement from nine states alone served in the U.S. Forces, brought most work to a standstill. Between 1915 and 1920 no national convention was held and few records were kept. The main strength remained in Pennsylvania, Maryland, New York and New Jersey. Calling together the Brooklyn convention for June 1920, F.J. Kress of Pittsburgh, the retiring Commander-in-Chief, gloomily reviewed the previous five years, citing various factors: non-cooperation from the Churches and many companies; the lack of money, leaders and literature; the absence both of policies and a standard uniform; and the low level of spirituality. He optimistically but wildly guessed the membership at 28,000 in 930 companies. The old problems, pinpointed by William Smith thirteen years before, still persisted:

> Our present system makes it so tempting for those who strive for rank, glittering uniform and display of authority, to be identified with the work for no other reason, and with little conception of the real purpose of it. Perhaps, this accounts for their sudden severance after a period of unsatisfactory results and misunderstandings.[41]

In the early 1920s Joseph Cudlipp, a redoubtable Anglo-American from Baltimore who succeeded Kress in 1920, tried to inspire and reform the U.B.B.A. along simpler lines. In many places, with a number of British immigrants opting to take up B.B. work in the U.S.A., this seemed possible. In 1932 the national administration moved to Baltimore under General Walter A. Koerber. Unsuccessful attempts were made to unite with the American Cadets of New York and the long established and highly successful Boys' Brigade of Neenah-Menasha, Wisconsin. 'Our work', wrote Frank Shattuck from Neenah-Menasha in 1934, 'has developed more on the British pattern', and he refused to be tempted into the U.B.B.A. From London, Edward Cooke, and later McVicker, refused to register American companies through Abbey House, hoping in return to see U.B.B.A. endorsement for a simpler Brigade structure in the U.S.A. Throughout the 1930s, however, Koerber had to battle with severe internal problems and with a strong nationwide and Church-based pacifism working against the U.B.B.A. By the mid-1930s membership had dwindled to 3,000 boys, and by 1940 was estimated at 2,000 in only eleven states. Contemporary correspondence and literature demonstrates that the hardcore remnant, although very American, was most sympathetic to persistent attempts by the Brigade in Britain and Canada to persuade their U.B.B.A. colleagues to introduce a more orthodox Brigade programme. Such attempts were, however, never entirely successful and, although the U.B.B.A. continued to be relatively strong in Maryland and Pennsylvania, the old structures had long outlived the realities.[42]

The Brigade work in Neenah-Menasha was soon to achieve a special place in the B.B. international fellowship, although it remained aloof from the U.B.B.A. for most of this century. Started in the First Presbyterian Church of Neenah in January 1900, the movement prospered under Frank Shattuck's long direction. In 1909 Shattuck visited Britain, met Sir William Smith and studied the B.B. method closely. He was 'impressed by the simplicity of the British organization and uniform in contrast to the overdone methods of the American organization [i.e. the U.B.B.A.] which had taken root in our middle Eastern States.' Nevertheless, although vastly simpler in rank-structure and uniforms than the U.B.B.A., The Boys' Brigade of the twin towns of Neenah-Menasha developed in a decidedly American idiom. An influential business and community-based Boys' Brigade Association was set up to support the single 'company'; buildings were developed and a campsite purchased at Onaway Island between Rainbow and Hick's Lakes, Wisconsin. In reality the B.B. in Neenah-Menasha became a community-based, interdenominational boys' club, retaining the object and many features of any large traditional Brigade company elsewhere. Its membership ran (and runs) into many hundreds and, although 'a boy's allegiance to and regularity at the church of his parents' choice' was demanded, the organization refrained 'from direct religious instruction, leaving such to the several churches whose boys are admitted to membership of The Boys' Brigade'. The religious climate was, however, never in doubt. The evolution of this successful isolated Wisconsin B.B. work, and its unqualified acceptance by the international B.B. fellowship since the 1930s, begs the question whether it might not have been used as a model for B.B. development elsewhere in the U.S.A. and, indeed, the world.[43]

In other parts of the global Brigade fellowship World War II brought more than evacuations, rationing, national service, blackouts and the absence of leaders. In the Channel Islands, Denmark and Amsterdam it meant either closure or underground meetings, near-starvation or, even worse, forced deportation and death. In Denmark the F.D.F. was at the forefront of 'a widespread underground youth movement', and by 1945 eleven leaders had lost their lives, and one hundred had been interned in Germany and elsewhere. Despite this the movement grew from 15,000 to 21,000 boys. The 1st Amsterdam, Holland's only prewar company (formed in 1935) operated disguised as a

'Jongens Gilde' (Boys' Guild) after 1940. At the union of the B.B. and the B.L.B. in 1926 the movement also inherited from the B.L.B. five Baptist companies in the Baltic Republic of Latvia: one in Riga, two in the port of Liepāja, one at nearby Grobina, and another at Ventspils in the north. This work did not survive the political upheavals of the 1930s. It was, however, the Brigade story in faraway Singapore which captured the imagination of the war-beleaguered movement in Britain.[44]

James Milner Fraser — 'Fraser of Singapore' as he was later called — grew up in the active 23rd Aberdeen Company under that famous captain, George White, before moving south as a qualified architect to work for the London County Council in 1925. He soon became an officer in the 23rd London, but his work took him to Singapore in 1927. In 1929, as we have seen, the B.B. work in Swatow ceased. The following year, on 12 January, Fraser, greatly encouraged by his former London captain, Jack Williams, started the 1st Singapore Company at Prinsep Street Presbyterian Church, aided by ex-Sgt. Quek Eng Moh, late of the 1st Swatow, whose father was pastor of the nearby Chinese-speaking Presbyterian Church. Progress was at first slow but sure as Fraser, assisted soon by Dong Chui Sing, a teacher and scoutmaster from St. Andrew's School (from 1938 the home of the 7th Singapore), and John McNeish (ex-76th Glasgow), strove to build his company on firmly orthodox B.B. lines. Although, as Fraser later recalled, 'these boys were poor boys, mainly poor boys', he insisted that 'we gave nothing away'. Their unofficial motto became 'Nothing for Nothing', and, as in South China, the local membership rose to the challenge. Formal enrolment followed in August 1930 with thirty to forty boys. Drill, Bible Class — the best attended events — concerts, wayfaring, signalling, 'Ambulance', swimming, single-stick fencing, tumbling and other forms of physical recreation formed the core of the B.B. syllabus. 'From the outset', too, 'the embryo Company became interdenominational . . . and Boys were enlisted from a wide area of Singapore.'[45]

Extension soon followed, spearheaded by McNeish, with the formation of the 2nd Singapore at Kampong Kapor Methodist Church in February 1931. McNeish later also initiated the 3rd Singapore at the Anglo-Chinese Continuation School of the Methodist Mission in 1933, and the 5th Singapore at Chuan Guan Presbyterian Mission School, Katong, in 1934. In the latter year the 4th Singapore, also sponsored by the pioneer company, began at Geylang Chinese Methodist Church, and the 6th at Paya Lebar Methodist Church. From the outset, Fraser notes, their aim was to train up Chinese boys and officers to run the movement. 'Everything seemed to spring from the first Company — either an officer or a Senior boy, NCO come Staff Sergeant' — these acted as eager extension emissaries. In 1931 B.B. camping started at the Singapore Volunteer Camp at Siglap, later the scene of many inter-company camps. The movement's association with the Singapore Volunteers was extremely close — Fraser was a member of the Scottish Company and in charge of the Singapore Searchlight Battery on the outbreak of war — and the Volunteers' drill hall became the venue for memorable drill competitions and reviews. Relations with the Y.M.C.A., Scouts, Toc H, the St. John Ambulance Association, schools, the Churches, successive governors and the colonial government were close and cordial. By 1970-71, it is reported, most of the office-bearers of the Prinsep Street Church had been members of the 1st Singapore. During the 1930s the B.B. became root-and-branch a Singapore institution, hailed in Britain as one of the gems in the Brigade crown, and proclaiming its work through the local magazine *Sure and Stedfast*.[46]

In 1933 two Singapore corporals, Tan Keng Kang and Choy Ah Soo, visited Britain for the Jubilee celebrations. They proved popular and enterprising ambassadors, the first of many such from their country. Haunted by B.B. people for autographs, the Singapore NCOs exacted sixpence a signature, raising enough money to equip a full bugle band. On their return Tan Keng Kang went to run the 5th Singapore and Choy Ah Soo became Captain of the 3rd Singapore. In 1936 the Singapore B.B. Battalion was raised 200 strong, and mustered seven companies and three Life Boy teams 340 strong by 1940. Fraser served as its President from 1936 until 1956. Since 1932, bowing to local schooling, custom and climate, the Singapore movement had adopted, a calendar year session. By the end of the decade the Brigade in Singapore — serving predominantly Chinese boys — was a model of European-Chinese joint leadership. In 1940 Fraser handed the captaincy of 1st Singapore over to one of his boys, S.P. Chua. Fraser maintained Singapore's international links on his trips to South Africa and Britain in 1936 and to Australia and New Zealand in 1941. In New Zealand in January 1941 he was an instructor at the North Island NCOs' Course at Rotorua, and spent three weeks touring the Dominion.[47]

By the end of 1941, however, with danger 'from bomb and threatened invasion' the situation in Singapore was desperate enough for Air Chief Marshal Brooke Popham to cancel his B.B. Review. The battle for Malaya was raging. Many officers were at the nearby front or on defence assignments. Alarmed, the Brigade in London cabled words of encouragement. The reply came back, 'Inspired by your message we will carry on.' On 15 February 1942, 'after the unequal struggle darkness fell on Singapore', and the 'fortress' capitulated to the Japanese. 'The dark days of "Soynan" ' (the Japanese name for occupied Singapore) had come, and would last for nearly four years.

The Brigade in Singapore suffered sorely. Choy Ah Soo, a member of the Volunteers, was shot, and many of his fellow-countrymen faced death, torture and extreme deprivation. A large number of Europeans, including Fraser, became prisoners-of-war. Though very sick with dysentry, Fraser maintained fellowship with captive B.B. members through secret 'Stedfast Clubs' in Singapore and Thailand. To avoid desecration the proud Singapore colours were destroyed, but some of the coveted drums were secreted away in a room at Prinsep Street Headquarters. 'Our brave Chinese allies', it was later reported, suffered more than many Europeans. One such ally to the Europeans was the redoubtable Life Boy Leader, Lucy Wong, who 'at the risk of unimaginable horrors . . . smuggled food to her British friends in the Japanese internment Camp'. In Britain the events of 1941-42 were watched with pride and horror: 'Thus has closed', noted the B.B. Gazette of April 1942, in its 'Salute to the Brave',

> a chapter — not, we are sure, by any means the last — in the history of the B.B. in Singapore. The lights are going out in the Far East. We have entered on another period of trial and danger and darkness . . . Amidst all the fury of the present day of tribulation, few events have moved us more than those which culminated in the fall of Singapore. In B.B. circles that name has long borne a special significance, and within the great tragedy of the stronghold's capitulation lies the lesser tragedy behind the pall which, for the time being, has blotted out our Singapore Battalion.

The unshakeable determination in conditions of adversity was reminiscent of Swatow in the late 1920s. 'We will carry on' remained the determined aim of the B.B. all over the world — and especially in Singapore.[48]

CHAPTER 7

'PLANS FOR ADVANCE'

The Boys' Brigade in Britain, 1939 to 1960

'A MAD FOOL'S FOLLY compels us to carry a shield in a little cardboard box,' exclaimed the news-sheet of the Brighton B.B. Battalion on the outbreak of the Second World War. The reference was to Hitler and gas masks. 'Our ears are tuned to a screaming siren. Prices are rising, food is rationed, plans are upset, holidays cancelled. BUT above all there is a call — loud and clear and insistent — CARRY ON! CARRY ON!'

The coming of war in September 1939 had initially overwhelmed The Boys' Brigade because of the severe strains imposed by the evacuation of their Life Boy membership from the cities and the 'call-up' of so many of their officers, warrant officers and staff sergeants. As the Overseas Secretary, William McVicker, took turns at U-boat 'look-out' on his ocean liner zig-zagging its way home through the Atlantic, he wondered what was to become of his plans for Brigade development in South Africa, from whence he had sailed only a week before war was declared. What would be the fate of the newly formed dominion administration of The Boys' Brigade in Canada, which he had visited ten months previously? How would the Brigade in the British Isles stand up to the unwelcome experiences of evacuation, blackout, requisition of company headquarters, departure of officers on service and the like? Only a week after the outbreak of war, the answer to this last question came when every company in Britain received a letter from Abbey House urging them to 'carry on' to the best of their ability. 'Until the position crystallizes it is not possible to give very definite advice,' wrote the Brigade Secretary, 'but if Officers keep before them the needs of the Boys — greater in many cases than under normal conditions — and use imagination and breadth of vision, they should find means of helping the Boys and of enabling the Boys to help their country.'[1]

Brigade Council meetings arranged for 9 September 1939 obviously had to be cancelled, but the Executive, meeting a fortnight later, made sober plans for continuing their work, in spite of the unprecedented circumstances in which they found themselves. They did so with some trepidation, since the outlook during the so-called 'phoney war' up to April 1940 appeared the more threatening because unknown. Many feared that H.G. Wells' prophecies of the destruction of London, as shown in Alexander Korda's 1936 film version of *The Shape of Things to Come*, were about to be realized. The following air-raid precaution issued to the 92nd London Company is characteristic of the exaggerated fears circulating during the early months of the war:

> In the event of an Air Raid Warning being given while a Company meeting is in progress, Boys whose homes are within five minutes walk of Headquarters will go home as quickly as possible. Younger Boys will be accompanied home by members of the Staff. The remainder will proceed quietly via the main door of the School to the boiler vault, which is well protected. It will be an advantage to have a pocket

torch, though Boys are reminded that torches must not be shone in the open. All Boys must bring their gas masks to any meeting they attend.

Significantly, by November 1940, the 5th Brighton Company for one was advising parents that in future their Bible Class would *not* be interrupted to take boys to a nearby air-raid shelter when the 'alert' was sounded during a class.[2]

'In the first place, the Executive hope that no Company will be allowed to close down at this juncture when the needs of the Boy population are so urgent,' ran a Brigade Memorandum. 'The absence of father or mother, the breaking up of homes consequent on evacuation, and the general disturbance of life caused by wartime conditions may have a demoralizing effect.' After the familiar call to 'carry on', there followed advice on the programme, the Brigade contribution to part-time national service, and on how companies should cope with boys in both evacuated and 'reception' areas of the country:

> Wherever a Company exists it should be the earnest resolve of Officers and Boys to keep the flag flying in these days of difficulty. Let us show that The Boys' Brigade is true to its high ideal, by setting an example of unflinching faith. We must be resolute and calm, cheerful and brave, having unshaken confidence in God. So we shall keep our Boys in the bewildering days through which they are passing and prepare them to play their part in the better days which we believe are in store for them.

Little did the Executive realize that, four years later, after the ordeals of Dunkirk, the Battle of Britain and the London Blitz, The Boys' Brigade would be able to record a greater increase of boy strength than ever before in a single session. For during 1942 to 1943, Diamond Jubilee Year, over 9,000 boys were added to the Brigade's totals, bringing their adolescent boy strength to 73,000 — an impressive figure during wartime.[3]

Before this revival in their fortunes took place, however, the Brigade in Britain went through severe trials and difficulties as a result of wartime conditions. The problems associated with air raids were numerous, not least being the wholesale disruption of company activities and a reduction in Life Boy numbers sustained through the consequent evacuation of the school-age population in many cities. Under the full blast of intensive air attack, many churches and their halls were destroyed, and as a result many companies were left homeless. The Boys' Brigade Diploma for Gallant Conduct was awarded to three boys of the 1st Great Yarmouth Company for their gallantry and disregard of danger on the night of 24-25 June 1940 when the local parish church where they were acting as fire-guards was destroyed by enemy action. Brigade boys attempted to fight the raging inferno caused by incendiary bombs and, despite the danger from flames and falling debris, these three managed to rescue the band instruments and other property of the company from the vestries of the burning church. When the diplomas were presented by the mayor of Great Yarmouth in the precincts of the ruined church, the vicar praised the conduct of the boys:

> Nobody knows better than I do how fierce the fire was. After fighting five fires in the Vicarage I watched the Boys struggling against the flames. I grew so anxious for their safety that I had to forbid them to continue the struggle, and even then some of them continued to enter the building and bring out valuables. If they could have possibly saved the building they would have done so. This is the crowning point of my forty years' connection with The Boys' Brigade and I am proud to be here today.[4]

Evacuation orders for entire schools in those cities threatened by German bombing also cut across Boys' Brigade and Church life, sweeping away nearly all potential recruits and many existing members, so that boy numbers declined by 30,000 between 1939 and 1941 before climbing steadily again. Some schoolboys moved out of London found temporary membership in companies belonging to the 'reception areas' where the evacuees were billeted. The 92nd London Company, in Streatham, was scattered far and wide by the War, many of the boys being evacuated to Eastbourne, some to very 'posh' lodgings indeed: one boy, to the amusement of his captain, was regularly taken for drives in the Rolls Royce of his temporary hosts, Sir Alex and Lady Maguire. For those boys left behind, Bible Class and club nights were still held every week for, although in the autumn of 1940, with air-raid casualties mounting, most London schools were closed down and their pupils sent away, some 279,000 children of school age remained in the evacuation area throughout the worst of the raids. Companies in this area set about 'blacking-out' their church halls so that weekday activities could be continued, doing their best to 'carry on' under the most adverse conditions.[5]

As the War progressed, members of The Boys' Brigade, no less than the rest of the civilian population, found themselves under fire from the Luftwaffe in the British Isles. Just as ordinary men and women carried on bravely under enemy air attacks in cities like London, Belfast and Liverpool in the autumn and winter of 1940 to 1941, the boys and officers of the Brigade faced danger and death in simply attending B.B. training activities. Over four-fifths of the casualties of air raids were in London, and the boys of the Mid-Surrey (Sutton and District) Battalion, for example, often went to and from company nights under heavy fire. In the summer of 1944, the passing of 'doodlebugs' or V1 flying bombs en route to the centre of London were an additional hazard; fortunately no casualties were reported, although the houses of two officers in Sutton were severely damaged by fire bombs. At the height of the London Blitz in the autumn of 1940, Abbey House, B.B. Headquarters in Westminster, suffered from continuous air raids as the capital was bombed every night by an average of two hundred German planes. Wardens and firemen trained the new Supplementary Fire Parties (S.F.P.), but this failed to capture a public imagination already much preoccupied with the Home Guard and Civil Defence. Fire watching was started to look out for incendiary bombs, but it was difficult to find S.F.P.'s willing to keep watch over private business premises, since it was uncomfortable, lonely and often dangerous work, and The Boys' Brigade was fortunate in having staff prepared to undertake this hazardous night-time duty. 'I can well remember the nights we spent on the flat roof of Abbey House, Westminster, watching the gun-fire and hearing the dreaded noise of bombs dropping all around,' recalls Tom Sharman:

> It was a nerve-wracking business but despite two near misses — bombs dropped on either side of Abbey House, all the windows were blown in several times — the Office was kept intact; although on very many occasions the Staff were prevented, by dislocation of railways and transport due to the effects of bombing, from being punctual in their daily attendance. One member of the Staff, a youngster from the South East of London, was killed by a bomb on his way to the Office.

The office boy was Kenneth Wiggins who belonged to a London B.B. company and, though only sixteen years old, had been on duty in the A.R.P. during many nights of the heaviest air fighting. 'We would have wished to have laid him to rest in his own native sunshine,' the *Gazette* memorably recorded his funeral:

> But there was a savage fitness in the threatening murk of the sky where droned the

enemy planes; in the shattered tombs around us, witnessing to the stark madness of the havoc; and in the angry thunder of the guns which at times drowned the padre's voice as he told us that God had looked upon this gallant Boy and loving him, had taken him to Himself. And as the gunfire died away, above us the song of a bird was heard.[6]

Several B.B. 'old boys' won awards such as the much coveted Victoria Cross during the War, and the B.B. Cross for Heroism and the National Service Badge were given to boys involved in fire-watching, messenger services, air-raid precautions and rescue work. The Cross for Heroism, for example, was awarded to eighteen-year-old Corporal Kenneth Clements of the 76th London Company for his outstanding bravery in attempting to rescue his aunt and other members of his family from a bombed and burning house in Forest Hill during a raid on the night of 11-12 September 1940. The first V.C. to be won by an 'old boy' during the War was awarded to Flight Sergeant John Hannah of the Royal Air Force, an ex-member of the 237th Glasgow Company, aged eighteen, and thus the R.A.F.'s youngest ever V.C. His Hampden bomber was attacking enemy barge concentrations at Antwerp when the bomb compartment received a direct hit from a shell. Instead of baling out with the other crew members, Sergeant Hannah remained and fought the fire with extinguishers, receiving burns to his face and eyes but enabling the pilot to bring the aircraft safely to its base. Tragically, Hannah died of tuberculosis, after being discharged from the R.A.F. on medical grounds, when he was only twenty-five. The V.C. was also awarded posthumously in 1946 to Guardsman Edward Charlton of the Irish Guards, who was an 'old boy' of the 32nd Manchester Company and a tank driver during the closing days of the War. On his own initiative, to retrieve his comrades from a dangerous situation, Charlton advanced alone up a road near Hamburg in full view of the enemy, firing his Browning gun from the hip, until he was fatally wounded. He died shortly afterwards in enemy hands. When he volunteered he had told his mother, 'Someday you will be proud of me.'[7]

On the domestic front, when the air-raid siren went on the parade evenings of the 1st Ipswich Company, in Suffolk, the lads were marched with exemplary precision into a nearby shelter and there they carried on class work until the 'all clear' signal sounded. Quite often the officers would have to dash off to report as wardens, and several of the older boys were themselves air-raid messengers and had to report for duty as soon as a warning sounded. The 64th Birmingham Company had their own team of messengers who reported to the Queen Elizabeth Hospital, Edgbaston, after an air raid, where they obtained a list of the casualties and sent this to their central headquarters in order that a comprehensive list could be compiled. Belfast received several terrible air raids in the spring of 1941 and, as a result, there was a brisk demand locally for the erection of the new 'Morrison' family shelters, which kept Brigade volunteers exceedingly busy throughout the summer on this aspect of national service. Meanwhile, the rationing of food, confectionery, petrol and clothing, and the wholesale shortage of supplies of nearly every kind, added to the hardship of these years of stress and strain. 'At this critical time in our Country's history every Boy will be keen to be of help and comfort to those in his home,' ran an Executive memorandum of July 1940 to captains of companies, recommending that parades be held for Home Defence Instruction:

> He can only render this service if he knows what to do in time of emergency or danger . . . The provision of such training will call forth an eager response from our Boys, so many of whom are deprived this summer of the interest of Camp, and the

Executive believe that parents too will be grateful that their sons should be given instruction which may well prove of inestimable value . . .[8]

The Boys' Brigade found its staff in both London and Glasgow drastically reduced by the 'call-up' and came to rely increasingly on local organizers, but every effort was made to see that companies did not close down. Life Boy teams were, in any case, the most seriously hit by Government measures such as evacuation. Where all the officers had left to serve in the Armed Forces, much of the work was carried on with the help of staff sergeants and NCOs, often functioning under great difficulties in urban areas, aided by the chaplain or some 'senior' friend. In August 1941, Stanley Smith recorded that the second year of hostilities had brought the War very close to many in the movement. 'The whole Brigade is proud of the gallant conduct of Officers and Boys who have shown true Christian Manliness in circumstances of peril,' wrote Stanley rhetorically. 'After two years of war The Boys' Brigade maintains its service to Boyhood. We have reason to thank God for all that He has given us strength to achieve during a time of unexampled difficulty.' It was generally felt by the leadership that The Boys' Brigade could best aid the war effort by keeping their activities at the highest possible state of efficiency and by extending their scope and appeal — even by opening their Home Defence Instruction parades to non-Brigade boys of twelve and over in the hope that they might eventually be attracted to apply for full membership. In addition to its supreme Christian purpose, the Brigade felt that it was already providing valuable pre-Service training: 'the B.B. is giving just that training which not only fits a fellow for national service, but gives him that something extra in his make-up which leads to being singled out for promotion'.[9]

Thus in March 1942 the Executive did not feel justified in sanctioning the affiliation of battalions and companies of the Brigade to the Army Cadet Force, as had been done during the First World War, for they held 'the view that it would not increase the effectiveness of such training, and might lead to the religious aims of the Brigade being compromised'. Boys could become members of the Cadet Force in an individual capacity, provided they had parental consent, whilst still maintaining their Brigade membership. The Boys' Brigade, in taking this position, continued to act as an extremely sensitive barometer of shifts in public and governmental attitudes towards the military in British society. Meanwhile, in Hertfordshire, the 1st Barnet Company had intended to follow Stanley Smith's advice in a memorandum of 4 February 1941 to battalion secretaries and form a local flight unit of the new Air Training Corps. The A.T.C. was the first ever State-directed, voluntary, uniformed, pre-entry training scheme, and it soon had accumulated 200,000 recruits. When this application fell through, a unit of the Cadet Corps was formed from the Company, with Brigade officers in charge, for boys of over fourteen years of age who had received church and parental consent. In 1943, however, the over-worked Brigade lieutenant running the unit, a local chartered accountant with an Army Cadet Force commission, was compelled to close it down, owing to his putting in seven days a week with either the Brigade or the Cadets, while changes in the running of the local Hertfordshire Cadets made it impossible to run both in tandem. 'I have weighed the position carefully in my mind,' he wrote explaining this decision:

> . . . and with considerable regret I have asked the Colonel Commandant to accept my resignation from the Cadets and to allow me to close the Unit connected with The Boys' Brigade. The B.B. Company is over 50 years old and I have been interested in it for over 20 so you will understand my feelings in that direction. You

know from what you have seen the standard of drill, gymnasium and other activities to which we attain, and it is because of this and because so many of our Old Boys have been so successful in their Army careers that I feel justified in following the B.B. rather than Army Cadets.[10]

Whether the Second World War was merely the occasion rather than the cause of social and economic changes in Britain, one outcome of emergency wartime planning was the Government's growing recognition of the importance of the social, cultural and physical welfare of the young as a necessary sphere of educational provision. Voluntary youth organizations, of which The Boys' Brigade was a pioneer, had long promoted the welfare of youth to the best of their often meagre resources but with little or no statutory recognition from central and local government, with the exception of the 'special areas' during the mid-thirties. All this changed on 27 November 1939 when the Board of Education issued its famous Circular 1486, 'In the Service of Youth', to Local Education Authorities (L.E.A.'s). Because of its far-reaching impact on the leisure of the young this Circular has become an important document in British social history. The Government was not concerned primarily with delinquency as in 1916 nor with physical fitness as in 1937 but with the 'all-round' development of Britain's nearly three million fourteen to twenty-one year olds who had left school and whose welfare had for too long been neglected by the State. A National Youth Advisory Council (N.Y.A.C.) was established and Youth Committees were to be set up in all areas by the L.E.A.'s, whose responsibility it was to see that adequate local provision was made for the recreational needs of the young. The Youth Service, as it became known, was born with this Circular, comprising all the voluntary organizations and the statutory services arrayed in 'the service of youth'. Since, in practice, Circular 1486 produced little in the way of local government involvement with the young, it was replaced with a more explicit directive soon after: Circular 1516, 'The Challenge of Youth', of 27 June 1940, which laid down in some detail the aims of the 'new' service and directed the L.E.A.'s to set up boys' clubs, youth centres, evening institutes, and other clubs. 'At a time like the present, when the nation is fighting for its life, the preparation of our youth for their full participation in the life of the nation assumes a new significance', the Circular concluded. 'In the days that lie immediately before us . . . we cannot afford to neglect the youth for whose free future the struggle is being waged.'[11]

Nonetheless, these circulars had largely failed to achieve their desired impact at the local level and were thus, in turn, supplanted by the far more sweeping Board of Education Circular 1577 of 20 December 1941, which recommended the registration of all youths of both sexes from sixteen to eighteen (in effect sixteen to seventeen) for national service, to be carried out through the local offices of the Ministry of Labour. Young people who registered by order under powers taken by Defence Regulation were invited to attend interviews conducted by representatives from the Home Guard, the Air Training Corps, local Youth Committees and the voluntary youth organizations. At these interviews those found to be 'unattached' were advised, though not compelled, to join a suitable youth movement or pre-service unit. This unusual interference by the State in the liberty of the adolescent has excited little comment from the historian and accounts differ as to how much pressure was brought to bear on those interviewed to 'serve their country' by joining a 'voluntary' organization. In any case, government coercion proved difficult to graft onto the established voluntary system even during wartime, although the Army Cadet Force was soon overwhelmed with recruits as a result of this Circular. The effects of the late 1941 Registration Order on The Boys' Brigade are more difficult to gauge accurately, but B.B. promotion leaflets were quick to define the movement as 'a Training Organization, approved for Boys registering at the age of sixteen to seventeen years, in which membership can be continued until the time comes to join one of the Services'. It is probably no coincidence that the largest ever increase in boy numbers during a single session was recorded for the Brigade in 1942 to 1943. Yet an analysis of the first 30,000 registrations in Birmingham revealed that while forty per cent of sixteen to seventeen year olds were undertaking some form of 'approved' activity or were in full-time education, sixty per cent were still 'unattached' and, even allowing for the popularity of the Cadets and the Air Training Corps among boys during wartime, only about twelve per cent of the 'attached' were in youth organizations other than pre-service units.[12]

It was the 'Butler' Education Act of 1944, which shaped the British state educational system for twenty years or more, that finally gave notice of the Government's intention to become a full and active partner in providing for youth work and that henceforth voluntary organizations were no longer sufficient for the social education of the adolescent. The sections of the Act relating to the Youth Service were designed to integrate it into the nation's educational structure and to formalize many *ad hoc* wartime practices by bringing an end to the voluntary principle which had allowed the L.E.A.'s to opt out of involvement in youth work. In future, every L.E.A. was to provide adequate facilities for recreation and training in its area — camps, holiday classes, playing fields, play centres — while having 'regard to the expediency of cooperation with any voluntary societies or bodies whose objects include the provision of facilities or the organization of activities of a similar character'. To implement this new policy of partnership, the Ministry of Education started making generous grants to the headquarters of the national voluntary youth organizations (in 1947-48 the total amount spent among nineteen such bodies was £164,552). So the outcome of the Board of Education Circulars from 1939 to 1941, and the sections of the 1944 Education Act dealing with the Youth Service, was much more direct government intervention in the field of youth work than ever before.[13]

As a result, Stanley Smith suggested quite seriously in February 1944 that the trend was towards advocates of compulsion forcibly attempting to herd all British youngsters into a monolithic state-controlled youth movement, and that this would seriously weaken the spirit of voluntarism. 'Thousands of men and women who are on active service just now are eager to come back and lead our young people,' he wrote in the *Listener*. 'I wonder what they would say if they thought that in their absence there was an idea of snuffing out the voluntary principle and bringing in compulsory membership of clubs, scouts, brigades, youth centres and pre-service corps?' It is evident, despite Stanley Smith's fears, that a regimented, compulsory state youth movement along Eastern European lines was never the intention of the Ministry of Education, which repeatedly stressed the desirability of partnership between the statutory and voluntary sides of youth work. In fact, there was little uniformity of pattern in the development of the Youth Service throughout the country, and the policy of partnership was variously implemented at local level. On the other hand, all the voluntary organizations certainly felt the benefit of the new wartime interest in the welfare of the younger generation, and, under the patronage of the Churches and the L.E.A.'s, many new Brigade companies came into existence with their autonomy and principles preserved intact. 'In this country we have been helped undoubtedly by the prominence given to youth work by the Government,' claimed Stanley more favourably at the Brigade's London Council. 'People are conscious of youth and the needs of youth as never before but our stability today is due primarily to the devoted service of Officers with the loyal support of NCOs and Boys.'[14]

The Boys' Brigade celebrated its Diamond Jubilee in 1943, the year of the invasion of Sicily, with special displays taking place at the Albert Hall in London and Hampden Park in Glasgow. Thanksgiving services broadcast on the overseas transmissions of the B.B.C. on the last day of the Brigade's sixtieth year were all that was possible as a world celebration during wartime, but local displays and services marked the event throughout Britain. The grand climax came on 16 October 1943 when King George VI became the first reigning monarch to conduct an inspection of the Brigade in person. This event had been arranged, to quote *The Times*, 'so that the King might personally pay tribute to this mainspring of disciplined youth training'. The King, accompanied by the Queen and Princess Elizabeth, inspected three hundred senior boys, the majority NCOs drawn from nearly as many London companies, in the quadrangle of Windsor Castle. Military restrictions on transport had precluded a large international assembly in London, as was originally planned by the Executive, and for security reasons no previous publicity could be given to the royal inspection in the press — it even came as a last minute surprise to many of the boys present. The King first proceeded down the ranks and the Queen and the Princess then made their own separate inspection. 'Many were the questions asked, many the interested comments made', as the *Gazette* breathlessly recorded:

> The Royal Family appeared to be absorbed in their task, while the Boys stood as veterans, vying in their rigid stillness with those immoveable Grenadiers. In the twenty minutes which the actual inspection lasted not a Boy faltered; not a Boy fell out. Meantime the Brass Band of the 88th London came into action, accompanying the Royal progress with a discreet and tuneful melody.

The command to form hollow square was given and the King, without benefit of a loudspeaker, gave an address (much quoted in subsequent Brigade literature) which was clearly audible throughout the quadrangle:

> When The Boys' Brigade was founded sixty years ago your Founder, Sir William A. Smith, builded better than he knew, for he started not only a great movement, but one from which all our present widespread youth training was destined to spring . . . I feel sure that the B.B. will go from strength to strength because it is built upon the twin pillars of religion and discipline, and so is meeting two of the greatest needs of the present time. Good luck to you and all your comrades. May all of you Boys live to see the centenary of this great movement.[15]

A few weeks earlier, on 4 September 1943, representatives of every battalion and district of The Boys' Brigade had been summoned to a special conference in London, in order to allay criticism of Headquarters and also to consider the interim report of the Development Committee's proposals for the consolidation and extension of the Brigade during and after the War. The Executive received this report in the light of the views expressed at the conference and approved certain specific alterations and additions to be referred to the Development Committee for inclusion in their report before it reached its final form. Then, in May 1944, with the Normandy landings fast approaching, the Executive published the final report as *Plans for Advance*, which was to become the blueprint for the postwar development of The Boys' Brigade. This document recommended the closest cooperation with the Youth Committees set up during the war by the L.E.A.'s, and regular consultation with their Youth Organizers, so that The Boys' Brigade might fully benefit from the new Youth Service through the provision of instructors, playing fields, gymnastic and games equipment, and finance. Brigade officers were told in no uncertain terms to play their part in the 'Service of Youth' plans for their localities. The report also proposed that the term 'County Administration' be replaced by 'Division'; that no boy be appointed to NCO rank before his actual age was fifteen; that the boys' uniform be standardized; that public relations and publicity should be improved; and that the upper age limit for warrant officers should be abolished. New regulations to give effect to most of these proposals were introduced once the War was over by the Brigade Secretariat. 'Great days lie ahead of us when our serving members will return,' exhorted Lord Home, Brigade President, in his foreword to *Plans for Advance*. 'The outlook and the ideas which they bring home will set The Boys' Brigade on its future course.' It is to these so eagerly anticipated postwar years that our account now turns.[16]

Immediately after the War, Britain was preoccupied with reconstruction, the nationalization of various industries by the incoming Labour Government, the creation of the National Health Service, and various methods of financing such ambitious projects, including the American Lend Lease loan, the 'austerity' budgets of Chancellor Sir Stafford Cripps, and the continued rationing of consumer goods. The Boys' Brigade had, therefore, to make a rapid adjustment to a rather sombre postwar British society, but returning soldiers, sailors and airmen quickly made up the strength of officers and provided the movement with enthusiastic leaders adequately trained in military drill. However, though prolonging conscription until 1961 assisted the Brigade by providing a continuous pool of drill instructors, many of whom became full-time B.B. officers, it also served to obstruct juvenile recruitment, in that the military image of the Brigade proved far less attractive in an age of compulsory National Service than it had in an age of voluntarism before the War. Yet the biggest problem which faced The Boys' Brigade in the late 1940s and 1950s, as far as recruitment was concerned, was to find ways of expanding into the new, more anonymous settings of new towns and suburban council estates, following the population movement away from the inner cities where the B.B. had once flourished. The absence of churches in many of the new postwar housing estates meant that, without halls to operate in locally, prospective companies could not even get off the ground. The loss to the movement of their inner-city recruits from strong working-class neighbourhoods in cities like Nottingham, Manchester, Newcastle and Glasgow, was never adequately replaced, although in some new towns, like Milton Keynes, the Brigade was to recruit in quite healthy numbers. 'In this war-weary world, in which anything which suggests military organization is suspect in many quarters and in which conscription and the widespread adoption of camping holidays have robbed The Boys' Brigade of much of the novelty which it offered the Boys of earlier generations,' pondered Dr J.W. McLeod, the ex-President of the Leeds Battalion, 'progress tends to be more difficult and there may be a temporary constriction of numbers.' Although Brigade strength rapidly increased to 90,000 adolescent boys in the U.K. by the closing years of the 1940s, the accuracy of this judgement was borne out by the trough of the mid-1950s when it settled at 80,000.[17]

In 1947 Sir Joseph Maclay, later Lord Maclay, a successful and pragmatic Scottish businessman, took over from Lord Home as Brigade President, and Roger Peacock announced his retirement from the position of Administrative and Financial Secretary at Abbey House in London. Peacock, Captain of the 76th London Company for nearly forty years, was at one stage in the 1920s Editor of the *Gazette*, Secretary for Administration, Secretary for Finance, *and* Secretary for Equipment. The originator of 'B.B. Week', he was for many years the indispensable right-hand man of Stanley Smith and, although some found him stern and unapproachable, his strong personality and gifts for leadership were placed unstintingly at the service of the movement he loved. Peacock's forty-five years as a loyal colleague, first of Sir William and then of his son, comprised the longest secretarial service in the history of the Brigade — for which the historian of the movement should certainly be grateful, since he left behind a wealth of invaluable documentary evidence.[18]

Meanwhile, the Brigade fulfilled one of the pledges made in *Plans for Advance* — to secure suitable accommodation for Brigade training schools in Scotland and England — by setting up Carronvale House in Larbert, Stirlingshire, and Felden Lodge, at Boxmoor, Hertfordshire, as National Training Centres. Scotland had lost its original training centre at Balrossie, Kilmacolm, when it was requisitioned for war purposes, so the announcement in 1946 that Carronvale had been acquired as a replacement was greeted with enthusiasm. The history of Carronvale can be traced back for over 150 years, and one of the many striking features of the Brigade's property is its magnificent woodwork. In the early nineteenth century the Hon. Duncan Robertson lined the rooms at Carronvale with mahogany grown on his Jamaican estate; when, towards the end of the century, extensive alterations were made by George Sherriff, a lifelong Boys' Brigade supporter, the original structure and woodwork were preserved. Carronvale was officially opened by Lord Home on 28 June 1947 and soon became a household word for training throughout The Boys' Brigade in Scotland.[19]

Felden Lodge in Hertfordshire was originally owned by Lord and Lady Cooper but during the Second World War it was converted to a hostel for Dutch and Belgian refugees. It then belonged to Oxford University for a short period until it was put on the open market again. The Boys' Brigade had providently set aside £14,000 for a postwar development fund, primarily to provide training centres, but assistance to the tune of £25,000 was needed from the South Africa Aid to Britain Fund — through the King George Jubilee Trust — before large country mansions such as Felden Lodge, with its thirty-two acres of ground, could be considered for purchase. 'This magnificent gift meant that the Brigade could "shop around" in quite a different market,' and, owing to the persistence of Sweyn Barnes, Secretary for Training, 'instead of inspecting fairly large suburban houses the [Training] Committee started to look at country mansions, and whereas they had previously been received by butchers and bakers they now found themselves taking tea with city magnates and dowager duchesses!' Felden Lodge was officially opened on 22 October 1949 by the Duke of Gloucester, who said in his speech that 'the acquisition of this fine new house now provides the Brigade with a training centre of its own, where its leaders can come and learn the secrets of their craft'. Felden quickly acquired an international reputation as officers, NCOs and boys from all over the B.B. world gravitated there for weekend training courses on almost every Brigade activity imaginable. It is thus hardly surprising, as the 1940s drew to a close with the opening of new National Training Centres in England

*During the Second World War, many members of the B.B. undertook
voluntary duties. These members of the Bournemouth Battalion
became Auxiliary Fire Service messengers.*

*King George VI, Queen Elizabeth and Princess Elizabeth
inspect the B.B. at Windsor Castle in 1943, the year of the movement's
Diamond Jubilee.*

At the end of the 1951 Relay Run celebrating the Festival of Britain, Sgt. R. Merritt presents George VI with a message from The Boys' Brigade. Behind the King stands Stanley Smith, the Brigade Secretary.

B.B. boys from all over the world came to the 1954 Founder's Camp at Eton, held to mark the centenary of the birth of William Smith.

(The Daily Record, Glasgow)

A contingent of officers and boys marches past
the Queen and Prince Philip at Balmoral during
the B.B.'s Seventy-fifth Anniversary celebrations in 1958.

The 750 Camp for senior boys in 1958 concentrated on sport and other
outdoor activities. The Commanding Officer was Sir John (now Lord)
Hunt, fifth from the left, back row; to his left is the Brigade
Secretary, Major General D.J. Wilson-Haffenden, and to his right, the
Rev. David Sheppard, now Bishop of Liverpool.

(Liverpool Daily Post and Echo Ltd.)

Prince Philip visits some B.B. boys on a Duke of Edinburgh Award
Scheme expedition. The Brigade became involved in a pilot 'Adventurous
Training' course in 1955, the success of which led to the launch of
the Award Scheme in the following year.

and Scotland and a healthy total of 90,000 boy members, that the decades to come were awaited with a quiet confidence by The Boys' Brigade. With the benefit of hindsight, this confidence may appear somewhat misplaced, for the late 1940s can now be seen as the summit of the movement's postwar recruitment in Britain.[20]

The following decade was to be marked by several important events in the Brigade calendar, such as the worldwide celebrations on the centenary of the birth of the Founder (1954) and the Seventy-fifth Anniversary celebrations (1958), which will be dealt with at a later stage of this narrative. Let us look first at the particular historical circumstances within which the Brigade was located in order to understand more fully both its own subsequent development and its contribution to national life during these years. At the outset of this period, the British were still governed by a political philosophy which was part collectivist, part moralist, and which espoused social as well as economic controls. As some small indication of how the social atmosphere was more inhibited than it is today, senior Brigade staff of Roger Peacock's generation would never expect to be addressed by their Christian names in the London Office. By the late 1950s, however, the nation was living through an era of unprecedented material prosperity, its overseas Empire was gradually being wound up, and liberal 'reforms' marked a retreat from the social controls imposed in the Victorian era by evangelism and Nonconformity. Affluence, with its attendant hire-purchase, 'consumer society' ethos, and the inability of the British to adjust to a changing international order, were to be the two major themes of British history in the late 1950s and early 1960s.

The Boys' Brigade thus found itself as a Christian, militarily structured organization, placed in a spiritual and cultural environment which was becoming increasingly materialistic, in which neither authority and discipline nor the Christian religion were taken any longer for granted. If the Brigade had been founded on the twin pillars of religion and discipline, it was now becoming apposite to ask whether or not those seemingly enduring pillars were in danger of crumbling. 'These are days of easy amusement and cheap distractions and low moral standards, of materialism when money is so tremendous an attraction to everybody and for many almost the only goal,' lamented Sir Donald Finnemore, Brigade Vice-President, in a 1959 address to a conference of Brigade chaplains. 'For thousands discipline has largely gone from home and school. We believe that for any proper life there are still written in the plainest possible and largest possible letters "Thou shalt" and "Thou shalt not".' How did a Church youth movement, dedicated to such moral imperatives and to the late nineteenth-century ideal of Christian manliness, come to terms with a rapidly changing, more secular and more affluent society? How far did the adolescent of 1959 differ from the young men who had gone to war twenty years earlier?[21]

'Glowing, good-to-look-at, bugle-blowing ranks of Boys' Brigades [sic], preceded by police motor-cycle escort, delighted my admiration as I drove through Brunswick Road the other Sunday afternoon,' wrote the columnist of a Gloucester local paper. 'The sight, by contrast, of the frowzy, slouching "Teds" sneering under the Co-op clock, was like a breath of slum air across a spring field.' The contrast between opposing versions of the adolescent as perceived by the 'respectable' adult in the mid-1950s could not be made with greater clarity, but it is the appearance of delinquent or rebellious youth, represented here by the teddy boy, that helps to explain the rejection of the voluntary youth organizations as an outlet for leisure by large numbers of their less rebellious and more law-abiding contemporaries.[22]

Earlier, in 1951, the year of the Conservative election victory, Stanley Smith gave a talk to the Athenaeum Club on the modish topic of 'Juvenile Delinquency', claiming that 'there is a dangerously soft attitude prevalent which whittles away all personal responsibility for wrong doing, and the child comes to regard himself not as sinful, but just as "a psychological case"'. The Brigade Secretary went on to call for a change in the moral environment of the offender through the restoration of the Christian faith as the dominant influence in every phase of British life. Yet by 1959, when crime rates among juveniles had reached the highest levels ever known in Britain, the Report of the Committee on Children and Young Persons set up by Parliament suggested that more than a decline in church attendance was to blame for rising crime figures:

> It is not always so clearly recognized what a complete change there has been in social and personal relationships (between classes, between the sexes and between individuals) and also in the basic assumptions which regulate behaviour. These major changes in the cultural background may well have replaced the disturbances of war as factors which contribute in themselves to instability within the family. In such a climate it is no wonder that many young people are bewildered or that some parents become uncertain what standards they should insist on or what ideals they should put before their children. It is more a matter for surprise that so few young people get into real trouble and that there are, on the whole, so few families which break down or otherwise fail their children.

Stanley Smith with his Calvinist upbringing may have rejected such a general approach as showing a dangerously 'soft' attitude towards juvenile crime and 'problem' families, but it was becoming increasingly evident that the duty of the State to help such families in carrying out their proper functions could not be evaded for much longer by the still inadequate social services.[23]

'That vast schemes of social welfare should co-exist with grave deterioration of moral standards must raise serious doubts in the minds of all capable of thought,' Roger Peacock declaimed of the changing times in 1954. 'That the Welfare State and God's Kingdom on earth do not seem to march in step, suggests that paganism is by no means bounded by the iron curtain. Indeed, the new order almost seems to be disorder on the grand scale.' It is apparent from a widely read study of rebellious youth in the Welfare State that Peacock was not alone in seeking to determine how the so-called 'affluent society' of the 1950s had somehow led to rising figures for juvenile crime in almost every West European country. T.R. Fyvel's *The Insecure Offenders* (1961) suggested that mass advertising, mass consumption and mass culture were to blame for creating a new commercialized youth culture which weakened family ties, created delinquent gangs, increased moral confusion and led to a materialistic outlook with which the youth services and the State in general were unable to compete. Collectively, these influences were seen as a sort of cultural 'downward pull' in postwar British society which, in many areas of the inner cities, had created pockets of juvenile lawlessness, exemplified in the 1950s by the teddy boy or 'cosh boy' subculture. Much later, when Fyvel came to look at the 'insecure offenders' in retrospect, he implied why a Church-related, morally authoritative youth movement would come to exert a declining appeal among postwar British youth (The Boys' Brigade lost over a third of its boy membership between 1949 and 1979):

> What I saw as finally crumbling by the fifties was the classical bourgeois capitalist society dominated by the urban upper middle class. This society consolidated its

status in the 19th century and was based on exclusive upper middle class economic privilege, buttressed by domestic servants. *It was filled with institutions and patriarchal figures embodying moral authority.* By the fifties, this society was being rapidly replaced by the British consumer society ... Before the new onrush of mass consumption, mass advertising and mass entertainment, the whole system of upper middle class exclusiveness, with its large houses and servants, was simply swept away. So, but more slowly, was its system of moral authority: deference to upper class and state authority; to employers, the law, the police, the churches and teachers, and to parents in the family which had held society together. A new authority was assumed by the advertisers, entertainers and other hedonistic voices of the consumer society. [my italics][24]

The undocumented assertion that economic and social privilege based upon land and wealth had somehow been replaced from the mid-twentieth century onwards by the spurious values and hidden power of the mass consumer society may appear a somewhat sweeping historical analysis. Yet the collapse of a 'patriarchal' system of moral authority such as Fyvel described would, if true, have done great harm to the progress of a youth movement whose Object recommended the 'promotion of habits of Obedience, Reverence, Discipline, Self-respect and all that tends towards a true Christian Manliness'. Not unexpectedly, Fyvel called in 1978 for the 'upward pull' of a 'reorganized' adolescent life, even if this had touches of regimentation, to prevent the weakening of discipline in family, school, work and elsewhere caused by the materialism of a mass consumption society. 'Instead of profound questioning about capitalist society and social deviance, a guided reorganization of adolescent life is more appropriate to the social needs of our time,' he argued in advocating the establishment of 'a strengthened organization for guiding adolescents towards getting on in society'. The Boys' Brigade could possibly take heart from this advocacy of a return to the discipline and spiritual values which the movement had so steadfastly upheld in the face of changing attitudes and shifting moral standards. Of course, not all the adolescents of the 1950s were juvenile delinquents, but mostly what Stanley Smith referred to as 'normal' young people. These were characterized in 1958 by novelist and essayist Colin MacInnes as much more lively, happy and classless than older age groups; not so much hostile to, as blithely indifferent to, the Establishment; irreversibly English despite the influence of American mass culture; and more internationally minded and more independently mature than previous generations. This author, unlike Fyvel, took the view that increasing juvenile delinquency could accompany a vast general improvement of social behaviour among the young. Fringe groups like the teddy boys, soon followed by the mods and rockers of the early 1960s, may have become more violently antisocial, but the conduct of the young as a whole, MacInnes claimed, had become much more happily adjusted to society — which might explain why each group of teenagers so fervently despised the others.[25]

More rigorous social surveys were also carried out during this period to discover why young people did not join youth organizations and why, of the roughly one-third who did join, so many left soon afterwards. The most renowned and far-reaching of these surveys in its impact on The Boys' Brigade was the Albermarle Report of 1959-60 on the Youth Service in England and Wales. Briefly, the Report recommended that such a service should be made available for all the nation's youth aged from fourteen to twenty; that the Ministry of Education initiate a ten-year development programme advised by a Youth Service Development Council; and that the Minister take steps to increase the existing pool of full-time youth leaders. All these proposals were accepted and, in time, implemented by the Minister. Critics of the Albermarle Report complained that these remedies did not really tackle the roots of the problem and felt that the committee who produced the Report were too much influenced by the 1958 riots in London and Nottingham, which had led to their seeing the issue of the behaviour of large sections of the adolescent population as largely one of deterrence and control. In any case, the historian would possibly regard the Committee's preoccupation with a 'crime wave among the young' as being somewhat premature, for 1958 and the previous decade served as little more than a prelude to what later came to be disting-uished rather unhelpfully as 'youth culture' and its corollary, the so-called adolescent and student 'rebellions' of the sixties. The expansion of the Youth Service which Albermarle set in progress was, on the other hand, to have severe repercussions for a movement like The Boys' Brigade, which relied upon the voluntary service of officers who might now be attracted away by youth clubs which paid them for their services.[26]

In 1950 the prospects for Britain's future looked much brighter than in the immediate postwar years of austerity. 'Reconstruction' was virtually over and peace could at last be savoured by the long-suffering British public. To celebrate this spirit, the outgoing Labour Government planned a Festival of Britain to be held on London's South Bank on the centenary of the Great Exhibition of 1851. To mark the occasion, The Boys' Brigade organized a 'Festival of Britain Run', on the same lines as the 1935 Royal Jubilee Run, in which relays of boy-runners on five routes from the extremities of the United Kingdom were to carry a message to reach King George VI on 10 May 1951 at Buckingham Palace. Since this Run reproduced many of the features already familiar from sixteen years earlier, it would be superfluous to give additional details of ceremonial transfers and civic ceremonies or of the many colourful incidents along the way reproduced in the souvenir of the Festival Run, *A Message to the King*; however, credit must be given to William Whiteley, Brigade Public Relations Secretary, who organized the whole scheme.[27]

The Festival Run reached its climax in brilliant sunshine, after days and nights of rain and storm along all five routes into London, when the final bearers with their escorts doubled in to Buckingham Palace to hand their batons to the King. Their entry was proceeded by the arrival of the Brigade Guard of Honour, headed by a silver band and a combined drum, fife and bugle band, which aroused the admiration of the crowds in the Mall as they marched with drums and fifes playing from Wellington Barracks in through the gates of the Palace. 'The months of preparation, organization and rehear-sal, the devoted service of countless Officers and the gallantry of the Boys, many of whom had run through darkness, rain and snow along lonely roads and across bleak moors,' eulogized the *Gazette* in an eight-page account of the Run, 'the well-planned organization and the willing cooperation of so many friends and well-wishers had surmounted all difficulties. The Run was over.'[28]

Close on the Coronation Year celebrations of 1953, which included the televised presence of the Duke of Edinburgh as Chairman at the annual Albert Hall Display, there followed another milestone in Brigade history: the worldwide events arranged for the centenary of the birth of the Brigade's Founder, Sir William Alexander Smith, in 1954. All over Britain planned events were held in commemoration, such as the Torch Run from Thurso, the Founder's birthplace, to Glasgow, where the Brigade Council was being held in September on a scale reminiscent of the 1933 Jubilee — including a massive 'Conventicle' in Hampden Park (18,000 boys and officers, 60,000 spectators), and an excursion by steamer down the Clyde. On 20 February 1954, Belfast Battalion staged a 'Cavalcade of Boyhood' in the King's Hall, and on 21 May an outdoor show, 'B.B. Fanfare', at Windsor Park, the city's largest football ground. The display of the Dundee Battalion in the city's Ice Rink surpassed all records, while the Edinburgh Battalion put on the pageant 'Scotland the Brave' at the Empire Theatre for a whole week. Another memorable pageant, 'Soldier of Christ', based on the life of the Founder and written by Thomas Henderson and Douglas Smith, son of Sir William, was performed by battalions and groups in many parts of the country. On a national scale, events really got under way on Saturday 19 June 1954 with 'The Festival of Boyhood' held at Wembley Stadium, organized by the London District, with about 3,000 boys from all over Britain taking part in a spectacular programme watched by ten times their number on the terraces and stands. 'As a spectacle the whole show was interesting, colourful and well presented,' wrote a visitor, John H. Rowley, for the *B.B. Gazette*:

> Each item in the packed programme was well conceived and carried out with exemplary precision. The sight of thousands of Boys, gathered together from all parts of the country, carrying out their allotted tasks with such polished efficiency, could not fail to arouse and hold the interest of the most casual beholder. This was 'Boyhood' in the arena. How could it fail to be a 'Festival'![29]

In August 1954 a special Founder's Camp was held for 2,000 boys in 400 tents parked on Eton's famous playing fields — the first ever Brigade International Camp. Heavy rain and mud failed to dampen the spirits of those present, but, as Eric Chapman (District Organizer and later Field Officer for the West of England District) remembers, it was often necessary to move the mess marquees because of 'the sheer odour of the stagnant mud and grass'. Boys came from overseas to represent the B.B. in Malaya, Africa, Canada, America, Holland, Denmark, Singapore and New Zealand: in the words of the B.B. song, 'a mighty band of brothers spreading out across the world' (see Chapter 8). All those present, from Commandant Sir Donald Finnemore to the youngest boy, had their own selective memories of the Camp which they looked back upon with gratitude in later years. Highlights of the Camp included the visitor's day held on Saturday to inspect the biggest B.B. camp ever, marred by a parade held in the pouring rain; Sunday camp church parades and services in formal uniform held in the two Eton College Chapels; the visit and inspection by the Brigade President on the Tuesday; the great parade to London by special trains for the service at Westminster Hall on the Wednesday; excursions to such places as Heathrow, Windsor Castle, and by river steamer to Marlow-on-Thames; and the climax of the Friday night torchlight parade and camp fire held in Windsor. 'It will sound rather good in later years to be able to say of another fellow, "Yes, we were at Eton together",' as the Official Souvenir rather quaintly put it, 'but there will be for all of us a deeper significance when we say, "We were both at the Founder's Camp in '54." ' The Camp was followed, as usual in the Brigade calendar, by Council in September, and then came the Old Boys' Reunion Rally of 22 October 1954 held in the Albert Hall, leading up to the culminating services of thanksgiving in St. Paul's Cathedral in London and the High Kirk of St. Giles in Edinburgh on Wednesday 27 October, the actual birth date, with Founder's Day Services held the following Sunday. 'So the great "year to remember" comes and goes and will, we pray to God,' a B.B. handout declared, 'prove an inspiration throughout the Brigade to advance in its dedicated purpose, in its efficiency and in its numbers.'[30]

The centenary of his father's birth was also the year during which Stanley Smith, Brigade Secretary since 1925, had chosen to retire and hand over the reins of office to a new incumbent. Aged sixty-five, but looking much younger, Stanley had lived with his brother, a fellow bachelor, at Wraysbury, near Windsor, since 1941, where his circle of young acquaintances had grown to include most of the boys of the village as well as many Etonians and the members of the local B.B. battalion. Stanley told the local newspaper that, free for the first time in his life from active participation in the Brigade, he intended to spend more time in his garden. He and his brother were an inseparable pair in their years of retirement, often holidaying together in their beloved German Black Forest, so that Douglas' illness and subsequent death in 1965 left a great void in his brother's life. Stanley spent his last years in a nursing home, dying peacefully three days before his eighty-sixth birthday on 25 November 1974. Not only in Brigade circles but also in his wider contacts with leading religious and public figures, Stanley Smith's vibrant personality and easy charm of manner won many friends for the movement he so ably represented. Administration may not have been his forte (there was always Roger Peacock for that), but his value to the Brigade was more as an exceptional ambassador for the organization, its Christian message, and indeed, for the cause of the Youth Service in general.[31]

The Brigade Executive appointed Major General D.J. Wilson-Haffenden in Stanley's place as Brigade Secretary. 'Haffy' was the son of a Baptist Minister and, after nearly thirty years in the Indian Army, eventually returned to England following Independence to become the Secretary of the Church Missionary Society. But for a year after leaving the Army in 1948, Wilson-Haffenden served as a missionary at the Christian Medical College at Vellore, South India, and in both 1954 and 1966 was the Chairman of the London Billy Graham Crusade — significant details in the light of his B.B. career. Since 1950 the General had been President of the London District and was also a Brigade Vice-President. An outgoing, robust Christian, the new Secretary personified a different style of management to that of his predecessor Stanley Smith, emphasizing that the Brigade was not just another organization for boys but must of necessity be evangelical in outlook: ' "We don't want any of that Billy Graham nonsense here," the retiring Secretary warned me. "Well, in that case you shouldn't have asked me," I replied.' Here is Wilson-Haffenden's own statement of his guiding aims, seen in retrospect long after vacating the post of Secretary but nonetheless convincing for all that:

> I had realized that the Brigade needed a new slant. They paid lip service to the Brigade Object but people were not doing anything very definite about advancing the Kingdom. Because as I've always said in The Boys' Brigade my own view was that if you want to advance a Kingdom you must create more citizens for that Kingdom — and I saw that as my main object in the Brigade — to recall them to their first Object as laid down by William Smith. To definitely go for an ardent evangelical thrust, to try to win boys for Christ.[32]

The introduction of a more 'ardent' approach to the religious policy of The Boys' Brigade did not recommend itself universally and could at times result in a clash between Scottish Calvinism and Gospel Evangelism on the Executive that Wilson-Haffenden did little to ameliorate during his period of office. In the early 1960s the Brigade Secretary became unpopular with a faction in the

London District as a result of his more aggressive views on the conversion of boys, but he never lost his aplomb, even when a meeting might be going against him, and he successfully fought off all attempts at ousting him from the leadership. On the whole, while Wilson-Haffenden may have alienated many of those who could not share his fundamentalist beliefs, there is no doubt that he did much to revivify a movement which was in danger of becoming averse to change and innovation. His decade as Brigade Secretary, from 1954 to 1965, spanned a period when not only was the Duke of Edinburgh's Award Scheme taken up with enthusiasm in Brigade work, but the internally momentous Haynes Committee was initiated and an appeal fund was launched to secure a more permanent Headquarters building in London. Much of the inspiration and drive for these different projects was supplied by the Secretary himself who, assisted by the full-time staff, possessed the attention to detail acquired from his Army training to carry most of them through.[33]

Only the new Award Scheme and the Seventy-fifth Anniversary celebrations fall within the scope of this chapter. The Boys' Brigade had been involved in a pilot scheme for the former at an early stage, preceding the Scouts, who were at that time preoccupied with their current Jamboree. In June 1955, for example, Wilson-Haffenden speaks in his confidential quarterly *Newsletter* of the approval given to start an experimental pilot course of 'Adventurous Training' for about forty-five Brigade boys of sixteen to twenty-one years during the coming summer in Snowdonia. The course was to be led by Sir John (now Lord) Hunt, leader of the successful 1953 Everest expedition. The idea of the Duke of Edinburgh's Award Scheme was not made fully public until 1956 when a series of committee meetings and press conferences were held, while the *Gazette* ran a series of articles explaining how the Brigade could benefit and how the idea could be integrated into existing Brigade activities. The success of the Capel Curig 'Adventurous Training' course for senior boys in August 1955, which introduced the Brigade to strenuous mountain leisure pursuits, did much to convince the B.B. Training Committee of the need for such a scheme to be taken up by the movement. 'I am sure that the Award Scheme dovetails in with Adventurous Training,' wrote Wilson-Haffenden to his District Organizers, 'and that it is development along these lines that is going to help us in holding the Senior Boy. I hope you will give all the encouragement you can to Companies that wish to try.' The Award Scheme was essentially designed both to attract those from outside the existing youth organizations and to provide an additional incentive to the older teenager already involved by appealing to his sense of competition and achievement. 'If we can develop this kind of work in The Boys' Brigade for Senior Boys we shall have better hopes of holding them,' wrote A.S. Maney in the *Gazette* of the Brigade's underlying strategy:

> As to the way in which the Brigade can provide these activities, there are different opinions, but there should be no doubt that we must do it somehow. Had the Founder been alive today, he would probably have been ahead of, and not behind, other organizations in this field.[34]

The Scheme now passed, as the Duke of Edinburgh's Award, to the districts and battalions, where every effort was made to fit it into the existing badge structure, so as to reduce the amount of extra work involved for the officers. In fact, the whole of the Award, with the exception of the expedition section — really an expansion of Brigade wayfaring and camping — could be carried out within the existing range of Brigade activities. In 1958 Don West replaced

Sweyn Barnes as Training Secretary for Engand and Wales, taking up the Scheme with renewed vigour. In June 1959 Wilson-Haffenden was able to report that The Boys' Brigade had achieved no less than forty Gold Awards, which 'had a great deal of effect on our publicity and on our general standing in the eyes of the public, so keep it up'. In the late 1950s and early 1960s, as drill declined in popularity among boys, the Duke of Edinburgh's Award Scheme was to have a transforming effect on the Brigade, doing much to arrest the loss of the senior boy to the movement — even if it could only slow down the process rather than reverse it altogether. The 1980-81 Annual Report instances 522 companies involved in the Scheme, with 1,615 boys making a start on the Bronze Award, 197 on the Silver, and 50 on the Gold. The Scheme has also been of great value to the Youth Service in general by setting up standards in award work which were national rather than peculiar to any one organization. On the other hand, a 1974 study by sociologists of Outward Bound Centres and the Award Scheme reached the conclusion that, contrary to the inflated claims made, there was little evidence to suggest that these particular methods of 'character' training had any real impact on the subsequent ethical or social behaviour of their participants. It is equally true that many youth workers saw the Award as offering the potential of challenge, adventure, opportunities for exciting leisure activities and more involvement with others in the local community. Sir John Hunt himself was convinced of the value of mountains as a gateway to an understanding of true and lasting values. Yet only if more young people were involved could the Scheme ultimately fulfil its potential of encouraging cooperation between the different local youth organizations and in developing community awareness among the young.[35]

The Seventy-fifth Anniversary celebrations of The Boys' Brigade were held in 1958. Though not on such a large scale as the events of 1933, or 1954, the Anniversary included several important happenings worldwide, and is a convenient point at which to close this chapter. Most significant in Britain was the 750 Training Camp for over 670 senior boys, mostly British, held in August 1958 at Lilleshall Hall Recreation Centre, near Newport, Shropshire. The Commanding Officer was Sir John Hunt, Secretary of the Duke of Edinburgh's Award Scheme, and the Rev. David Sheppard, who had played for England in twenty-two test matches and was to become in time Bishop of Liverpool, acted as Chaplain of the camp. Wilson-Haffenden, who was also present, remembered the camp for its 'spiritual activity', in particular the success of his discussions with boys of their 'spiritual problems' after 'lights out' one evening. The presence of Sir John Hunt and a full coaching staff also ensured ample time was devoted to canoeing, expedition work and various sports. Large international camps were also held during 1958 in New Zealand and the West Indies, while from the Brigade Council held in Aberdeen that year, the Queen received a large contingent of officers and boys for inspection at Balmoral Castle in honour of the celebrations. 'The real value of celebrating an anniversary, particularly of a great movement such as The Boys' Brigade, lies not so much in rejoicing over the past achievements — great though they may be — as in setting a sound course for the future,' wrote Sir John Hunt, giving his timely afterthoughts on the 750 Camp in the *Gazette*:

> In every movement which continues to thrive during 75 years in a period of tremendous change — social, economic, political — there is an essential core which must not, on any account, be tampered with. We all know that the essence of The Boys' Brigade is the Christian Faith. To me the presence of this Faith throughout

our Camp, and among all ranks, will remain an inspiring and unforgettable fact . . .
But in other respects *a movement must adapt its ways to the changing times, if it is to
capture the imagination and hold the allegiance of the young people in each generation*. I
believe boys and girls of today are seeking and needing — some of them
desperately so — outlets to a spirit of enterprise and adventure which is in them
still, both despite of and because of the encroaching walls of material progress. The
opportunity to provide for this urge is one which the B.B. and other spheres of
youth should not miss, even though it may mean changes in existing training
programmes, even training policy. [my italics]

The challenge of the next quarter century of Brigade history was indeed to be
how far the movement could succeed in adapting its ways to the changing
times in order to meet the expectations and spiritual needs of the coming
generations of boys.[36]

The Boys' Brigade had emerged from the Second World War in much better
shape numerically and financially than it had from the First. Financially, the
amounts collected during 'B.B. Week' had risen progressively throughout the
War and by 1946 had reached £72,000, while the generous financial assistance
offered by the Ministry of Education to voluntary youth organizations in 1944
continued into the postwar period. The wartime Board of Education Circulars,
in drawing attention to the Youth Service in general, also did a great deal to
promote the cause of The Boys' Brigade in particular, as Stanley Smith was
compelled to recognize. Numerically, although boy membership in Britain
totalled some 90,000 in 1949, excluding the Life Boys, prewar figures of several
thousands over this number were never again to be reached. Even in the 1950s
a much higher proportion of children were exposed to the rudiments of
Christian teaching than in later decades, and so the maintenance of Brigade
strength during this period should perhaps be seen more as a symptom of
Church and Sunday School stability than as a sign of the widespread appeal of
religion and discipline to the youth of the nation. The Boys' Brigade set out to
meet the challenges of postwar British society with a confidence deriving from
its manifesto, *Plans for Advance*, and founded on the dubious assumption that
'youth' would somehow remain preserved in the acquiescent mould of the
prewar years, having respect for elders and the authority of parents, police-
men, teachers and youth leaders. Hence the worried editorials and speeches of
the 1950s became obsessed with the teddy boy and the juvenile delinquent,
figures who, in the light of the teenage gangs that were to follow, now seem
much less menacing than they did to their contemporaries.

Changes in society and the economy which are customarily grouped under
the label 'affluence' were also seen as threatening the spiritual and military
values of The Boys' Brigade with materialism and lack of discipline. The
Brigade attempted to overcome the crisis of self-confidence caused by social
and cultural upheavals over which it had no control by attempting to revive
past triumphs. The 1951 Festival of Britain Run invited memories of the 1935
Royal Jubilee Run, and the 1954 celebrations of the Founder's Centenary
aroused strong parallels with the 1933 B.B. Jubilee, particularly during Brigade
Council in Glasgow. On a more positive note, the appointment in 1954 of
Major General Wilson-Haffenden to replace Stanley Smith as the new Secretary of The Boys' Brigade might be interpreted as a brave attempt to inject a
more dynamic evangelical force into a movement that was, perhaps, suffering
from a stiffening of the joints, or at least not moving ahead with the same
forward thrust which it had once possessed in abundance.

CHAPTER 8

'AN INTERNATIONAL MOVEMENT'

The Boys' Brigade Overseas, 1945 to 1982

ON 16 JUNE 1947, R. Alec Mason, a member of the Brigade Executive and the Overseas Committee, faced an inquiring audience of B.B. officers at the Y.M.C.A. in Wellington, New Zealand. Mason was part-way through a whistle-stop Australasian tour which, in New Zealand alone, would take in nine battalions, numerous meetings, and over two thousand miles of travel. What, he was asked, was the Brigade's policy in New Zealand and overseas? The admission was enlightening:

> Brigade Overseas has like the proverbial Topsy just 'growed up'. In other words the overseas section has just grown up unorganized.
> We have at present a whole time employee in Nigeria. We have 45 Companies [session 1946-47] in Northern Nigeria — 1,000 Boys waiting to join.

At the same time the British Executive, so great was the emphasis about to be placed upon overseas work, was releasing William McVicker from all other duties to concentrate on the expected expansion abroad. In Australia and New Zealand the Brigade's leaders were pressing for a visit from McVicker to help resolve their problems of growth and isolation. In Northern Nigeria the Rev. F.B. Whale, as full-time B.B. Field Organizer (supported from Britain and North America) was attempting to cope with a rapidly expanding mission-based indigenous movement. By 1947-48 there were 3,300 members in 60 companies in Northern Nigeria, and in 1948 New Zealand reported 4,700 members (including Life Boys) in over 200 companies and teams. As Whale recalled at the end of his long missionary and B.B. service in 1957, 'Nigeria and New Zealand seem to have grown up (B.B.-wise) like a couple of youths.' These two dissimilar countries, thousands of miles apart, neverthless became leaders in B.B. affairs, both within their regions and in world affairs after the Second World War.[1]

As early as 1944-45 McVicker was reporting, somewhat sanguinely, that the War had taught 'the Dominion B.B. organizations . . . to depend largely on their own resources'. In the colonies, too, the newly emergent spirit of 'initiative and enterprise' would be badly needed in the not-too-distant future if the movement was to develop. 'Valuable service', it was concluded by the Brigade Executive in 1948, 'could be rendered in other mission fields if similar B.B. missionaries [like F.B. Whale] were available.' Yet at that time there were still only three full-time B.B. professionals concerned with Brigade affairs internationally: McVicker in London, Howard L. Trotman in Wellington, New Zealand (as Dominion Secretary), and Whale in Nigeria.[2]

By 1950 it was the clear policy of the British Brigade Executive to cajole the dominions into a greater, preferably total, acceptance of financial and organizational responsibility for their countries and regions, whilst Britain diverted its main resources into the colonies, particularly in Africa and the Caribbean. With the rapid drives towards decolonization in Africa, Southeast Asia, South America and the Caribbean from the late 1950s onwards, the strategy for full-time B.B. organizers and field staff in the colonies proved a wise and ultimately fruitful one. On the other hand, the intractable sociopolitical problems of South Africa, and the haste to thrust 'home' structures onto vast and still relatively weak B.B. countries like Australia and Canada, initially only served to retard and frustrate real B.B. development in those dominions. The frustration tended to be enhanced by the failure of many (but certainly not all) high-placed visiting B.B. officers from Britain to understand that even the so-called developed Commonwealth countries needed to evolve systems of Brigade government and operations which reflected their own social and religious conditions. Immigrant British officers were officially (and perhaps often too optimistically) seen as one means of hastening the assumption of local responsibilities and the setting up of national B.B. Councils modelled on the British system. But, with the exception again of New Zealand (where effective local control had been assumed tacitly, if not officially, since the 1930s) and perhaps Australia, the immigrant-officer approach often proved counterproductive. Many Australians and Canadians, for instance, increasingly saw British models of social organization as less relevant to their immediate problems in many spheres of life. The Boys' Brigade proved no exception. Britain's entry into the Common Market and its search for new political, commercial and military alliances emphasized the increasing and real independence of the old Commonwealth, particularly of faraway Australia and New Zealand. South Africa and Rhodesia (now Zimbabwe) inevitably suffered some isolation, even in B.B. affairs, as political and other sanctions were applied internationally to their governments over sociopolitical issues, and South Africa is still not immune. Just as the appointment of indigenous organizers and secretaries became vital to the continuation of the movement in the newly independent Commonwealth nations of the Third World, so too did the complete and *actual* achievement of B.B. independence from Britain prove necessary to the developed nations of the Commonwealth.[3]

By 1958, however, the year in which the Boys' Brigade Australian Council received its 'charter' from The Boys' Brigade in Britain, the only 'self-governing administrations' set up in accordance with Article 17 of the Brigade Constitution were those in New Zealand, Australia, Canada and Jamaica. In the context of prevailing political realities and the sheer pace of overseas B.B. expansion, continued British 'oversight, guidance and development', unaccountable locally, could not last much longer in the remaining thirty Brigade territories. The Seventy-fifth Anniversary of the movement in 1958, with its theme 'All One — B.B. round the World — Brothers All', marked a turning point in the Brigade's search for the truly independent, consultative and international way of conducting its affairs. The outcome, after over twenty years of much necessary goodwill on all sides and the occasional painful lesson in 'cutting the apron strings', was the World Conference, that global fellowship which today unites 'into a closer working relationship' The Boys' Brigade and its kindred organizations in over sixty countries throughout the world. Another related development was the formation from the early 1960s onwards of eight autonomous 'Regional Fellowships' to liaise on more local matters and to provide representation on B.B. affairs to the World Conference. The eight Fellowships are West Africa, East and Central Africa, Southern Africa, East Asia, the Pacific, North America, the Caribbean, and Europe.[4]

Statistically overseas growth in the postwar years was impressive (see Appendix 3). In 1947-48 the overseas membership (all ranks but excluding Life Boys) was 14,855 among 404 companies. Forty-eight per cent of that membership was in Nigeria and New Zealand and a further twenty-two per cent in Canada and South Africa. In the same session, 58 new companies were formed outside Britain. By 1950-51 international members totalled 18,000 in the Boys' Brigade (all ranks) and a further 4,700 in the Life Boys. Sixty-five per cent of boy membership was in Nigeria (5,850), New Zealand (2,400) and South Africa (2,230). A decade later, by the session 1960-61, 1,040 new overseas companies had enrolled through London Headquarters, and the membership amongst forty-eight countries outside the United Kingdom stood at nearly 62,200 (all ranks) in 1,191 companies and 546 teams. The Nigerian Brigade membership had rocketed to over 21,000 (347 companies) and New Zealand reported the formation of 150 new companies in the same period, and a membership of nearly 11,800 (all ranks). Despite many losses on aggregate, impressive expansion was also taking place elsewhere: between 1950-51 and 1960-61 over 140 companies were formed in Australia (membership in 1960-61 was 8,600); over 130 in the West Indies (where Jamaica's membership alone was over 2,000); and South Africa recruited 4,600 people into the movement. In Nyasaland (now Malawi; independent 1964) membership reached over 2,000 and the Brigade made notable strides in the Gold Coast (now Ghana; independent 1957) and Uganda (independent 1962).

Ten years further on the total overseas membership (all ranks) had increased by fifty per cent to just over 90,000 with 55,000 boys in The Boys' Brigade and nearly 25,700 in the Life Boys. There was now a much healthier ratio of Life Boy to B.B. membership overseas than at any time previously. (The adoption by most overseas B.B. territories of the Haynes recommendations on restructuring [See Chapter 9] undoubtedly aided this trend.) In the 1960s 1,119 companies were enrolled, and the movement now boasted 1,888 companies in over fifty countries and territories. The attrition rate, clearly, was also still high. In the Federation (later the Republic) of Nigeria (independent 1960) internal dislocation and the civil war between the Federal Government and Biafra (1967-70) affected the Brigade, especially in the former Eastern Region, although some 300 companies were formed in the 1960s. In Malaya (independent 1957) and Uganda, civil problems prior and subsequent to independence often interrupted the movement's work in certain areas. With the secession of Singapore from the new Federation of Malaysia in 1965 the Brigade faced some major reorganization. In other parts of Africa in the 1960s, Brigade growth was experienced in Ghana, Kenya, Malawi, Zambia (formerly Northern Rhodesia), the Federal (now United) Republic of Cameroon, and Sierra Leone (independent 1961). In the West Indies (including Jamaica) another 130 companies were formed, and in Australia, where the membership rose to 10,600 an astounding total of 224 companies were formed. In 1970-71 just over a third of the total Brigade world membership (excluding kindred organizations) was outside Britain.

In the 1970s international expansion increased steadily beyond the 2,000 company and 100,000 member marks. In 1974-75 there were nearly 145,700 overseas Brigade boys and leaders in 2,441 companies. By 1976-77 there were 2,725 companies in existence and nearly a half of world B.B. membership was outside Britain. World Conference statistics are now taken triennially. By 1981-82, however, despite considerable losses in some countries (notably the Solomons and Papua New Guinea), The Boys' Brigade was active in a greater diversity of countries, among a greater multiplicity of cultures, races and languages, than in the previous nine decades of its existence. Brigade growth peaked in Australia and New Zealand in the late 1960s and early 1970s. B.B. Canada never regained the numerical strength it had enjoyed in the immediate prewar years. By the late 1970s and into the centennial decade the dynamism of The Boys' Brigade outside Europe no longer lay with the Old Commonwealth. Following developments and trends in the Churches, the initiatives in ideas, programmes and forward thinking seem to be passing rapidly to the new Commonwealth and the Third-World B.B. countries of Africa, Asia and, to some extent the Caribbean.[5]

The immediate postwar years were devoted to determined reconstruction and the establishment of viable national councils rather than to the necessarily slow moves towards the new consultative internationalism. The one clear exception, of course, was Europe, where international cooperation had its roots in the very close links which had already blossomed in the 1930s between the British movement and the F.D.F. in Denmark. In May 1946 a thirty-eight-strong contingent from Denmark visited Britain, performing with considerable acclaim at the Albert Hall display. In July 1945 McVicker and his wife went to Denmark, meeting with F.D.F. leaders and visiting the great national Brass Band Festival at Odense and the 'Comradeship Camp' at Jomsborg, attended by five hundred young people. McVicker was deeply impressed by 'the strength and vitality of the Danish movement':

> While there are many minor diversities in method, due to differences of national outlook and environment, F.D.F. and B.B. are out for the same goal, and have much to learn from each other. Both sides are eager that the link between us should be strengthened.[6]

As both Britain and Denmark moved towards national recovery in the postwar years, the momentum of exchanges in training, camps, band tours and other events increased at national, battalion and company level. The B.B. in Britain also showed considerable interest in providing some help to the Christian Church in British-occupied Germany. Visits of German pastors to training courses and camps were arranged 'with a view to infusing them with something of the B.B. spirit'. Although Brigade units did start in some places for the sons of British soldiers, the movement never gained a foothold in Germany — understandably, given the attitude of many Germans after 1945 towards uniformed youth. Out of these early links with Denmark, however, developed the present European Fellowship. On the occasion of the Sixtieth Anniversary of the F.D.F. in October 1962, McVicker and A.E. Milan, a member of Brigade Executive, represented the U.K. movement at a consultation with the Danish movement and two other kindred organizations, the Poikien Keskus of Finland and the Ansgarsförbundet of Sweden. These kindred movements are today full members of the World Conference.[7]

It was, of course, one thing to develop close working relationships between autonomous national movements in Europe, but quite another to hammer out a real partnership between the branches of The Boys' Brigade in the British Commonwealth. It required tact, skill, and infinite patience on all sides. During his tour of New Zealand in 1947 Alec Mason, whose visit has been mentioned above, demonstrated how, initially at least, shock tactics might work.

Throughout New Zealand Mason was politely and eagerly received. B.B.

men in the Dominion had seen their movement go through difficult times organizationally in the immediate postwar years and they were keen to gain help and advice for its reconstruction. There was no lack of boys or even officers willing to serve, and they looked to Britain for assistance in training and new ideas. However, what they got from Mason caused some shockwaves of disquiet and disbelief. In his official report Mason was blunt — almost, it seemed, to the point of tactlessness:

> As a general conclusion I feel bound to say that the B.B. is not really being properly used in N.Z. since, with the exception of a small minority of cases, the motive in forming Companies seems to have been to provide week-day activities for boys already in the Sunday Schools and Bible Classes rather than to draw more boys into the sphere of influence of the church. Evidence for this is found in the almost complete abandonment of the B.B. Bible Class, the acquiescence in a very low average Company strength (17 boys) and the acceptance of one night a week as the standard for Company activities.

He even struck at the historical roots of the Brigade in New Zealand: 'I think that the B.B. "got off on the wrong foot" in the present era in New Zealand.' He found that the main problem lay in the attitude of Church leaders towards the ideal Brigade movement as he conceived it:

> . . . there exists in N.Z. in connection with each Protestant denomination a very well organized 'Bible Class Union' to which most Churches' Bible Classes are affiliated. It seems that the average Minister is so anxious that his Bible Class shall make a good showing in comparison with others in the Union that he will not allow his B.B. Company to have a separate class, preferring that B.B. boys should be distributed between the Sunday School (12-14) and the Bible Classes (14 upwards).

On the two other critical points of low company numbers and one-night-a-week activities he was quite scathing. His recommendations carried the sting: One alternative is to reconstitute the B.B. in the Dominion as an independent body with a different name. The reformed movement would then be a New Zealand counterpart of the Danish F.D.F., with its aims, methods and constitution suited to the particular needs of the country.' If the B.B. in the Dominion wanted to stay in the Brigade mainstream, it should address itself, Mason insisted, to the Bible Class and numbers problems first, and secure 'officer-training by experienced men', i.e. men from Britain. He also recommended that McVicker visit the Dominion as soon as possible.[8]

'Your report', wrote the Dominion Secretary Howard Trotman, in February 1948, 'has raised a lot of controversy.' Particular exception had been taken in a country priding itself on its 'British allegiances' to the recommendation that the B.B. in New Zealand should 'consider reforming as the F.D.F.' All were agreed that 'an aggressive Officer Training policy was required', but the matter of forming B.B. Bible Classes in New Zealand proved intractable, and led to isolated and sometimes bitter quarrels. Mason, for all his incisive, justified criticism of the other problems ailing the movement in New Zealand, could not grasp the strength of the long-established, entrenched and effective New Zealand Bible Class movement. Educationally, too, New Zealand was in some respects still in advance of Britain, with its higher school-leaving age and the greater demands it made on a boy's leisure time through sport and Bible Class activities. (The New Zealand 'Bible Class' was a weekly social and religious activity, with its own camps and denominational Unions.) Mason was frankly aware of the furore he caused. 'I could', he told Trotman, 'with equal justification be just as hard on a large proportion of the Brigade at home . . . B.B. N.Z. doesn't need to develop an inferiority complex.'[9]

And neither did it. The movement responded admirably to Mason's well-intended strictures. In 1949 Leo W. Lewis, Brigade Executive member, and E.A. Robertson ('Robbie') of Leigh-on-Sea, Essex, travelled over seven thousand miles throughout the Dominion giving eighty-eight lectures on B.B. methods in nine centres. Their knowledge, urbanity, charm and tact 'did much to inspire keenness in B.B.' throughout the country. Between 1949 and 1955 the membership rose from just under 5,000 to 7,750 (all ranks). In 1951 McVicker at last came to New Zealand, spending ten weeks studying administration, meeting government and B.B. officials, and visiting many companies, battalions and courses. His impressions were most favourable:

> The B.B. in N.Z. at the end of 25 years' existence is firmly established, true to the basic principles of our movement and loyal to the Brigade at home ... It is conscious of its shortcomings, which are mainly due to the lack of the B.B. tradition and experience, from which we at home so continually benefit.

More clearly than Mason, he was able to see New Zealand's social and economic position: 'The standard of living is higher than at home, and the majority of Boys stay at school until 16 and often to 18.' The population was thinly scattered and more mobile, both for work and recreation.[10]

New Zealand soon assumed wider B.B. responsibilities and leadership in the South Pacific. In 1949 the training talks of Robertson were illustrated and published as *The Plan*, a 48-page booklet outlining the B.B. method and a boy's progress through the movement. This was perhaps the most influential Brigade publication to date in the Antipodes. It was reprinted again (10,000 copies) in 1957, and used widely in Australia and New Zealand. In 1952 Frank Weedon, a young physiotherapist from Dunedin, went to Britain on a British Council scholarship to study Brigade training and administration. The following year he became Brigade (N.Z.) Training Officer. In the wider sphere New Zealand also enhanced its responsibilities. Over the New Year period 1950-51 the Brigade Silver Jubilee Camp was held at Waipara, near Christchurch in Canterbury. Nearly 1,400 attended this camp — despite a national rail strike — including contingents from Australia, the Cook Islands and Nauru. This major event tested B.B. organization in the Dominion. It also provided an excellent opportunity for informal dialogue between the Australian leaders and New Zealanders concerning their future relations and responsibilities in the Pacific. The embryo of the Pacific Regional Fellowship was developing.[11]

We have already seen in Chapter 6 how McVicker shifted some of the financial burden for Pacific extension to the B.B. in New Zealand during World War II. In 1948 Bob Challis, the 'father' of The Boys' Brigade in the Pacific, moved to Auckland. In the Cook Islands, Pastor Teariki Maka was now appointed B.B. Organizer. During his Antipodean visit in 1951 McVicker negotiated Challis's appointment as part-time Liaison Officer for the South Pacific responsible to the Overseas Committee in London. With substantial help from the Overseas Extension Fund in Britain, Challis conducted a major training school in Samoa in 1951 attracting some candidates from Niue. From New Zealand the financial commitment to the Pacific was gradually increased, especially for work in the Cooks and Niue. Each September New Zealand units held a 'Pacific Week', raising £280 ($560) in 1953 and increasing tenfold to over $5,000 by 1967. In 1954 Pacific Island B.B. membership stood at 2,000 and in 1956 reached 2,500.[12]

The main catalyst towards greater regional cooperation in Australasia and the Southwest Pacific was, however, the Founder's Centenary Camp at Eton in 1954 (see Chapter 7). The Centenary Camp was of course very important for the whole course of international B.B. cooperation; that its impact on the remote Antipodean movement was to prove so great was largely due to the calibre and size of the contingents which travelled the twelve thousand miles to Britain from Australia, New Zealand and the Cook Islands. A whole generation of young leadership was affected, directly or indirectly. The British 'B.B. tradition' was experienced at first hand, and the enthusiasm and vitality of the postwar Brigade in Australasia was, in turn, an inspiration to the British movement.

New Zealand began its preparation for the Centenary Camp in 1951. An International Camp Committee was set up under Mervyn T. Dearsly, an astute accountant of Palmerston North. A New Zealand Vice-President by 1951, Dearsly had been active in national administration since 1940. He had learned much from Frederick Scott Miller and Roland Hill about Brigade methods and 'politics'. By the early 1950s he had become one of the most influential B.B. men in New Zealand — where he assumed the Presidency in 1955 — and by the 1960s he was the recognized spokesman for the Pacific region in all international B.B. forums. He was to leave his mark decisively on the Pacific Regional Fellowship (P.R.F.) and helped to shape the independence and consultative status of the World Conference. Ironically he never went to Eton in 1954. Nevertheless, he influenced New Zealand's contribution and understood the important implications of that visit as few others did at the time in his country. He became one of the most outstanding Brigade leaders of the postwar period.[13]

Ninety-three New Zealanders and fifteen Cook Islanders travelled by sea to Britain in 1954. They went via Australia, receiving B.B. hospitality at each landfall. Already in Wellington they had received a state farewell from the Prime Minister, Sidney Holland, and in Britain their reception was 'overwhelming'. The Australian contingent under their Honorary Organizer, Robert McEwan, numbered fourteen. The Eton experience itself was important for all future international cooperation. But the most seminal events of the tour were the informal consultations held between the New Zealand leaders, Howard Trotman and Bruce Patchett (the contingent's commanding officer) and the Australians McEwan and Doug Adam, and also their discussions with McVicker, Leslie Rawson and Lionel Pearce at Brigade Headquarters in London and Glasgow. The Australians, as was their intention, secured credits and improvements in their trading relations with London. Most officers attended the Brigade Council in Glasgow where the overseas work of the B.B. was the theme. Many officers, staff sergeants and senior NCOs also attended training courses in Britain, some at Felden Lodge or Carronvale. In his report to the Australian movement, McEwan said that he felt they had achieved more by coming to Britain than they could have done at home. For New Zealanders it was a B.B. odyssey from which the movement in their country never looked back. It was to prove so for many other overseas countries.[14]

It was made plain to the New Zealand leaders who conferred in September 1954 with the Overseas Committee at Merchant's House, Glasgow, that as the largest B.B. centre in the Pacific they must face up to assuming control in the development and supply of B.B. work in the Pacific region. It was one price to pay for getting trading concessions. Fifteen B.B. countries were represented at the Founder's Centenary Camp, and Brigade leaders in Britain, especially the Overseas Committee, recognized the importance of the event for international development. Their incursion into B.B. affairs in New Zealand had proved effective and acceptable. Soon Australia and South Africa, it was hoped, would go the same way, having been given the same help. Clearly 'the great efforts' at home and abroad to foster Eton as 'the first international gathering' were designed to bear greater results in strengthening 'the worldwide solidarity of the Brigade':

> Boys' Brigade members in the British Isles, having had so many overseas members as their guests and having met them face to face for the first time, have become more conscious than ever of the Brigade's worldwide character. They have realized afresh the responsibility this brings, as eyes from many places round the world turn naturally for guidance and example to the B.B. in the United Kingdom, where our Founder started his work which was destined to be for the benefit of boyhood everywhere.

It was all a prelude to a further shift, a further step in developing international responsibilities.[15]

At the Glasgow meeting on 10 September 1954 each country represented gave an account of 'its growth and development' and its 'difficulties and future prospects'. Canada alluded to 'the question of distance' hindering developments, and the two representatives from South Africa ('one from the Rand Battalion, mainly controlled by white people, and the other from Port Elizabeth which is mainly a development among the coloureds') spoke of their strengths and problems. As B.B. Organizer, the Rev. Tua Pittman represented the Cook Islands, and others spoke from Australia, Southern Rhodesia, Singapore, Jamaica and Nigeria. It was all consultative discussion: no formal commitments and no binding decisions were made.

At the Brigade Council in Bute Hall, University of Glasgow, the overseas guests had their moment of genuine and more public acclaim on Saturday 11 September. Presented by McDiarmid, Chairman of the Overseas Committee, representative leaders came forward from Denmark (the F.D.F.), the United States (representing Neenah-Menasha), Australia (representing a movement of 2,500), Canada, New Zealand, South Africa, Singapore, the Cook Islands, Jamaica and Nigeria. At the Centenary Camp itself the international representation had been even more impressive: Australia (14), Canada (16), New Zealand (94), South Africa (29), Southern Rhodesia (7), Nigeria (7), Singapore (25), Bahamas (4), British Guiana (2), Jamaica (7), Cook Islands (15), Falkland Islands (11), Denmark (30), Holland (18) and the U.S.A. (6). With their 285 representatives, the overseas contingents made up just over fourteen per cent of the campers at Eton, who numbered over 2,000 in all. The inspiration and generosity of the Brigade in Britain, the shared problems, and the genuine postwar desire for worldwide cooperation — all of these were apparent in the events of 1954, and they motivated the Brigade movement more strongly than it had been at any time before.

The significance of 1954 was appositely summarized by Howard Trotman of New Zealand:

> After hearing these statements and the difficulties that are being faced in these countries, things that we thought were problems in New Zealand just cease to exist. We appear to have no problems in comparison with these other countries who are greatly hindered in their growth by lack of permanent offices and permanent staff to organize and gather up the work . . . we in New Zealand must develop a missionary outlook as far as the development of B.B. work in the Pacific is concerned.

The lesson was plain: the richer and more developed B.B. countries should shoulder and share the burden with Britain:

The amount of finance that London requires to just touch the development of B.B. work overseas in these countries is something that is far beyond their resources at the present time and anything we can do to assist them in the husbanding of these resources is something I feel we must look at seriously.[16]

In all the speeches and expressions of gratitude, one man's name predominated — that of William McVicker. For him and his Assistant Overseas Secretary, R. Leslie Rawson, this Founder's Centenary Year proved a golden opportunity to further their growing cause, to display its potential and to seek, both at home and abroad, the resources so vitally needed for overseas expansion. New Zealanders returned home convinced of their responsibilities. The movement in Britain, in that first decade of rapid decolonization, was called upon to provide the personnel and mobilize even more resources:

From several countries in Africa where the B.B. does not yet exist, or does only to a very small extent, strong indications have come that the development of B.B. work would be appreciated. The whole of life on that great continent is on the move. The present time affords a wonderful opportunity for the Brigade to play a great part in the evangelism and Christian training of the Boys who will be the men of tomorrow's new Africa.

Britain was now putting its resources into maintaining overseas organizers, British expatriate B.B. men who would, it was hoped, hand over a properly organized and trained movement to the indigenous B.B. leaders of the near future. The Glasgow overseas delegates and the Eton campers took home much food for thought and many ideas for development in 1954.[17]

One immediate outcome was the formal assumption by B.B. New Zealand of Pacific Islands extension in 1955. As Dearsly (now Brigade N.Z. President) actively promoted this policy, Challis became part-time Pacific Organizer, and for several months each year between 1956 and 1963 visited the two Samoas (Western and American), Niue and the Cooks, laying the basis for local B.B. administration with full financial support from New Zealand. In 1959 the Rev. Ta Upu Pare returned to the Cooks after two years training in Brigade and youth work in Britain. In the two Samoas a booming birthrate aided recruitment into the B.B. By 1951 there were 800 members in the Brigade in Samoa, and in 1965 1,300 (all ranks) in twenty-three companies. In 1960 Pastor Tepa Faletoese became Samoan Organizer after training in New Zealand, and in 1967 he conducted extension work in the Tokelau Islands, north of Samoa. By 1969, 2,000 members were in the movement in the Samoas.

Relations between the B.B. in the Pacific Islands and in New Zealand were greatly affected by the strong tide of Island migration to the latter country. On the tiny island of Niue, Brigade work was made especially difficult because of the high incidence of emigration. In the Cook Islands the Brigade achieved its maximum development by the early 1970s. Here, as in Niue, there was a close relationship between State, Church and Brigade. Many old B.B. boys became prominent in the government and community services. The Hon. Tangaroa Tangaroa, a former Brigade President, entered the Cabinet as Minister for Education and Cultural Development, and Vaine Rere Tangata Poto, the current Brigade President (1982), served as a member of the Cook Islands Legislative Assembly. Similarly in Western Samoa (independent 1963) the Hon. Fiame Mata'afa, the former Prime Minister, gave the movement considerable support as Brigade President.

In 1960 the New Zealand Brigade led the advance into Melanesia with the appointment of a New Zealand officer, Derek G. McKay, as Organizer in the

British Solomon Islands. Based initially at Goldie College, Banga Island, McKay travelled by canoe, on foot and occasionally by air as he rapidly extended the Brigade in the scattered and remote islands of the Solomons. In 1962 he was succeeded by another New Zealander, Ron Dickey, who set up his headquarters at Munda. In the same year Gordon Siama, a native Solomon Islander, was appointed Organizer after training in New Zealand. By 1963 there were 700 members in the movement in the Solomons. Siama was later elected to the Solomon Islands Legislative Assembly and appointed to the Governing Council. By 1969-70 the Solomons B.B. membership had peaked between 1,200 and 1,300.

In 1963 Ron Dickey became full-time Pacific Organizer, and was wholly supported from New Zealand. He introduced the movement into the New Hebrides (now Vanuatu) and extended it in the Tokelaus and Ellice Islands (now Tuvalu). In 1967 Dickey retired after seven years as a 'B.B. missionary' in the Pacific. At its peak in the 1970s Brigade work in the Pacific Islands (excluding Papua New Guinea) was reaching 5,500 members.

New Zealand's 'Pacific Venture', adopted so readily in the mid-1950s, had proven one of the most successful Brigade outreaches undertaken wholly and solely by any B.B. country outside Britain. In the eight Pacific island states reached by the Brigade, the training, upward mobility and opportunity provided to many B.B. boys and leaders came at a vital time in the emergence of those islands towards self-government and independence. In the Cook Islands the B.B. pervaded almost all facets of life. These developments have not been, of course, without their critics but, whatever the viewpoint taken, the effects of the Brigade in some Polynesian territories are undeniable. One New Zealand Brigade visitor to Aitutaki (Cook Islands) in 1982 remarked how often he was 'stopped by men and given a B.B. handshake and welcome'. 'It appears', he noted, 'that B.B. and ex-B.B. men run most things, particularly Government Departments.' Religion, kinship and tradition are strong motivators in the Pacific.[18]

New Zealand's major partner in developing the Pacific region in the 1960s was Australia. Postwar B.B. development in that vast country proved, however, slower to achieve. There were several keys to eventual success: the recognition of the federal nature of most national enterprises, the building up of Brigade strength state by state, and, as in New Zealand, the inspiration initially provided by B.B. leaders from Britain. In 1947 Alec Mason visited New South Wales and Victoria. He urgently presented the Brigade Executive's case for establishing a 'Dominion Council'. Leo Lewis and E.S. Robertson followed in 1948-49. As one local officer wrote, they 'showed up just what we didn't know about the B.B. — an amazing lot'. As in New Zealand, their impact on training in the Eastern States and South Australia was seminal. In 1948 Victoria also acquired the organizational services of an immigrant, Guy Lester, formerly Captain of the efficient 23rd West Middlesex Company (this company had directly inspired the introduction of the B.B. into Holland before World War II). In Victoria and New South Wales, immigrant B.B. officers were in many cases able to adjust swiftly to Australian conditions. The turning point for Australia was McVicker's tour of 1951.[19]

'Mac' spent five weeks in Australia, covering 2,900 miles and visiting all the battalion and officer councils. He had been intimately involved in Australian affairs since the 1930s, and through Robert McEwan, Honorary Organizer since 1948, was fully briefed on local problems. He knew that great tact and a

The International Camp at Glenalmond in Scotland in 1963 was held in the same year as the World Conference was formally established, although the latter body only achieved full autonomy in 1976.

The 1st Bahamas Company parades through Nassau in 1953.

A B.B. pyramid in Nyasaland in 1959. Although the B.B. started in Nyasaland as long ago as 1910, the movement no longer exists in what is now Malawi.

Church parade at the 1962 Sierra Leone National Camp at Kenema.

The 4th Kigezi Group Band Competition, Uganda, in 1962.

The Boys' Brigade on the South Pacific island of Niue.
The top picture shows a Life Boy team on parade.

B.B. uniforms are often adapted to local conditions and customs. These Samoan boys are wearing the traditional Polynesian lava-lava.

William McVicker inspects the Auckland Battalion of the New Zealand Brigade in 1951. As Overseas Secretary from 1933 to 1966, McVicker did more than any other man to extend the B.B. idea round the world.

The Boys' Brigade parade through Penang, Western Malaysia. The B.B. has successfully recruited from all ethnic groups in Malaysia.

superior kind of B.B. statesmanship were required to deal with interstate rivalries, suspicions and susceptibilities.

Beginning their extensive tour in Sydney and Brisbane in July 1951, McEwan and McVicker gained tacit support for their ideal of a federal or commonwealth executive. The idea had been in McVicker's mind since the 1930s when Canada had set up a similar structure (see Chapter 6). In Melbourne, McVicker preached the same stern messages he was to repeat in four state capitals: the B.B. must not be 'apologetic or half-hearted'; they must attract non-church boys, train dedicated officers, and improve standards all round. 'Officers' Councils ought not to be cluttered up with dead heads [and] an officer leaving England is no longer an officer until taking up the work again here or elsewhere.' In Adelaide he announced the registration of the new Battalion and, as in Victoria, rallied support for a Commonwealth equipment depot and national full-time organizer's fund. With strong diplomacy McVicker, aided and abetted by McEwan, raised the thinking of the Brigade in Australia onto a new national plain. It was no mean achievement.[20]

The direct outcome was the establishment, in December 1951, of a peculiarly Australian system of B.B. consultative administration. It was called the Provisional Federal Advisory Council (P.F.A.C.). McEwan was its coordinator, responsible directly to McVicker and the Overseas Committee in London. Its task was to woo, inveigle and cajole resources and some power away from the states to form a federal secretariat and office in Sydney. Representatives were ultimately elected by the Brigade in each state, though some, where the B.B. was weak, were appointed. The P.F.A.C. operated in Australia until 1958. It made significant steps forward in training and extension, and also in the standardization of uniforms, badges and administration. Suspicion and reticence were gradually worn down. In 1953, through Neil McLean of Adelaide, the P.F.A.C. promoted the movement in remote Western Australia. Based upon the principle of parity of state representation, regardless of the Brigade's size locally, the Council gradually succeeded. It had its crises. Once, frustrated by criticism and sniping, McEwan threatened to resign with his secretary Alwyn Innes; happily McVicker's diplomatic intervention averted this disaster. The Life Boys were also extended under the P.F.A.C. and an Australian Life Boy consultant was appointed. By 1955 the movement's Australian membership (all ranks) rose to nearly 3,000 and over £1,800 was raised in B.B. week.

After the Eton Camp, McEwan was determined to secure a full-time Australian Organizer. National feeling in a now prosperous postwar Australia rejected prolonged dependence on London, and demanded more democracy in the Brigade's national administration. How long, some wondered, would it take to acclimatize a 'Pom' to organize the B.B. in Australia? Others felt a young Australian should be appointed. In Britain in 1954 tacit agreement had been reached that Australia would, before long, accept responsibility for B.B. extension into the territory of Papua and New Guinea. In 1956 a draft constitution for B.B. Australia began to circulate, drawn up by Robert Tait of Queensland, by now a less reluctant 'federalist' (see Chapter 6). The document enshrined states' rights whilst adopting the most relevant parts of similar national B.B. constitutions in Britain and New Zealand. 'With our great distances separating us', wrote Tait, 'it is essential to form State Councils' to represent 'their own local body' and conditions. In June 1957, with the movement 4,300 strong, the P.F.A.C. adopted an Australian Constitution setting up the Australian Council and Executive as the principal national governing bodies. With effect from January 1958 the Brigade Executive in London, on the recommendation of the Overseas Committee, was ready to pass responsibility for B.B. administration in Australia to Sydney and the Australian Council. In 1958 McEwan handed the movement over to the first Australian President, Robert Tait. It was a monument to the patience, hard work and perseverance of McEwan and his co-federalists, and to the behind-the-scenes promptings of McVicker.[21]

Within three years B.B. Australia had appointed John Bernard Gowman, then living in Hornchurch (Essex), as its first Organizing Secretary. Reared in the famed 88th London, Gowman faced one of the most daunting full-time Brigade jobs anywhere. Australia remained a country politically sensitive over most internal issues. State and federal politicians of whatever persuasion often view each other with suspicion and a certain scorn as they vie for the unusually rich slices of their country's vast economic cake. In the 1960s and 1970s Australia enjoyed unprecedented wealth: with good reason was it known as the 'Lucky Country'. Great wealth, however, did little to alleviate political and economic distrust between the federal government and the states or between the states themselves. To a greater or lesser degree such divisions permeate all facets of Australian life. The Boys' Brigade proved no exception. Despite this the movement grew remarkably, especially in New South Wales, Queensland and Western Australia. Extension soon followed to Tasmania and the Northern Territory. In 1961 total membership stood at 9,185 (all ranks), in 1964 at 10,426, and in 1969 at 11,960.

For all their internal wranglings — even in Brigade circles — the Australians achieved much throughout the 1960s and 1970s. Most remarkable perhaps, were their great series of triennial international Pan Australian Camps: these were held in Sydney, New South Wales (1962-63); Southport, Queensland (1965-66); Stanwell Tops, New South Wales (1968-69); Rabaul, Papua New Guinea (1971-72); Perth, Western Australia (1977-78); and Melbourne, Victoria (1980-81). The maintenance of a federal B.B. structure is sometimes most precarious but it is never allowed to diminish the strength of the State Councils. At state level lies the real muscle of B.B. Australia. In 1976 Gowman recognized this in accepting appointment as Executive Officer for New South Wales. Today state and territorial offices and depots are the main links that companies have with the wider movement. To the outsider the operation seems almost Byzantine in its complexity. But Australia is a complex, federal entity, and the Brigade reflects all the checks and balances, the tolerances and stresses, inherent in that country's make-up. Today the national movement is part-time and maintains a low profile. Admittedly many Australians (although not all) prefer to see most federal entities in that position. Federalism waxes and wanes in B.B. Australia. In 1981 an Honorary Federal Liaison Officer, based in Canberra, was appointed to further aid national cooperation. National consciousness can indeed be aroused for great Australia-wide events like Pan Australian Camps and Brigade anniversaries. Independent and left alone, B.B. Australia evolved its own *modus operandi*. A similar development might have taken place in B.B. Canada if it had been as far-removed from Britain as Australia. The problems, French Canada apart, are very similar for the Brigade in both countries.[22]

We can now consider B.B. Australia's own Pacific experiment: extension into Papua New Guinea. The experiment arose partially out of a coordinated

Pacific policy agreed between Australia and New Zealand through the Pacific Regional Fellowship (P.R.F.). The P.R.F. was formed in February 1962 at Blackheath, New South Wales, with founding members from B.B. Councils in Southeast Asia, Australasia, and the Pacific Islands. By 1962 the P.R.F. in those areas embraced a membership of 26,000.[23]

Brigade work in Papua New Guinea was restarted in the 1960s by expatriate missionaries. Being in an Australian territory (it was known as the Territory of Papua and New Guinea until independence in 1975), companies there tended to seek registration through Sydney. As early as 1954 a new company on the phosphate-rich island of Nauru, northeast of the Solomons, had sought affiliation with Australia. In 1963 Australian Headquarters began to receive applications for enrolment from Rabaul in New Britain and from the New Guinea mainland. As in New Zealand a Pacific Extension Fund was started in Australia to which teams and companies made annual contributions. The Methodist Overseas Mission in Rabaul gave further impetus to Australia's commitment in the Territory by requesting the dispatch in 1963 of a B.B.-trained field officer to work under their auspices. B.B. Australia chose Brian England, Captain of the missionary-conscious 14th New South Wales (West Ryde) Company in Sydney.

In 1964 John Gowman visited the Territory on a fact-finding tour. The need for an organizer was pressing. England's dispatch northwards, however, was thwarted by the withdrawal of the Methodist Mission's offer of funding, and B.B. Australia was forced to look to its own resources. By 1965 £2,560 had been raised from within the movement. Assured of funding, Brian and Marjorie England spent six months training in Sydney. In 1966 the P.R.F. defined more precisely Australia's area of responsibilities as the Territory of Papua and New Guinea other than the islands of Buka and Bougainville, leaving B.B. oversight there and in the nearby Solomons and in the New Hebrides to New Zealand. All over the Territory companies were ready to open. When they did, harassed officers were often deluged with hundreds of eager 'boys' — B.B. age limits were ill defined in the Territory.[24]

England established his headquarters at Malmaluan, a centre for Christian education near Rabaul, in July 1966. The first months were spent in extensive travel, made relatively easier in the rugged terrain of Papua New Guinea by the selfless service of the Missionary Aviation Fellowship. By 1968 a B.B. family dwelling had been constructed at Rapolo, a village near Rabaul. Fundamental to England's B.B. missionary strategy was the need to train 'dedicated indigenous leadership'. The problems, however, were vast. 'Tremendous differences' in ethnic composition, language and in social and economic evolution existed between localities, reported England. In some places European involvement spanned more than a century, in others 'first contact was just a matter of a few years ago'. Added to this, Papua New Guinea was slowly preparing for self-government and eventual independence. Political unrest, particularly on the Gazelle Peninsula, was rife. It was a society in flux. By 1968 overall B.B. membership stood at 650 in nineteen units. The greatest strength lay in New Britain, particularly on the Gazelle Peninsula, where a battalion was gazetted in 1969. England, with the movement well established in the islands of New Britain, New Ireland and New Hanover, was now ready to tackle the urgent problems of the Territory's mainland.[25]

The publication of B.B. literature in Pidgin — the lingua franca of that multilingual country — was started. European assumptions in 'programming, times and general organization' were not, however, Territory norms:

. . . it has to be borne in mind [reported Brian England] that B.B. as we know it in our own country is not necessarily the most effective and profitable for New Guinea Companies. Whilst we naturally maintain the Brigade objectives, all training and activities must be geared to the local conditions.

After 1970 the Brigade expanded dramatically on the New Guinea mainland. England travelled frenetically all over the Territory in response to pleas for help; to East Sepik, the Western District, the Southern Highlands, and Manus Island. Expansion soon followed, too, in the capital, Port Moresby. By 1971 fifty companies with a membership of 1,500 were operating. On 1 January the fourth Pan Australian Camp, attended by four hundred from Australia, Papua New Guinea, New Zealand, Singapore, the Solomons and the United Kingdom was opened at Rabaul, climaxing five furious years of expansion. Exhausted and drained, Brian England nearly lost his life after a thirty-foot fall while searching for lost B.B. personnel in the rugged terrain around the campsite.

After an enforced convalescence in Australia, England returned to the field in November 1972. With membership now over 2,000, local field officers were appointed. The first was the 'tall, ever-smiling' Oliver To Matlaun, a pastor of the Gazelle, and the second, Amenoni Izod, field officer for Papua. In 1975 B.B. Headquarters were moved to Boroko, Port Moresby, where Walo Ani was appointed in the same year. On 16 September 1975 Papua New Guinea, with the Brigade prominent in the celebrations, achieved independence. B.B. membership in the new nation now numbered 2,500 in over seventy companies. In 1976 a national executive was set up to administer the movement. B.B. Australia's formal commitment, although not its economic and moral responsibilities, was over.[26]

In the intervening years the movement has declined sharply in Papua New Guinea. New nationhood has brought urgent demands for leadership resources, new economic and political alignments, and a rethinking of youth work and missionary activity. The Brigade, apart from initial European-sponsored expansion, never achieved in the Melanesian territories of the Pacific the same degree of indigenous acceptance and leadership as it had over a considerably longer period in parts of Polynesia. Today, responsibility for these areas is a partnership shared through the Pacific Regional Fellowship and the World Conference with local officers.

With Australia so heavily committed to the development in Papua New Guinea, it fell to the B.B. in New Zealand to take the main lead in P.R.F. affairs. By the 1960s it had a very strong base indeed from which to work. In 1956 Alford Dornan, Training Officer in Northern Ireland from 1945 onwards, was appointed Training and Extension Officer to New Zealand. A former boy and captain in the 3rd Ballymena Company, and greatly influenced by McVicker, his fellow-Ulsterman, Dornan had been closely associated with the New Zealand contingent at Eton, finding them 'friendly, open and personable types'. Through the direct mediation of McVicker, Dornan was sent to New Zealand, thus abandoning a clearly effective career in the wider B.B. training sphere in Britain; his work in Northern Ireland had been particularly influential. Together with Mervyn Dearsly, Dornan made the movement in New Zealand one of the most innovative and model Brigade organizations outside Britain.

Between 1954 and 1968 the membership rose from 7,500 to 12,500. In 1958 the great Ardmore Camp in Auckland held to celebrate the Seventy-fifth Anniversary attracted 1,650 campers from all over the region. Dearsly with great foresight initiated the Pacific programme, streamlined the Brigade's mode of government, and backed Dornan's intensive training and extension programmes. National officer and NCO training was introduced. National week-long Christian Leadership Development Courses for NCOs were started in 1957 and continue today, providing some of the most intensive training for young men anywhere in the Brigade movement. Well over 2,000 NCOs have passed through these 'schools', supplying many leaders for the Brigade and the community. In 1960 Dornan became Brigade (N.Z.) Secretary. Between 1962 and 1967 the Governor General of New Zealand, Sir Bernard Fergusson (later Lord Ballantrae), who was a Brigade Vice-President before leaving Britain, lent his unswerving support to a buoyant high-profile B.B. movement in New Zealand. He opened Government House to Queen's Men once a year, supported the National Relay Run in 1963, and visited the Brigade in the Pacific. On his departure in 1967 he was described as 'a staunch friend, a wise counsellor and one whose example encouraged us all'. By the late 1960s the B.B. in New Zealand compared with the best anywhere in the world. To such a movement the Pacific and the new B.B. internationalists inevitably looked for a lead. In Dearsly, Dornan and Challis they found it.[27]

The Founder's Centenary Camp in 1954 provided, as we have seen, the first really important step forward in international consultation in the Brigade. The next opportunity came with the great Seventy-fifth Anniversary Caribbean International Camp at Kingston, Jamaica, in April 1958. The same year the Jamaican Council was granted full autonomy. Before considering the outcome of the informal deliberations in 1958 we must briefly examine the rise of the Brigade after the Second World War in the Caribbean.

By 1949-50 the total boy membership in the West Indies in only seven territories stood at less than 900 among thirty-five companies. Well over half that membership, in twenty-three of the companies, were in Jamaica. The following decade, 1951 to 1961, saw a great leap forward: fifty-eight companies were formed in Jamaica, and over seventy elsewhere throughout the region. By the session 1960-61 boy membership in just over one hundred companies had risen dramatically to slightly under 3,000 throughout more than twenty islands and territories. Life Boys were also strong in most places. The hub of the B.B. in the Caribbean was still Jamaica, with over fifty companies, more than twenty teams, and nearly 1,800 boys. In November 1953 John R. Edbrooke was sent from Britain as Training and Organizing Secretary for Jamaica.[28]

In 1954-55 five Group Councils were formed. Within three years the Caribbean B.B. trebled in membership. In 1955 a Tercentenary Jamaica B.B. Run, conveying a special message from the Brigade President, Lord Maclay, covered over four hundred miles night and day around the island. The Run attracted wide publicity and did much to enhance B.B. morale locally. The movement's great supporter in many ventures was the Governor, Sir Hugh Foot. In 1958 he chaired the organizing committee for the greatest test yet to face the B.B. in Jamaica, the International Caribbean Camp, which was to be attended by representatives from twenty-four countries. Already Edbrooke was much in demand elsewhere throughout the region, including Haiti, the Bahamas, St. Kitts, the Leewards, and British Guiana. In 1959 he was appointed Organizer for the Caribbean and, with full Jamaican B.B. autonomy the same year, Karl McDonnough became full-time Organizer on the island. It was a measure of the esteem in which the Brigade was held in Jamaica that, with independence in August 1962, the B.B. was chosen to 'show the flag' on another major run around the island. Over five hundred members took part before the black, green and gold flag of the new nation was presented to the Prime Minister, the Rt. Hon. Sir Alexander Bustamante.[29]

International camps in Britain and overseas provided the best opportunities to encourage the growing internationalism in the B.B. from the 1950s onwards. The Annual Report of 1954-55 lauded the importance of 'self-governing and self-supporting B.B. administrations'. Britain was generously pouring huge sums into the appointment of Overseas Organizers. 'The policy of such appointments', it was affirmed in 1955, 'has passed the experimental stage.' In the session 1956-57 Leslie Rawson was made Joint International Secretary with McVicker. More and more overseas B.B. personnel, particularly from Asia and Africa, came to study professionally in Britain; a few came specifically to receive B.B. training. Indigenization of the movement's leadership, as we shall see, was proceeding in Africa, especially in Nigeria. The Australasian and Pacific branches were almost wholly self-sufficient. By the session 1959-60 the B.B. outside Britain had doubled in eight years. 'One Boy in every four of our total B.B. membership is outside the United Kingdom', it was reported that year, 'and three-quarters of these belong to the coloured races.' The new jet age left even Australia and New Zealand only twenty-four to thirty-six flying hours away from Britain. Africa, the Caribbean and Asia were correspondingly closer. At the 1958 Caribbean camp in Kingston, Jamaica, the B.B. representatives 'inside and outside the British Commonwealth' demanded a significant advance in international B.B. administration. The first change had to be in attitudes on the home front.[30]

In May 1958 Brigade Executive asked Archdeacon J.H.L. Phillips to prepare a memorandum entitled 'The B.B.'s International Development'. It was a seminal single-page document. The Overseas Committee, overburdened and fully-stretched, was a mere 'sub-committee of the Home Executive'. The largely informal Jamaican discussions showed that 'a new pattern must be evolved'. Representatives from inside and outside the Commonwealth 'were insistent that their work was hampered, if they were merely to be part of a sub-committee run from Abbey House'. In Ghana and the Caribbean, for instance, 'nationalist feelings' were strong, and there was 'a deep feeling of independence':

> It will make all the difference to B.B. work in these countries, in terms of Government support alone, if they can rightly claim to be part of an international movement rather than part of an essentially British movement. An international basis will also greatly facilitate the introduction of the B.B. idea into countries where it is not known.

Phillips boldly suggested the setting up of two distinct executives, 'one International, the other Home'. The Overseas Committee, at least to begin with, might comprise the core of the International Executive, with overseas B.B. countries nominating their own representatives, possibly from within Britain. Problems would be legion. Did the movement and the Executive, Phillips asked, have the vision to face them?[31]

The Brigade Secretary, whose own quarterly bulletins to 'All District and Overseas Organizers' were regular sources of inspiration, had some misgivings. Wilson-Haffenden pointed out that Brigade Executive represented 'the largest single contingent in the International Movement' which supplied 'the bulk of the funds necessary', and therefore that body should provide the nucleus for any International Executive. Such an executive could only be advisory, 'as all decisions or recommendations would need to be ratified by all self-governing members of the united body'. Dependent countries would remain the Brigade Executive's responsibility. McVicker commented that all 'other similar Boys' organizations in countries outside the Commonwealth' must find a place within any new 'international Framework (possibly some type of Federation)'. Finance and 'control' were paramount difficulties. Currently, £3,750 came from the Brigade General Fund annually 'for overseas administration at the home base'. Field costs came from the denominational missionary auxiliaries of the B.B., the missionary societies themselves, the Overseas Extension Fund (through bursaries and grants), trusts, and some overseas governments. In essence they had two choices: 'a loose federation of entirely independent boys' movements all with [an] essentially Christian aim', or 'a body which through a name, an emblem, or a specific aim and basis, unites its member organizations in a more definite way'.[32]

McVicker prepared a 'state of the nations' addendum to his remarks on Phillips's memorandum. Only Australia, Jamaica, Canada and New Zealand were self-governing (in B.B. terms) in 1958. Overseas B.B. councils with no enrolment powers existed in the Bahamas, the Federation of Malaya, Ghana, Nyasaland, the Northern Antilles, the regions of Nigeria, Samoa, and Southern Rhodesia. Niue and Singapore formed a third group with battalion status. In South Africa, the Cook Islands and the Federation of the West Indies no coordinating administration had yet been developed, and 'guidance and control' came from London. The longest, most revealing list consisted of fourteen B.B. countries, including Haiti and the Netherlands West Indies, whose 'guidance and control' came unequivocally from Abbey House. McVicker was convinced that the 'International Committee', however constituted and manned, must remain under home control. There was one concession: the self-governing administrations might appoint consultative non-voting members.[33]

The tempo of international events and the depth of local feelings soon swept away this cautious procrastination and the matter was referred to the B.B. overseas in the form of questions concerning international extension and organization. Mervyn Dearsly prepared New Zealand's reply. The 'larger overseas councils', he insisted, should have 'a direct voice in deciding the policy of the movement'. A 'World Council' meeting every five years with 'overseas representatives' present was the ideal. Brigade Executive must canvass overseas opinion on common issues before reaching a decision. New Zealand was giving notice of its intention to take full and sole responsibility for the Pacific Islands. 'There should not be the same need for well established Councils to communicate through the Overseas Committee on all matters.' With these and other replies on hand 'a galaxy of overseas office-bearers' was summoned to an 'Overseas Consultation' at Leeds in September 1960. Twenty-six delegates represented the movement in sixteen of the forty-three B.B. countries outside Britain. They included expatriate clergymen and B.B. organizers, nationals from Africa, Asia, Canada and the Caribbean, and observers from the F.D.F. From Singapore came Cheong Hock Hai, Vice-President of the Singapore Battalion and Deputy Director of Education, and from Nigeria Archdeacon I.O.S. Okunsanya (Western Nigeria Council) and Mallam Gwamna, Chief of Kagoro (Northern Nigeria Council). As Dearsly immediately wrote home:

> There was no lack of candour in expressing difficulties experienced in the present set-up. There was universal acknowledgement of the need for a wider organization

of the B.B. yet an earnest desire on the part of all countries to maintain any close association and contact with the U.K. from which the main impetus and guidance will still come. It was a humbling experience to realize that out of some 23 actual speakers only 3 of us represented European groups.[34]

Under Lord Maclay's chairmanship a 'Concensus of Opinion' was prepared. The Brigade Executive was requested to note overseas aspirations towards international government and devise a mechanism to satisfy these. A 'consultative World Conference' to safeguard at all times the movement's Aim, Object and methods as a uniformed church-based movement was recommended. At the regional level, 'Brigade events' were to be encouraged. Then, in November 1960, the Brigade Executive reconstituted the Overseas Committee as the International Committee. Whilst in Britain in 1960 Mervyn Dearsly had made it abundantly plain that New Zealand would not be fobbed off with the 'status quo', in which the World Conference would only be a 'talking session', 'still leaving the Executive in U.K. the controlling body, with the power of veto'. As he recalled in 1977, he was 'hauled over the coals' for his outspokenness. He remained unrepentant. It was his opinion that the B.B. in Britain — or the leaders in overseas affairs at least — did not want to consider international autonomies seriously. Dearsly, however, aligned himself and his country firmly with the arguments expressed earlier by Archdeacon Phillips. The 'political climate' in some countries demanded the setting up of international B.B. structures. In due course the World Conference 'will have to become a policy-forming body of the B.B.' He demanded and got the transfer to the Pacific and New Zealand of such residual 'powers' as remained with London and, in consultation with colleagues from Hong Kong, Malaya, Singapore, and the South Pacific, took the first steps in 1961-62 to constitute, in the most widely dispersed B.B. region of the world, the Pacific Regional Fellowship. It became a model for all other extra-European B.B. fellowships, and worked in its original form until 1975, when the East Asia Fellowship was formed (Singapore, Malaysia, Hong Kong, and ultimately Brunei). Dearsly's was a long view. In 1961-62 he definitely felt that the convening of a World Conference meeting in Britain in 1963 was too early. 'It may take a long time to work this out, perhaps 10 years, but I do not think we should rush into it without very long and full deliberations.'[35]

The World Conference was formally established at Mayfield Hall, Dundee, Scotland, on 3 September 1963 by representatives from twenty-three countries. Although a World Conference Committee was set up to work by correspondence between full meetings, it took, as Dearsly predicted in 1961, over ten years for the international body to achieve full autonomy. As he said then, the ideal progression was from national autonomous councils to functioning Regional Fellowships, and thence to a truly independent World Conference. That evolution took exactly thirteen years: Singapore became the venue for the first truly independent World Conference in November 1976. In that time the world had changed considerably, and the British B.B.'s attitude towards and appreciation of international realities inevitably changed too.[36]

In all his deliberations Dearsly stressed on behalf of all overseas countries their 'great debt of gratitude for many years of fullest cooperation and assistance' from London Headquarters. Although New Zealand and Australia and their B.B. dependencies in the Pacific could do without London's direct assistance from the late 1950s onwards, this was not true of the rest of the world. We now turn, therefore, to a consideration of the developments in other Regional Fellowships of the B.B. world.

Brigade policy towards Africa, the Caribbean and South America, particularly after 1954, was in reality an intensification of the missionary fervour of the 1920s and 1930s. It was also essentially a race against decolonization if the Brigade was to survive, be reconstructed or gain footholds in new countries. The new indigenous Churches, for all their gratitude for services rendered in the past, had themselves to perform credibly within the internal political and social realities of their new nationhoods. In Africa it was (and is) an intensely political time of national reawakening. It is to the everlasting credit of the international Brigade leadership in London that their policy now became increasingly pragmatic and deliberately flexible to meet the changing realities. A three-phase programme was clearly stated in the Annual Report of 1964-65. The first phase was 'leadership training at all levels', providing, if necessary, a training organizer from Britain to establish B.B. infrastructures and 'train a suitable local officer' to succeed him. The second stage, using grants from the Gulbenkian and Leverhulme Trusts and other sources, was to train such indigenous organizers in Britain for a minimum of four months. A third line of policy was to send to 'selected countries overseas experienced officers from Britain to conduct concentrated refresher training tours of several months duration'. From this time onwards the terms 'partnership', 'consultation' and 'advice' began to appear more frequently in international B.B. parlance, in place of the old terms 'control', 'guidance' and 'dependence'.[37]

Nigeria, the greatest and most populous former British colony in Africa, was the model proving-ground for this postwar B.B. policy. Nigeria became to the Third World what New Zealand was to the old Commonwealth in terms of B.B. leadership. The Rev. F.B. Whale in Northern Nigeria cooperated closely with missionary societies, trained Nigerian leaders, and trebled the movement within three years between 1945 and 1948. By 1949-50 Nigeria had a membership of 3,500. In April 1951 Daniel Macmillan went to Southern Nigeria and soon the movement was nearly 6,000 strong. During Macmillan's twelve years of service the Lagos and Western District Nigeria Council and the Eastern Nigeria Council were established. His successor in 1963 was Sam Ola Maraiyesa, an 'old boy' of the famed 1st Ijebu Company. The policy of appointing Nigerian assistants-in-training started in the mid-1950s. In 1958-59, for instance, Asuquo J. Udo was appointed to assist Macmillan in the Eastern Region, whilst Maraiyesa had begun his work in the Western Region several years earlier. Udo became National Secretary in 1981. By 1955 B.B. membership in Nigeria stood at just under 13,500 and on national independence in 1960-61 at 16,000. Prior to independence the Rev. Climie Hewitson became Organizer in Northern Nigeria, handing over five years later to David Ossabo. As in many other emerging Commonwealth nations the Brigade celebrated Nigerian Independence in November 1960 with a major national relay run involving 750 boys. Full Brigade autonomy followed in 1962 after the setting up of regional B.B. councils and of a Nigerian Executive Committee with Maraiyesa as National Secretary. By then the movement totalled 21,500 members in 415 companies.[38]

Whale, Macmillan and Hewitson, wrote Maraiyesa in 1978, 'counted not the cost in their untiring efforts to lay the bedrock on which the modern Boys' Brigade work in Nigeria was laid'. Their efforts, however enlightened, would have had little effect without African leadership and cooperation. Such leadership came, for instance, from Bishop Okunsanya, first National President of the Nigerian B.B. and founding President in 1969 of the West African Regional Fellowship. Okunsanya introduced the B.B. into Ondo State when bishop there. Another 'Mellor man' was Chief E. Oye Sofudu, later President of the Ogun State B.B. Council. A later B.B. 'convert' and enthusiast was the Most Rev. J.O. David, sometime President of the B.B. Council in Eastern Nigeria. In the 1960s and 1970s Nigeria evolved rapidly from a federation of four regions into a republic, experienced almost three years of tragic civil war, and in 1976 became a federation of nineteen states. Throughout this period the 'bedrock' of the B.B.'s foundation was tried and proven, although not without disruption. In 1966 total boy and officer membership stood at nearly 27,000; in 1971, after the war, at 26,000; and in 1974 at 80,000. After further political unrest in 1978 it declined again to 50,000.

Throughout these viscissitudes the Brigade in Britain, through the International Extension Fund and other agencies, continued to give generous aid towards the reconstruction of the Nigerian movement. Leadership resources became scarcer and few state councils could any longer afford full-time organizers. In 1978 one thousand members attended a Nigerian B.B. Seventieth-Anniversary camp which helped greatly to restore a sense of unity within the movement. With a National Headquarters in Lagos, and vocational, agricultural and other training programmes evolving to meet the needs of a modern young African state, the movement enjoys considerable prestige and support from most governments, both state and federal. Changes in attitudes have taken place since independence, wrote Maraiyesa in 1978, most obviously among leaders:

> In those days [the 1950s and 1960s] being a leader in a voluntary organization counted much whenever one seeks [sic] reference for any job or for promotion or for pursuit of education. People now offer to serve as Youth Leaders voluntarily or for pay, according to one's conscience.

Much the same might be said for any well-established B.B. country, and certainly as a vast, delicately balanced federation, Nigeria shares many similar problems of B.B. government with Malaysia, and even Canada and Australia.[39]

Nigerian leadership in West Africa was crucial and unstintingly given. In Ghana (then the Gold Coast) and Sierra Leone postwar development recommenced in earnest in the 1950s. In Ghana a number of companies were formed in the 1950s in the Western, Central and Eastern Regions, in the towns of Ashanti and in Greater Accra. In 1956 a Ghana Council was established and in the following year Mathew S. Stewart began service from Britain as Organizer. As in Nigeria, the policy was to replace the British expatriate in due course with an African. In 1961, the Rev. E.K. Dadson succeeded Stewart on secondment from the Methodist Church and served until 1967. From its independence in 1957, Ghana experienced a rapid constitutional and political evolution, similar to that of Nigeria. By the late 1970s it had achieved a B.B. membership of over 3,500, due in large measure to the dedicated service of Daniel Fei, now the full-time Organizer, and his voluntary leaders. As in most of the Third World, one crucial contribution to local development was the award of United Kingdom B.B. bursaries for national officers to train in Britain. Since the 1960s the B.B. membership in Sierra Leone has waned and the Brigade there has depended in recent years upon honorary organizing and training personnel, prominent among whom has been Eardley J.A. Norman.

Late in 1956 Leslie Rawson was in West Africa following up Macmillan's exploratory visit to Sierra Leone from Nigeria several years earlier. In the 1960s

Maraiyesa visited the Gambia, where the earliest development took place in the Methodist and Anglican Churches of Banjul (formerly Bathurst). The B.B. in Gambia was later nursed 'into maturity' by the Ghanian Council, but has never achieved the numerical base to support full-time staff. In the 1960s the Brigade spread to the French-speaking Ivory Coast and to the Cameroons. In September 1969 the West Africa Fellowship was constituted at Takoradi, Ghana. One of its outstanding leaders in the 1970s was Dr G.B.A. Coker, a former Nigerian High Court Judge from Lagos, who contributed significantly to the drafting of the final World Conference Constitution at Singapore in 1976. The important place of the West Africa Fellowship in the Brigade sphere was recognized in 1982 when the World Conference Committee met in Lagos. Nigeria has indeed already considered extension into the Niger Republic and the Republic of Benin.[40]

The problems and potential for the movement are no less in those countries which constitute the East and Central African Fellowship: Kenya, Uganda, Burundi, Rwanda, Zambia, Zimbabwe (formerly Southern Rhodesia) and Malawi. The first consultation and first regional camp were held at Kigezi, the home of the movement in Uganda, in August 1963. A second meeting followed in 1968 in Malawi whilst Leslie Rawson was on a tour of the Region.[41]

In Uganda a dozen companies were established in Kigezi between 1957 and 1960. Geoffrey Hewitson, formerly of the 1st Cambridge Company, spent seven years in the country as the first full-time organizer before handing over in 1965 to John W. Bagorogoza, an 'old boy' and Captain of the long-established 1st Kigezi Company. The B.B. Council of Uganda was formed in 1964 and, despite internal unrest and upheavals, the movement grew to 140 companies and a membership of 8,000 in the 1970s. The Brigade, as in many parts of Nigeria, has been largely supported by the Anglican Communion (here the Church of Uganda) with the objective of establishing a full-time worker and office in each diocese. 'What magnificent work is done by Field Officers', reported Canon Jim Hamilton in 1981. Even today few workers have their own transport and rely either on their feet (walking anything up to fifty miles), buses, taxis or friends with cars. B.B. Uganda has been privileged to have highly experienced indigenous leaders, especially from the 1st Kigezi Company, among them J.N. Bikangaga, National Chairman and World Conference representative. Today, at the request of the Churches, strenuous efforts are being made to extend the movement beyond the B.B. heartlands of the Southwest, Kampala, and the West Nile region.[42]

Uganda enjoys close fellowship with the B.B. in the neighbouring Republic of Kenya. Here the movement serves a largely rural and economically deprived membership. Communication between the villages and the principal B.B. centres (Eldoret in the west, Meru near Mount Kenya, Chogoria, Mombasa and the Taita Hills) is often poor. Programmes have evolved accordingly. In 1967, at the request of the National Christian Council in Kenya, John Chappell of Halifax went as a full-time B.B. organizer to examine the potential for extension. In 1968 only one unit was in existence. Despite a strenuous programme of training and extension the immediate response was discouraging:

> The Brigade was new to nearly everybody and the Training and Organizing Secretary had to do a lot of talking in churches and with individuals. Most of the newly trained officers thought the Brigade would provide employment to all officers. The leaders lost interest after a short time of active company work.

But such misunderstandings and suspicions soon died. Chappell travelled thousands of miles. Within a year forty companies were active and a Coast Battalion was formed in 1970. Into the 1970s the growth continued with membership recently reaching 2,700. After six years Chappell handed over his task to William Kithara and a Kenyan Management Committee. Today the local programme emphasizes 'self-support and self-employment':

> The idea is to encourage the boys to use their hands and imagination as early as possible in life, since many will have to earn a living on a self-employed basis. Small projects are, therefore, being developed in different localities, such as mat and basket making in Mombasa, craft work using tins and cans in Nakuru, and the growing of cash crops — coffee, tea and cotton in Chogoria and Meru.

Training is increasingly geared to employment: bricklaying, block making, and carpentry. 'Group projects' will, it is hoped, assist boys 'if they wish to join a cooperative venture when the time comes to earn a living'.[43]

International Brigade literature today increasingly emphasizes the need to gear programmes to local realities, particularly concerning employment and other social issues. The vitality and rapid expansion of the Churches in most Third World countries ensures a strong spiritual base for the B.B., but the shaky dependent economic status of many new nations leaves little room for boys to afford the now costly outward accoutrements and equipment of traditional Brigade programmes. Valuable foreign exchange is easily eaten up by imported equipment. In a six-month tour of Ghana, Nigeria, Kenya, Uganda and Zambia, two Danes, Anni and Erik Fyhn, found an urgent need to 'Africanize' those youth organizations that had been introduced and subsequently dominated by Europeans. In Zambia (formerly Northern Rhodesia), as a result of initiatives by the Rev. Wellington Chishimba, Brigade Secretary, twelve acres of land have been given to the B.B. in Luapula Province for a community-based agriculture project. At B.B. Headquarters, Kaniki, Ndola, the Zambian Government helped set up the Brigade's twenty-five-acre property as an agricultural and skills training centre. In Zambia it was the President, Dr Kenneth Kaunda, who actively promoted the development of the movement from 1964 onwards.[44]

In 1964 the Rev. Christopher Hancock was appointed Training and Organizing Secretary for Zambia. Expansion in Zambia was swift, especially in the towns of the job-rich Copperbelt to which many families migrated, and where boys found themselves without 'the restraining influences of traditional family life and tribal ties'. In 1971 Hancock handed over an autonomous, well-organized B.B. movement 1,500-strong, to Maurice Chauluka. Today the movement has about 2,500 members with companies in all seven provinces. The new economic self-help agricultural schemes — a full-time agriculturalist was appointed in 1980 at Kaniki — are helping to make the Zambian movement self-sufficient and more relevant to African needs.[45]

In other parts of the Regional Fellowship, British organizers have played an important role, among them Stewart McCullough in Malawi in the 1960s. His years of service and training and those of his successor John Mattenje have made a valuable contribution to the leadership of the Church there. Although B.B. work no longer exists in Malawi, in Rhodesia (now Zimbabwe) the membership reached over 4,500. The experience of former B.B. organizers has proved invaluable to the work of the International Committee (then responsible for the British movement's world relations) and to the World Conference. A Pan-African B.B. Conference in Nigeria in 1975 greatly aided continental awareness of the Brigade movement. In August 1979, Derek Creighton,

Captain of the 1st Coleraine Company, Northern Ireland, went to Lesotho, Southern Africa, under the auspices of the World Conference and the United Society for the Propagation of the Gospel. As a 'Church Boys' Worker' with the Anglican Church in Maseru he has been conspicuously successful in forming many B.B. units.

In South Africa the movement has been strong in the Rand Battalion since the 1940s. From there an equipment depot served all the provinces of the Union (later the Republic) from the mid-1950s onwards. In South Africa's sensitive sociopolitical and racial climate the long search for a permanent full-time organizer has proved elusive, despite the offer of some overseas financing. Throughout the 1950s membership climbed to nearly 3,000, and at the time of the first South African consultation in August 1961 stood at over 3,700. In the late 1940s the movement began to gain ground amongst urban blacks. In different parts of the country it has had a strong following from whites and coloureds, depending upon local circumstances. In April 1968 the multiracial South African Council was reconstituted, but multiracial companies have rarely been formed in South Africa. In the Transvaal in recent years joint activities including parades, training courses and competitions have been held. The Southern African Fellowship still remains unique in its formal 'political' isolation. It is, however, a full and participating member of the World Conference, and individual contacts are strong.[46]

Between 1959 and 1962 John Edbrooke worked as Caribbean Organizer, initially with Trinidad as his base. 'What we must do', he wrote in July 1959, 'is to make each individual local Council a strong working unit.' Travelling thousands of miles throughout this dispersed B.B. region, Edbrooke brought new life and expansion to the movement through training courses, extension campaigns, and his own personal dedication to the B.B. cause. Councils were formed and morale and numbers rose as a result throughout this sprawling, ever-expanding, multilingual and interdenominational Brigade territory. Especially encouraging were developments in the non-British islands: the Republic of Haiti (where a major national camp was held in 1960), the Netherlands Antilles, and the U.S. Virgin Islands (St. Thomas). Extension was also undertaken in Spanish-speaking Costa Rica, into French-speaking St. Martin, and into Surinam, Curaçao and Aruba. In September 1962 Carlyle Jackson, a Barbadian, succeeded Edbrooke as Organizer for the Eastern Caribbean.[47]

In 1963 a limited Caribbean consultation was held in Trinidad, and in November 1966 the Caribbean Fellowship was inaugurated in Barbados, attended by eleven B.B. countries from British Honduras to Surinam. For William McVicker it was his valedictory overseas tour as International Secretary. The occasion was crowned by a major regional training course for over 140 officers and NCOs from eighteen Caribbean countries. Full-time organizers continued the development throughout the region into the 1970s with membership reaching 7,000. But it was in the face of continued chronic unemployment and dwindling government resources. The Brigade's response has been to pilot vocational training schemes for boys, in which the World Conference is also cooperating.[48]

The B.B. in Canada, despite strenuous efforts from within and without, never could attain the membership of the prewar years. Several Canadian organizers were appointed including George Barron in the 1960s and later Paul Montacute and Danny Reesor. The movement's strength remained in the Atlantic Provinces, Quebec and Ontario (particularly in Toronto), but membership rarely rose above 1,000 to 1,200. The U.B.B.A. has maintained its work principally in Pennsylvania, Maryland, California and Texas. But it is fragmented and, by North American youth-work standards, its membership is low. In Neenah-Menasha, Wisconsin, the organization has retained its position as the 'largest single B.B. unit' in the world. Through the North American Fellowship — which includes Bermuda — the scattered remnants of a once formidable B.B. movement in North America maintain close links in camps and other exchanges. The inescapable conclusion is that the Brigade, except in Neenah-Menasha, failed to 'Americanize' or 'Canadianize' itself early enough, at a time when the opportunity was ripe.[49]

'Dawn in Singapore' came quickly for the B.B. after the Japanese surrender in 1945. Very soon Chua Siak Phuang (more popularly known as S.P. Chua) revived his old company, the 1st Singapore. He was joined almost immediately by James Fraser. British companies and teams raised £700 for the speedy Singapore recovery, and by 1950 the Battalion had regained its old strength. In 1954 twenty-five Singaporeans went to the Founder's Centenary Camp at Eton, and by 1957 the membership had risen to 500. Meanwhile Singapore was providing help to advance the movement on the nearby Malay Peninsula. The B.B. had begun there at Penang in 1946. One architect of this new advance was the educationalist, Geh Hun Kheng, Captain of the 1st Penang. On Malayan independence in August 1957 there were six companies in the new Federation. The following year a Malayan Council was established. These early days were, however, not easy for the movement in Malaya — this was the time of the Malayan emergency and the 'confrontation' with Indonesia. Even today in parts of the country insurgency is not unknown. The movement continued to expand after independence throughout the Malay Peninsula (known as Malaysia from 1963), reaching most of the major centres such as Ipoh, Malacca and the capital, Kuala Lumpar, and finding a place even in rural communities. In 1961 it spread to Kuching in Sarawak (later part of East Malaysia) and afterwards to the other Borneo state of Sabah. Between 1954 and 1962 nearly thirty companies were registered in Malaya. In 1963 the first Pacific Regional Camp was held at Port Dickson, West Malaysia, attracting 250 campers from as far away as New Zealand and Samoa. Throughout this period cooperation with the still growing Singapore Battalion was close and cordial. In 1964, the year following Singapore's incorporation into the Malaysian Federation, S.P. Chua became founding President of the Malaysia Council. The Singapore Battalion, always at the hub of East Asian B.B. affairs, became temporarily the Southern District of B.B. Malaysia. At this time the Malaysian movement had a membership of over 2,000 (B.B. and Life Boys), in nearly forty companies and teams. In 1965 Singapore seceded from the predominantly Moslem Malaysian Federation. The movement in Singapore became in time an autonomous self-governing national Battalion.[50]

The new political division had little or no effect on the movement's advance, especially after the appointment in 1966 of Edgar Ramalingam, Captain of the 6th Singapore Company, as B.B. Organizer for Malaysia and Singapore. It had long been thought that, as elsewhere, a European would initially be appointed — expatriate officers like Len Strange of Singapore and Paul Juby of Johor Bahru were highly respected leaders in the movement locally — but the B.B. in the region had by then matured way beyond such an interim arrangement.

Ramalingam became responsible to a Joint Consultative Committee in both countries. It was a remarkable example of regional cooperation. In Malaysia the movement grew to nearly forty companies and a membership of 1,800 by 1970. Known as the Beriged Putera Malaysia, the Malaysian movement strove very hard to remain multiracial in an increasingly Malay-conscious society. The literature was slowly translated into Malay, and over ninety per cent of the recruits were non-Christian. 'There is a great vigour', reported Paul Juby in 1967, 'in the multicultural society of Malays, Chinese, Indians, Eurasians, Sarawakians and Sabahians.' The B.B. consciously worked closely with the government to assimilate itself into Malayan society. The leadership and membership, however, remained predominantly Chinese. In Singapore the same multicultural society was being built up, but under strong Chinese leadership. The B.B. reflected this ethnic make-up, and the leadership and membership remains mostly Chinese. Strong nationalism, and an identification with the determination to build a virile, self-sufficient island republic in a troubled part of the world became characteristic of The Boys' Brigade in Singapore. At all levels the success was remarkable. As Cheong Hock Hai, Chief Examination Officer in the Ministry of Education in Singapore and an ex-Battalion Vice-President, wrote in 1969:

> The strength of the B.B. in Singapore . . . lies in its adaptability. Founded in an alien land which, through the dictates of colonial history, gave the pattern to several aspects of present Singapore life, the B.B. can still be used as one more weapon for the forging of Christian values in a fundamentally non-Christian society. Nationalism embraces us all, including the B.B., and all organizations are assessed today according to how they can contribute to a better national life. A youth organization in an intensely civic environment is measured by the yardstick of its capacity for contribution to the welfare of the whole country. That is what the challenge to the B.B. in Singapore today is.[51]

Nation-building, industrialization and intense educational competition characterized Singapore in the 1960s and 1970s. Already in 1962 the Founder's Badge had replaced the Queen's Badge. In 1970 small-arms training (locally termed musketry) was introduced into the B.B. syllabus after much controversy, and the movement undoubtedly survived because it responded to rather than resisted national service. Cooperation with government was rewarded by assistance and recognition. The President of the Republic, Dr B.H. Sheares, became B.B. Patron in 1971, and no major event in Singapore lacks attendance by a minister or senior government official. By 1980, the fiftieth year of the B.B. Singapore, the movement was active in over twenty companies with a membership of over 2,000. With a highly professional headquarters B.B. Singapore is a leader in regional and world affairs.

In 1958-59 Jim Fraser revived the B.B. in Hong Kong. Today the movement there is predominantly Cantonese speaking and serves nearly one thousand boys, many in high-rise, low-cost housing areas. In 1966 Fung Shiu Wing became the first Organizer, and in 1975 a government grant allowed the establishment of a headquarters shared with the Girls' Brigade. Hong Kong today contributes with Malaysia, Singapore and Brunei to the affairs of the East Asia Fellowship, which split amicably away from the Pacific Regional Fellowship in 1975.[52]

The following year, under gentle pressure from the United Kingdom, the International Committee and elsewhere, the World Conference Committee met in Singapore, the first time it had convened outside Britain, to consummate the new spirit of B.B. internationalism in a more formal yet truly independent consultative management arrangement: the World Conference.[53]

In September 1968 the World Conference Committee met in Northern Ireland and issued invitations to the kindred organizations in Denmark, Sweden, Finland and the U.S.A. to become full members. In 1976 the International Committee reviewed the whole structure of the World Conference in the light of 'the meaning of mission today' and the 'translation of the B.B. to meet the needs of different cultures, different societies, different thought forms around the world'. The B.B. could no longer ignore the changing world order. The meeting in Singapore in November 1976 ensured that 'the international outreach of the B.B. will never be the same again'. It was resolved that from 1 January 1978 the World Conference Committee would assume 'overall responsibility for world development'. Leslie Rawson, the personal heir to McVicker's ideas and vision and the co-architect of many of the developments of the 1970s, was appointed as Executive Secretary to the World Conference. The Conference was given its own budget and a Standing Committee. The latter consisted of the representatives of the European Fellowship on World Conference Committee together with any other members of this Committee able to attend. Its brief was to oversee policy between the three-yearly meetings of the World Conference Committee. In 1977 the Brigade Council resolved to transfer those responsibilities still vested in the International Committee to the World Conference, and the Brigade in Britain became, more formally, a partner member of the Conference.[54]

In May 1979 an international consultation was held at Center Sjaelland, Denmark, to consider *inter alia* the movement in the 1990s — programmes, leadership, and Christian education and worship. The Committee and European full-time staff meanwhile also considered the role of an international youth movement in the 1980s. In the intervening years, through travel bursaries, extension follow-up, Regional Fellowship meetings, vocational training and many other grants and projects, the World Conference has touched every corner of the Brigade and kindred world. The movement has now spread to Brazil and Bangladesh, and Scandinavian leaders are making significant contributions to the 'partnership-in-mission' through the World Conference. (The F.D.F. had already been active in extension overseas, especially through Danish-based missions. In 1953, for instance, a group was enrolled at the Kidugalo leprosy village at Sikonge, near Tabora, in what is now Tanzania.) No longer is it assumed that all the expertise resides in Britain. Singapore and Canada, for instance, have sent senior staff and office-bearers in recent years to study the B.B. in New Zealand and Australia. In November 1982 the West African and European Fellowships arranged a project entitled 'Youth Work in a Changing World', during which twenty-eight Europeans and twenty-eight Africans shared life and work in Nigeria. In August 1982 the World Conference Committee met in Lagos, Nigeria. No longer do European ideas, values or even money dominate Brigade decision-making. 'The Gospel', wrote Heening Iburg Andersen of Denmark before that meeting, 'was sent out from Europe.' Thereupon:

> Technology and money followed. The stronger ones [Andersen maintained] helped the weaker ones. Today we must stop and consider: who are the stronger ones — and who are the weaker ones — People who have their age-old traditions and cultural background reaching generations back? — Or those who have developed incredible technological and economical structures but lost their roots

and their very basis as human beings? The answer is not clear 'either-or'.[55]

The future of The Boys' Brigade in the developed countries, where numbers in general are in decline, and in the developing or Third World countries, where every year new potentials are being opened up, shows that there is indeed no clear answer. A dynamic and growing Church in the Third World may well lead The Boys' Brigade into a more intensive internationalism in the movement's second century. The greatly enriched and wider, more 'liberal' European base of the World Conference is already having a marked effect on traditional B.B. thinking throughout the world. These two forces will undoubtedly enhance the mood of experiment and change, and extend it into the 1980s and beyond.[56]

CHAPTER 9

'THE WINDS OF CHANGE'

The Boys' Brigade in Britain, 1960 to 1982

'PRESENT DAY WONDERS — television, sputniks, and the rest — sometimes blind us to the fact that the problems of youth are the problems of youth!' stressed a B.B. publication entitled *Discipline Outdated?*:

> So long as children have to grow into adults, so long will they need guidance during the period of transition; and the B.B.'s basic tenets of discipline and religious training are as relevant to the growing boy of 1961 as ever they were to his great-grandfather in 1883.

As The Boys' Brigade entered a period in British history during which that relatively new phenomenon, the 'teenager', was apparently becoming more hostile to authority and traditional values, the dilemma the Brigade found itself in was much more pronounced than this opening quotation suggests. 'The young today are different from you and me. They are also different from us when we were young,' asserted Colonel J. Hughes to an Annual Council Meeting of the Northern Ireland District. 'They are different from any younger generation that has ever existed before. They are the object of a cult.' In the early 1960s there was no lack of authoritative pronouncements on the tremendous impact of social changes on the lives of children and young people, and on the institutions which sought to serve them. While boys will always be boys, the young were certainly regarded by many contemporary commentators as being the most sensitive barometers of social change in an era in which traditional authority was weakening, moral standards rapidly changing, and family and community ties becoming looser. Other important factors in this period were the increase in affluence and the widening opportunities for the young in education, work and leisure.[1]

'At no time in human history have the forces for change been more far reaching or more powerful in the influences they exercise on the material, moral and spiritual life of the young,' claimed the Haynes Report on the B.B. in 1964. This Report, whose recommendations are discussed at greater length later in this chapter, also recognized that the basic religious purpose of The Boys' Brigade was opposed by strong undercurrents of feelings and attitudes in modern British society:

> The general loosening of standards and restraint and the greater stimulation through the mass media of entertainment, information and advertisement, can be powerful solvents of the young person's will to assert and sustain a steady purpose in life. For many, the challenge of the Brigade may be unwelcome or unacceptable. Under present conditions it cannot hope to make the popular appeal which some organizations can make far more easily since they are not held by so strong a religious and restraining purpose and can more readily come to terms with fluctuating moods and desires.

These years were to see a profound questioning of traditional values combined with a search for new values felt to be more appropriate to life in a rapidly changing, materialistic and scientific civilization. The term 'permissiveness' came to be widely used in the press, and by Churchmen and other opinion-formers, to decry certain freedoms, especially sexual freedom, and its use implied a reaction against the rate of change in the moral and social behaviour of the young. In this social climate, it began to be asked whether the purposeful, disciplined, openly religious stand of The Boys' Brigade was as genuinely relevant to the modern boy as it had been to earlier generations.[2]

'The pace of change and its openness were affected by a decline in authority. Freedom is constrained by authority and sees authority as an enemy,' wrote one commentator, 'but in postwar Britain authority was unusually at a discount.' A younger generation was growing up in the 1960s which *did* believe that discipline was becoming outdated, and refused to give the same unthinking obedience and respect to its elders as they had been accustomed to receive in the past. In a political culture where nearly all forms of authority — from the Lord Chamberlain's powers of censorship over the theatre to the running of University administrations — were being brought into question by iconoclastic youth, it would have been surprising if The Boys' Brigade had remained exempt from criticism. Hence the B.B. was seen by many outsiders as a 'closed' self-perpetuating group, composed mainly of 'respectable' working-class and lower middle-class members — a kind of 'freemasonry of the Youth Service' — as well as the most tradition-orientated youth movement, resistant to change and sticking to quaint uniforms and quaint drill movements. Because of the nature of the training and the self-effacing, unassuming characteristics which were bred by Christian commitment, the Brigade did not seem to be an outgoing or lively organization possessed of the 'fashionable' public image which many regarded as desirable. That this was not an entirely accurate representation of the Brigade during this period of its development will become apparent when we examine its activities as a movement in more detail and, in particular, look more closely at how far the recommendations of the Haynes Report were carried out in practice. The mere survival of The Boys' Brigade as a uniformed, Church-orientated, militarily structured, adult-led, single-sex organization might be considered a sufficient achievement in itself in a society which evinced such an uncritical adulation of youth for its own sake. 'Today we worship youth,' wrote one B.B. officer:

> 'Temples' are erected to its honour — glittering Carnaby Street, dim-lit discos, Top of the Pops T.V. programmes, opinion panels also on T.V., and that non-stop anthem of praise to the 'beautiful people' — the gospel according to Radio One. No one seems to reflect that, as a result of all this, we are being submerged in a deluge of shoddy goods, immature thinking, half-baked notions about how society should be changed, unhygienic hairstyles, and a refusal to recognize any form of authority.[3]

With such an active emphasis on its uncompromising religious purpose and the strict discipline of the drill parade, it is not surprising that the B.B. found its objective of advancing Christ's Kingdom among boys far more difficult to attain than in the past. For not only did The Boys' Brigade emphasize — in direct opposition to the prevailing 'youth culture' — such character traits as obedience, reverence, self-respect and discipline, it also maintained order and hierarchy as prominent features in its system of self-management. Added to this, the Brigade was regarded by many as an Establishment organization, perpetuating Victorian ideals of patriotism and military discipline. 'There is no doubt in my mind that the image we are creating in the public mind at the moment is of an exceedingly efficient movement, slightly conservative and rather old-fashioned,' wrote Secretary Wilson-Haffenden in 1962 in uncharacteristically self-critical mood:

> Discipline and religion, drill and uniform, Bible Class and Badge work are inherent in the B.B., but there is no reason why these should not be up-to-date and attractive to the modern Boy. The cap, belt and haversack were an attraction in 1883. I am not certain that they are today and if not, we must substitute something else that is.

The Secretary's evident awareness that The Boys' Brigade needed to improve its public image in order to attract new recruits and to retain the older teenager was to lead to a major reassessment of both the direction and the organization of the movement in Great Britain.[4]

In January 1963 the Executive Committee of The Boys' Brigade appointed the Haynes Committee, chaired by Sir George Haynes, Director of the National Council of Social Service,

> to investigate the difficulty of The Boys' Brigade . . . in attracting and holding a greater number of Boys at a time when the Boy population has increased. The Committee are asked to consider all relevant aspects of Brigade work, including recruiting, programme, church relationships, uniform and age limits, should they consider any or all of these have any effect on the problem, and to report to the Brigade Executive.

This important committee, a precursor of similar investigations by all the major uniformed youth movements, held its first meeting in February 1963 and approved its final report in January 1964, having met in all on six occasions. The Committee, with only six members (including the Chairman) out of fifteen not having an intimate connection with The Boys' Brigade, made its deliberations more in the manner of an internal 'audit' than as an outside study undertaken by an independent body. Nevertheless, Haynes was genuinely animated by the desire to take a fresh look at the Brigade as an established youth movement faced with an important task of reappraisal in the light of changing historical circumstances. Indeed, such was the subsequent impact on the Brigade of the Committee's conclusions, that it is virtually impossible to see more recent Brigade history in terms other than before or after the Haynes Report.[5]

Sir George himself, introducing his Report to Brigade Council in 1964, mentioned the great changes coming over the British educational system as a result of the various official government reports of the early 1960s, such as the Crowther Report (1959) on fifteen to eighteen year olds, the Albermarle Report (1959-60) on the Youth Service in England and Wales, the Kilbrandon Report (1960) on Children and Young Persons, the Robbins Report (1963) on Higher Education, and, finally, the Newsome Report (1963) on Secondary Education. These forward-looking reports provided an impressive re-examination of the basic educational and youth services, and called for, in Haynes' words, 'an urgent mobilization of greater resources to meet these needs [of the adolescent] and for a more generous and imaginative approach to young people'. Haynes broadly agreed with the conclusions reached by most of these reports, particularly where they emphasized the challenge presented to the Youth Service by changing social and economic conditions.[6]

At the outset, the Haynes Committee made it clear in their unanimous Report that The Boys' Brigade stood or fell by its continued adherence to its primary religious purpose, and that this should not be toned down to fit more congenially in with prevailing attitudes for the sole purpose of attracting a larger membership. Instead, the Committee recommended that The Boys' Brigade should make a stronger appeal to the increasing numbers of 'young people' impatient with 'soft' options and ready to accept the challenge of something more positive and demanding. The Haynes Committee was convinced that many young men wanted to play a more constructive and responsible social role and believed that The Boys' Brigade could become an important channel for the expression of the spirit of enterprise and practical idealism that was the obverse of the irresponsible, rebellious and selfish side of 'youth' so often portrayed in the media. (The distinction made here between 'young people' and 'youth' was both social and cultural in its implications.)[7]

The Brigade could also make some contribution towards preserving order, Haynes implied, in a society threatened by 'moral panic' because of the activities of those 'folk devils' of the 1960s, the teenage gangs of mods and rockers. 'You don't need a Judge to tell you of the quite appalling conditions among the senior teenage Boy today, and the wave of violence and destruction which affects so many of the present generation,' Sir Donald Finnemore told Council, with the 1964 Bank Holiday Weekend clashes between mods and rockers clearly in recent memory. Thus Judge Finnemore saw the new Senior 'Brigade' recommended in the Haynes Report as the Committee's *raison d'être*, because he felt that discipline was needed for a much higher age range than it had been years ago when he first joined the movement from the Boys' Life Brigade. In presenting his Report to the Council, however, Sir George Haynes drummed home quite a different message: that contemporary youth and the youth of the 1880s were quite different and that any movement which was going to advance had to be aware of the changes which had taken place during the interval. 'I think you must let the winds of discussions and thought and interest play-in [sic] a little more into your Councils,' he gently admonished the officers present. Whether the recommendations of the Haynes Report were seen as improving the techniques for managing the young within the Brigade or as supplying the young with a more challenging faith to live by in a society that treated them too indulgently, the publication of the final Report led to wide-ranging internal discussions and a certain amount of criticism from those within the movement resistant to change.[8]

The Brigade Executive set up a sub-committee to examine the Haynes Report in detail and to prepare a resolution recommending its adoption in time for the next Brigade Council in Cambridge; subsequently a more detailed motion to implement the Report's proposals was to be put in 1965 to Council at Southampton. Haynes proposed several sweeping changes in the age-composition of the Brigade, as well as substantial changes in uniform, and suggested placing less emphasis on drill and more on outdoor activities. The Report recommended a three-tier age structure (subsequently modified) which involved the contentious scrapping of the Life Boy movement for a new Junior 'Brigade' and the setting up of a new Senior 'Brigade' which was to raise the upper age limit: Junior Brigade for nine to eleven year olds; The Boys' Brigade for twelve to fifteen year olds; and the Senior Brigade for sixteen to nineteen year olds. Haynes also suggested that the Brigade Executive set up a special committee to advise on the uniform for all three tiers of the modified organization. The whole Brigade training scheme was to be reviewed and revised in the light of these recommendations on the future management and development of the movement. At the 1964 Council Meeting, Sir Donald Finnemore, Brigade Vice-President, moved that Council give its general approval to these proposals but, during the ensuing debate, perhaps quite naturally, the majority of the speakers were either against the Report in its entirety or felt that parts of it, particularly the proposals in regard to the Senior 'Brigade', were unnecessary and should be dropped altogether. Many B.B. officers present also opposed the disappearance of the long-established Life Boys, although the lack of continuity between the two movements had contributed to the fact that only about half of the Life Boys ever reached Brigade membership. In parallel with other youth movements at this time, The Boys' Brigade was aiming to promote more of an upward flow of younger members into its teenage sections and it was this process which the new Junior 'Brigade' was expected to enourage.[9]

Such was the resistance to the Report from some quarters of the Brigade that, until persuaded by Dr J. Martin Strang, Scottish Vice-President, to withdraw their opposition, there was a fear that several Scottish Battalions would actually vote against the resolution to implement Haynes. 'I think the underlying feeling,' reflected Wilson-Haffenden with some understatement, 'is that something is going to be forced on someone which they do not want to do.' At this juncture in the Council meeting, Finnemore spoke again to wind up the debate, making it quite clear that Council would have either to reject or accept the whole of the resolution which the Executive was putting forward to implement Haynes, and that this meant acceptance or rejection of the Junior and Senior 'Brigades' or 'Sections' (as they were to become). The newly installed Brigade President, Lord Bruce, asked for a show of hands for the Executive's resolution and, as only thirty officers present voted against, it was deemed that Council had given its general approval to the Executive's proposals. To clear up certain misunderstandings that had arisen, especially with regard to the 'third tier', the Brigade Executive in March 1965 sent out a letter to captains of companies pointing out that the 'third tier' would be 'on an experimental and optional basis'. It was stressed that there was no intention whatever to make it obligatory for any company to adopt a pattern with which it was not in full agreement. Then, in June 1965, a booklet entitled *Proposals for the Implementation of the Haynes Report* was drawn up by the Executive to enable officers and leaders to understand fully the operation of the new three-section company which, with effect from 1 September 1965, was to be revised as: Junior Section for eight to twelve year olds, Company Section for eleven to seventeen year olds, and Senior Section for sixteen to nineteen year olds.[10]

At Brigade Council in Southampton that year, approval was eventually given to this new three-section company structure, including, from 17 September 1966, the integration of the Life Boys with The Boys' Brigade as the Junior Section. A keen debate on age limits was enlivened by an historical event when Ana Simpson of Paisley became the first woman leader to address Council. She made cogent arguments for dropping the term 'Life Boys', spoke of the necessity for integrating training, and assured Council that 'there was no danger of the womanly tail attempting to wag the male dog'. Since the first and so far only woman, Daphne Pickford of the 1st Loughborough Company, did not appear on the Brigade Executive until 1975, this was undoubtedly an accurate prediction. During this debate, the spokesman for the Executive pointed out that the overlap in ages between the sections not only gave company and church a certain amount of discretion but it also enabled different parts of the country to cope with varying educational ages. Lord Bruce, Brigade President, said that even the Executive was not entirely happy about the names for the three new sections — Junior, Company and Senior — but that they would serve until something better emerged. The President believed that The Boys' Brigade had to try out this type of experiment in practice and hoped that companies would find that the age limit resolution, which had been passed by an overwhelming majority, was in line with the needs of young people generally. Three years earlier, the Executive had authorized the optional use of an alternative full uniform of navy blue shorts or slacks, navy blue shirt and a white lanyard, together with other normal items of uniform. A referendum on the question of whether the Brigade should adopt a single uniform with a basis common to all three sections was to be held in January 1966 and debated at that year's Council. Only fifty-four per cent of voting papers sent to all captains of companies were returned, but on the decisive question of whether officers agreed that the Brigade should have a full uniform, thirty-four per cent of all companies polled replied in the affirmative and twenty per cent in the negative.[11]

The Executive, meeting on 12 February 1966, therefore agreed to go ahead and replace existing uniforms with the proposed new full uniform, at the discretion of individual companies, in Company and Senior Sections. But at Brigade Council in Edinburgh that year, a motion put by the Glasgow Battalion resolved that 'the results of the Referendum on Uniforms are not sufficiently decisive and that the whole question be referred back to the Brigade Executive for further consideration'. The majority of the Scottish district and battalion presidents did not accept the Executive's interpretation of the referendum results, and it was the strong contention of the Glasgow Battalion that to introduce a radical change in uniform was basically wrong unless it was widely accepted throughout the movement. The ensuing debate not only crystallized the eternally contested question in The Boys' Brigade of whether to wear the full uniform or the accoutrements over 'ordinary' clothing, but also the perennial problem of what actually qualified as 'ordinary' clothing. For the Executive, Thomas Henderson inveighed against the strength of tradition and resistance to change on the uniform issue:

> This was an age of change not only in methods and ideas but in dress. All the uniformed organizations were looking at themselves and advocating changes in uniform. The real issue was not one between North and South, but whether we were going to move forwards or backwards.

By a clear majority, however, the Glasgow resolution referring back the whole question of uniform to the Executive for further consideration was passed. This meant that the leadership's decisions on uniform had been effectively reversed by the democratic forum of Council. To cut a long story short, the Executive eventually decided after lengthy discussions that, until 31 August 1971, the Junior Section would retain the old naval-style uniform of the Life Boys, the Company Section would continue with haversack, leather belt and forage *or* field service hats worn over 'ordinary' clothing, and the Senior Section would remain experimental, since there was still no current official uniform for this Section. The non-member might find this apparent obsession with styles of dress difficult to comprehend, but to the member of The Boys' Brigade it was — and is — of crucial importance in helping to determine a sense of organizational loyalty and cultural identity.[12]

New uniforms for 'Lady Officers' and the proposed new field service style hats for boys in all Sections had been approved in 1969 in a motion carried by a large majority at the Liverpool Council (existing hats and caps were in use up to 31 August 1971 after which only the new hats could be worn). Thus, to the evident sorrow of many an 'old boy', the familiar pillbox cap which had served to identify a member of The Boys' Brigade for generations was at last abandoned. New uniforms were also designed for Junior Section boys in 1971 which consisted of a blue jersey with turtleneck and grey shorts or trousers. These uniform changes indicate that the full implementation of the Haynes Report was to take until the end of the decade and, in the case of some of its recommendations, even into the 1970s. The lack of extensive consultation with officers and boys over the Report, however, and the slow response from captains and other leaders who *were* consulted are both to some extent responsible for whatever failures occurred in giving effect to its recommendations. Most companies, for example, had introduced the new Senior Sections by 1967, but many officers, owing to a lack of information and training, were inadequately prepared and unaware of what sort of programme to provide for this older age group. Since the number of Senior Section boys had, excluding age overlap, declined from over four thousand on its creation to under a thousand in 1980, its formation can hardly be accounted a major success. The Junior Section, on the other hand, proved much more attractive as an experiment and maintained a consistent membership of 70,000 throughout the 1970s with a programme that was popular among both officers and boys. The introduction in 1977 of a Pre-Junior Section (known as Anchor Boys from September 1982) for six to eight year olds was, if measured simply in terms of numbers enrolled, another conspicuous success for the Brigade.[13]

The launching by the Brigade Secretary, Wilson-Haffenden, of an Appeal Fund to secure a permanent Headquarters building in London was, in some districts and battalions, to have an impact in the early 1960s equal with that of the Haynes Report. When Wilson-Haffenden first became Secretary in 1954, the lease of Abbey House in Westminster was to expire in 1966, when it was due for rebuilding. Hence he drew the obvious conclusion that it would be necessary for the Brigade to acquire a more permanent site for its Headquarters. The then Brigade President, Lord Maclay, did not agree with buying new property in the capital, and strongly opposed such a move at Executive meetings. The Secretary got around this obstacle by persuading London District to put forward a resolution at Brigade Council in 1959 demanding that the Executive take immediate steps to secure new accommodation, and this was agreed unanimously. The first meeting of the Appeal Committee, chaired by Lord Luke of Pavenham, was held in December 1959, and it was decided to launch an appeal to raise £100,000 from 1 March to 4 October 1961. Since the proposal for a permanent Headquarters had come from the body of the 1959 Council, the actual responsibility for the success of the appeal rested with Council members. A company target was set ranging from 2/6d. (25p) per head for twelve-year-old boys to £1 for officers. With a renewed emphasis on 'youth' as a result of the recent Albermarle Report on the Youth Service, The Boys' Brigade hoped to raise contributions of at least £10 per company for the Appeal Fund, and by March 1961 over £14,000 had been received towards the target. Wilson-Haffenden told his staff that the Appeal occupied 'most of my working hours and many during the night as well'.[14]

To collect further much-needed cash for the Appeal Fund, the Executive decided to resort to that old standby, 'The Great Relay Run', which it was planned would end at Mansion House on 11 May 1961 where the Lord Mayor of London would receive the runners. Fifteen final runners, covering the last stages of the five routes, were to represent over 2,500 of their comrades running a total of over 3,000 miles from John O'Groats, Northern Ireland, Fishguard, Land's End, and Cromer in Norfolk. The achievements of the various runners along the five routes was eloquently summarized by the *Gazette*:

> Boys who have traversed their Ulster countryside through day and night, converging on Belfast, and then the sea miles to Glasgow; Boys who have trotted across the Scottish Highlands in torrential rain, day and night; Runners who have slogged across the Yorkshire Moors in a howling gale; Teams in the South who have sweated it out along dusty roads and the fume laden atmosphere of towns, in summer heat — all converging upon the heart of the Commonwealth, laden with Civic Greetings and generous gifts from B.B. well wishers. All these combine to make the Run an outstanding success.

Despite the *Gazette's* optimism, the Run received less coverage than expected in the national press — certainly in comparison with the 1935 Silver Jubilee Run — and at Mansion House, Lord Luke announced the total received for the Fund to date as only reaching £31,000, including cheques donated on the Run. However, the figure had increased to over three times that amount by the end of the year. Sir Cyril Black M.P., a prominent temperance advocate and moral crusader who became Brigade Treasurer in 1962, offered to act for the Brigade by making sure that they got the right building at the right time at the right price. He invested the Appeal Fund money in short-term government loans, so that when a suitable property came on to the market a deposit could be put down almost immediately.[15]

After several years of long and diligent search all over London for suitable accommodation, a site was eventually discovered at Parson's Green, Fulham, which was zoned for office and light engineering work. At that time, the Board of Trade had a regulation concerning the acquisition of office property, and what was known as a Development Permit or 'change of use' license was essential if the site was to be developed for a Brigade Headquarters. Wilson-Haffenden narrated the events which followed, in his confidential quarterly *Newsletter*, in terms which suggest a hidden 'old boy' network at work in bureaucratic circles:

> You will remember that in speaking of the new Headquarters, Sir Cyril Black mentioned that a difficulty had arisen over the necessity for an Office Development Permit. One morning in my Quiet Time I was convinced that I should write personally to the Foreign Secretary, Michael Stewart, who was not only at Christ's Hospital [Wilson-Haffenden's old school] but is also my own M.P. and is the new M.P. for Hammersmith in which the proposed new Headquarters is situated. I asked Sir Cyril's permission to write and I handed in my letter to the Foreign Office personally. The following day we received three telephone calls from the Board of Trade referring to my letter and asking for further information. Then I discovered that the official at the Board of Trade dealing with the application was also an old B.B. Boy. Twenty-four hours later we were told that the O.D.P. would be issued and two days later it was issued. The final hurdle is the Planning Permission from the Borough council and I am going with Sir Cyril to see the Mayor this week, so we're hoping now for a quick decision . . .

Planning permission was received in due course, and the purchase of the building to be called 'Brigade House', which with improvements cost £220,000, was made official at last. The new Headquarters was meant for the joint use of The Boys' Brigade, its London District, and the newly formed sister organization of the Girls' Brigade.[16]

The Appeal Fund had raised most of the money needed for Brigade House, with some contributions from private industry, and on 9 December 1966 the new offices were officially opened by Princess Alexandra, deputizing for the Queen. 'It is with real regret that I am unable to come to Brigade House to see this new Headquarters of The Boys' Brigade and the Girls' Brigade,' ran the Queen's letter from Buckingham Palace:

> On the occasion of the Diamond Jubilee of The Boys' Brigade in 1943 my father forecast that it would go from strength to strength, because it was built upon the twin pillars of discipline and religion and so was meeting one of the greatest needs of the present time. *I believe that in a swinging age it is still important to have a basis of faith and discipline in order to keep one's feet on the ground.* The establishment of positive standards of value is becoming increasingly difficult for young people, who find it hard to know what or whom to respect. [my italics]

A few years after the two Brigades had moved to Fulham, in 1971, a hostel was built on the site to accommodate visiting Brigade members. During the ninetieth anniversary celebrations of The Boys' Brigade on 22 February 1973, the Queen and Prince Philip were able at last to visit Brigade House for themselves, a most memorable occasion for those present.[17]

In October 1966, William H. McVicker, who had received an O.B.E. in that year's Birthday Honours, retired from full-time service as Secretary of the B.B.'s International Committee. Son of the founder of the 1st Belfast Company, 'Mac' was considered by many to have been one of the most influential men in the movement. He had been Secretary for the Life Boys' from 1933 (a post he relinquished to B.M. Steward in 1947) and Overseas Secretary until his retirement. From Brigade Headquarters in London, as development abroad gained momentum, McVicker made tours of the B.B. overseas in Canada, South Africa, New Zealand, Australia and the West Indies. Many overseas B.B. leaders have told how 'Mac' gave them friendly advice in a paternal manner, keeping the 'youngsters' on the rails without them being aware of it, and his humility coupled with his capacity for friendship endeared him to men and women all round the world. Not only was he outstanding in the contribution he made in propagating the B.B. overseas, as has been shown elsewhere in this book, but he was intimately associated with various aspects of the work in Britain and formed many links between the B.B. and world missionary societies. His death in November 1975 marked the end of an era in B.B. history. The immense increase in the B.B.'s work overseas was ultimately his finest memorial.[18]

Having seen the Haynes Report published and the Appeal Fund reach its objective, Wilson-Haffenden himself retired as Secretary of The Boys' Brigade, and was succeeded by Ian G. Neilson with effect from January 1966. Popular with his full-time staff at Abbey House, not least for establishing proper pay scales in line with youth workers generally, Wilson-Haffenden acted as a strong evangelizing force within the Brigade, and with his strength of personality and military bearing was to be a difficult man to follow. 'You have said on several occasions recently that there are many things you would have liked to have done, that there were often occasions when you had much opposition from different sources, and so on,' Wilson-Haffenden was consoled by the Eastern District Organizer:

> We believe very sincerely that you have done a great deal for the movement which we all love so much — much more than perhaps most people will realize — but I believe that your greatest contribution has been to make the movement aware,

once again, that it is an integral part of the living Church of Jesus Christ and, as such, must of necessity be evangelical in outlook; that we are not just another organization for Boys. This is what makes the movement stand head and shoulders above all others and we have to thank you for reminding us of this time and time again during your term of office.

Ian Neilson, his successor, had been educated at Glasgow Academy, and was commissioned in the Royal Artillery during World War II, eventually commanding a War Crimes Investigation Unit. He had also had extensive administrative experience, being Senior Under-Secretary with the Royal Institute of Chartered Surveyors at the time of his appointment. Perhaps a less conspicuous, more subdued Secretary in contrast to his flamboyant predecessor, Neilson was a capable administrator who skilfully guided The Boys' Brigade through the changes initiated by the Haynes Report recounted earlier in this chapter. Another change in leadership had taken place in 1963, when the Earl of Elgin and Kincardine (then Lord Bruce), a witty and popular Scot, took over from the much-respected Lord Maclay as President of The Boys' Brigade. Two issues which Ian Neilson had to cope with almost immediately on taking office were the matter of drafting a new constitution for the movement and the vexed issue of Church relationships.[19]

The Church connection could sometimes be a constraint on The Boys' Brigade in the sense that it limited the formation of companies mainly to church premises, the physical base, and required that leadership should be sought from within the church membership. There were exceptions, but this was generally the case and Brigade Headquarters could only approve (occasionally with reluctance) but not appoint the officers of a company. The fact that the company operated within the church tended to breed an inward-looking mentality and hence a reluctance to operate away from base. Thus a Special Committee on Church Relationships was set up by the Brigade Executive in February 1966 on the advice of its Organization and Administration Committee, 'to study and report on the present and future relationships between The Boys' Brigade and the Churches'. Chaired by the Bishop of Portsmouth, the Special Committee held eight meetings, and in April 1967 its Report was published with a main recommendation that a Churches' Advisory Panel should be established at national level by the Brigade Executive as the chief point of contact between the representatives of the Churches and the Brigade. It was felt that there had to be greater mutual understanding and cooperation between The Boys' Brigade and the Churches, based on more up-to-date knowledge and more frequent contact at all levels. The Denominational Committees of the Brigade, set up immediately after World War II to provide liaison with the Churches, were to continue to function, but would now work in close cooperation with the new Churches' Advisory Panel. The Report was approved unanimously in September 1967 at Brigade Council in Birmingham. The Special Committee confirmed the pre-existing procedure for the appointment of officers by getting the approval of Council for a binding amendment to the Constitution that:

> The Church or any other organization of which the Company is a part shall nominate for enrolment all Officers of the Company. They shall be members or adherents of a Church or other Christian organization and shall be desirous of promoting the Object of the Brigade.[20]

The revised Constitution, which replaced that published in the 1960 Officers' Manual, was only adopted after countless drafts and numerous amendments had been submitted for consideration by members of Council.

Curiously, of sixteen amendments submitted for consideration by Brigade Council on 31 August 1968 in Belfast, half came from the Dublin Battalion. Passing over such constitutional niceties as the regulations affecting the formation and enrolment of companies and the powers of battalions and districts, the reader's eye may be caught by the schedule showing electoral areas for the election of the Brigade Executive, the movement's ruling body. The United Kingdom and the Republic of Ireland were divided into eighteen electoral areas, only four of which were entitled to elect more than one member, according to their strengths: London District (three); Lancashire and Cheshire (two); West of Scotland, including Glasgow (three); Northern Ireland, including Belfast (two). Appendix 4, based upon The Boys' Brigade Register of Directors, gives an occupational breakdown of the Executive's membership from 1916 to 1979 from which it will be seen that whereas the dominant groups until the 1930s were men from professional and merchant backgrounds, after this date managerial occupations replace the merchant class and, while professionals are still in the majority, schoolteachers or those with a white-collar background begin to play a more active role. The other major constitutional change from the 1960 edition of the Manual was the gradual phasing out of divisions (the old county administrations) and groups, leaving behind a simpler structure of company, battalion and district. (The last year in which divisions were listed in the Annual Report was the session 1966-67.) The drafting of the new Constitution was one of the major achievements of Ian Neilson's period as Secretary of The Boys' Brigade, involving considerable hard work in committee and the reconciliation of opposing interpretations of regulations. 'It was a matter of starting really from two different points of view,' Neilson said in retrospect:

> One was to say, 'What are we out to achieve in this new constitution — what kind of a structure are we producing?' and the second thing was to say, 'This is what is in the book at the moment, how much of it ought we in fact to preserve?' If we can, under a new sort of format and wording [provided] it fits into the revised structure we are after [sic], and I think that we produced, though I say it myself, a reasonable document in 1968 and I think that, by and large, it worked.[21]

The Boys' Brigade continued to register the seismic shock waves of the Haynes Report, both in terms of new uniforms and new awards and activities being introduced, as it moved into the uncertain and unpredictable years of the 1970s. The Junior Section continued to expand but the Senior Section showed a marked falling-off in numbers despite the apparently more quiescent, less rebellious adolescent lifestyles of many 'young people' during this decade. A drop in numbers in the sixteen-to-eighteen age group raised some considerable doubts as to the movement's ability to attract older boys, who in the past had been the backbone of the NCO leadership of the Brigade. In the late 1970s, only a third of the eighteen districts in Great Britain and Ireland managed to hold their own or show any increase in boy strength: Wales, West Lowland, North Scottish, Northern Ireland, Republic of Ireland, and the North of England. The location of these more successful districts would tend to suggest that The Boys' Brigade, as it drew closer to its centenary, was retreating into its traditional geographical bases of support. Greater London and the Midlands, for example, could only muster between them about 30,000 boys in all sections, whereas the total for Ireland — both North and South — was over 21,000 and for Scotland over 52,000. In Scotland and Northern Ireland, the B.B. attracted approximately six times as many boys in proportion to population as in England and Wales. In Northern Ireland, recruitment proved unexpectedly resilient during this decade, which was a remarkable achievement in view of the difficulties under which the Brigade's work in the Province had to be carried on.[22]

The recruitment of suitable officers into the organization also remained a persistent problem due both to the competition provided by the advent of paid professional youth workers in the postwar years, and to the decline in the pool of potential recruits with a church affiliation of some kind. In 1964 the Haynes Report had claimed that some ninety-five per cent of Brigade officers had graduated from the ranks which, to the outsider, could give the movement a rather self-perpetuating, self-enclosed look. Statistics taken from officer enrolment forms during the mid-1970s, when occupational details were requested, tend to show that The Boys' Brigade was no longer recruiting its officers from the ranks of the business and professional middle-class, as in William Smith's day. The bulk of the officer recruits came from white collar or skilled working-class backgrounds and the lowest proportion from unskilled and middle-class backgrounds (see Appendix 5). The social, occupational and geographical mobility of the postwar generations, together with declining church attendances and the loss of middle-class Nonconformist leadership, made it unlikely that The Boys' Brigade would find sufficient officers to cope with the potential demand in some areas of the British Isles.[23]

This was confirmed by an information survey conducted among battalion secretaries in 1978 which found that the major problems facing the movement were a high turnover of personnel and a difficulty in finding sufficient leaders, combined with declining local interest due to a lack of publicity at national level. (The B.B. did not have a full-time publicity officer during this period on the Headquarters staff.) Nearly all those who answered the survey agreed that there were plenty of boys available in their areas, if only dedicated officers could be found to recruit and hold them. None admitted that it was a problem to attract modern youth to a church-related organization. A Birmingham company officer saw the major problem in terms of changing moral values and the efforts of the Churches to cope by making changes in their forms of service and methods of teaching. A Scottish officer felt that boys were maturing earlier than in the past, were more affluent and tended to leave the Brigade at an earlier age. Several made reference to the gradual reduction in the size of companies in the inner-city areas and the difficulties of starting them in new, suburban housing estates. City centre rebuilding schemes and some Brigade successes on new-town estates and in rural areas helped offset the decline in urban recruitment, although it is difficult to generalize since some battalions were more successful in industrial and commercial centres than in the surrounding rural areas or suburbs. The provision of leisure activities by youth clubs with paid staff, Cadet units with free equipment, facilities and uniforms, and schools with a wide range of extra-curricular interests were all seen as obvious sources of keen rivalry for the allegiance of the boy, a rivalry which had not been so prominent in earlier decades.[24]

What did it mean and how difficult was it to be a specifically Christian and church-based organization for boys during the period dealt with in this chapter? In 1967 Pearl Jephcott published *Time of One's Own*, the findings of a project initiated by the Kilbrandon Council based on a sample of 600 adolescents from three areas in Scotland: Dennistoun and Drumchapel in Glasgow, and Armadale in West Lothian. Despite the fact that forty-three per cent of the sample had regular association with a church and as many as one in three had taken part in some kind of religious activity in the previous week, many found the church in their area old-fashioned and out of touch: 'kids went to Sunday School, old people to Church' — it was no place for anyone of their age. The Church was also associated with social class and, in Glasgow at least, with sectarian divisions, although those who actually belonged to a church organization disputed this. The rejection of church-linked organizations, such as the B.B., did not seem to stem from hostility to the Church as such but from an association of the Church with social class — 'The Church youth organizations are for snobs.' The adolescents interviewed also mistrusted any youth group if they thought of it as a bait to step up church membership. Only about one in three of those in the sample belonged to any of the Scottish youth groups on offer in their areas. The chief objection to the Youth Service centred on what was seen as its over-authoritarian set-up: youngsters complained that they were bossed around too much and that it was the adults' show, not their own. All this in no way decried the special value of a movement like The Boys' Brigade, but the author believed that the Youth Service had to provide for youngsters and their families who were anti-school and anti-church, as well as those from more 'respectable' church-going families.[25]

Most contemporary historians would now accept that the message that the Churches sought to promote and the attitudes and values that they tried to encourage no longer formed a significant element in the life of the nation. The Boys' Brigade continued to exist in an increasingly secular, pluralist society in which church-going declined dramatically and parents no longer sought to provide religious instruction for their children. In 1953 nearly eighteen per cent of the children in England between the ages of three and fourteen were on the books of Church of England Sunday Schools alone, and if you add Nonconformist Sunday Schools to these, certainly more than a third of children attended Sunday School. By the late 1970s the proportion was probably less than fifteen per cent in total, and in many churches the Sunday School had almost been allowed to die out. The proportion of English fifteen year olds confirmed as Anglicans was below twenty per cent by the mid-1970s (in 1952 the figure was about twenty-eight per cent), and only forty-seven per cent of the children born alive in England were baptized during 1973 in the Church of England (in 1950 it was sixty-seven per cent). An even more rapid decline had set in for the Nonconformist Churches in England and Wales. The Methodists lost a third of their membership between the early 1950s and the mid-1970s, the Baptists nearly half, while the Congregationalists and Presbyterians in the amalgamated United Reformed Church had one third less members than the Baptists. (In 1980 there were roughly 240,000 Baptists, 600,000 Methodists, 157,000 United Reformed Church.) A general fall-off in voluntary involvement in the religious and youth activities of all denominations can, therefore, be traced back to the seemingly inexorable decline of organized religion in Britain. This fall-off was particularly difficult to reverse in a movement, such as The Boys' Brigade, whose units were constitutionally bound to be part of a church or other Christian organization approved by the Brigade Executive and whose officers were appointed by that church. Yet, as regards the boys themselves if not their officers, this decline in active church membership may not have been as crucial for the Brigade as it at first sight appears; for while a large proportion of B.B. boys have, and still do, come from so-called 'church families', a great many do not. The Boys' Brigade recruited large numbers of boys with no church connection whatsoever from an early stage in its historical development, once the organization moved out of its mission and Sunday School environment, as in the Liverpool and Sheffield Battalions. With the continuing decline in church attendance, however, the only link many families preserve with their local church is often through their son's or daughter's membership in the particular youth organization which that church embraces.[26]

On the other hand, despite pronounced secular trends in modern British society, The Boys' Brigade was still supported by a non-institutionalized form of religion that permeated much of the nation. In 1978 a Market Research Survey showed that about sixty per cent of the British mainland population still described themselves as belonging to the Church of England, although only about a tenth of that number attended church every week. While the age profile of the Nonconformist Churches showed a strong bias towards the elderly, it is notable that the Anglicans held their ground in the number of children going to church each Sunday: in Greater London about one third of churchgoers were actually under fifteen. Thus there were some signs of an imminent revival in the Church of England where the numerical decline was not only halted but reversed and an increasing number of young people were attracted to church every Sunday for worship. (Albeit this did not offer much consolation for The Boys' Brigade since, in 1980, a quarter of Brigade companies were Methodist, over a quarter Scottish Presbyterian, nearly seventeen per cent Baptist, and only just over eleven per cent Anglican.) A large proportion of the population, in other words, wished to regard itself as Christian but could not see any connection between that and involvement in institutional forms of Christian activity — going to church on a regular basis. Even if society had moved away from the old ways of expressing it, Britain was still apparently a deeply religious nation.[27]

A national survey on the religious attitudes of young people, also appearing in 1978, however, found a rapid decline in the credibility of Christianity among the young compared to a similar survey four years earlier. The most striking change detected was in the authority with which the Bible was regarded among the nearly one thousand teenagers questioned: in 1974 of those surveyed three-quarters disagreed that 'the Bible is out of date', in 1978 the proportion was only half. Nonetheless, the Survey did confirm that the young retained a great deal of interest in, and goodwill towards, the Bible and Christianity. Conversely, a lack of interest in institutionalized religion was also confirmed by the Survey, which showed that of the thirty per cent in one sample taken who considered religion very or fairly important, most never, or only occasionally, went to church. It would therefore appear, from the evidence of declining church attendances (outside Anglicanism) and surveys of religious attitudes, that to remain a church-based organization dedicated to the advancement of Christ's Kingdom among Boys' was not liable to court wide popularity among the young, whatever their social and educational background. Yet the degree of Christianity in Britain did not, as we have seen, exist as an objective, scientifically measurable quantity, evident in terms of church attendance alone. Rejections of regular church or chapel worship did not necessarily say anything about the rejection of Christian values or teaching in the wider community. Half the 1978 Survey of young people, for example, said they 'belonged' to Christianity, even if only twenty-one per cent went to church once a month or more.[28]

Ian Neilson was succeeded as Brigade Secretary in April 1974 by Alfred A.J. Hudson, a genial, open-minded Christian, then a wing commander in the

R.A.F. Regiment. Hudson had a background in Scouting, having held the position of District Commissioner, and he was also a member of the Church Missionary Society and the Officers' Christian Union. The issues confronting the new Secretary may best be approached through a consideration of the September 1976 Brigade Council held in Aberdeen, at which several important areas of policy were discussed and usefully resolved. The Report of the Working Party appointed in May 1975 to examine the Brigade's organization, management, financial policy and future development was presented to this Council. Group D (Development and Public Relations) of this Working Party was responsible for a motion which, in effect, amended the Constitution to make it possible for women to become officers in any Section of the Brigade and indeed to become company captains, although the latter would only apply in a small minority of cases, in particular companies which only consisted of a Junior Section. While this may not have done a great deal to meet the deficit in Company Section officers, it belatedly struck a blow for female equality in an organization long dominated by males. Five years later, when there was an encouraging growth of 352 officers and 223 warrant officers in the Brigade, 260 (over forty-five per cent) of them were women. Group B (Organization and Management) of the Working Party made several important recommendations: a smaller delegate Brigade Council which would abolish company representation and voting; a smaller biannual Brigade Executive; and increased responsibilities — including financial — for districts. Perhaps not surprisingly, these recommendations were not accepted by the officers present at Aberdeen. A new group, Group E, was appointed in February 1977 to examine the future organization of the Brigade in Scotland, and an examination of the operation and function of Brigade Headquarters was to be undertaken by Group A (Financial Policy) of the Working Party. In general, the Report of the Working Party presented to Council did not fundamentally change the 1970 view of Development Committee that 'the Brigade must remain a Church-centred organization, with the purpose of helping Boys to achieve a true Christian faith and to become full members of the Church'.[25]

Those present at this historic meeting of Council also received a memorandum entitled 'A Pre-Junior Organization?' which stated the case for and against the Pre-Juniors and gave some background information on the Northern Ireland District motion proposing their formation. The latest Working Party to consider the matter, set up by the Brigade Executive in January 1976, made recommendations on such fundamental matters as age, title, uniform, leadership and programme. The idea of such a Section had first been tried out in the Northern Ireland District in the mid-1960s for boys from six to eight years old, who were known locally as 'Robins'. At Brigade Council in 1974 the Executive reported that 690 B.B. companies had Pre-Junior Section groups in their churches but that only thirty-three battalions had replied to a questionnaire on the subject, resulting in a decision to take no further action in the matter of introducing a proper national organization. It was only with the possibility of under-eight activity being started in the Scout Association that the Executive set up the Working Party to advise them on the implications of extending Pre-Junior work to England, Wales and Scotland. The chief arguments used against the Pre-Juniors at the 1976 Brigade Council in Aberdeen were that they might distract officer attention away from the work of the Company and Senior Sections, and also that taking very young boys into the Brigade might give the movement a more juvenile image which would put off older boys not wishing to be associated with a predominantly 'little boys'

Three former Secretaries of the Brigade,
whose combined tenure of the office spans nearly fity years.
From left to right: Major General D.J. Wilson-Haffenden (1954-65),
Ian G. Neilson (1966-74), and G. Stanley Smith (1925-54).

President Éamon de Valéra takes the salute of the march past
of the Dublin Battalion of the B.B. during the Council meetings
in Dublin in 1962. Next to de Valéra is Lord Maclay,
President of The Boys' Brigade from 1947 to 1963.

The B.B. parading in Leeds in 1960. Lord Maclay takes the salute,
while behind him stands Brigade Secretary Wilson-Haffenden.

The Boys' Brigade today.

organization and consequently leaving. The advantages, as time proved, were that boys were able to join The Boys' Brigade at the same age that girls could join the Girls' Brigade or the Brownies, and also that the Pre-Juniors became a considerable source of recruits for the Juniors, giving common membership to a very large number of unofficial existing groups and bringing more boys into the Churches through the Sunday Schools. Swayed by the arguments in favour of a Pre-Junior Section, Council approved their introduction from 1 September 1977. Pre-Juniors were expected to attend Sunday School, a church or some other service as well as the weekly meeting of their Section for a play hour consisting of games, singing, story-telling or simple handwork. The Pre-Juniors were one of the great success stories of the late 1970s for the Brigade, with over 29,000 members by 1980, offsetting a decline of over 2,000 in the Junior Section.[30]

A discussion paper for officers on 'The Christian Aims and Influence of the Brigade's Work and the Christian Commitment of its Officers' was also reported to Brigade Council in Aberdeen, having since the previous November been distributed throughout the movement. It posed such questions as whose policy should determine the teaching given at Bible Class, and what led men to want to become Brigade officers. The aims of the paper were to examine the place of the Brigade in the Church and its contribution to the Christian education of the boys, and to encourage officers to examine their Christian commitment and leadership. 'Read not to contradict and confute, nor to believe and take for granted,' the paper quoted from Francis Bacon, 'but to weigh and consider.' An apt summary of the generally welcoming and widespread response to this document is provided by the Glasgow Battalion report:

> The value of the discussion document should not be assessed on the basis of the conclusions to which it has led. The paper has provided a valuable stimulus to discussion and will form the basis of useful discussions in the future. The issues raised by it are important and timely. In an increasingly secular and pluralist society, Officers in the Brigade must be encouraged to find a satisfactory answer to the fundamental question of what it means, not only in theory but in practice, to be a specifically Christian and Church-based organization for Boys in the last quarter of the twentieth century.

Introducing the Brigade's response to the discussion paper at Aberdeen, the Rev. Dr D. Steel, Brigade Vice-President, said it represented the accumulation of nearly ten years work and thinking about the Christian commitment of the movement. 'The Brigade is a Christian organization and we have unashamedly to recognize and unequivocally to witness this,' said Dr Steel in his address. He drew the attention of Council to a proposal for reconvening the Churches' Advisory Panel to consider the spiritual and vocational development of the officers and to examine and advise on all aspects of relationships between the Churches and the Brigade. The proposal also required the Panel to prepare a consultative document covering all aspects of the Christian education of boys in the Brigade. 'A study of those reports [received from sixty per cent of battalions in response to the Christian Commitment Paper] leaves the reader with an overwhelming impression of the great depth of devotion to our Lord Jesus Christ, the spiritual strength, unity of purpose and sense of oneness which is present throughout the Brigade,' ran the final report for consideration by Council at Aberdeen.[31]

One issue that the Christian Commitment Paper did not really confront was that the pluralism of a multiracial society in Britain was beginning to make

Christianity into just one religious tradition among many others, particularly in the rapidly changing inner-city areas. The Muslim, Sikh and Hindu communities together constituted the most exotic variant to the pattern of religious belief in the last quarter of the twentieth century, but we know neither the numbers actually practising these faiths, nor the extent of their commitment. The Boys' Brigade drew a large number of its recruits in the inner cities from among boys with a West Indian background, so that in 1975 the Brigade Executive invited serving officers to comment on their experience with boys from ethnic minorities. The Brigade produced an interesting study which summarized these reports and considered the changing pattern of company membership in several deprived inner-city areas with large immigrant populations. In twenty years the composition of one such company had changed from being entirely indigenous to a 1975 membership in which fifty-five out of sixty-three boys and three out of thirteen staff were of West Indian origin. In other words, where an urban area had become a mainly 'West Indian district', the Brigade company could be expected to reflect such shifts in the ethnic make-up of the population.

There were, of course, strong historical reasons why West Indian families had in the past retained a deep regard for Christianity, and boys from such homes were brought up in an atmosphere of strong Church connections. 'These are perhaps now being eroded by the apostasy by which they are surrounded in Britain,' admitted the study entitled *Brigade Work in Areas of Ethnic Minority Populations* (1976), but added, 'There is no doubt that The Boys' Brigade has welcomed many Boys of Afro-Asian and West Indian background and continues to do so.' This leaflet, intended to provide guidelines for company captains, betrayed a certain ethnocentric bias in outlawing 'positive' discrimination in favour of ethnic minorities: 'If the Boys are all British, then a firm, understanding line must be decided upon by the Captain and his staff and applied impartially to all members of the Company.' This meant that if a boy of any race or creed wished to belong to the Brigade, there were certain conditions that had to be observed, not only in terms of Christian education, but also in matters of punctuality, regular attendance and keeping the company rules. 'Running a Company which has a mixture of racial groups may have meant in the past that Captains have occasionally overlooked attendance, disciplinary and contribution problems, making "special cases" of immigrant Boys,' but, the guidelines declared, 'such discrimination should now cease.'[32]

In December 1977 the full-time staff at Brigade Headquarters in London had formed a National Action Group. This small representative group of five then lobbied the Brigade Executive to initiate a nationwide development campaign to increase recruitment. By 1979 this had resulted in the biggest campaign for new membership ever undertaken by The Boys' Brigade, launched under the slogan, 'The Boys' Brigade, First For Boys'. It is much to the credit of the Brigade Executive that they responded enthusiastically to their full-timers, and it is to be hoped that the Brigade will use its full-time staff more actively in the future than they have in the past — all too often the Brigade have merely regarded them as consultants. The Development Campaign Committee reported directly to the Brigade Executive on progress, under the general oversight of the Brigade Secretary, and was coordinated by John Edbrooke, Secretary for Development, formerly B.B. Organizer in the Caribbean. As part of the campaign, intended to extend up to the Centenary, districts, battalions and companies were urged to participate in promoting the movement and given free materials to do so. Besides publicity, important matters such as programme content, awards, uniforms and the quality of leadership were given serious attention in the context of Brigade development. In its second year, the recruitment campaign spent £26,000 on publicity materials, such costs being wholly met from sources outside the Brigade, by sponsorship, services freely donated, and financial contributions. Also in 1979, in response to some of the general historical developments this chapter has outlined, the Brigade Executive set up a Programme Study Group, chaired by John Edwards, 'to study the programme and environment which members experience in The Boys' Brigade'. The intention of this Group was to provide a thorough conceptual reappraisal of the whole Brigade programme, seeking to identify factors and trends likely to influence the ability of the Brigade to fulfill its Object, and asking whether the existing programme would still meet the needs both of boys and of the Churches in the 1980s.[33]

The Interim Report of the Programme Study Group, presented to Brigade Council at Canterbury in 1980, outlined various stratagems to meet the 'environmental' problems conditioning the future programme of the Brigade, such as the limited availability of government financial support for youth work and the problems of the Christian Church in a multi-faith, multiracial society. The Report proposed changes in the age structure of the Brigade, a more integrated award scheme, changes in promotion, procedures and ranks, more 'family' activities in companies, and the incorporation of 'themes' into the Brigade programme. The Programme Study Group were aware that if they were to meet such problems as the growing social and economic pressures upon the pattern of home and family life (manifested, for example, in the growing numbers of one-parent families) and the increasing ethical challenges faced by young people, then they had to do their best to prevent the reduction of numbers in the B.B.'s potential 'market' by providing 'motivators' for the appropriate age groups. Such radical proposals, couched as they were in the zealous vocabulary of market research and advertising, did not meet with the wholehearted approval of Brigade officers, as the correspondence columns of the *B.B. Gazette* amply testify. The more 'progressive' wing of the Brigade felt that the Report was not radical enough. It failed, for example, to jettison the late Victorian Brigade Object: 'There is little point in modernizing our programme to meet partially outdated objectives,' argued the Captain of the 50th Liverpool Company. 'It seems to us that we are swimming against the tide of a rapidly changing society in promulgating to such an extent concepts of obedience and discipline for example.' The more 'traditionalist' wing of the Brigade from north of the Border felt that in such a society there was all the more reason to stick to tried and trusted ways, leaving at least one constant and stable force in an insecure world. 'Let's leave something solid and dependable on which our young men and officers can fall back on,' pleaded the Captain of the 5th Aberdeen Company, 'The virtues [the Object] does demand are a sound and unshakeable foundation for Christian faith.' While some officers regretted the substitution of the Junior Section for the Life Boys and the phasing out of drill from the Brigade programme, others greeted the 'forward-looking' Report with approval, finding the change of emphasis from company drill to ceremonial drill on special occasions only long overdue, and particularly liking the concept of the B.B. 'family'. This 'family' concept was of the B.B. company sections behaving as a whole, not as four separate watertight compartments, so bringing greater cohesiveness to the movement and overcoming the separateness of officers in many companies.[34]

In a sense, the history of The Boys' Brigade as it drew closer to its Centenary was dominated by the attempts of the Executive and the Secretariat to reconcile these two viewpoints, labelled here as 'progressive' and 'traditionalist'. Hence the final Report of the Programme Study Group could be expected to have a similar impact on The Boys' Brigade in the closing decades of the twentieth century as the Haynes Report had for its development in the late 1960s and 1970s. If it was the less effective companies, lacking continuity of leadership and failing to hold Company Section boys, who were most in need of a new programme, even the efficient, strong companies who retained their Seniors were living in a rapidly changing society, and the Group's Report aimed at providing a programme relevant to their future needs. The full Report, approved by the Executive and entitled *The Boys' Brigade in the 1980s: a Strategy for Programme Development*, was presented by John Edwards to Council at York in September 1981 to general acclaim. The actual recommendations of the Report were expected to take effect, once they had received the approval of Council, by 1984 — the beginning of a second century for The Boys' Brigade. Since the Report set out to assess both the role which The Boys' Brigade already played in national life and its strategy for meeting the social conditions of the future, its publication represents a convenient point at which to bring our account of the history of the movement over the last hundred years to a close.

The Report of the Programme Study Group, it is fair to say, honestly faced up to the difficulties and challenges confronting The Boys' Brigade at this stage in its historical development. Particular emphasis was given to the Churches' need for youth work that would lead to a good flow of boys into church membership, the growing moral challenges facing young people, the problem of youth unemployment, and the almost total demise of Brigade work among the over-sixteens. The Report also recommended a far more positive and aggressive approach in, for example, formulating a strategy for the formation of new companies in rural areas and new housing estates. Less stress was to be placed on the activities of large companies in Brigade literature, and the range of activities open to small rural companies that would help provide for their extension and development was to be examined more closely. In a further endeavour to extend the movement, the Report also suggested that where new housing estates did not have established churches and church premises, consideration should be given to numerically smaller 'satellite' groupings. The entire Brigade movement, from individual companies right up to the Brigade Executive, were told to concentrate their efforts upon meeting the challenge of serving older boys and younger men. 'Rather than ignore the "senior" we must seek a more challenging programme for him,' exhorted the Report:

> . . . rather than ignore 'promotion' wastage we must seek ways to make this an exciting and useful time for the eleven year old; rather than let small Companies fade away we must recognize that they can serve and we must design programmes that work in small units; rather than accept high Officer turnover we must work to make their training and programme opportunity a challenge to commitment; and we must be more positive in our outward relations to show what quality it is that we offer.

Specific changes which the Report proposed, and which were to define the parameters of debate within the movement into the 1980s, included altering the age structure to frame a substantial shift in emphasis. For membership statistics as of 30 April 1981 revealed stunning evidence that nearly seventy-eight per cent of the total boy membership was now under fourteen years of age. The new age structure might be: Anchor Boys for the six-to-eight age group, Juniors for eight to eleven, Seniors for eleven to fifteen, and Cadets for fifteen to seventeen. The Report did not, however, advocate joint Boys' and Girls' Brigade Companies or girls serving as members of the B.B. More positively, it suggested that districts and battalions should regularly examine their competitive programme to prune over-burdened calendars, and that a 'Stedfast Fellowship' be set up to retain and increase the number of adults, especially 'old boys', interested in the work of the Brigade.

Altogether, the Programme Study Report was a worthy and constructive attempt to examine the relevance of the Brigade method and its traditions to the forseeable needs of boys and of the Churches in the 1980s and the decades to follow. As the authors of the Report put it in suitably concise terms:

> The Boys' Brigade is a highly diverse Movement of large and small Companies, rural and urban, well-manned and under-manned, spanning many Christian denominations, working within their different educational systems, and operating in their different regional cultures. This diversity is obvious in the range of responses received [to the Interim Report]. We have tried to suggest that the major component required of the Brigade is a mental flexibility to adjust to these changes and conditions.

This verdict is a fitting appraisal of The Boys' Brigade on the verge of its Centenary, and we leave it looking forward with anticipation, mingled with a justifiable pride in past achievement, to a second century of 'the advancement of Christ's Kingdom among Boys'.[35]

CONCLUSIONS

The Boys' Brigade in Historical Perspective

'FIFTY YEARS OF WORK in training the boys of our nation in habits of discipline, self-respect, and manliness represented a contribution to the national welfare which could not be expressed in mere words,' ran *The Times'* report of the speech given by Prince Arthur of Connaught at the 1933 B.B. Jubilee celebrations held in the Albert Hall:

> The Boys' Brigade was the pioneer of all the great voluntary movements for boys, and its history showed that it was a movement of wonderful staying power . . . He claimed that The Boys' Brigade was a movement which gave expression to the British qualities of perseverance, doggedness, and staying power. Their motto was 'Sure and Stedfast' and certainly there was nothing passing or ephemeral about such work as the Brigade was doing. Its influence upon the lives and characters of the boys who joined was equally enduring and permanent . . . At no period was such training more needed. History showed that national indiscipline and the lowering of national standards had resulted in the past in the fall of nations. The Boys' Brigade and the organizations following its example were forming a barrier against the encroachment of influences which did not make for the national well-being.

Such praise, delivered in the year Adolf Hitler became German Chancellor, must be forgiven its alarmist excesses, but from our vantage point fifty years further on, the 'staying power' of The Boys' Brigade is not something which can be seriously doubted. It is a task beyond the scope of this history to measure the influence of the B.B. upon the lives and characters of the boys who have joined over the years, although it may be asked whether this influence has really been as enduring and permanent as the Prince appears to have believed. It is possible, however, to speculate on why boys should have joined the organization in the first place and what they expected to get out of membership. For the success of a youth movement cannot be gauged solely by the speeches of figures in authority sympathetic to its aims, but must also take into account the reaction of the membership to the activities on offer. After all, a mass movement like the B.B. cannot be sustained over such a lengthy period without the participation, interest and acceptance of its rank and file.[1]

This leads us on to a further key question, namely, how successful has the B.B. been in attracting boys into the Church, the purpose for which it was originally instituted? Did it retain boys in the Sunday Schools until they were old enough to pass into the young men's organizations connected with the local churches and missions? Following on from this, it is appropriate to ask why the officers so willingly gave, as they still do, such substantial time and unpaid effort to the movement. In these closing pages, it may also prove useful to consider once again the validity of the perennial charges of militarism that have been levelled at the movement almost since its inception. And finally, in drawing up some sort of crude balance sheet, an attempt will be made to assess the part the B.B. has played in Britain's national life and in cementing international unity since it was started one hundred years ago. For when William Smith first started The Boys' Brigade for fifty-nine boys in a mission hall in a working-class area of Glasgow in 1883, he little imagined that less than a century later it would have spread to some sixty countries throughout the world.

There is no shortage of plausible answers to the initial questions of why the boys joined and what they expected to get out of membership. The Boys' Brigade, as this account of its history will have demonstrated, fulfilled several expectations of the adolescent boy, whether he be from a church or a non-church background. It combined all the glamour of the military — in style, ethos and nomenclature — with a deliberately simple and inexpensive uniform and, until 1926, the opportunity in some companies to drill with a dummy rifle. It provided leisure facilities, such as a club room, football, camping and bands, virtually unobtainable elsewhere for the average state-educated adolescent until well into the present century. Schools, for example, did not seriously compete with the recreational functions of youth organizations until after the First World War in most cities; prior to that school activities were defined strictly in terms of 'academic' education, while character building or 'social' education was seen — except in the private sector — as the prerogative of voluntary agencies. Thus when Tom Sharman, who served as a full-time B.B. staff member for fifty years, was asked in 1980 whether the movement had a future, he replied:

> I think it will always have an attraction for boys, to go into a movement with other boys, like I did, to play a bugle, beat a drum, jump over the horse, swing on the parallel bars, play football, play cricket, go swimming. All of these things you can do in The Boys' Brigade, you see, and most companies manage to do them, in their own ways. So I think the B.B. certainly has a future, which they have only got to carry on . . . It's difficult to know but I think there will always be a place for The Boys' Brigade, 'if we faint not', as they say . . .[2]

The Boys' Brigade may not always have been in the vanguard in responding to social change, but in many sporting and leisure activities it had the reputation of being the leader among youth movements, particularly in youth football and swimming galas, and more recently in rock-climbing, sailing, skiing and badminton. Not all boys, of course, will have taken to the essential principle of Brigade training — the development of discipline through religious instruction and formal drill — and for them the controlled individualism of the Boys Scouts may have been more suitable. It is however a notable fact that drill and discipline have held an attraction for many boys in the past, although there is now little emphasis on drill in the average weekly programme. It is also true that in the companies of The Boys' Brigade where the most rigid demands were made on the members in terms of military obedience, the attendance was often better as a result; for, 'at the bottom of their hearts, many boys want and like traditional forms of authority and efficiency'. This may not be true of all boys, but many youth leaders fail to get a response from boys because they pitch their demands too low.[3]

The Boys' Brigade also provided the opportunity for the socially aspiring member to 'get on', a factor not to be discounted in looking at what the ambitious boy may have got out of the movement. In 1921 R.W. Campbell published a novel, *Jimmy McCallum*, whose eponymous hero is recruited into the 99th Glasgow Company of the B.B. by Sir William Smith himself. The author provides the following convincing reasons for a Glasgow street boy like Jimmy wanting to become a member of The Boys' Brigade:

This Boys' Brigade idea gave Jimmy no rest. It captured his imagination and his soul. Being one of the hunted and despised, he saw in it an avenue for 'getting on', a dream ever present in the Scots boys' heart. The native military genius was tickled too; he hungered for the bonnet, belt, and gun. Somehow he thought it a social lift, and he would be equal with 'the toffs'. Jimmy bore no resentment against the well-to-do. Nevertheless he believed he had the right to be 'weel aff'. Doubtless he would have been in The Boys' Brigade before, but he was not connected with any church. His clothes, always in rags, prevented attendance; while the 'unco guid' apparently did not seek him out . . . He was like the rookie, raw; nevertheless he thought he was a fine sodger. And those daydreams — fighting sham-fights at Maryhill, and killing all the laddies in Govan and Pollock-shaws!

In the course of the novel, Jimmy advances from railway porter, a post secured by his B.B. captain, to clerk in the railway head office; if nothing else, evidence of the occupational mobility eased by a smart appearance and the benefits of B.B. training. The desire to move up in the world by wearing a clean collar and polished boots, via the informal labour exchange operated by many B.B. officers, should not be underestimated as an element in the appeal of the movement. 'Anyone who will take the trouble to enquire personally into the matter', wrote Lord Roberts to the 12th Earl of Meath in 1898,

> cannot fail to recognize the benefit conferred on the boys who belong to the [Boys'] Brigade. Not only are they cleaner, brighter, and better mannered than boys of their class generally, *which shows that they have risen above their fellows on the social scale*, but those by whom they are employed bear strong testimony to their increased usefulness and their uniform good conduct. [my italics][4]

The success of the B.B. in attracting boys into the Church is a more difficult question to answer satisfactorily, and the extent of its success has always been a matter of lively debate within the organization. Nonetheless, it is not difficult to find evidence from the B.B.'s early years that many boys did in fact join the Y.M.C.A., often the means of transfer from youth to adult church activity, and that Sunday School attendance was markedly improved as a result of membership of the Brigade. The entry of B.B. boys directly into Y.M.C.A. branches in Scotland is recorded at Alexandria, Ayr, Callander and Edinburgh for the session 1889-90, and in Dublin a Y.M.C.A. branch was specifically formed a few years later to take forty boys from the 2nd Dublin Company. This success rate was reflected in Glasgow itself where in 1891 a committee consisting of B.B. office bearers and district presidents was appointed to confer with the Y.M.C.A. regarding the drafting of Brigade boys into local Y.M.C.A. branches. The sentiments of the President of the North Woodside branch of the Y.M.C.A. in the city, W.A. Campbell, can be found echoed elsewhere when in 1886 he said that he 'could not help believing, from past experience, that but for the B.B. these ten young men would not have been here this morning enrolling themselves as members of a Y.M.C.A.' When, at a conference of Belfast officers held in 1890, each captain gave a short report on his company's work, it was remarked almost without exception that since the B.B. had commenced there had been a significant improvement in attendance at Sunday School. The success of the B.B. in filling the gap between Sunday School and the Y.M.C.A. is, however, more clearly recorded prior to 1900, indicating either a less marked degree of success after that date or the availability of less firm information as membership continued to increase.[5]

On the question of church attendance, figures taken from annual reports before 1900 indicate that as the B.B. grew and ceased to enlist new members primarily from Sunday Schools, the proportion of members who regularly attended the sponsoring church declined:

Table 1:
Boys attending church with which B.B. company is connected, 1887-1896*

Year	Number in church	Total B.B. boys	%
1887/88	8,125	10,388	78.2
1888/89	10,424	14,372	72.5
1889/90	11,494	16,752	68.6
1890/91	11,992	17,259	69.4
1891/92	14,524	21,002	69.1
1892/93	17,140	26,033	65.8
1893/94	19,614	29,849	65.7
1894/95	20,466	32,372	63.2
1895/96	19,547	32,862	59.4

*From B.B. Annual Reports

These figures, in so far as they are reliable, suggest that whereas in 1887-88 almost eighty per cent of members were regular churchgoers, by 1890-91 this had fallen to below seventy per cent and by 1895-96 to below sixty per cent. The annual reports stopped printing these figures in the same format after this last date but a progressive decline from a remarkable peak of early attendance can be inferred.

Information about the proportion of B.B. members who were or became regular churchgoers during the present century is, therefore, less accessible to the historian simply because after 1896 the Brigade only published collective figures for boys attending church, Sunday School or other religious meetings in addition to meetings of their company. In 1953, boys' club historian W.McG. Eagar took a positive view of the B.B.'s success in attracting boys to church membership which the movement itself would endorse:

> The Bible-Class-Brigade, Sunday-weekday link has never been broken, and in that particular the Brigade Movement has solved one part of the problem of boy-welfare in which other movements have failed, namely how to transfer their members, when they grow out of boyhood, to effective membership of a related adult organization.

Five years later an independent survey sponsored by the Church of Scotland claimed that the B.B. was attracting boys who would not otherwise have been attending Bible Class and that nearly fourteen per cent of all Sunday School or Bible Class attenders in Scotland were enrolled in a B.B. Bible Class. On the other hand, the estimate by Brigade Secretary Wilson-Haffenden that in the 1950s and early 1960s one in three senior Brigade boys were full church members seems exaggerated and could certainly not be sustained twenty years later. The actual proportion of B.B. 'old boys' becoming church members at a later date, after their B.B. careers were over, is a different question and has not been formally investigated by the movement.[6]

That the B.B. continued, as it still does, to promote church or chapel membership cannot be doubted, but it has to be accepted that the strength of the organization, in this particular aspect of its endeavours, has diminished in parallel with the decline of the Christian Churches themselves, at least in the British Isles. Any youth group which has to be constitutionally linked with a church or other Christian organization, such as the local B.B. company, must expect its fortunes to wax or wane with the corresponding rise or fall of the parent body. That the B.B.'s strength has not been affected in the same proportion as the Churches, particularly in the first half of the twentieth century, is indicative of the influences, other than the purely spiritual, which have contributed to the formation and development of the movement. If the exact gains to the Churches of the B.B.'s existence cannot be accurately quantified, various reports and opinions from both the clergy and within the Brigade itself indicate a measure of success in holding the adolescent to an age when membership of a young men's society or church congregation became possible. One sincere indication of the efficacy of B.B. training is given by the testimony of F.J. Marriott, a former London Vice-President, looking back in 1980 over his experience with several London companies:

> The aim of The Boys' Brigade is the advancement of Christ's Kingdom and it was for this reason that I joined. One might perhaps ask: and what result comes from that? One hesitates very greatly and one doubts if it is wise at any time to attempt any assessment of spiritual results, so I will just say what I know. I know that a number of boys in the B.B., in my companies of the B.B., developed into fine Christian men, some of them doing a considerable amount of Christian work, some of them in the B.B. I also know that a number of boys in my companies, who were as it were feeling their way towards some form of religious belief, found that belonging to a B.B. company was a great help to them. I know that no boy who ever joined a company ever left it without at least hearing the call to a Christian life. I think one can leave it at that.[7]

Having looked at the motivation of the boys, we may now turn to the question of why men volunteered to become officers in the B.B. Most of the early officers in Glasgow, it will be recalled from the opening chapters, were Volunteer officers in their thirties, often men from a business or professional background, who were actively involved in church or mission work among the young. In some towns and villages a local Nonconformist businessman or large shop owner might be the dominant figure in the local battalion, providing both leadership and financial support for many years. A typical officer of the following generation, on both sides of the Border, was more likely to be a relatively younger man of 'respectable' working-class or lower middle-class background, a former or existing Sunday School teacher, an ex-Territorial, or a Cadet Corps member while at school. For leaders from this social milieu a permanent commitment to the local company was likely, whereas for young officers from a wealthy, upper middle-class, Established-Church background in a city like Edinburgh, the B.B. was possibly only a passing interest or even a social obligation. The attraction of becoming a B.B. officer for the lower middle-class white-collar worker, so prominent in late twentieth-century enrolment forms, may be related to the desire to affirm social respectability, a form of vicarious identification with middle-class values; but it may be just as reasonable to assume that the lower middle classes were particularly active in B.B. work because of their higher rate of involvement in Nonconformist worship and church office. By the last quarter of the twentieth century, the profile of the average officer exemplified the continued trend away from the professional middle-class leadership of the early Glasgow companies. The majority of B.B. officers in the mid-1970s came from white-collar or skilled working-class backgrounds: engineers, draughtsmen, bank clerks, school teachers, technicians and fitters. The lowest proportion of B.B. officers came from the ranks of the unskilled working class or from professional middle-class backgrounds (see Appendix 5). Thus in asking why church members were so willing to give extra time and effort to the B.B., it has to be taken into account that the 'typical' B.B. officer — apart from the first generation — can be largely identified with a skilled working-class or lower middle-class profile. To become a leader in the Brigade, officers had to be church members, and to remain as such they would require religious conviction and a genuine concern for the welfare of the boys under their care.

It is not really possible to conclude a book on The Boys' Brigade without considering how much truth there is to the charge levelled at the movement throughout almost its entire history that it encouraged the military spirit. As the preceding chapters have demonstrated, the B.B. is a movement for the young which defies being categorized as either primarily 'religious' or 'military' — for, firmly Christian in its aims, it was undeniably military in its methods of achieving them. The ambiguity of the B.B. — and incidentally part of its interest to the social historian — lay not only in the seeming contradiction between using military means to achieve religious ends, but also in the fact that a Church youth movement firmly based on the Sunday School or Bible Class was initially led by men with a part-time military training. Thus the Brigade has been criticized by the historian H.J. Hanham for securing a greater degree of Church and Nonconformist recognition for the military values of the Volunteers than they might otherwise have found, so providing a sort of link connecting the Volunteers and the Army with the everyday life of the country. It stands accused not only of helping to prepare the way for the recruiting drives of the First World War but also of helping to undermine the essentially civilian system of values which had guided English Nonconformity for two centuries. This is, perhaps, unfairly to load the burden of guilt onto what was, and is, basically a church-orientated youth movement which happens to have employed military methods of boy management to achieve its religious aims. 'To accuse it of encouraging the military spirit is the most vulgar of misconceptions,' wrote the Rev. Edgar Rogers in 1908 of the Church Lads' Brigade, 'they had merely entered the field of religious education in the most scientific and modern fashion.' Military methods of management and organization were simply considered fashionably 'modern' and 'scientific' during the 1900s, an antidote to symptoms of national decadence and inefficiency in the face of the growing military and economic threat from Germany that so preoccupied Baden-Powell and other youth leaders. Furthermore, in Britain at least, the actual course of the relationship between the B.B. and the military authorities was far from being a smooth one, as is testified by the War Office's frustrated attempts from 1909 to 1911 to link up the Brigade with the Territorials by transforming them into a military Cadet Corps.[8]

In this respect, the history of the B.B. before 1914 shows a marked divergence from the Anglican, proto-military Church Lads' Brigade. Their difference of opinion on the issue of whether or not to submit to the War Office can be interpreted either as a reflection of the B.B.'s dissimilar origins — arising as it did from the Scottish liberal dissenting tradition — or as an outcome of the firm leadership provided by William Smith in the crucial years prior to the First World War. For when Smith felt that the Minister for War in the Liberal Government, R.B. Haldane, was about to undermine the religious basis of the movement he had founded, he was openly prepared to depart from the canons of middle-class respectability and patriotism — values that Professor Hanham accuses The Boys' Brigade of upholding at the expense of individual conscience. Writing to the Secretary of the Sunday School Union in 1912, Roger Peacock, the B.B.'s London Secretary, underlined Smith's attitude:

The stand which The Boys' Brigade took last year against the Army Council Cadet Scheme, by which the Brigade gave up some most valuable privileges rather than accept the least suspicion of connection between the Brigade and the military authorities, must I think have finally dissipated the old suspicion against the Brigade on the score of alleged 'militarism'.[9]

Yet William Smith was not opposed to military training in itself, but was of the opinion that until the nation had the courage to face up to compulsory military training for young men, rather than for boys, it was only trifling with the subject. He also found that it had never strengthened the Brigade's position to minimize or apologize for the military features of its work, frankly accepting military organization and drill as the basis of B.B. training. To set the historical record straight, however, it should perhaps be mentioned that William Smith's definition of the 'military spirit' was considerably at variance with that of his pacifist detractors, as is indicated by the following newspaper report of one of his speeches, made at a B.B. demonstration in Carlisle in 1894:

So long as England required an Army it would be better surely if that Army should be recruited from the ranks of boys like those in this Brigade. Many of the boys joined the Volunteers and he thought that this was a good thing for the boys, and for the Volunteers and for the country (cheers). When people said they were creating a military spirit it depended on what they meant by a military spirit. If by a military spirit they meant a spirit which taught a boy to come to parade to the minute, with his uniform neatly put on and his hands clean, and to salute his officer whenever he met him, then he said they were doing so (cheers). If this meant prompting a boy to be obedient to his parents, his teachers, and his master, and true to God, then he admitted they were creating that sort of military spirit (cheers).[10]

'Cannot some better way of keeping their old scholars together be laid before Sunday-school teachers,' inquired a correspondent to the Peace Society's journal in 1887, 'than teaching boys how to kill and maim their brethren?' If it is unreasonable to condemn the B.B. for the militarism with which it was accused by sections of pacifist opinion, it is still possible to see how the marching and drilling with dummy rifles must have aroused the fears and hostilities of their accusers. Exaggerated pacifist claims, such as the belief that the B.B. was incubated at the War Office under the auspices of Lord Wolseley and the Duke of Cambridge, can easily be refuted, but the suspicion that the B.B. had strong military links lingered on among the more pacifist Nonconformist Churches. The terms adopted by the Brigade, the ranks, saluting and drill, the qualities of smartness, obedience and discipline which William Smith sought to encourage, had all been most highly developed in the Army and the Volunteers. Naturally, church youth workers and Sunday School teachers wishing to apply the same classic methods of training to unruly teenage boys would at once lay themselves open to charges of encouraging the military spirit. Yet while there is no doubt that outwardly the B.B. wore a military air, there seems little evidence for thinking that it has helped in the past to create a warlike attitude. So the question of how far the B.B. helped to nurture militarism and how far on the other hand the B.B.'s military style was an effect of the preponderance of militarism in late Victorian and Edwardian society cannot be answered with any real precision. One can only repeat that the B.B.'s adoption of some of the Volunteers' military methods — drill, camp, parades, bands, inspections — was done primarily as an effective means of attaining the Brigade Object, not as an end in itself. The B.B.'s willingness to abandon the use of the dummy rifle and to sever all links with the Government's Cadet Scheme in 1924, together with their amalgamation with the anti-military Boys' Life Brigade two years later, are fairly conclusive evidence of their lack of real attachment to the military ethos. Since the Haynes Report in 1964, drill has declined in importance in the weekly programmes of most companies and the emphasis has shifted to such activities as the Duke of Edinburgh's Award Scheme. Thus throughout the postwar period the movement has relied less and less on military methods while maintaining a consistent allegiance to its spiritual aim.[11]

In our account of the historical impact of The Boys' Brigade, the development of the movement beyond the United Kingdom — helping to spread the Christian message among non-European peoples, as well as white settlers of British descent — has been given its rightful prominence for the first time. The Brigade was actually exported surprisingly quickly to the British dominions and to North America, where it followed British migration overseas, particularly among skilled artisans and professionals, many of them Scottish in origin. The first phase of B.B. overseas development in the late Victorian period also benefited considerably from the fervour of a shared evangelical revivalism associated with Moody and Sankey, and also from the enthusiasm of such B.B. 'ambassadors' abroad as Lord Aberdeen and Henry Drummond. During the 1900s, the B.B. made much of its role in helping to consolidate the British Empire in its official publications, but William Smith and his Executive in Glasgow adopted a relatively pragmatic approach which made no attempt to coordinate overseas policy and which lacked the imperial spirit often evinced by other contemporary youth organizations. Seen from the outposts of the British Empire, however, the B.B. was clearly more of a factor in promoting Imperial unity than when viewed from Headquarters in London or Glasgow. Speakers from the dominions or missionaries on leave from their colonial duties constantly reminded the U.K. Brigade Council that the movement had become more than national, it had become imperial. Yet, at this stage in its historical progress, the B.B. lacked the necessary organization and resources to promote international youth work cooperation on the scale required to cement ties within the British Empire. Unlike Baden-Powell, who travelled the world extensively visiting Scouting movements both before and after the First World War, William Smith never got further than brief visits to Canada and America to encourage his followers.

Since it was always Smith's policy as Secretary not to interfere directly in overseas practice nor to advocate strict adherence to the British model of B.B. development, the Brigade did not play such a direct role as the Boy Scouts in assisting their overseas branches before 1914. On the other hand, William Smith's attempts, when they did occur, to exert some control over developments outside of Britain were never as autocratic, imperialist or centralizing as those of the Chief Scout, although this did not mean that the B.B. in a dominion such as Canada was allowed complete freedom to develop a style of management and ethos more suited to national conditions. Even before 1914, the Brigade had grown too large both at home and abroad for Smith, with his limited staff, to manage alone, and the Scouting movement was far quicker than the B.B. in learning that a proper structural framework was required to govern its overseas branches. Hence the scattered remnants of the poorly organized U.B.B.A. were not to survive the harsh realities of American geography and organizational scale, problems also evident in such a vast country as Canada. It is of course possible that a firmer hand before 1914 from

Britain might have prevented the unsuccessful adaptation of the B.B. to American conditions or diminished that vulnerability of the B.B. in Australia and New Zealand which made it difficult for them to resist government pressures to become uniformed Cadets. Generalizations are made difficult on such matters because of the sometimes marked divergence between official B.B. policy in London or Glasgow, local B.B. practice overseas, and the response taken towards youth organizations by the respective indigenous governments. After 1914 the B.B. in the mother country was more concerned with problems of wartime survival and internal reorganization than with overseas development, and into the 1920s little was done to coordinate international B.B. policy. Even this disappointing period from the overseas viewpoint held the seeds of the eventual emergence of independent national B.B. councils and the rise of strong local B.B. traditions in the dominions.

The revival of the B.B. overseas after the First World War saw numerous mission-sponsored, European-controlled companies spring up in China, India and Africa, and missionary workers in the field for long periods were not averse to training local leaders to run their own companies. It was not, however, until the renewed momentum of the late 1920s and early 1930s boosted company formation that the Brigade Executive in Britain was compelled to adopt a more positive approach towards its overseas branches, highlighted in 1933 by the appointment of William McVicker as Overseas Secretary. Until his arrival at Brigade Headquarters there was no staff officer with the responsibility of handling correspondence with overseas companies. The willingness of B.B. officers like McVicker to travel extensively between the Wars also did a great deal to encourage overseas expansion, particularly in Canada and South Africa in the 1930s. One effect of the Second World War was to make many overseas B.B. branches more self-sufficient, and in the self-governing dominions there emerged an autonomous, independent-minded B.B. leadership which paralleled the political changes in the relationship of these territories with the United Kingdom — although Canada and South Africa were not to achieve the same level of development in this respect as New Zealand and Australia. Further waves of overseas expansion took place in the 1950s, as we have seen, with new companies being set up regularly in the Pacific, East Asia, West Africa and the Caribbean. Consultation and partnership between the Brigade in the U.K. and its overseas branches slowly replaced control and direction, symbolized in 1963 by the setting up of the World Conference Committee which eventually took over the responsibility for overseas development. In the late 1970s the international membership came close to overtaking that of the B.B. in the British Isles, with Nigeria alone contributing over 50,000 boys to the total. Then in 1978 the responsibility for overseas development was transferred to the World Conference, a body divided into eight Regional Fellowships which has made an attempt to bring the B.B. and its overseas equivalents into a closer working relationship than hitherto. Thus where the B.B. did play a part in helping to build up or consolidate the British Empire, later the Commonwealth, it was largely an unintended effect of their overseas development rather than a necessary concomitant of Brigade policy. Because of its international spread, however, the B.B. played an unquantifiable but nevertheless significant role in promoting friendship and understanding between nations.[12]

The Brigade in Britain, meanwhile, claim to have sent at least two million youngsters out into the world with some instruction in military drill and the

Christian religion. It is an inescapable fact that a large proportion of them will have been influenced in their general outlook and behaviour by the military training and, more importantly, by the religious teaching they received while wearing the B.B. uniform. Nearly three out of five British males, on being interviewed by Mass Observation in 1966, said they had belonged to one or more uniformed youth groups when young. The impact of youth movements on the pattern of social and cultural behaviour in twentieth-century Britain must, therefore, have been considerable. One prominent example of this impact can be seen in the area of outdoor activities. The introduction of camping holidays by the B.B. from 1886 onwards undoubtedly contributed a great deal to the popularity of this form of open-air leisure activity among the young. The annual camp did much to relieve the monotony of an often grim urban existence for the boy confined for most of his working week to the dirt and noise of the industrial conurbations. 'We with our fair conditions of life at home and school do not realize even one little bit what the poor lads of our busy manufacturing towns have to live amongst and endure,' wrote a B.B. officer in 1903 of his company camp. 'The B.B., its drill and festivities, and more than all, its summer camp, is indeed a boon and a blessing.' The movement also did much to make the adoption of camping as an adult pastime more widespread between the Wars among a generation which had been the first to grow up under B.B. influence. In an earlier chapter it has also been suggested that the highly organized structure of competitive B.B. football was often the first introduction many boys received to their local company, if not to the game itself. The role the B.B. has played in encouraging band music among young people has equally to be recognized. Unless the organization had been sufficiently adaptable to introduce modern leisure activities it could not have retained its share of the youth market. The B.B. officer hoped to lead the boy towards the B.B.'s religious aim, via attendance at Bible Class, from the starting point of such purely recreational activities as football, camp and bands — as one boy put it, 'It's worth sticking the Bible Class for a good game of football.'[13]

The possible ecumenical effects of the B.B.'s interdenominational nature are of course more speculative, but since the organization has held to this path from the outset it may have contributed to a better understanding among the Protestant Churches over the past hundred years. In Scotland, particularly, the close cooperation among the Nonconformist Churches and B.B. companies may have smoothed the way to union between the Free Church and the United Presbyterian Church in 1900 and between the United Free Church and the Church of Scotland in 1929. As The Boys' Brigade developed it became not only a bridge for the adolescent between Sunday School or Bible Class and full church membership but also a way in which the Churches might reach the community itself. The B.B. injected a colourful, lively element into local village and town life, though street processions and battalion parades may have played a greater part in people's memories of the B.B. than they did in the annual programme of a company. From the 1920s onwards 'B.B. Week' also brought the movement before the public in the most practical and necessary way, raising money for both local and national finances. As church membership declined, Brigade recruits did not fall off in proportion, and thus the B.B. could be seen in the present century as a mechanism for reaching families with no church connection but whose sons were enthusiastic company members. Home visits by B.B. officers have in the past led families to a closer connection with their local church, hence the current B.B. slogan: 'Attract a boy, win a family'. The Brigade has, therefore, enlivened many individual church congregations — not simply by encouraging young men to take up church membership, but also by drawing in families on the periphery of the religious life of the community.

The historical role of The Boys' Brigade in promoting voluntary work among boys and young men has over the years led to an important contribution to the life of the nation — the creation of the voluntary and statutory Youth Service. William Smith has never really received the credit he deserves in the public mind as the instigator of what was to become the Youth Service in Britain. For too long he has been overshadowed in reputation by the more ostentatious figure of Baden-Powell — who did not actually come on to the youth work scene until nearly a quarter of a century after the foundation of The Boys' Brigade. As the first voluntary uniformed youth movement, the B.B. was not only to provide the inspiration and the prototype for the many derivative 'brigade' organizations that followed in the 1890s — the Church Lads' Brigade, the Jewish Lads' Brigade, the Boys' Life Brigade, the Catholic Boys' Brigade — but it was also to be among the first to run Boy Scout troops in Britain (see Chapter 4). The B.B. stimulated the even more revolutionary turn-of-the-century idea of uniformed girls' organizations, for it was a B.B. captain who in 1900 started the Girls' Guildry in Glasgow as a female equivalent to the B.B., the forerunner of the present-day Girls' Brigade. Thus the B.B. has played a pioneering role in the development of the national Youth Service, not only because it was the first voluntary uniformed youth movement but also because it provided the model for so much of what followed, actively assisting in the emergence of the Boy Scouts, a movement that was to outstrip all the other uniformed youth organizations put together by the outbreak of the First World War.

Whatever else the B.B. may have achieved in terms of its contribution to youth work or its effect in bringing young men into full church membership, it did provide the poorest street boy with an opportunity to blow a bugle, parade on the streets, wear a uniform, and also to take part in a wide range of recreational activities. The Boys' Brigade, in other words, gave status and the recognition of that status to adolescents who had never achieved it before. Finally, in considering what part the B.B. has played in the life of the nation and whether or not there is any way to measure its influence upon the lives and characters of those boys who have joined, it is fitting to remember the words that round off Roger Peacock's 1954 biography of the Founder, Sir William Smith:

> One of the most marked features of the B.B. has always been its extraordinary hold upon the Boys' affections, and the way in which it develops the best that is in him. It has never feared to make high demands upon him, nor to call for high standards of duty and sacrifice. It is because much is expected of him that he so freely gives his service and loyalty, not only during his Boyhood, but in numberless cases throughout life. An appreciable percentage of the nation's manhood has passed through the ranks. To vast numbers of these men the B.B. is not only a happy Boyhood memory, but it is an abiding influence which has led them to a life of Christian service.[14]

On his visit to a B.B. camp on the Isle of Wight over twenty-five years later, journalist Ian Jack asked an officer's wife if it was not dispiriting, this effort to promote true Christian manliness among present-day youths of sixteen. 'Oh no,' she replied, 'even if we keep only one boy, his spirit is precious to Our Lord.' Later he asked a sixteen year old if the prospect of unemployment did not worry him. No, he said, he was more scared of nuclear war: 'But I've got faith — it's that that keeps me going really.' Conversely, we may also agree after considering its history that The Boys' Brigade, as Henry Drummond once put it, would have been worth starting were it only for the sake of the young and not so young men who acted as its officers, and who dedicated themselves so wholeheartedly to its declared Christian Object through a hundred years. Even now a new generation of boys is learning to sing of the B.B. Motto that gives this book its title:

> Sure and stedfast, the Brigade Boys' motto clear
> That's our watch word when troubles and trials are near.
> Sure and stedfast, to the flag that flies above
> In all that we do we'll try to be true to the Anchor that we love.[15]

Appendix 1: U.K. Boys' Brigade Strength since 1884: Company Section only‡

Year	England & Wales Coys	Boys	Scotland Coys	Boys	Ireland Coys	Boys	Total Coys	Officers†	Boys†
1884			1	30			1	3	30
1886	4	191	40	1,808			44	136	1,999
1888	37	1,516	183	8,872			220	716	10,388
1890	122	5,023	260	11,109	12	620	394	1,250	16,752
1892	212	9,248	245	10,293	33	1,461	490	1,618	21,002
1894	371	16,718	239	10,552	64	2,579	674	2,354	29,849
1896	435	18,711	264	11,522	64	2,629	763	2,676	32,862
1898	468	18,823	259	12,858	59	2,528	786	2,828	34.209
1900							906	3,319	41,096
1902							1,100	4,164	49,561
1904							1,161	4,829	50,456
1906							1,237	5,402	53,486
1908							1,324	6,044	58,090
1910							1,386	6,429	61,660
1912							1,298	6,039	55,819
1914							1,360	6,503	60,244
1916	770	28,374	468	23,205	108	4,022	1,346	6,368	55,601
1918	548	21,890	442	21,600	88	3,096	1,078	4,947	46,586
1920	618	25,033	491	23,712	79	2,839	1,181	5,653	51,584
1922	612	26,190	542	27,335	85	3,259	1,239	6,264	56,784
1924	641	26,250	594	28,577	94	3,533	1,329	6,708	58,360
1926	694	27,514	640	29,012	102	3,696	1,436	7,437	60,222
1928	1,371	46,037*	671	29,375	115	4,360	2,157	10,117	79,772
1930	1,434	46,366	700	28,811	123	4,162	2,257	10,467	79,339
1932	1,518	49,558	736	30,405	141	5,070	2,395	11,500	85,033
1934	1,662	54,854	809	35,922	157	5,986	2,628	12,808	96,762
1936	1,678	50,327	872	35,201	167	5,951	2,717	12,810	91,479
1938	1,694	50,941	889	35,061	173	6,136	2,756	12,718	92,138
1940	1,558	44,530	779	26,655	161	5,564	2,498	11,718	76,749
1942	1,255	37,466	694	23,034	146	4,274	2,095	10,251	64,747
1944	1,424	43,804	721	27,396	195	6,798	2,340	11,225	77,998
1946	1,518	45,251	777	29,422	231	7,829	2,526	11,717	82,502
1948	1,657	50,400	872	32,468	232	7,554	2,761	13,132	90,422
1950	1,660	47,318	887	32,208	237	7,354	2,784	13,460	86,880
1952	1,659	45,157	915	30,770	239	7,364	2,813	13,158	83,291
1954	1,665	42,376	932	30,391	248	7,553	2,845	13,140	80,320
1956	1,701	42,977	971	32,338	261	8,491	2,933	13,512	83,806
1958	1,738	41,818	968	30,434	282	8,817	2,988	13,673	81,067
1960	1,803	47,418	972	34,948	295	9,568	3,070	14,382	91,934
1962	1,815	45,197	988	33,318	307	9,287	3,110	14,431	87,802
1964	1,769	39,525	981	31,116	317	8,945	3,067	13,933	79,586
1966	1,683	36,320	946	29,007	319	8,956	2,948	13,172	74,283
1968	1,693	33,663	918	27,559	324	8,905	2,935	18,110	70,127
1970	1,617	30,348	900	25,317	331	8,315	2,848	16,698	63,980
1972	1,594	30,713	867	24,916	331	8,444	2,792	16,603	64,073
1974	1,591	30,854	850	23,430	330	8,081	2,771	16,125	62,365
1976	1,514	30,538	799	22,541	329	8,107	2,642	15,863	61,186
1978	1,513	28,933	813	22,097	335	8,474	2,661	16,095	59,504
1980	1,535	27,979	804	21,282	346	8,237	2,685	16,842	57,498
1982	1,540	25,429	803	19,329	359	8,259	2,702	17,330	53,017

‡ Source: Figures supplied by B.B. Records Section, London.
† Total all sections, excluding warrant officers, instructors and staff sergeants.
†† Company Section boys only. Excludes: Boy Reserves (1917-26), Life Boys (1926-66), Junior Section (1966-), Senior Section (1966-) and Pre-Juniors (1977-).
* Large increase due to 1926 amalgamation with the Boys' Life Brigade.

Appendix 2: U.K. Boys' Brigade Strength since 1917: Junior Section only‡ (including Boy Reserves and the Life Boys)

Year	Teams	Boys	Year	Teams	Boys
1918	59	1,573	1952	2,344	59,652
1920	209	5,998	1954	2,508	64,045
1922	294	8,406	1956	2,681	69,595
1924	419	12,632	1958	2,790	70,999
1926	646	18,928	1960	2,883	68,676
1928†	1,098	29,129	1962	2,944	68,404
1930	1,440	42,085	1964	2,985	68,283
1932	1,731	51,701	1966*	2,932	68,362
1934	1,903	53,607	1968	2,960	74,657
1936	1,914	50,310	1970	2,946	71,152
1938	1,990	53,150	1972	2,936	75,245
1940	1,547	35,782	1974	2,926	74,081
1942	1,272	33,414	1976	2,879	73,642
1944	1,621	42,868	1978	2,907	70,232
1946	1,746	46,499	1980	2,966	70,050
1948	2,077	57,463	1982	2,957	61,865
1950	2,233	58,113			

Pre-Junior Section (Anchor Boys) since 1977

	England & Wales		Scotland		Ireland		Total	
Year	Sections	Boys	Sections	Boys	Sections	Boys	Sections	Boys
1978	466	7,577	225	4,559	220	4,203	911	16,339
1980	776	13,218	398	8,730	284	5,656	1,458	27,604
1982	932	14,041	436	9,650	322	5,739	1,690	29,184

Senior Section since 1966

	England & Wales		Scotland		Ireland		Total	
Year	Sections	Boys	Sections	Boys	Sections	Boys	Sections	Boys
1968	296	1,831	137	1,140	34	339	467	3,310
1970	206	1,074	112	773	39	353	357	2,200
1972	133	818	70	513	25	193	228	1,524
1974	104	570	45	277	9	57	158	904
1976	91	499	35	279	12	61	138	839
1978	91	530	34	277	11	77	136	884
1980	84	486	28	202	10	93	122	781
1982	101	530	32	269	6	79	139	878

‡ *Figures supplied by B.B. Records Section.*
† *Following union in 1926 with B.L.B. Lifeboys, the Boy Reserves became the Life Boys.*
* *The Life Boys became the Junior Section in 1966.*

Appendix 3: Boys' Brigade Strength Overseas since 1888†

Session	Companies	Officers*	Boys	Life Boy Teams	Life Boy Leaders	Boys	Total all ranks
1888/89	7						
1890/91	33						
1892/93	302		8,000				8,000
1894/95	651	350	25,000				25,350
1896/97	755	2,460	33,500				35,960
1898/99	788	2,511	34,852				37,363
1900/01	786	2,439	32,040				34,479
1902/03	802	2,418	36,094				38,512
1904/05	803	2,171	39,544				41,715
1906/07	933	2,567	45,011				47,587
1908/09	954	2,558	46,878				49,436
1910/11	974	2,301	47,957				50,258
1912/13	1,018	included	51,882				51,882
1914/15	931	in boy	47,681				47,681
1916/17	1,116	figure	64,260				64,260
1918/19							
1920/21							
1922/23							
1924/25	35						
1926/27	62						
1928/29	65						
1930/31	84						
1932/33	119						
1934/35	157	568	5,043	56	107	1,133	6,851
1936/37	210	808	7,116	73	133	1,717	9,774
1938/39	294	1,054	9,424	95	196	2,122	12,796
1940/41	350		11,000				11,000
1942/43	400		12,000				12,000
1944/45	400		12,000				12,000
1946/47	400		13,500				13,500
1948/49	429	1,809	14,613	187	362	3,892	20,676
1950/51	465	1,938	16,014	198	401	4,299	22,652
1952/53	493	2,419	18,149	210	412	4,409	25,389
1954/55	593	2,951	23,108	252	569	5,203	31,831
1956/57	752	3,745	28,134	347	782	7,966	40,627
1958/59	943	4,368	33,748	445	1,024	9,360	48,500
1960/61	1,191	5,498	42,980	546	1,313	12,403	62,194
1962/63	1,481	7,017	50,049	648	1,605	14,638	73,309
1964/65	1,508	7,040	57,397	646	1,457	13,573	79,467
1966/67	1,684	8,866	56,089			14,344	79,299
1968/69	1,650	8,946	50,561			22,121	81,628
1970/71	1,888	9,383	55,030			25,686	90,099
1972/73	2,145	10,237	58,334			30,348	98,919
1974/75	2,441	12,802	91,422			41,471	145,695
1976/77	2,725	13,207	91,797			38,022	143,026
January 1978			WORLD CONFERENCE				
1979	2,219	12,053	102,093				114,146
1982	2,940	11,793	111,894				123,687

* The figure for officers also includes warrant officers and staff sergeants and from 1967 also includes the former Life Boy leaders.

†*Note: Owing to the difficulties of distance, communications etc. these figures can in no way be taken as accurate. Figures for the years prior to 1917 have been obtained by simply subtracting the returns for the British Isles from an estimated worldwide figure and are heavily inflated by the inclusion of unreliable figures for the United States of America. Except for the years of World War II the figures quoted for 1934/35 onwards are reasonably correct. From the 1st January 1978 when the World Conference was set up it was decided that statistical returns be obtained every three years. The figures quoted are for the Boys' Brigade overseas only and do **not** include the U.B.B.A., Neenah/Menasha, F.D.F/F.P.F., Ansgarsförbundet or Poikien Keskus, although they are members of the World Conference.*

Appendix 4: Years of Entry to B.B. Executive: Occupational Breakdown, 1916-79†

Occupation	1916-1918	1920-1929	1930-1939	1940-1949	1950-1959	1960-1969	1970-1979	Totals	%
Landed	1	1	2	1		1		6	2.6
Manufacturers and shipowners	4	4	3	2	2			15	6.6
Company directors	3	1	1	2	1	2	1	11	4.8
Merchants	6	6		1		2*		15	6.6
Bishops and clergy		4	4	1	1	2	2	14	6.2
Managerial			4	5	3	6	3	21	9.3
Professional	8	6	5	8	8	7	6	48	21.3
School teachers and headmasters	1			4	3	4	3	15	6.6
White collar, e.g. clerical		3	1	4	7	4	3	22	9.7
Skilled, e.g. engineers	2	3	1	5		1	3	15	6.6
Retired					2	2	1	5	2.2
Unclassifiable	4	6		5	4	6	6	31	13.7
Not given	1	3	2			1		7	3.1
Totals	30	37	23	38	31	38	28	225	99.3

†Source: B.B. Register of Directors, 1916-79, B.B. H.Q., London.
* coal, steel

Appendix 5: Officer Enrolment Forms: Occupational Breakdown 1972-76†

Occupation Given	Total in each Category	%
Professional Middle Class		
Accountants	23	
Surveyors and draughtsmen	17	
Lecturers	4	
Chartered and civil engineers	5	
Other professional or executive	25	
	74	7.0
White Collar/Lower Middle Class		
Managerial	40	
Supervisory, e.g. stock controllers	32	
School teachers	31	
Technicians	15	
Civil Service	27	
Local Government	12	
Secretaries & typists	27	
Salesmen/sales representatives	25	
Shopkeepers/tradesmen	17	
Shop assistants/sales assistants	13	
Bank clerks	29	
Other clerical	73	
Others	19	
	360	34.0
Skilled Working Class		
Engineers	72	
Hospital workers, e.g. nurses	25	
Electricians	15	
Carpenters and joiners	20	
Fitters	19	
Apprentices	26	
Others	118	
	295	27.9
Unskilled Working Class		
Drivers, incl. ambulance	20	
Other manual	38	
	58	5.4
Miscellaneous		
Students and schoolboys	41	
Housewives	94	
Police/Forces/Firemen	23	
Retired	3	
Not Given	25	
Unclassifiable	84	
	270	25.5
Totals	1,057	99.8

† *Source: B.B. H.Q., London*

Appendix 6: B.B. Week Totals in Real Terms, 1921-80†

Year	Companies	Company Section Boys (Collectors)	Actual Total Raised £	Total at 1980 values	Purchasing power of pound‡	Amount raised per head £
1921	1,199	52,748	2,855	28,855	1.00	54p
1925	1,380	60,280	7,316	93,645	1.28	1.55
1930	2,257	79,339	11,696	167,253	1.43	2.11
1935	2,673	92,509	15,157	239,481	1.58	2.59
1940	2,498	76,749	18,081	————	not available	————
1945	2,389	78,917	62,804	————	not available	————
1950	2,784	86,880	85,553	607,426	0.71	6.99
1955	2,878	80,891	115,147	656,338	0.57	8.11
1960	3,070	91,934	149,078	760,298	0.51	8.27
1965	3,014	76,877	154,128	662,750	0.43	8.62
1970	2,848	63,698	178,700	607,580	0.34	9.53
1975	2,664	61,176	258,233	490,643	0.19	8.02
1980	2,685	57,498	304,275	304,275	0.10	5.29

† *Compiled by John Digby, Brigade Finance Secretary, and David Evans.*
‡ *Central Office of Information Figures.*
* *Movement away from traditional collecting cards to other forms of fund raising.*

Appendix 7: Brigade Personnel, 1885-present

Brigade Presidents:

James Carfrae Alston	1885-1909
Lord Guthrie	1909-1919
Colonel John A. Roxburgh	1919-1933
Earl of Home	1933-1947
Lord Maclay (Sir Joseph P. Maclay)	1947-1963
Earl of Elgin and Kincardine (Lord Bruce)	1963-

Brigade Honorary Presidents:

Earl of Aberdeen (Marquis of Aberdeen and Temeir)	1889-1919
Prince Arthur of Connaught	1919-1938
Earl of Home	1947-1951
Duke of Hamilton and Brandon	1963-1973
Lord Clydesmuir of Braidwood	1973-

Brigade Secretaries:

Sir William Alexander Smith	1885-1914
H. Arnold Wilson (Honorary)	1914-1925
G. Stanley Smith	1925-1954
Major General D.J. Wilson-Haffenden	1954-1965
Ian G. Neilson	1966-1974
Alfred Hudson	1974-

Brigade Treasurers:

John Lammie	1885-1898
T.W. Cuthbertson	1898-1904
David Laidlaw	1904-1905
James D. Robertson	1905-1910
H. Arnold Wilson	1910-1915
John A. Roxburgh	1915-1918
Samuel Osborn	1918-1925
H. Arnold Wilson	1925-1938
The Marquess of Clydesdale (Duke of Hamilton and Brandon)	1938-1962
Sir Cyril Black	1962-1969
Sir Alfred Owen	1970-1973
Leonard Boyle	1982-

NOTES AND REFERENCES

Preface

1 'Letters', *The Daily Mail*, 6 May 1982; 'Boys of the Old Brigade', *The Daily Herald*, 30 June 1933.

2 Ian Jack, 'Youth: Scenes from the Life of a Beleaguered Generation', *The Sunday Times Magazine*, 1 November 1981, p.35; T.W. Laqueur, *Religion and Respectability: Sunday Schools and Working Class Culture, 1780-1850* (Yale, 1976), p.249; Helen Meller, *Leisure and the Changing City, 1870-1914* (London, 1976), p.171. See also: ed., M.R.D. Foot, *War and Society* (London, 1973), pp.172-174.

3 Brian Harrison, *Separate Spheres: the opposition to women's suffrage in Britain* (London, 1978), pp.16-17.

4 Reports of clergy or superintendents, 1st Aston Manor Company, Birmingham, *Company Log Book, 1894-1897* sessions (B.B. H.Q., London).

5 See: chap. 4 infra for the B.B. and Cadet issue in the U.K. in the 1900s; Michael E. Hoare, '"Our Comrades Beyond the Seas": Colonial Youth Movements, 1880-1920', *The Turnbull Library Record*, Vol. 12, No. 2 (October 1979), pp.82-83; John Barrett, *Falling In: Australians and 'Boy Conscription', 1911-15* (Sydney, 1979), passim.

6 Frederick P. Gibbon, *William A. Smith of The Boys' Brigade* (London, 1934); Roger S. Peacock, *Pioneer of Boyhood: the story of Sir William A. Smith, Founder of The Boys' Brigade* (Glasgow, 1954).

Introduction

1 See: D.A. Reeder, 'Predicaments of City Children: late Victorian and Edwardian Perspectives on Education and Urban Society' in: ed. D.A. Reeder, *Urban Education in the Nineteenth Century* (London, 1977), pp.75-94; ed. Geoffrey Crossick, *The Lower Middle Class in Britain 1870-1914* (London, 1977), pp.11-60.

2 See: François Bedarida, *A Social History of England, 1851-1975* (London, 1979), pp.100-103; R.K. Webb, *Modern England, from the 18th century to the present* (London, 1969), pp.373-379.

3 William Smith, holograph, Bible Class or Young Men's Society notes on 'Joshua', n.d. (1900s?) (Archives of 1st Glasgow Company); C.A. Oakley, *The Second City* (London, 1946); S.G. Checkland, *The Upas Tree: Glasgow, 1875-1975* (London, 1977).

4 See: Kathleen Heasman, *Evangelicals in Action: an appraisal of their social work in the Victorian era* (London, 1962), p.111; John Kent, *Holding the Fort: studies in Victorian revivalism* (London, 1978), chap. iv.

5 T.C. Collings, 'A Chat with Major W.A. Smith', *The Boys' Own Paper*, Vol. 21, No. 1039, 10 December 1898, p.174; T.W. Laqueur, *Religion and Respectability: Sunday Schools and Working Class Culture, 1780-1850* (Yale, 1976).

6 Clyde Binfield, *George Williams and the Y.M.C.A.: a study in Victorian social attitudes* (London, 1973); David Macleod, 'A live Vaccine: the Y.M.C.A. and Male Adolescence in the United States and Canada 1870-1920', *Social History*, Vol. 11, Pt. 21, Canada (May 1978), pp.5-25.

7 Lilian Lewis Shiman, 'The Band of Hope Movement: respectable recreation for working-class children', *Victorian Studies*, Vol. 17, No. 1 (September 1973), pp.49-74; 'Temperance Work', entry in *B.B. Manual for the Use of Officers* (London and Glasgow, 1936), p.48.

8 Victor Bailey, 'Salvation Army Riots, the "Skeleton Army" and Legal Authority in the Provincial Town', in: ed. A.P. Donajgrodzki. *Social Control in Nineteenth Century Britain* (London, 1977), pp.231-253; John Springhall, *Youth, Empire and Society: British Youth Movements, 1883-1940* (London, 1977), pp.43-44.

9 William A. Smith, *The Story of The Boys' Brigade* (Glasgow, 1888), p.9; Norman Vance, 'The Ideal of Manliness', *The Times Educational Supplement*, 28 September 1973, p.24; J.A. Mangan, *Athleticism in the Victorian and Edwardian Public Schools* (Cambridge, 1982).

10 See: Olive Anderson, 'The Growth of Christian Militarism in Mid-Victorian

Britain', *The English Historical Review*, Vol. 86 (January, 1971), pp.46-72; Douglas H. Johnson, 'The Death of Gordon: a Victorian Myth', *The Journal of Imperial and Commonwealth History*, Vol. 10, No. 3 (May, 1982), pp.285-310.

11 See: John R. Gillis, *Youth and History: tradition and change in European age relations, 1770 to the present* (New York, 1981 edn.), chap. iii; G. Stanley Hall, *Adolescence, its psychology and its relations to physiology, anthropology, sociology, sex, crime, religion and education*, two vols. (New York, 1904); Dorothy Ross, *G. Stanley Hall: the psychologist as prophet* (Chicago, 1972).

12 See: James Walvin, *A Child's World: a social history of English childhood, 1800-1914* (London, 1982), p.186; Martin Barratt, 'The Foundation and Early Years of The Boys' Brigade: an aspect of the social history of youth', M.A. Dissertation, September 1976, University of Leicester School of Education, chap. i.

Chapter 1

1 Commission papers (George III, 1810 and 1813) and family papers (B.B. H.Q., London).

2 W.R.O. Campbell to G. Stanley Smith, 7 April 1925 (B.B. H.Q., London); British Consul in Swatow to Archibald Campbell Cameron, 10 January 1868 (B.B. H.Q., Glasgow).

3 *The Scottish Law Review of 1905*, referring to Glasgow as 'The Oppressor of the West'; Geoffrey Best, 'The Scottish Victorian City', in *Victorian Studies*, March 1968, p.338.

4 Mss. autobiographical notes, 1869 (B.B. H.Q., London); Register of Companies (Scottish Business Archives, Edinburgh); Alex Fraser to William Smith, 5 February 1895 (B.B. H.Q., London).

5 H. Cunningham, *The Volunteers* (London, 1975), p.28.

6 J.J. Bell, *I Remember* (Glasgow, 1932), n.p.

7 *1st Lanark Rifle Volunteers Gazette*, vol. 10, No. 1, 25 November 1895 (Cameronians Headquarters, Hamilton). 1st L.R.V. eventually became the 5-8th Volunteer Battalion, The Cameronians (Scottish Rifles).

8 Grove Street Home Mission Institute, Annual Report 1886 (Mitchell Library, Glasgow).

9 Ib.; cf. Smith's diaries, 1875 (B.B. H.Q., London).

10 Annual Reports and Compendium of Ob-ject, Operations and Management, Glasgow Foundry Boys' Religious Society (Merchants' House, Glasgow).

11 1875 Diary, ib. (1st Glasgow Co.). Smith marked the crucial events of 1874 in red ink in this diary to underline their significance.

12 William Clow, *Dr George Reith: A Scottish Ministry* (London, 1929), p.101.

13 Dr Herbert Gray, 'The Founder as I knew him' (B.B. H.Q., London); Free College Church Annual Reports, 1877-88 (Scottish Record Office, Edinburgh).

14 Mss. Roll Book 1884-85 (B.B. H.Q., Glasgow), and Census Returns 1881, 1891 (Scottish Record Office, Edinburgh). Registrar General's division into five social classes according to standing of occupations in the community.

15 Deacon's Court Minutes, 3 June and 1 July 1885, Adelaide Place Baptist Church, Glasgow.

16 Mss. register of company enrolments (B.B. H.Q., London); Census Returns 1891 (Scottish Record Office, Edinburgh).

17 Henry Drummond, 'The Brigade as a Field of Work for Young Men', n.d. (B.B. H.Q., London).

18 W.A. Smith to R. McNair, Calton, Glasgow, 16 February 1887, Smith's letter book (B.B. H.Q., London).

19 G.F.B.R.S., Merchants' House, Glasgow.

20 A.N. Russell, Mss. notes and article 'The Man He Was', n.d. (B.B. H.Q., London).

Chapter 2

1 Paper given by W.A. Smith to World Sunday School Convention, possibly 1887 (B.B. H.Q., London).

2 Cited in: *Christian Leader*, 7 October 1886.

3 W.A. Smith to J. Carfrae Alston, 27 September 1886 (B.B. H.Q., London).

4 Oliver Hind to Roger Peacock, Asst. Brigade Sec., London, 24 October 1913 (B.B. H.Q., London).

5 *Carlisle Journal*, 23 February 1894.

6 Brigade Annual Report 1891-92; Sheffield Battalion Annual Report 1892-93 (B.B. H.Q., London); *Royal Commission on Physical Training (Scotland)*, 1902, Mins. of Evidence, Cd. 1508, xxx, 123, 562 (Mitchell Library, Glasgow).

7 N.M. Bain, Mss. Enrolment Registers, 24 May 1889 (B.B. H.Q., Glasgow); S. Ogilvie Skea, *The Fourth Aberdeen*, 1968, 80th Anniversary Leaflet (B.B. H.Q., London).

8 R.Q. Gray, *The Labour Aristocracy in Victorian Edinburgh* (Oxford, 1976), p.19; Mss.

Enrolment Registers (B.B. H.Q., Edinburgh).

9   Mss. log. of 1st Aston Manor Company (B.B. H.Q., London).

10 Smith's letterbook, and mss. documents on Trust Fund drawn up by Messrs. McGrigor, Donald & Co., Glasgow, April 1888 (B.B. H.Q., Glasgow).

11 W.McC. Eager, *Making Men*, (London, 1953), p.12.

12 Henry Drummond, *First*, 1889, Christmas Gift Booklet for Boys (B.B. H.Q., London).

13 John Gorst, *The Children of the Nation — How their health and vigour should be promoted by the State* (London, 1906), p.1.

14 William Sharpe, taped reminiscences, 1974 (B.B. H.Q., London); William Sharpe's memories are as a boy and not a leader. He was not an officer in the organization. Cuthbert Lennox, *Henry Drummond* (London, 1901), p.205.

15 W.A. Smith to W. Blott, Wellingborough, 19 February 1887, Smith's Letter Book (B.B. H.Q., London).

16 Cited: Muriel Ellis, *Banging the Drum: the story of Boys' Brigade Bands*, 1980, n.p. (B.B. H.Q., London).

17 Annual Report 1893-94, p.16 (B.B. H.Q., London).

18 Free College Church Report 1883-84 (Scottish Record Office, Edinburgh); *The Chronicle*, Edinburgh Battalion magazine, January 1914 (B.B. H.Q., Edinburgh).

19 Rev. P.E. Thomas, 1st Blackburn (Lancs.) Company to W.A. Smith, 21 February 1896 (B.B. H.Q., Glasgow).

20 *B.B. Gazette*, June 1979.

21 *The Times*, 4 July 1907, when publishing an appeal for camp funds.

22 *The Down Recorder*, 22 July 1892.

23 *The Free Church Monthly*, July 1886 (1st Glasgow Company Archives).

24 West Kent Battalion papers; 1st Witney Company, camp records, 1905-10 (B.B. H.Q., London).

25 William Smith's Camp Diary, 1892; 1st Blackheath Company, *Company Chronicle*, July 1900 (B.B. H.Q., London).

26 *B.B. Gazette* January 1904; *B.B. Gazette*, September 1903.

27 W. Sharpe, taped reminiscences, 1974; Mss. essays, 1st Hamilton Company, in possession of the Captain, Mr Frank Gardiner.

28 *The Brigade*, C.L.B. Magazine, Vol. 1, No. 1, April 1894 (C.L.B. H.Q., London).

29 *Church Times*, 30 March, 1893.

30 Charles A. Magnus, *E.M.J. — The Man and his Work*, a collection of reminiscences on Ernest Martin Joseph, a leading Jewish youth leader and J.L.B. officer, for private circulation (London, 1962), (J.L.B. H.Q., London); Sidney Bunt, *Jewish Youth Work in Britain*, (London, 1975).

31 J.L. Paton, *John Brown Paton: A Biography by his son*, (London, 1914), p.315.

32 M. Lochead, *A Lamp Was Lit: Girls Guildry through fifty years* (Edinburgh, 1949), p.21.

33 Annual Report 1891-92 (B.B. H.Q., London).

Chapter 3

1   Smith to A.B. Field, 11 October 1906, *Australian Boys' Paper*, 1 January 1907, pp.113-14. The known Australian letters of the Founder are reproduced in M.E. Hoare, *Boys, Urchins, Men: A History of The Boys' Brigade in Australia and Papua New Guinea, 1882-1976* (Sydney, 1980), p.267; Brigade President's address, *B.B. Gazette*, November 1907.

2   G.A. Smith, *The Life of Henry Drummond* (9th ed., London, 1907), pp.440-61; H. Drummond's writings on the B.B. include 'Manliness in Boys — by a new process', *McClure's Magazine*, December 1893, pp.68-77, and 'The Secret of Managing Street Boys', *Review of Reviews*, 3 (1891), p.155. For the career of the Aberdeens see John Campbell and Ishbel Gordon, *'We Twa': Reminiscences of Lord and Lady Aberdeen* (2 vols, London, 1929). From the 1890s onwards the Brigade took a close interest in mission support, especially — as in the case of Dr Arthur Lankester of London and the Rev. P. Walsh — where the missionaries in question were former Brigade officers themselves; see e.g. *B.B. Gazette*, October 1894, January and March 1901, November 1902, and January 1903.

3   Hoare, *Boys, Urchins, Men*, pp.36-53; R. Baden-Powell, *Boy Scouts beyond the Seas: 'My World Tour'* (London, 1913); Longstaff papers (Archives of British Columbia, Add. MSS 677); *B.B. Gazette*, February-April and October, 1902, February-June and December 1903, and April 1904.

4   *B.B. Gazette*, January and October 1902, and January 1904.

5   John Barrett, *Falling In: Australians and 'Boy Conscription', 1911-1915* (Sydney, 1979); James F. Findlay, *Dwight L. Moody, American Evangelist 1837-1899* (Chicago, 1969), pp.118-80; J.S. Pollack, *Moody: A Biographical Portrait of the Pacesetter in Modern Mass Evangelism* (New York, 1963), pp.127-177; Kathleen Heasman,

Evangelicals in action: an appraisal of their social work in the Victorian era (London, 1962), pp.107-23.

6   'Overseas Register', United States companies, 1887-91 (B.B. H.Q., London); Charles B. Morrell, *Handbook of The Boys' Brigade containing full directions for organizing and conducting military Companies in Churches, with a history of The Boys' Brigade* (Cinncinnati, 1893), pp.174-5; *B.B. Gazette*, 1889-93.

7   'The Boys' Brigade in America, Interview with Professor Henry Drummond', *B.B. Gazette*, December 1893; 'Important statement by the Rev. John Q. Adams, Brigade President, U.S.A.', and Henry Coates to Smith, Perth, 4 January 1894, *B.B. Gazette*, April 1894; David MacLeod, 'Good Boys made better: The Boy Scouts of America, Boys' Brigades, and Y.M.C.A. Boys' Work, 1880-1920', Ph.D. thesis, 1973, University of Wisconsin, pp.28-30. MacLeod wisely advises caution in reading contemporary U.B.B.A. statistics.

8   *Brigade Boy* ('Official organ of The United Boys' Brigades of America'), 1902-06; *B.B. Gazette*, 1894-1900; MacLeod, op. cit., pp.30-57.

9   'Lieutenant-General H.P. Bope, Our new Commander-in-Chief', *Brigade Boy*, January 1902; J.H. Cudlipp, 'Impressions of an American Officer', *B.B. Gazette*, 1 December 1905.

10 W.A. Smith to Stanley and Douglas Smith, Baltimore, 30 May 1907 (B.B. H.Q., London); *B.B. Gazette*, October and December 1907, and February 1908; *American Brigadier* ('The Maryland or American Brigadier: A monthly magazine devoted to the interests of the B.B. of Maryland'), 1906-09.

11 'Overseas Register', Canadian companies, 1889-93; Fotheringham papers, 1889-1914, New Brunswick Museum, St. John, New Brunswick; *Daily Telegraph* (St. John), 14 June 1904; *B.B. Gazette*, September 1889-October 1902.

12 Ed. John T. Saywell, *The Canadian Journal of Lady Aberdeen 1893-1898* (2 vols., Toronto, 1960), entries for 21-22 January 1894, vol. 1, pp.60-62; Haddo House MSS, B.B. Correspondence, 1893-98, 1/48-9, Bundle 2; 'Overseas Register', Ottawa companies, 1894.

13 'Overseas Register', Canadian companies, 1893-4.

14 Ed. Saywell, op. cit., entries for 20 February, 6-7 March, 23 March 1895, vol. 1, pp.199-200, 208-10, 212; *The Globe* (Toronto), 27 March 1895; *The Gazette* (Montreal), 21 February 1895; *B.B. Gazette*, April and June 1895.

15 Longstaff to William McVicker, 25 October 1946, Longstaff papers, Box 407/376 (Archives of British Columbia); Nisbet's correspondence with Lord Aberdeen, 1893-97, Haddo House MSS 1/43, Bundle 3, 1/48-9, Bundle 2 and 1.50, Bundles 1 & 2; *B.B. Gazette*, May 1895; comp. F.V. Longstaff, Annual Report 1910-11 (The Boys' Brigade in Canada), (Victoria, British Columbia, 1911), 16pp.

16 Taylor Statten, 'The genesis of work with boys in Canada', *Canadian Welfare*, vol.16, No.2 (16 May 1940), pp.15-18; J. Campbell, 'Colonial Companies and Battalions: Toronto', *B.B. Gazette*, October 1899; McKim to Longstaff, 23 February 1913, *B.B. Gazette*, May 1913; *Boys' Clubs of Honolulu: Successors to The Boys' Brigade: Report for 1905* (Honolulu, 1906); T. Richards, 'Development of boys' work in Honolulu', *The Friend* (Honolulu), vol.98 (September 1928), pp.107-08.

17 A.H. Sovereign, 'Boys' Camps on the Lower Mainland of British Columbia' (Vancouver City Archives); *Vancouver Province*, 21 May 1898, and 28 November 1950; *The Canadian Boy* ('A Journal of Incident, Story and Self-Help'), (Cobourg, Ontario), 1901-02.

18 Longstaff, 'An outline of The Boys' Brigade in Canada from 1889 until 1907', Longstaff papers, file 375; biographical notes on Longstaff (Archives of British Columbia).

19 *New Star* (St. John), 5 September 1910; *Citizen* (Ottawa), 1 September 1910; *Quebec Chronicle*, 9 September 1910; *Manitoba Free Press*, 20 August 1910; newspaper cuttings, Longstaff papers, files 1 & 376 (Archives of British Columbia); Longstaff, Annual Report 1910-11; comp. W.A. Smith, *The Boys' Brigade in Canada* (brochure issued by order of the Brigade Executive, Glasgow, 1911).

20 A.S. Roberts, 'North-West Canada', *B.B. Gazette*, March 1907, pp.104-05; Oliver W. Hind, 'Emigration of Boys', *B.B. Gazette*, January 1912, p.72; 'The Canadian Boy', *B.B. Gazette*, June 1912, pp.132-33.

21 Longstaff, 'Notes for tour of Canada in the interests of The Boys' Brigade Canada, 1912'; Longstaff to Smith, 9 and 16 October 1912, 12 April 1913, 24 March and 17 April 1914; Smith to Longstaff, 2 April 1913 and 5 May 1914; Longstaff correspondence with Adjutant General, Ottawa, 23 September 1912, 5 March, 11, 19 and 30 April 1913; G. Rees (Captain 1st Nelson, B.C.) to Smith, 20 May 1914, Longstaff papers, files 217 and 375 (Archives of British Columbia).

22 *B.B. Gazette*, May 1915; F.V. Longstaff,

Occasional notes of The Boys' Brigade in Canada (Victoria, 1911).

23 M.E. Hoare, *Faces of Boyhood: An Informal Pictorial Record of The Boys' Brigade in New Zealand* (Wellington, 1982); Hoare, ' "Our Comrades Beyond the Seas": colonial youth movements, 1880-1920', *Turnbull Library Record*, Vol. 12, No. 2 (October 1979), pp.73-94; B.B. New Zealand Archive, MS Papers 2024 (Turnbull Library, Wellington).

24 G.A. Smith, *Life of Henry Drummond* (1907), pp.293, 368; Hoare, *Boys, Urchins and Men*, pp.34-48, and the sources cited therein.

25 Barrett, op. cit., pp.7-12; Hoare, *Boys, Urchins, Men*, pp.49-57.

26 Hoare, *Boys, Urchins, Men*, pp.53-62.

27 'Overseas Register', South African companies, 1889-1901 (B.B. H.Q., London); *B.B. Gazette*, March 1890-April 1901.

28 *B.B. Gazette*, October 1894-November 1902.

29 *B.B. Gazette*, October 1891-September 1899; John C. Harris, 'The Boys' Brigade in South Africa: The Transvaal Battalion', *B.B. Gazette*, May 1901.

30 'Overseas Register', African companies, September 1910-April 1914; S. Ola Maraiyesa, National Secretary, The Boys' Brigade in Nigeria, response to International History Information Survey, May 1978; The Boys' Brigade in Ghana, response to Information Survey, 1978.

31 'Overseas Register', Asian companies, 1903-10; *B.B. Gazette*, February 1894-June 1912; Baden-Powell, *Boy Scouts beyond the Seas* (London, 1913), p.102.

32 'Overseas Register', West Indian companies, 1892-1912; *B.B. Gazette*, December 1899 and April 1902.

33 'Overseas Register', 1894-1912; The Boys' Brigade in Jamaica, response to Information Survey, 1978; Henry Robson, 'The B.B. in Jamaica', *B.B. Gazette*, May 1911.

34 *B.B. Gazette*, December 1899-February 1912.

35 H. Tornöe to Stanley Smith, 6 June 1953 (B.B. H.Q., London).

36 The Ansgarsförbundet in Sweden was founded by Karl Fromen in 1946 and works closely with the Lutheran Church there. The organization is much less strong than in Denmark but with closer Diocesan control. Membership in the 1970s was around 14,000 boys in 200 local units. Finland followed Sweden in establishing the Poikien Keskus (Boys Centre) as a branch of Y.M.C.A. work. Again it is closely connected with the Lutheran Church and coordinates its activities with the Y.M.C.A. sections and to a lesser extent the Scouts. As with its Swedish and Danish counterparts it takes a keen interest in Brigade methods and activities through the World Conference. The present strength is around 62,000 boys in 3,200 units.

37 *B.B. Gazette*, December 1908.

38 *B.B. Gazette*, October 1913 and April 1914.

Chapter 4

1 Death certificate and precognition report (Scottish Records Office, Edinburgh, and B.B. H.Q., London).

2 *Glasgow Herald*, 5 September 1908.

3 H.B. Brandish on behalf of C.B.B., cited in: F.P. Gibbon, *William A. Smith of The Boys' Brigade* (London, 1934), p.152.

4 Mansion House Committee files (Constitution and minutes) and London District Council minutes, 1910-12 (B.B. H.Q., London).

5 W.A. Smith to Mr Gray, n.d., Smith's Letter Book (B.B. H.Q., London); *B.B. Gazette*, July 1907, from a speech in Philadelphia, U.S.A., 23 May 1907; *Herald of Peace*, Vol. 22, No. 489, 1 May 1890, pp.62-63. The Peace Society unsuccessfully attempted to have the Sunday School Union of Liverpool reject the Brigade at this time.

6 Mss. Enrolment Registers, Lt. Porter to W. Smith, 10 February 1894 (B.B. H.Q., Glasgow); *Carlisle Journal*, 23 February 1894.

7 Plymouth Battalion Annual Report, 1889-90 (B.B. H.Q., Glasgow).

8 *Regulations Governing the Formation, Organization and Administration of Cadet Units by County Associations*, (H.M.S.O., London, 1910), pp. 5-6. See also accompanying *Circular Memorandum No. 262 of the War Office*, instructing the refusal of facilities to organizations not applying for recognition (B.B. H.Q., London).

9 W.A. Smith to R.S. Peacock, 25 February 1910; R.B. Haldane to Lord Guthrie, 27 June, 1910 (B.B. H.Q., London).

10 *Glasgow Herald*, 4 March 1911; correspondence between Smith, Gee and Haldane, March 1911 (B.B. H.Q., London).

11 Baden-Powell, *Scouting for Boys* (London, 1908), p.267.

12 *The Times*, 6 May 1903; Baden-Powell, 'Scouting for Boys', *B.B. Gazette*, 1 June 1906, p.150; B.B. Glasgow Battalion, Memorandum by the Committee appointed by the Battalion Council to consider Scouting for Boys, 29 January 1909 (B.B. H.Q., Glasgow).

13 Baden-Powell to W.A. Smith, 9 December 1909 (Scout Headquarters, London); Baden-Powell to W.A. Smith, 25 December 1909; W.A. Smith to Baden-Powell, 28 December 1909 (B.B. H.Q., London).

14 W.A. Smith to F.P. Gibbon, 16 December 1913; W.A. Smith to R.S. Peacock, 12 November 1913 (B.B. H.Q., London).

15 Sir Francis Belsey to W.A. Smith, 17 March 1914, and copy of Resolution (B.B. H.Q., London).

16 B.B. Gazette, June 1914; Chief Constable's Report, 24 June 1914 (B.B. H.Q., London); A.S. Jackson, A. Reid, taped interviews, n.d. (B.B. H.Q., London).

17 B.B. Gazette, June 1914.

18 W.M. Gee, quoted in C.L.B. Magazine, The Brigade, July 1894 (C.L.B. H.Q., London).

19 Alfred Plummer and Richard Early, The Blanket Makers, 1669-1969 (London, 1969), p.124.

20 William Smith, holograph notes, Bible Class exegesis on 'Joshua', n.d., p.7 (Archives of 1st Glasgow Company). See: J.H. Hanham, 'Religion and Nationality in the Mid-Victorian Army', in: M.R.D. Foot ed., War and Society, (London, 1973), pp.172-174.

21 The Boys' Brigade Executive, 'A Word About the War to the Boys of The Boys' Brigade', 1914 (B.B. H.Q., London).

22 Arnold Wilson, 'Memo to Officers Commanding Companies', 27 August 1914 (B.B. H.Q., London).

23 The Boys' Brigade, 'Rest and Refreshment Huts', leaflet n.d. (B.B. H.Q., London); George Barclay to Roger S. Peacock, 5 October 1915 (B.B. H.Q., London).

24 Memos of 22 January 1917 and 25 January 1917 by Southern Committee (B.B. H.Q., London); R.S. Peacock, Pioneer of Boyhood (London, 1954), pp.130-131.

25 Glasgow Post, 7 March 1915: 'Over 100,000 old Boys' Brigade members now serving in the trenches or with the Fleet'. See: G.A. Crompton, 'A Concise History of the Glasgow Boys' Brigade Battalion, 1914-1919', Wolfson College, Michaelmas 1980 (B.B. H.Q., London).

26 D.H. Rowlands, For the Duration: The story of the 13th Battalion, The Rifle Brigade (London, 1932), p.701; interview with R.E. Thompson, ex-2nd Enfield Company.

27 Interview with W.H.A. Monckton, ex-38th London Company, July 1975.

28 The B.B., 'Proposed Recognition as Cadets', Executive circular, 10 March 1917; Manchester Officers, 'The Boys' Brigade Proposal to obtain Recognition of Cadets', 16 March 1917 (B.B. H.Q., London); Captain 1st Hamilton Company to Secretary of The Boys' Brigade, 5 April 1917 (1st Hamilton Papers, Scotland).

29 Roxburgh, Executive Minutes, 14 September 1918 (B.B. H.Q., London).

30 Douglas Pearson Smith, 'The Life Boys' Fortieth Anniversary', B.B. Gazette, October 1957; B.B. Leaflet, '1917 Boy Reserves to Junior Section 1977' (B.B. H.Q., London); interview with Mrs Dora Stirling (formerly Miss Dora Webb), 2 November 1981, Scotland.

Chapter 5

1 'Council Meetings', B.B. Gazette, October 1921, p.28; Anon., (R.S. Peacock), B.B. Week: the Story of a Great Endeavour (1966), passim (B.B. H.Q., London).

2 B.B. Official Statistics, compiled by Muriel Ellis, Brigade Archivist, Brigade House, London. See Appendix 1.

3 Rev. Edgar Rogers, The Making of a Man in the Church Lads' Brigade (London, 1919), p.72; F.G. Marshall, St. Mary, Lewisham, Church Lads' Brigade, 1892-1929 (London, 1930), pp.24-25.

4 A.M. Josselyn to Secretary, the War Office, 12 January 1923; 'Administration of Cadet Units', Army Council Instruction 583 of 1923; B.B. Executive Minutes, 21 January 1923, and 10-11 May 1924 (B.B. H.Q., London).

5 B.B. Executive Minutes, 10 May 1924 (B.B. H.Q., London).

6 'Arguments re Model Rifle', B.B. Gazette, June 1924; 'Council Meetings', B.B. Gazette, October 1924, pp.27-30.

7 'Council Meetings', op. cit.; B.B. Executive Minutes, 10-11 January 1925.

8 Report of the Conference Between Representatives of the B.B. and the B.L.B. (March 1920); B.B. Gazette, April 1920, p.110; Edward Cooke to R.S. Peacock, 23 March 1920 (B.B. H.Q., London).

9 'The B.B. and The B.L.B.', B.L.B. Chronicle, May 1926, pp.131-132; Report of Meeting of Representatives of the Executives of the B.B. and the B.L.B., held in Glasgow 21 June 1924; Arnold Wilson to A.H. Angus, 17 July 1924 (B.B. H.Q., London).

10 Tables in B.B. Gazette, October 1926, p.25; F.P. Gibbon to A.H. Angus, 21 July 1924; F.P. Gibbon to Arnold Wilson, 18 July 1924 (B.B. H.Q., London).

11 B.L.B. Chronicle, May 1926, p.133; Report of Joint Sub-Committee, 'Proposed Scheme of Union', B.B. Executive Minutes, 23-24 January 1926; 'Proposed Un-

ion of The B.B. and B.L.B.', *B.B. Gazette*, 1 April 1926, p.107; B.B. Executive, 'Proposed Union with The B.L.B.', Memorandum for Members of Brigade Council, 21 May 1926, p.7 (B.B. H.Q., London); 'The B.B. and The B.L.B.', *B.L.B. Chronicle*, April 1926, p.113; 'Council Meetings', *B.B. Gazette*, October 1926, pp.24-26.

12 Arnold S. Clark to London District Officers, cyclostyled, January 1927; *B.B. Gazette*, cited: *B.L.B. Chronicle*, October 1926, p.19; Roger S. Peacock, *Pioneer of Boyhood* (London, 1954), p.139.

13 Anon., *The B.B. as an Auxiliary of the Church of England* (London, 1923), pp.12-13.

14 Anon., *From Paternoster Row to Parson's Green*, B.B. leaflet, May 1979, passim; *Report of the Organization and Administration Committee*, 12 August 1929, B.B. Executive Minutes (B.B. H.Q., London).

15 A.E. Morgan, *The Needs of Youth* (London, 1939), pp.297 and 312; Anthony J. Jeffs, *Young People and the Youth Service* (London, 1979), p.17; J.O. Springhall, *Youth, Empire and Society: British Youth Movements, 1883-1940* (London, 1977), passim.

16 'Forward', *B.L.B. Chronicle*, October, 1926, p.18; 'Council Meetings', *B.B. Gazette*, October 1924, p.28; F.P. Gibbon, *Sportsmen or Mugs?*, B.B. pamphlet (c.1930), p.5; B.B. Executive Minutes, 14-15 January 1928 (B.B. H.Q., London).

17 See: Keith Robbins, *The Abolition of War* (London, 1977); Martin Ceadel, *Pacifism in Britain, 1914-1945* (London, 1980); Donald S. Birn, *The League of Nations Union, 1918-1945* (Oxford, 1981); *The Torch of Peace*, B.B. leaflet, (c.1930), (B.B. H.Q., London).

18 B.B. Executive Minutes, 23-24 January 1932, and 28-29 May 1932 (B.B. H.Q., London); Charles Hovell to Headquarters, 19 February 1977; *Programme of Arrangements for the Fiftieth Annual Meeting of Brigade Council and Jubilee Celebrations*, 8-11 September 1933.

19 'Jubilee Celebrations in Glasgow', *B.B. Gazette*, October 1933, pp.22-36; *The B.B. Jubilee Film Commentary*, transcript (1933), p.2.; Anon., *The B.B. Jubilee Book* (1933), p.47 (B.B. H.Q., London).

20 Interview with Arthur Jackson, 1978; *The B.B. Jubilee Book*, op. cit., p.86; *B.B. Gazette*, October 1933, p.31.

21 *Notes for Officers, The B.B. Jubilee Review and Convention* (n.d.), p.20; 'The Scottish Conventicle', *The B.B. Jubilee Week Programme* (1933), pp.38-40 (B.B. H.Q., London).

22 *The B.B. Jubilee Film Commentary*, op. cit., pp.3-4; *The B.B. Jubilee Book*, op.cit., p.67.

23 Interview with Eric Chapman, 1979; Charles Hovell, op. cit.; *The B.B. Jubilee Book*, op. cit., pp.70-73; *B.B. Gazette*, October 1933, p.34.

24 'Address by the Brigade President', B.B. Wolverhampton Battalion typescript, n.d., McVicker Papers (B.B. H.Q., London).

25 C.L. Mowat, *Britain Between the Wars, 1919-1939* (London, 1955), pp.463-468; Anthony Jeffs, op. cit., pp.16-17; Annual Report, 1934-35, p.14.

26 John Chalmers, 'Special Areas: B.B. Development in the North of England', *B.B. Gazette*, April 1935, p.131; B.B. Executive Minutes, *Development Committee Reports*, 19 January 1935 and 18-19 May 1935; *Tyne Valley Battalion Council Meetings*, Minutes, 18 February 1935 (B.B. H.Q., London).

27 'King George's Jubilee Trust', *The Festival of Youth Programme* 3 July 1937, pp.5-6; B.B. Executive Minutes, op. cit., 18-19 May 1935 and 20 September 1935 (B.B. H.Q., London); Anthony Jeffs, op. cit., p.22; Bryan H. Reed (compiler), *Eighty Thousand Adolescents* (London, 1950), pp.1-3.

28 C.L. Mowat, op. cit., p.533.

29 D.G. Webb, taped interview, 1977, transcript, p.10.

30 Anon. (F.P. Gibbon), *The Boys' Brigade and the Silver Jubilee* (1935), p.4 (B.B. H.Q., London).

31 'Recreative Physical Training', *The Festival of Youth Programme*, 3 July 1937, p.7 (B.B. H.Q., London).

32 'At the Festival of Youth', *B.B. Gazette*, September 1937, p.5.

Chapter 6

1 *B.B. Gazette*, June 1917; Annual Report, 1919-20.

2 M.E. Hoare, *Boys, Urchins, Men: a history of The Boys' Brigade in Australia and Papua-New Guinea, 1882-1976* (Sydney, 1980), pp.60-62; 'For Fifty Years', *Anchor* (magazine of 1st Glasgow Company), 1933; Smith's testimonial on Orr, 9 April 1912 (1st Brisbane Company archives, Brisbane, reproduced in *Boys, Urchins, Men*, p.268); interview with Robert Tait, Brisbane, 1969.

3 *B.B. Gazette*, December 1911 and June 1914; 1st Brisbane Company archives.

4 *Boys, Urchins, Men*, pp.61-67; Pattersen to Robert McEwen, 1949 (The Boys' Brigade Australia archives, Sydney); 1st Brisbane Company archives; personal papers of

Albert Green and interview with Green, Adelaide, 1967.

5 *Boys, Urchins, Men*, pp.67-69, and address by the Rev. James Gibson at dedication of memorial window to Orr, 14 December 1930 (1st Brisbane archives, reproduced in *Boys, Urchins, Men*, pp.269-71).

6 S.G. Culliford, *New Zealand Scouting: The First Fifty Years, 1908-1958* (Wellington, 1958); G. McInnes, *The Road to Gundagai* (Melbourne, 1967), especially 'We are Scouts of Toorak', pp.164-200; *Boys, Urchins, Men*, pp.96-113.

7 Anon., *A Record of Heroism: The Story of The Boys' Brigade in China* (The Boys' Brigade, London, 1929), pp.3-5, and 'The Heroes of South China', *Stedfast Magazine*, No. 134, December 1964.

8 *Record of Heroism*, pp.5-9, and Gamble's address to Brigade Council, *B.B. Gazette*, December 1929.

9 *Record of Heroism*, pp.9-16; *Stedfast Magazine*, December 1964; George G. Barnes, *In the Furnace: Stories of Chinese Christians in Revolution Years* (London, 1929).

10 McVicker's hand in overseas events is clear, not only from the overseas records of B.B. Headquarters, London, but also from the many letters, contemporary B.B. publications and newsletters etc. held in B.B. archives, repositories and private hands outside Britain. See e.g. the references in *Boys, Urchins, Men* and Hoare, *Faces of Boyhood: An Informal Pictorial Record of The Boys' Brigade in New Zealand* (Wellington, 1982). The statistics cited here were given by McVicker, on his New Zealand tour, in the *Gisborne Herald* (N.Z.), 2 June 1951.

11 S. Ola Maraiyesa, National Secretary, The Boys' Brigade Nigeria, response to International History Information Survey, May 1978; 'Overseas Register' (B.B. H.Q., London); Annual Reports, 1925-35; *B.B. Gazette*, October 1933.

12 *B.B. Gazette*, October and November 1933, October and December 1936 and June 1937; S.O. Maraiyesa, op. cit.

13 *B.B. Gazette*, December 1936 and January, February and June 1937; Stanley Smith's correspondence (B.B. H.Q., London).

14 *B.B. Gazette*, September 1936 and June 1937; Annual Reports, 1936-40; S.O. Maraiyesa, op. cit.; International History Information Survey, Sierra Leone, 1978.

15 *B.B. Gazette*, May 1934, September 1935 and February 1938; International History Information Survey, Uganda, 1978.

16 *B.B. Gazette*, June 1937; 'Overseas Register' (B.B. H.Q., London); Annual Reports, 1930-40.

17 Annual Reports, 1923-33; 'Overseas Register'.

18 Dermott Monahan, *The Story of Dichpalli: Towards the conquest of leprosy* (London, 1949), pp.26-49.

19 Ib., pp.70-77; *B.B. Gazette*, April 1933.

20 Monahan, op. cit., pp.58, 74, 98-108; *B.B. Gazette*, April 1936 and June 1938.

21 Annual Reports, 1940-50; 'Overseas Register'.

22 T. Wemyss Reid (comp. & ed.), *A man like Bati: The Rev. Reginald Bartlett, O.B.E. The story of his missionary work in Papua and Samoa as told in his letters home* (London, 1960), pp.11-79; *B.B. Gazette*, November 1901 and January 1906; *Boys, Urchins, Men*, pp.44-54.

23 Reid, op. cit., pp.82-208: Reid drew extensively on letters provided by McVicker; *B.B. Gazette*, November 1940 and October 1942; *Boys, Urchins, Men*, p.215.

24 R.L. Challis, *Memorandum and diary of The Boys' Brigade in the Cook Islands, 1935-44* (B.B. Archive, Turnbull Library, Wellington); Interview with Challis 1976; *B.B. Gazette*, December 1935, January and November 1936, March 1937 and September 1938.

25 Challis, *Memorandum and diary*; 'Overseas Register' (B.B. H.Q., London); Annual Report (The Boys' Brigade NZ Dominion Council), 1944, p.6; McVicker to F. Scott Miller, 25 May 1944, with enclosure 'The Boys' Brigade in the Cook Islands, South Pacific' by R.L. Challis; McVicker to Roland Hill, 25 May 1944 (B.B. NZ Archive, Turnbull Library, Wellington); *B.B. Gazette*, February 1942 and February 1946.

26 Obituaries of Challis in *New Zealand Herald* and *Auckland Star*, 8 July 1980, and *Cook Islands Times*, 17 July 1980.

27 Horace Grocott, 'Early days of The Boys' Brigade in New Zealand', typescript, 2pp. 1940; interview with Roland Hill, Mervyn Branks and others, Dunedin, January 1976, typescript transcript, 12pp; Minute Book, Dunedin District Council, 1926-30; Headquarters correspondence, 1931-32 (B.B. NZ Archive, Turnbull Library, Wellington); *The Brigade Boy*, 1929-33.

28 The Boys' Brigade New Zealand Dominion Council (Inc.), Annual Reports 1934-44; *Faces of Boyhood*, op. cit., passim.

29 'Statement of Policy: The relationship of The Boys' Brigade with Bible Classes and Sunday Schools', 14 May 1934 (B.B. NZ Archive, Wellington); *The Council Table* (Official Organ of The Boys' Brigade NZ Dominion Council (Inc.)), 1933-41; Annual Reports 1934-44.

30 Correspondence re registration of name, 1933-63, including legal opinion (1933); Brigade (UK) solicitors' correspondence, 1933-35 (B.B. Australia Archives, Sydney); Hoare, *Boys, Urchins, Men*, pp.27-33 and 70-73.

31 Correspondence re registration of name, 1933-63; Correspondence McVicker and Tait, May and June 1936 (Queensland B.B. H.Q., Brisbane); Hoare, ib., pp.73-76.

32 Hoare, *Boys, Urchins, Men*, pp.79-115.

33 'Overseas Register' (B.B. H.Q., London); Notes on Vancouver and Winnipeg Companies, Longstaff Papers, file 375 (Add MSS 677, Archives of British Columbia, Victoria, B.C.); *B.B. Gazette*, October 1933 and May 1934.

34 Interview with J.H. Richardson, Montreal, 31 March 1978; J.H. Richardson, 'The Boys' Brigade in Montreal and District', typescript notes, 1978; *Montreal Gazette*, 7 May 1973; *B.B. Gazette*, March and December 1936, January and September 1937.

35 F.V. Longstaff, 'An outline of the work of The Boys' Brigade in Canada, from 1889 until 1937', typescript, 29 June 1937, Longstaff Papers, file 375; newspaper cuttings, correspondence, minutes, annual reports etc. 1937-44, Longstaff Papers, files 298 and 376 (Archives of British Columbia); 'Minutes and Financial Reports of the Canadian Dominion Council', 1937-54 (Canadian B.B. H.Q., Scarborough, Toronto); *B.B. Gazette*, January 1939, December 1940, April 1941, and October 1943.

36 Interview with Richardson, 1978, and *Montreal Gazette*, 7 May 1973.

37 Annual Reports, 1918-35; *B.B. Gazette*, January 1934 and November 1935.

38 Annual Reports, 1936-46; *B.B. Gazette*, November 1936, May and September 1937, October 1940, and December 1941.

39 Annual Reports, 1918-39; 'Overseas Register'; *B.B. Gazette*, June 1937.

40 Annual Reports, 1940-45; International History Information Survey, Jamaica, 1978.

41 National Association and Board and Trustee Minutes, 1899-1915; Kress's report to U.B.B.A., Pittsburgh, 1 June 1920; Correspondence files and reports of U.B.B.A. National Headquarters (Highfield Methodist Church, Baltimore, Maryland).

42 Correspondence, reports etc., U.B.B.A. National Headquarters (Baltimore), esp. H.Q. Correspondence 1932-40; New York Divisional Correspondence, 1930-36; Correspondence Koerber and Shattuck, 1934; International Correspondence (particularly with McVicker), 1934-37; Miscellaneous Correspondence, 1929-32 (particularly of Koerber and Cudlipp); Borleis to National Youth Administration, N.Y., 10 August 1940; interview with W. Koerber, Baltimore, 1978; *Boys' Brigade Advance* (1921); *The Brigader* (1941); *B.B. Gazette*, September 1935.

43 The Boys' Brigade Association, *The Boys' Brigade History and Songbook* (Neenah-Menasha, Wis., c.1963), 87pp.

44 Annual Reports, 1926-34; 'Overseas Register'; *B.B. Gazette*, January and September 1936, June and September 1937, and October 1945.

45 Interview with J.M. Fraser, 1976, typescript transcript 11pp. (B.B. H.Q., London); J.M. Fraser, 'Sketchy B.B. History', *H.Q. Echo* (Singapore), 1971, pp.1-6; 1st Singapore Company, First Annual Report, 1930-31, typescript (B.B. H.Q., Singapore); *B.B. Gazette*, May 1931.

46 'Overseas Register'; interview with Fraser; 'Sketchy B.B. History', *H.Q. Echo*, 1971, pp.7-12; *B.B. Gazette*, May and November 1936; 'The Boys' Brigade in Singapore', *50 Years On . . . The Boys' Brigade Jubilee Souvenir Magazine* (Singapore, 1980).

47 Interview with Fraser; *B.B. Gazette*, December 1933, April 1934, and December 1939; *50 Years On*, pp.86-9.

48 Interview with Fraser; 'Sketchy B.B. History', pp.13-14; Cheong Hock Hai, 'In the days of thy youth', typescript, 3pp. (B.B. H.Q., Singapore); *B.B. Gazette*, February and April 1942, and April 1946.

Chapter 7

1 Brighton Battn., *Breezes*, Vol. 17, No. 8/9 (Sept-Oct 1939), n.p., courtesy of Peter Ford, Brighton; William McVicker, 'The B.B. and the War, 1939-1944', typescript for *B.B. News*, New Zealand, to F. Scott Miller, 15 August 1944; Circular, 'The War', 8 September 1939 (B.B. H.Q., London).

2 'The A.R.P.', typed memo., 92nd London Co., 10 September 1939 (B.B. H.Q., London); 5th Brighton Co., *Broadcast*, weekly news-sheet, No. 285, 3 November 1940, n.p., courtesy of Peter Ford, Brighton.

3 Executive Memo. to Captains of Companies, 30 September 1939 (B.B. H.Q., London).

4 'Awards for Gallantry', *B.B. Gazette*, July/August 1940.

5 A.E. Milan, 92nd London Co., to Eric

Holdaway, 15 September 1939 (B.B. H.Q., London); Henry Pelling, *Britain and the Second World War* (London 1970), p.98.

6 Anon., *History of the Sutton and District Battn.*, January 1976, p.8; Pelling, op. cit., pp.202-205; Tom Sharman, 'Paternoster Row to Parson's Green: a resumé of events and personalities in the B.B., 1922-1972', address delivered to Wigan Battn., 29 October 1979, p.8; Kenneth Wiggins' obituary, *B.B. Gazette*, November, 1940.

7 'Award for Gallantry', *B.B. Gazette*, October/November 1940; 'For Valour: Our First V.C.', *B.B. Gazette*, November 1940; 'War Hero's Widow to Launch Rescue Boat in Husband's Name', *Leicester Mercury*, 25 May 1977; 'Service Awards: Another V.C.', *B.B. Gazette*, June 1946.

8 A.C. Saunders, *Before the Memories Fade: a short history of the 1st Ipswich Co.*, The B.B. (Ipswich, 1978), p.28; Brian Fraser, 'The Origins and Early History of The Boys' Brigade, 1883-1914', Ph.D. thesis, Strathclyde University, 1981, p.470; William Kelly, *Firm and Deep: a history of the Belfast Battalion*, The B.B. (Belfast, 1978), pp.62-65; Memo to Captains of Companies, 'Special Parades for Home Defence Instruction', July 1940 (B.B. H.Q., London).

9 Secretary, 'Opening of the New Session, 1941-1942', Circular, August 1941; The B.B., 'A Word to Senior Boys', 1943 (B.B. H.Q., London).

10 Memo, 'The B.B. and the Cadet Force', 31 March 1942; Memo, 'The New A.T.C.', 4 February 1941; 1st Barnet Co., The B.B./22nd Herts. Cadets correspondence, May 1942-July 1943; Lieut. R.H. Milnes to Major B.M. Barr, 26 July 1943 (1st Barnet Co. Records).

11 Circular 1486, 'In the Service of Youth', 27 November 1939; Circular 1516, 'The Challenge of Youth', 27 June 1940, Board of Education (Official Publications Room, British Library).

12 Circular 1577, 'Registration of Youth', 20 December 1941; Circular 1585, 'Registration of Girls', 6 March 1942; Circular 1600, 'Registration of Young Persons Aged Sixteen', 5 August 1942, Board of Education (Official Publications Room, British Library); B.B. Leaflet, 'The B.B. in the War', 1942 (B.B. H.Q., London); Bryan H. Reed (comp.), *Eighty Thousand Adolescents: a study of young people in the city of Birmingham* (London, 1950), p.47.

13 Public General Acts of 1944, *Education Act*, Chap. 31 (7 & 8), Geo. VI, section 53 (Official Publications Room, British Library); See: N.Y.A.C., *The Youth Service After the War* (London, 1943), passim.

14 G. Stanley Smith, 'The Youth Service', *The Listener*, Vol. 31, No. 788, 17 February 1944, p.176; ib., 'How We Stand', speech of 25 November 1944, London District (B.B. H.Q., London).

15 'B.B. Diamond Jubilee', *The Times*, 17 October 1943; 'The Royal Inspection at Windsor', *B.B. Gazette*, December 1943, pp.20-22.

16 Development Committee's Report, Executive Minutes, 5 September 1943; The B.B., *Plans for Advance: Executive proposals*, May 1944, foreword (B.B. H.Q., London).

17 Information collected from survey of opinion among battalion secretaries, 1978, and private discussion with B.B. officers on postwar recruitment problems; Dr J.W. McLeod, Foreword, *B.B. Handbook of the Leeds Battalion*, c.1952, p.3 (B.B. H.Q., London).

18 On Peacock: 'Obituary', *B.B. Gazette*, December 1965, p.42; taped interviews with Gerald H. Walker, London Secretary, 1977, and Tom Sharman, ex-staff officer, 1978.

19 Anon., 'Carronvale: new training centre in Scotland', *B.B. Gazette*, June 1947, p.80.

20 Anon., *A Short History of Felden Lodge as the B.B. National Training Centre*, n.d.; 'Official Opening of Felden Lodge', *B.B. Gazette*, December 1949, p.38. On 26 June 1963 the B.B. in Northern Ireland officially opened Rathmore House, Larne, as a Training and Conference Centre. In addition, a number of provincial battalions have their own, mostly non-residential, training centres.

21 Arthur Marwick, *Britain in the Century of Total War: War, Peace and Social Change, 1900-1967* (London, 1968), p.409; Sir Donald Finnemore, 'The B.B. Method', Address, 1959, p.2 (B.B. H.Q., London).

22 'Journal Padre', 'Socialism, Evangelism and The B.B.', *Gloucester Journal*, c.1954.

23 Stanley Smith, 'Juvenile Delinquency', talk to Athenaeum Club, 15 January 1951, typescript (B.B. H.Q., London); *Report of the Committee on Children and Young Persons*, Cmnd. 1191, 1959-1960, Pt. 1, Chap. 1, vii (Official Publications Room, British Library).

24 Roger S. Peacock, *Pioneer of Boyhood: Story of Sir William A. Smith* (Glasgow, 1954), pp.166-167; T.R. Fyvel, *The Insecure Offenders: rebellious youth in the Welfare State* (London, 1961), passim; ib., 'The "Insecure Offenders" in Retrospect', *New Society*, 20 July 1978, pp.128-129. I am grateful to the author for permission to cite this article.

25 *New Society*, op. cit., p.129; Colin MacInnes, *England, Half English: a polyphoto of the fifties* (London, 1961), pp.57-60.

26 Cmnd. 929, *The Albermarle Report on the Youth Service in England and Wales*, 1959-60, chaps. i, iii, x (Official Publications Room, British Library); Anthony Jeffs, *Young People and the Youth Service* (London, 1979), chap. ii.

27 Anon., *A Message to the King: souvenir of the Festival Run of the B.B.*, May 1951 (B.B. H.Q., London).

28 'B.B. Festival of Britain Run', *B.B. Gazette*, June, 1951, pp.94-100.

29 The B.B., '1954 Celebration Year', leaflet; typescript, '1954 is here indeed', n.d.; The B.B., *The Founder's Centenary Year: a record of some of the great events held in commemoration of Sir William Smith*, 1954; Thomas Henderson and Douglas Pearson Smith, *Soldier of Christ: a pageant to commemorate the centenary of the Founder's birth* (Edinburgh, 1954), (B.B. H.Q., London); John H. Rowley, 'A Visitor's Jottings', *B.B. Gazette*, August 1954, p.107.

30 Eric Chapman interview, 1977, transcript; 'Founder's Camp' in *The Founder's Centenary Year*, ib., pp.16-28; typescript, '1954 is here indeed', op. cit.

31 'Close-Up' No. 36, 'Movement that Circled the World', *The Windsor, Slough and Eton Express*, 30 April 1954; W.H. McVicker, 'Son of the Founder', *B.B. Gazette*, February/March 1975, p.60; 'The Brigade Secretaryship', ib., December 1954, p.34; interviews with Hugh Vaughan-Thomas, Tom Sharman, Gerald H. Walker, etc.

32 'Haffy', *B.B. Gazette*, December 1965, p.24; handout on retirement, February 1965; interview with Wilson-Haffenden, 23 January 1980.

33 Interview with Ronald Hewstone, 19 April 1980; personal information to author.

34 Wilson-Haffenden's quarterly *Newsletter*, No. 3, June 1955, n.p.; ib., No. 9, September 1956; 'The Duke of Edinburgh's Award', *B.B. Gazette*, October 1956, p.3; December 1956, p.26; February 1957, p.88; October 1957, p.11.

35 The B.B., *The Duke of Edinburgh's Award in the Boys' Brigade*, 1970, Brigade Executive; Wilson-Haffenden's *Newsletter*, No. 20, June 1959, n.p.; Kenneth Roberts, Graham E. White and Howard Parker, *The Character Training Industry: Adventure-Training Schemes in Britain* (Newton Abbot, 1974), passim; Alison Taylor, *For and Against the Duke of Edinburgh's Award* (London, 1967), p.56.

36 *Souvenir Handbook, The B.B. 750 Camp, 16-24 August 1958* (B.B. H.Q., London); Sir

John Hunt, 'Afterthoughts on the 750 Camp', *B.B. Gazette*, October/November 1958, p.12.

Chapter 8

1 Report of meeting held in Y.M.C.A., Wellington, on Saturday 16 June 1947 (4pp); Whale to Dornan, Glendale, California, 8 June 1957 (B.B. Archive, Turnbull Library, Wellington); Annual Reports (U.K.), 1945-48, and Annual Reports (N.Z.), 1945-48.

2 Annual Reports (U.K.), 1944-48.

3 The attitudes of Brigade officers in the dominions towards British B.B. expatriates who refused to accept local norms and conditions varied from total frustration, through resigned acceptance, to (though this was rare) outright hostility. These attitudes are made clear in a wide range of interviews I have conducted in Australia, New Zealand, Canada, and even the U.S.A. McVicker always reported, if informed, the emigration of B.B. men to the host country. Success, however, usually depended heavily on the reaction of the immigrant rather than the bending of the hosts. Many British officers contributed significantly to Brigade development overseas. Some never bothered to surface, others grumbled their way into B.B. oblivion. For some of the many successes, see Hoare, *Boys, Urchins, Men* (Sydney, 1980), and Hoare, *Faces of Boyhood* (Wellington, 1982), passim.

4 Memorandum to Brigade Executive on Overseas Development, 27 October 1958 (B.B. H.Q., London). Information brochure on the World Conference (London, n.d.)

5 Annual Reports (U.K.), 1947-81, and reports (many unpublished) of national councils; *B.B. Gazette*, 1946-80. Statistical analyses kindly supplied by Muriel Ellis (B.B. H.Q., London).

6 *B.B. Gazette*, June and October 1946.

7 Annual Reports (U.K.), 1946-47 and 1963-64, and *B.B. Gazette*, December 1962.

8 R.A.S. Mason, 'Report and Recommendations on his visit to Australia and New Zealand, April to July 1947' (B.B. Archive, Turnbull Library, Wellington).

9 Trotman to Mason, 10 February 1948, and Mason to Trotman, 29 February 1948 (B.B. Archive, Turnbull Library, Wellington).

10 'Report by Overseas Secretary on his Tour [to Australia and New Zealand] March to September 1951' (B.B. Archive, Turnbull Library, Wellington).

11 *B.B. News* (New Zealand), February, 1951; Annual Report (The Boys' Brigade N.Z. Dominion Council Inc.), 1948-52, and records of Silver Jubilee Camp, 1950-51 (B.B. Archive, Turnbull Library, Wellington).

12 Annual Reports (N.Z.), 1950-70; interview with R.L. Challis, 1976.

13 Interview with M. Dearsly, 1977.

14 Hoare, *Boys, Urchins, Men*, pp.174-75; Minutes, Provisional Federal Advisory Committee (B.B. Archives, Sydney); Hoare, *Faces of Boyhood*, pp.43-51; H. Trotman, 'Official Report of the International Camp Contingent', 1954 (49pp); minutes and correspondence (B.B. Archive, Turnbull Library, Wellington) and Annual Report (N.Z.), 1954.

15 Trotman, 'Official Report of the International Camp Contingent', 1954, and Annual Report (U.K.), 1954-55.

16 Verbatim report of proceedings in Trotman, op. cit., 1954.

17 Annual Report (U.K.), 1954-55.

18 Reports of Pacific Organizers, 1956-72, and minutes of Pacific Committee (N.Z.) (B.B. Archive, Turnbull Library, Wellington); interviews with Challis, 1976 and Dearsly, 1977; Annual Reports (N.Z.), 1950-80 and *B.B. News* 1952-80. Hoare, *Faces of Boyhood*, especially Chapter 9, 'Pacific Venture, 1935-1982'; Geoff Skilton, 'Pacific Regional Fellowship: Cook Islands Visitation, May 1-15, 1982', Mimeograph report, Wellington 1982 (30pp.).

19 Hoare, *Boys, Urchins, Men*, pp.79-138.

20 Ib., pp.94-96, 109-10, 120 and 131-32.

21 Minutes of the Provisional Federal Advisory Committee (P.F.A.C.), 1951-56; correspondence, accounts and notes of the P.F.A.C., 1951-57, and Honorary Organizer's reports, 1951-57 (B.B. Archives, Sydney); Hoare, *Boys, Urchins, Men*, pp.169-81.

22 The period of the Australian Council from 1958 is treated more fully state by state and nationally in *Boys, Urchins, Men*, pp.182-214. See also the bibliography and sources therein cited, pp.276-82.

23 *Boys, Urchins, Men*, pp.215-17.

24 Interviews with England, 1972 and 1975, and Gowman, 1976; *Australian B.B. Gazette*, 1962-66; Hoare, *Boys, Urchins, Men*, pp.218-23.

25 Reports of training officer to Australian Brigade Executive, 1966-68 (B.B. Archives, Sydney); *Australian B.B. Gazette*, 1966-68; Hoare, *Boys, Urchins, Men*, pp.223-30.

26 Reports of training officer, 1969-75; *Australian B.B. Gazette*, 1969-76; Hoare, *Boys, Urchins, Men*, pp.230-40.

27 Interviews with Dearsly, 1977, and Dornan, 1977; Annual Reports (N.Z.), 1956-67; Hoare, *Faces of Boyhood*, pp.120-23.

28 Annual Reports (U.K.), 1959-61, and *B.B. Gazette*, 1948-61.

29 Annual Reports (U.K.), 1953-62; International History Information Survey, Jamaica, 1978; *B.B. Gazette*, October 1962; Report of the Kingston Battalion, 1962 (B.B. H.Q., London).

30 Annual Reports (U.K.), 1954-61.

31 J.H.L. Phillips, 'The B.B.'s International Development', 1958 (B.B. Archive, Turnbull Library, Wellington).

32 D.J. Wilson-Haffenden and W. McVicker, comments on Phillips' memorandum, September 1958, appended to Phillips, ibid.

33 McVicker, notes for consideration at secretaries' meeting, 28 September 1958, appended to Phillips' memorandum.

34 'Leeds Consultations — September 1960 — Replies to Questions, 11 January 1960', prepared by the Brigade (N.Z.) President, M.T. Dearsly; Dearsly to Dornan, 16 September 1960 (B.B. Archive, Turnbull Library, Wellington); *B.B. Gazette*, October 1960.

35 Paper prepared by Dearsly for the New Zealand Executive on the World Conference, 1961; report to New Zealand B.B. Council on Overseas Consultations, 1961; 'Concensus of Opinion', Leeds Consultation, 1960; P.R.F. correspondence and Pacific Committee minutes (N.Z.), 1960-70 (B.B. Archive, Turnbull Library, Wellington); interview with Dearsly, 1977.

36 *B.B. Gazette*, October/November 1963, and Annual Report (U.K.), 1963-64. The World Conference Committee initially consisted of ten members. It was serviced by the two International Secretaries of the International Committee.

37 *B.B. Gazette*, 1960-76; Annual Reports (U.K.), 1963-76; international correspondence, especially with African and Asian Councils, 1960-70 (B.B. Archive, Turnbull Library, Wellington).

38 *B.B. Gazette*, December 1960, August 1961, August 1962 and February/March 1963, and Annual Reports (U.K.), 1945-63.

39 *B.B. Gazette*, April/May 1980; Annual Reports (U.K.), 1965-75; statistical returns, 1975-78; S.O. Maraiyesa, response to International History Information Survey, Nigeria, May 1978.

40 *B.B. Gazette*, 1954-80; Annual Reports (U.K.), 1954-75; International History In-

formation Survey, Gambia, Ghana and Sierra Leone, 1978.

41   *B.B. Gazette*, December/January 1967 and June/July 1968.

42   *B.B. Gazette*, June/July 1980 and December 1981/January 1982; Annual Reports (U.K.), 1957-75; International History Information Survey, Uganda, 1978.

43   *B.B. Gazette*, December 1970/January 1971 and June/July 1980; Annual Report (U.K.), 1968-74; International History Information Survey, Kenya, 1978.

44   *World Conference News*, February and December 1981.

45   Ib; *B.B. Gazette*, December 1969; Moffie J. Musonda, response to International History Information Survey, Zambia, 1978.

46   Annual Report (U.K.), 1945-75; *B.B. Gazette*, 1979-82; *World Conference Report and News*, 1976-81.

47   Caribbean Newsletters, Reports and correspondence, 1959-62; Annual Reports (U.K.), 1959-70.

48   Caribbean Reports; Annual Reports (U.K.), 1970-82; *B.B. Gazette*, August/September 1962, February/March 1967, June/July 1970 and October/November 1981; *World Conference News*, December 1981.

49   J. Edbrooke, memoranda and notes, 1959-61; personal interviews with Howard Richardson, Montreal, 1978, and Frank Butt, Baltimore, 1978; Tom Sharman, 'The biggest B.B. H.Q. in the World', *B.B. Gazette*, February/March 1981.

50   Interview with J.M. Fraser, 1976; 'Overseas Register' (B.B. H.Q., London); Lim K. Tham, 'The Singapore Retrospect', in B.B. in Singapore, *50 Years On . . .* (Singapore, 1980), pp.17-19; *B.B. Gazette*, 1945-46 and April/May 1971.

51   Personal interviews with Singapore and Malaysian officers, 1970-71; *B.B. Quarterly* (Singapore), June 1969; *B.B. News* (Singapore), 1981-82; *The Anchor* (B.B. Malaysia), December 1964; *B.B. Gazette*, October/November 1966 and June/July 1967; Annual Reports (U.K.), 1960-70.

52   Minutes, reports, statistics, publications of B.B. Singapore 1953-81 (National Archives, Singapore); B.B. in Singapore, *50 Years On . . .*; Annual Reports (U.K.), 1970-75; *B.B. Gazette*, October/November 1979; personal interviews with Hong Kong officers, 1970-71.

53   Leslie Rawson to World Conference Committee members, 10 February 1976, and background paper (B.B. Archive, Turnbull Library, Wellington).

54   *B.B. Gazette*, April/May 1977; Annual Reports (U.K.), 1966-78.

55   Martha Pedersen, *Joy cometh in the morning* (London, 1962); *World Conference News*, 1977-82; World Conference Reports (1979) on International Consultation (Center Sjaelland) and Conference (Silkeborg High School); *World Conference Report 1976-79* (London, 1979); *B.B. Gazette*, 1979-82.

56   *World Conference News*, 1979-82; *B.B. Gazette*, 1979-82 (especially reports on the work of the Programme Study Group); B.B. N.Z., *Beyond 100: A Development Plan* (Wellington, 1981), 125pp.

Chapter 9

1   Anon., *Discipline Outdated?* (B.B. Publications, 1961), p.19; Colonel J. Hughes, 'As Others See Us', *B.B. Gazette*, May 1974, p.53.

2   The B.B., *The Report of the Haynes Committee on the Work and Future of The Boys' Brigade*, February 1964, pp.7, 9 (B.B. H.Q., London); Arthur Marwick, *British Society Since 1945* (London, 1982), chap. ix.

3   Peter Calvocoressi, *The British Experience, 1945-1975* (London, 1978), pp.233, 238; Col. J. Hughes, 'The Youth Cult', *B.B. Gazette*, June 1974, p.66.

4   Wilson-Haffenden, *Newsletter*, No. 33 (September 1962), n.p. (London District Archives, B.B. H.Q., London).

5   *Haynes Report*, op. cit., p.6.

6   Sir George Haynes, 'Points from the Speeches', *B.B. Gazette*, October 1964, p.147.

7   'Conclusions and Recommendations', *Haynes Report*, op. cit., p.59.

8   'Points from the Speeches', op. cit., pp.147-148; Stanley Cohen, *Folk Devils and Moral Panics: The creation of the Mods and Rockers* (London, 1972), passim.

9   *Haynes Report*, op. cit., pp.52-55, 61; 'Brigade Council', *B.B. Gazette*, October 1964, p.144.

10   Wilson-Haffenden, *Newsletter*, No. 43, June 1965, n.p.; 'Brigade Council', loc. cit.; Brigade Secretary, *The Brigade Executive Proposals Regarding the Implementation of the Haynes Report*, March 1965; ib., June 1965 (B.B. H.Q., London). Full minutes of the 1964 Council are not available.

11   'Brigade Council', *B.B. Gazette*, October 1965, pp.7-8; ib., April 1966, p.80.

12   Minutes of Brigade Executive, 12 Febru-

ary 1966 (B.B. H.Q., London); 'Brigade Council', *B.B. Gazette*, October 1966, p.13; Wilson-Haffenden, *Newsletter*, No. 19, March 1959, n.p.

13 See: Muriel Ellis, *The Boys' Brigade Uniform: Then and Now*, rev. November 1977, passim; K.E. Afful, 'Developing a Corporate Strategy for The Boys' Brigade', M.Sc. dissertation (June 1981), pp.23-24.

14 Interview with Wilson-Haffenden, Hyde Park Gate, London, 23 January 1980; Wilson-Haffenden, *Newsletter*, No. 27, March 1961, n.p.

15 'Brigade Headquarters Appeal: the Great Relay Run', *B.B. Gazette*, June/July 1961, pp.98, 100. Sir Cyril Black had been Girls' Life Brigade Treasurer since 1939.

16 Wilson-Haffenden, *Newsletter*, No. 44, September 1965, n.p.

17 Anon., *From Paternoster Row to Parson's Green*, leaflet, May 1979; *B.B. Gazette*, February/March 1967, pp.47-53; April/May 1973, pp.72-4.

18 Obituary in *B.B. Gazette*, February/March 1976, p.75; B.B. handouts, February 1951, September 1959, 3 November 1966 (B.B. H.Q., London).

19 Matt and Christine Stewart to Wilson-Haffenden, 29 December 1965, cited with permission; on Neilson: *B.B. Gazette*, October/November 1965, p.4; interview with Neilson, Cripplegate Foundation, London, 6 January 1981.

20 The B.B., *Report of the Special Committee on Church Relationships* (1967, reprinted 1971), pp.7-8; DES Course N891, Priorities in the Youth Service, *Pre-Course Activity: Overall Assessment of the Youth Service Provided by The Boys' Brigade* (July 1981), p.3, kindly loaned by the Brigade Secretary.

21 The B.B., *The Constitution of The Boys' Brigade, as approved by Brigade Council at Belfast* (September 1968), n.p.; Ian Neilson interview, op. cit.

22 Source: Membership Statistics in Annual Reports, 1977-1981; Commentaries on Annual Statistics supplied by A.D. Weir, Brigade Executive Member for Mid-Scottish District, 1978-80.

23 *Haynes Report*, op. cit., p.21; Officer Enrolment Forms, 1972-76, Appendix 5.

24 Condensed version of replies received from survey of battalion secretaries, questionnaire circulated August 1978 by author.

25 Pearl Jephcott, *Time of One's Own: Leisure and Young People* (Edinburgh, 1967), pp.100-101, 123.

26 Bryan Wilson, 'How Religious Are We?' *New Society Social Studies Readers* (1977),

pp.19-21; personal communication from Brian Fraser, 2 December 1981; 'Churches Still Losing Support', *The Guardian*, 12 September 1980.

27 'The Mystery of Religious Motivation', *The Times*, 11 September 1978; 'A Good Year for Church', *The Guardian*, 25 January 1979; Statistics for 1977, *Church of England Year Book*, C.I.O. (London, 1979); Bryan Wilson, *Religion in a Secular Society* (London, 1966); ed. David Martin, *Sociological Year Books of Religion in Britain* (London, 1968-70).

28 Sponsored by 'Buzz' Magazine, The Bible Society and The Scripture Union, *National Survey of Religious Attitudes Among Young People*, 1978; Leslie Francis, 'Teenage Values Today', *New Society*, 28 September 1978, pp.687-688.

29 Report by the Brigade Working Party, *Brigade Organization and Financial Policy, 1975-1985*, 1 September 1976, 12 pp.; Motion 11, 'Officership', *Minutes of the Annual Meeting of Brigade Council held at Aberdeen*, 4 September 1976; 'Brigade Organization', Annual Report, 1976/1977, p.10; on Alfred Hudson: *B.B. Gazette*, April/May 1974, p.62.

30 Motion 12, 'Pre-Junior Organizations', *Minutes*, op. cit., 4 September 1976; 'A Pre-Junior Organization?' *B.B. Gazette*, August/September 1976, pp.136-138; Memo, 'A Pre-Junior Organization', circulated to Council members, 4 September 1976, 4pp.

31 Report on Discussion Paper, *The Christian Aims and Influence of the Brigade's Work and the Christian Commitment of its Officers*, 4 August 1976, 10 pp; 'Christian Commitment Paper', *Minutes*, 4 September 1976, op. cit., p.6.

32 Guidelines for Captains, *Brigade Work in Areas of Ethnic Minority Populations*, 1 September 1976, 3 pp.

33 See: 'First for Boys' campaign literature; articles on Programme Study Group in *B.B. Gazette*, December 1979–January 1981; personal communication from John Edbrooke on National Action Group, 15 January 1982.

34 The Brigade Executive, *Programme Study Group: Interim Report*, February 1980, pp.2, 4-7; 'Letters to the Editor', *B.B. Gazette*, February/March 1980 and April/May 1980; Programme Study Group, *Guidelines*, 15 July 1980 (B.B. H.Q., London).

35 Brigade Executive, *The Boys' Brigade in the 1980s: A Strategy for Programme Development*, enclosed in *B.B. Gazette*, June/July 1981, p.8. This is the final report of the Programme Study Group.

Conclusions

1 'B.B. Jubilee', *The Times*, 4 May 1933.

2 Tom Sharman, taped interview, 10 April 1980, recorded at B.B. H.Q. London.

3 A.E. Morgan, *The Needs of Youth* (London, 1939), pp.313-314.

4 R.W. Campbell, *Jimmy McCallum* (Glasgow, 1921), pp. 86-87; Lord Roberts to the 12th Earl of Meath, 18 January 1898, Meath Papers, Killruddery, Bray, Co. Dublin, Ireland.

5 Brian Fraser, 'The Origins and History of The Boys' Brigade from 1883 to 1914', Ph.D. thesis, 1981, Strathclyde University, pp.483-484; *Minutes of Conference of Officers of Companies in Belfast and District*, 22 February 1890, Public Record Office of Northern Ireland, Belfast.

6 W. McG. Eager, *Making Men: the history of boys' clubs and related movements in Great Britain* (London, 1953), p.323; Brian Fraser, op. cit., p.485, footnote 1.

7 F.J. Marriott, taped interview, 10 September 1980, recorded at St. Helens, Isle of Wight, by G.L. Wooderson, Brigade Honorary Vice-President.

8 H.J. Hanham, 'Religion and Nationality in the Mid-Victorian Army' in: M.R.D. Foot ed., *War and Society* (London, 1973), pp.172-174; Edgar Rogers, 'The Church Lads' Brigade', in: *Pan-Anglican Papers* (London, 1908), p.2.

9 Roger S. Peacock to Carey Bonner, 4 October 1912 (B.B. H.Q. London).

10 *The Carlisle Journal*, 23 February 1894.

11 'Military Conscription in embryo', *The Herald of Peace*, No. 457, 1 September 1887, p.269. The B.B. turned down an invitation to appear at the Royal Tournament in London in 1978 owing to the latter's paramilitary image: *B.B. Gazette*, December/January 1978-79, p.43.

12 Sections on the overseas history based on: Michael Hoare's 'Notes on writing the overseas/international history', 4 April 1982, and personal communications; M.E. Hoare, *Boys, Urchins, Men: a history of The Boys' Brigade in Australia and Papua New Guinea 1882-1976* (Sydney, 1980), pp.259-264; B.B. material from the Regional Fellowships of the World Conference; Baden-Powell, *Boy Scouts Beyond the Seas* (London, 1913).

13 Mass Observation Ltd., a sample of 2,000 adults for the Baden-Powell Scout Guild, Press Release, *Were You Ever A Boy Scout?* 14 April 1967; A. Hume Smith, 'A Company Camp', *B.B. Gazette*, Vol. 12, 2 March 1903, p.102.

14 Roger S. Peacock, *Pioneer of Boyhood* (Glasgow, 1954), pp.173-174.

15 Ian Jack, 'Youth: Scenes from the Life of a Beleaguered Generation', *The Sunday Times Magazine*, 1 November 1981, p.55; chorus of 'The Anchor Song', *B.B. Songbook* (B.B. H.Q. London), n.p.

BIBLIOGRAPHY

The relatively few secondary sources touching on The Boys' Brigade are referred to in the chapter reference notes. The bibliography lists primary sources or manuscript collections consulted by the authors which will provide the raw material for any future research on the history of the movement. It is organized as follows:

1. Held in Scotland
2. Held in England
3. Held in Australasia and the South Pacific
4. Held in North America and the Caribbean
5. Held in Asia
6. Material on B.B. in Africa
7. Interviews recorded on tapes
8. Theses and dissertations

1 Held in Scotland:

Brigade Headquarters, 168 Bath Street, Glasgow

Roll-books and documents relating to 1st Glasgow Company, 1883-88
Register of Companies (Scotland, England, Wales and Ireland), 1885-1911
Register of Companies (Scotland and Ireland), 1911-14
Glasgow Battalion Registers, 1883 onwards
Glasgow Battalion Minute Books, 1885 onwards
Glasgow Battalion Letter Book, 1887-91
Glasgow Battalion Annual Reports, 1885 onwards
William A. Smith, Diaries, 1888-99

Edinburgh Battalion Headquarters, 7 Victoria Terrace, Edinburgh

Papers relating to 1st Edinburgh Company
Edinburgh Battalion Minute Books, 1887 onwards
Register of Companies and Officers, 1887 onwards
Annual Reports, 1891-92 to 1914-15

1st Hamilton Company, Lanarkshire

Company Roll-books, 1886-94
Boys' application forms, 1888-90
Financial Records: Balance Sheets, 1891-1914
Papers relating to Cadet recognition, 1914-18
Records of field days, reviews, competitions and prize-winners
Miscellaneous letters and papers

1st Glasgow Company, Kelvin-Stevenson Memorial Church, Glasgow

William A. Smith, Diaries, 1875 and 1904
William A. Smith, Camp Notebooks, 1886-88
William A. Smith, Letter Book, 1894-1901
Jubilee Papers, 1933
Company cards, squad lists and miscellaneous documents, 1883-1914
Booklet, 'For Fifty Years', 1883-1933

The Mitchell Library, Glasgow

Diary of Sir Michael Connal, 1835-93
Grove Street Home Mission Institute — Annual Reports, 1886 onwards
Glasgow United Y.M.C.A. — Annual Report, 1883

Salvation Army (Scotland) — Annual Report, 1882

Sabbath School Union Report, 1883

Sabbath School Association Report, 1883

Association for Promoting the Religious and Social Improvement of the City, *Report on the Religious Condition of Glasgow*, 1871

Rev. J. Johnston, *Religious Destitution in Glasgow*, 1870

Clerk to the Board, *The Evening Schools of the School Board of Glasgow*, 1891

Historical Publishing Company, *Industries of Glasgow*, 1888

Series of sketches republished from 'Fairplay', a shipping magazine, *Clydeside Cameos*, 2nd Series, 1885

Post Office Directories, 1883-88

Strathclyde Regional Archives (formerly City of Glasgow Archives), John Street, Glasgow

Glasgow School Board — Summary of Work, 1873-82

Minutes of Glasgow School Board, 1873-79

J.A. Fairley, 'The Effect of the 1872 Education (Scotland) Act', from compilation entitled *Schooldays in Glasgow 100 years ago*, 1972

Glasgow Foundry Boys' and Girls' Religious Society — Cumberland Street Branch Report, 1889

Anon., *The Buchanan Institution — An Historical Sketch*, 1913

Glasgow Foundry Boys' and Girls' Religious Society, Merchants' House, Glasgow

Compendium of Objects, Operations and Management

Annual Reports, 1866-1914

Scottish Record Office, H.M. General Register House, Edinburgh

Free College Church, Glasgow — Annual Reports, 1877-88

Census Enumerators Returns, 1881 and 1891

Haddo House Manuscripts, Aberdeen

Earl of Aberdeen, correspondence as Canadian B.B. President, 1894-98

Other Records:

Adelaide Place Baptist Church, Glasgow — Minutes of Deacons' Court, 1885

Wellington Church of Scotland, Glasgow — Sunday School Society Minute Book, 1885

Kelvinside Botanic Gardens Church of Scotland, Glasgow — *4th Glasgow — For Fifty Years*, 1935

Elgin Place Congregational Church, Glasgow — *14th Glasgow Co. of the B.B.*, 1935

Sherwood Church, Paisley — Records and papers of 22nd Paisley Company

Free Church of Scotland, The Mound, Edinburgh — Annual Reports, 1883-1914

Church of Scotland, 121 George Street, Edinburgh — Reports of the General Assembly, 1883-1914

Reports of the United Presbyterian Church of Scotland, 1883-1901

Reports of the United Free Church of Scotland, 1901-14

2　Held in England:

Brigade Headquarters, Parsons Green, London

Brigade Executive Minute Books, 1916 to present

William A. Smith, Diary, 1914

William A. Smith, Letter Books, 1885-87, 1894-1901 (copies)

Boys' Brigade Annual Reports, 1883 onwards

Company Records — 2nd West Kent (Bexleyheath) Company; 1st South Essex (Leytonstone) Company; 1st Witney (Oxfordshire) Company; 1st Blackheath (Kent) Company; 1st Aston Manor (Birmingham) Company, etc.

Battalion Records — Tyne Valley Battalion Council Minute Books; North Midland District Council Minute Books

George Stanley Smith, Diaries, 1908-13, 1925-58; miscellaneous correspondence; notes for addresses and speeches; photograph albums; miscellaneous souvenirs

Douglas Pearson Smith, school and career details; sketches; letters at time of death

Brigade Magazines — *The Boys' Brigade Gazette*, 1889 to present; *The B.B.* (for boys), 1895-1900; *The Brigadier*, 1901-04; *The Boys' Bulletin*, 1918-20; *Stedfast Magazine* (for boys), 1953-79; *Life Boy Link*, 1961-65, then *Junior Stedfast Magazine*, etc.

Special Event Files — Mansion House Advisory Committee, 1913; death of Founder, 1914; reorganization scheme, 1914-15; Jubilee celebrations, 1933; Silver Jubilee Run, 1935; Royal Inspection, 1943; Founder's Centenary, 1954; Haynes Report, 1964; Royal Visit, 1973, etc.

Correspondence — Union with B.L.B., 1914 and 1920-26; Cadet recognition and withdrawal, 1910-14, 1916-17, 1923-24; Smith to Baden-Powell, 1909-10

Photographs — comprehensive collection from earliest days

London District Archives — Minutes of the London Committee from 1901 onwards; Minutes of London Council meetings; Minutes of Finance Committee; early letters and photographs; annual reports, etc.

Collection of company magazines, mostly 1920s and 1930s

Collection of company and battalion histories published locally

Register of companies (England and Wales), 1911 to present

Overseas Register and enrolment and registration records of overseas companies, 1889-1978

1st Enfield Company, Enfield, Middlesex

Holograph drafts of Annual Reports, 1907-15
1st Enfield Company Magazine, 1921-50
Enrolment Books, 1888-94
Admissions Register, 1890-1908
The Enfield Battalion Souvenir Handbook, 1888-1948 (Enfield 1948)
Miscellaneous items

Brighton and Hove District Battalion Archives, 6 Stone Street, Brighton

Battalion Executive Minutes, 1900-49 (six books)
NCOs Council Meetings Minutes, 1948-61
Local Magazines — *The Grasshopper* (Battalion), 1906-19; *B.B. Breezes* (Battalion), 1922 to present; *Broadcast* (5th Brighton Company), 1931-42 (weekly)
Miscellaneous items

The British Library, London

Company Histories — 76th Glasgow (1937); 14th West Kent, Bexleyheath (1954); 1st Glasgow (1933)
Magazines — *West London Battalion Gazette*, 1908-10, and *Camp Journal*, 1902; *B.B. Gazette*, 1889 to present
Girls' Life Brigade — *G.L.B. Chronicle*, 1925-67; *G.L.B. Magazine*, 1935-65; Annual Reports, 1927 onwards; etc.
Girls' Guildry — Annual Reports, 1930 onwards; *G.G. Gazette*, 1909-32; *Lamp of the G.G.*, 1932 onwards; Marion Lochead, *A Lamp was Lit* (Edinburgh, 1949)

Scout Association Headquarters, Cromwell Road, London

Press Cuttings — Vol. 1 on Brownsea Island and early Scouting
Correspondence — Stanley Smith to Scouts Association, 1951
Miscellaneous items relevant to B.B. in Scout archives

3 Held in Australasia and the South Pacific:

The Boys' Brigade Australia, Australian Headquarters, 103-105 Queen Street, North Strathfield, Sydney, New South Wales

Provisional Federal Advisory Council — minutes, agendas, correspondence, Honorary Organizer's reports, 1951-57
Australian B.B. Council — minutes, annual reports, Life Boy Committee records, Management Committee minutes, drafts of constitutions, 1958-82
Registration of the name in Australia — correspondence, legal opinions, 1933-65
State Councils, Battalions and Groups in Australia — reports, correspondence, 1946-82

The Boys' Brigade Australia, Queensland State Council, Heaquarters Office, Brisbane

1st Brisbane Company — roll-books, correspondence, records, 1913 onwards
Registration of name in Queensland — correspondence, 1935-57
Brisbane Officers' Council — minutes, 1941-60
Queensland State Council — records, 1960 onwards

Other Australian Records

Minutes and records of State Councils, battalions and groups are held in the Headquarters Office of the respective states. For a fuller listing see M.E. Hoare, *Boys, Urchins, Men* (Sydney, 1980), pp.276-79.

The Boys' Brigade in New Zealand Inc., 62 Brougham Street, Wellington

International Committee — minutes, records, 1978-82
B.B. New Zealand — Headquarters correspondence, records, reports, newsletters, 1978-82
Pacific Regional Fellowship — Secretary's records, minutes, correspondence, 1978-82

The Alexander Turnbull Library, P.O. Box 12-349, Wellington: MS Papers 2024

Dominion (National) Council — minutes of Council, Executive and Committees; Headquarters correspondence (particularly with overseas B.B. Councils), 1927-77
Life Boy Committee — records, minutes, correspondence, 1935-68
South Pacific Committee — correspondence, reports from organizers, diaries of tours, 1955-77
Battalions and Groups — correspondence with B.B. H.Q., 1945-77
Companies in New Zealand — records, charters, correspondence, 1946-77
Ardmore Camp — records, 1957-59

4 Held in North America and the Caribbean:

The Boys' Brigade in Canada, National Headquarters, St. Andrew's Presbyterian Church, 115 St. Andrew's Road, Scarborough, Ontario

Canadian Dominion Council — minutes of Council, Executive and Board of Directors, correspondence and financial records, 1937-72
Toronto Battalion — minutes of Council and Executive, 1948-70
John France (former Dominion Secretary), personal papers, 1908-60

Mr J. Howard Richardson, 50 Melbourne Avenue, Montreal, Quebec

Montreal Officers Council and Battalion — minutes, 1936-55
Montreal Battalion — correspondence, 1937-51

Provincial Archives of British Columbia, Victoria, B.C., Canada

Longstaff, Frederick Victor — Papers (Add MSS 677). These papers of the former Canadian Secretary form the most comprehensive record of the B.B. in Canada. The Boys' Brigade material forms only a small part of the total collection of Longstaff's papers:
Notebooks on Longstaff's B.B. activities, 1912-39 (vol. 217)
Pamphlets and newspaper cuttings on B.B. and youth work, 1895-1939 (vols. 1 & 23)
Notes on Longstaff's inspection of Canadian companies, 1941; Canadian Executive minutes and notes, 1941-43 (vol. 308)
Notes and statistics and drafts on Canadian B.B. history; correspondences with W.A. Smith, 1912-14 (vols. 375-78)

Vancouver Municipal Archives, Vancouver B.C., Canada

Vancouver Battalion — miscellaneous notes, correspondence and reminiscences, 1946-54

Records of the United Boys' Brigades of America, Highland Methodist Church, Baltimore, Maryland, U.S.A.

National Association, Board & Trustees — minutes, 1899-1915
Regiments and Divisions — records and correspondence, including Philadelphia Division, 1930-32; Pittsburgh Division, 1930-32; Philadelphia Regiment, 1933-40; New York, 1930-32; Virginia Division, 1933-37
Headquarters Correspondence, 1941
International Correspondence, 1934-37 (includes correspondence with W. McVicker)

U.B.B.A. Headquarters, Pittsburgh, Pennsylvania

A selection of U.B.B.A. materials is in the custody of Messrs. Guy Smith and John Schlee, Swissvale, Pittsburgh
Photographs of U.B.B.A. personalities
New York Division — records, 1930

The Boys' Brigade in the Caribbean

(copies in possession of Dr M.E. Hoare)
Caribbean Newsletters, 1959-61

Quarterly Reports of the Organizer, 1959-62
Miscellaneous reports and correspondence, 1959-63

International History Information Survey

Response from B.B. in Jamaica and Bermuda, 1978

5 Held in Asia:

National Archives and Records Centre, Singapore

Singapore Battalion — minutes of Executive, Council and Annual meetings, 1949-68 (microfilm NA 557)
The Boys' Brigade in Singapore — records, 1968-81 (microfilm NA 558)

6 Material on B.B. in Africa:

International History Information Survey

Responses from B.B. in Gambia, Ghana, Nigeria, Kenya, Sierre Leone, Uganda and Zambia, 1978

The Alexander Turnbull Library, Wellington

Correspondence between B.B. Organizers and Councils in many African countries and the B.B. in New Zealand, 1947-77, is deposited in the Archive of The Boys' Brigade in New Zealand, MS Papers 2024

7 Interviews Recorded on Tape:

Great Britain, 1971-82

Transcripts on deposit at Brigade Headquarters, London, and at the New University of Ulster History Film and Sound Archive
I.L. Bawtree (1975); Terry Bonfield (1982); John Chalmers (1978); Eric R. Chapman (1976); Maurice Cole (1980); James M. Fraser (1976); Vivian Garstang (1977); Ronald Hewstone (1980); Bert Hoey (1980); Arthur S. Jackson (1978); F.J. Marriott (1980); William H. McVicker (1971); W.H.A. Monckton (1975); Ian G. Neilson (1981); Arthur Primmer (1982); Leslie Rawson (1979); Arthur Reid (1977); Tom Sharman (1980); William Sharpe (1974); Dora Stirling (1981); Dr Alfred Swindale (1978); Robert E. Thompson (1975); Hugh Vaughan-Thomas (1980); Gerald Walker (1980); Norman Warters (1978); Dennis Webb (1977); D.J. Wilson-Haffenden (1980); Gordon Wooderson (1980)

Australia, New Zealand and the Pacific, 1969-77

Transcripts in possession of Dr Michael E. Hoare, Wellington, New Zealand
Mervyn Branks (1976); Robert Challis (1976); Mervyn Dearsly (1977); Alfred Dornan (1977); Brian England (1972, 1975); R. McEwan (1969, 1974); J.B. Gowman (1976); Roland Hill (1976); Archie McDonald (1969); Robert Tait (1969)

Canada and America, 1978

Transcripts as above
Francis Butt; Walter A. Koerber; Danny Reesor; J. Howard Richardson and B.B. officers in Toronto and Montreal

Singapore, Malaysia and Hong Kong, 1970-71

Transcripts as above
S.P. Chua; Paul Juby; Edgar Ramalingam; Len Strange; Ken Thornton

8 Theses and Dissertations:

Kenneth E. Afful, 'Developing a Corporate Strategy for the Boys' Brigade', M.Sc. Dissertation, 1980-81, Anglian Regional Management Centre, Chelmsford
Martin Barratt, 'The Foundation and Early Years of The Boys' Brigade: An Aspect of the Social History of Youth', M.A. Dissertation, 1976, University of Leicester School of Education
S.C.H. Besley, 'Youth Movements and Militarism', M.A. Dissertation, 1980, Thames Polytechnic

Bibliography

Michael Blanch, 'Nation, Empire and the Birmingham Working Class, 1899-1914', Ph.D. thesis, 1975, University of Birmingham

F.M. Brodhead, 'Social Imperialism and the British Youth Movement, 1880-1914', Ph.D. thesis, 1978, University of Princeton

I.L. Burt, 'Physical Education in The Boys' Brigade, 1883-1914', M.Ed. Dissertation, 1975-76, University of Manchester

Christopher J.P. Farmer, 'The Foundation of The Boys' Brigade: Social Discipline or Heavenly Design?' B.A. Dissertation, 1973, University of Keele

Brian M. Fraser, 'The Origins and History of The Boys' Brigade from 1883 to 1914', Ph.D. Thesis, 1981, University of Strathclyde

David MacLeod, 'Good Boys Made Better: The Boy Scouts of America, Boys' Brigades, and Y.M.C.A. Boys' Work, 1880-1920', Ph.D. Thesis, 1973, University of Wisconsin

John Springhall, 'Youth and Empire: Studies in the Propagation of Imperialism to the Young in Edwardian Britain', D.Phil. Thesis, 1968, University of Sussex

Paul Wilkinson, 'A Study of English Uniformed Youth Movements, 1883-1935: their origin, development, and social and political influence', M.A. Thesis, 1968, University of Wales

INDEX